高雄右京

To Heart 2

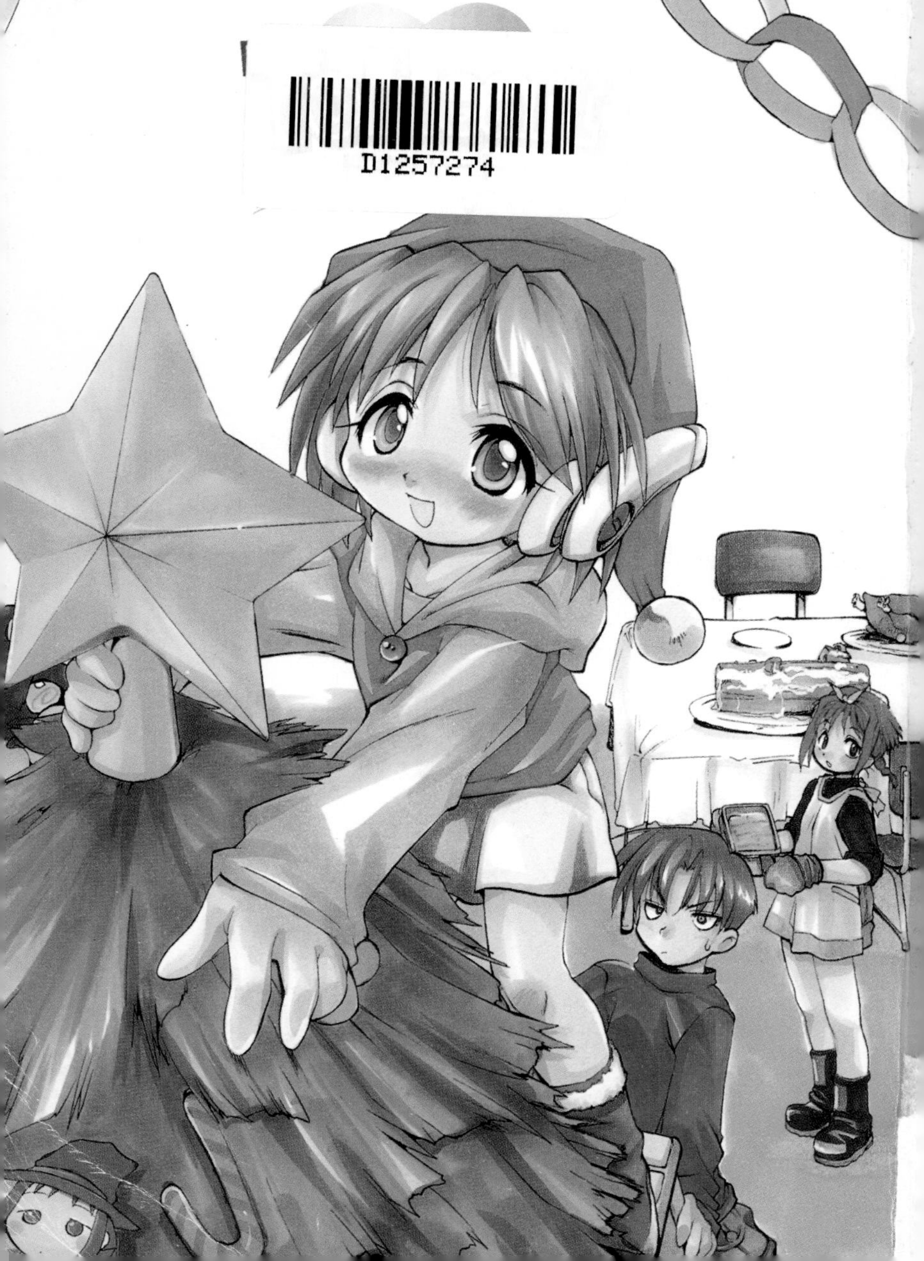

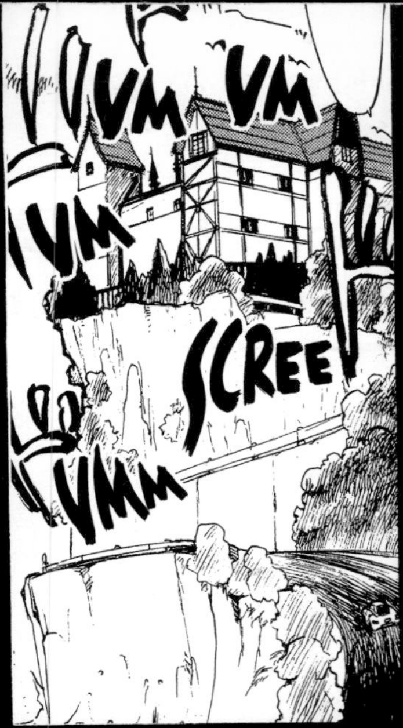
VUM VUM
VUM
SCREE
VMM

Episode 4
『The Girls of Summer』

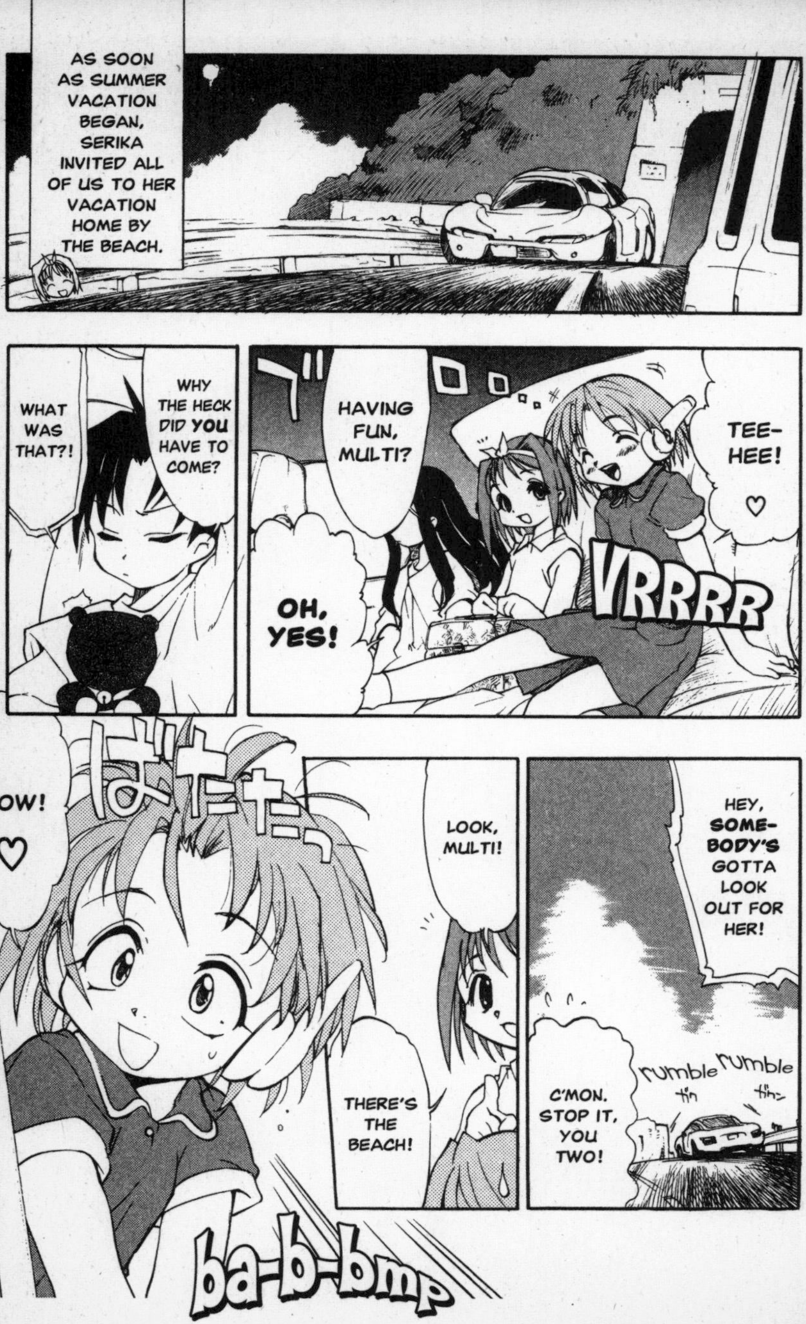

AS SOON AS SUMMER VACATION BEGAN, SERIKA INVITED ALL OF US TO HER VACATION HOME BY THE BEACH.
WHAT WAS THAT?!
WHY THE HECK DID YOU HAVE TO COME?
HAVING FUN, MULTI?
OH, YES!
TEE-HEE! ♡
VRRRR
LOOK, MULTI!
THERE'S THE BEACH!
WOW! ♡
ba-b-bmp
HEY, SOMEBODY'S GOTTA LOOK OUT FOR HER!
C'MON. STOP IT, YOU TWO!
rumble rumble

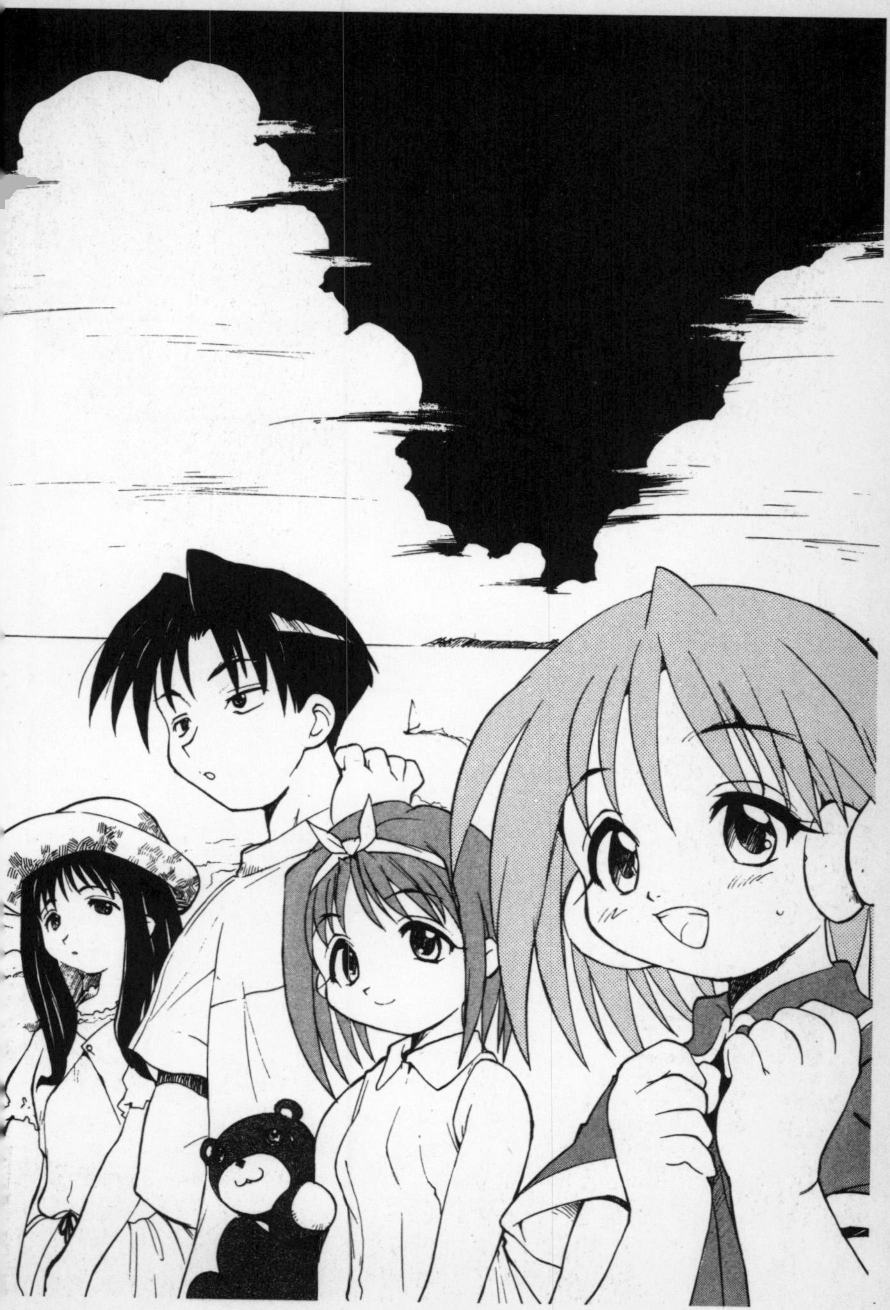

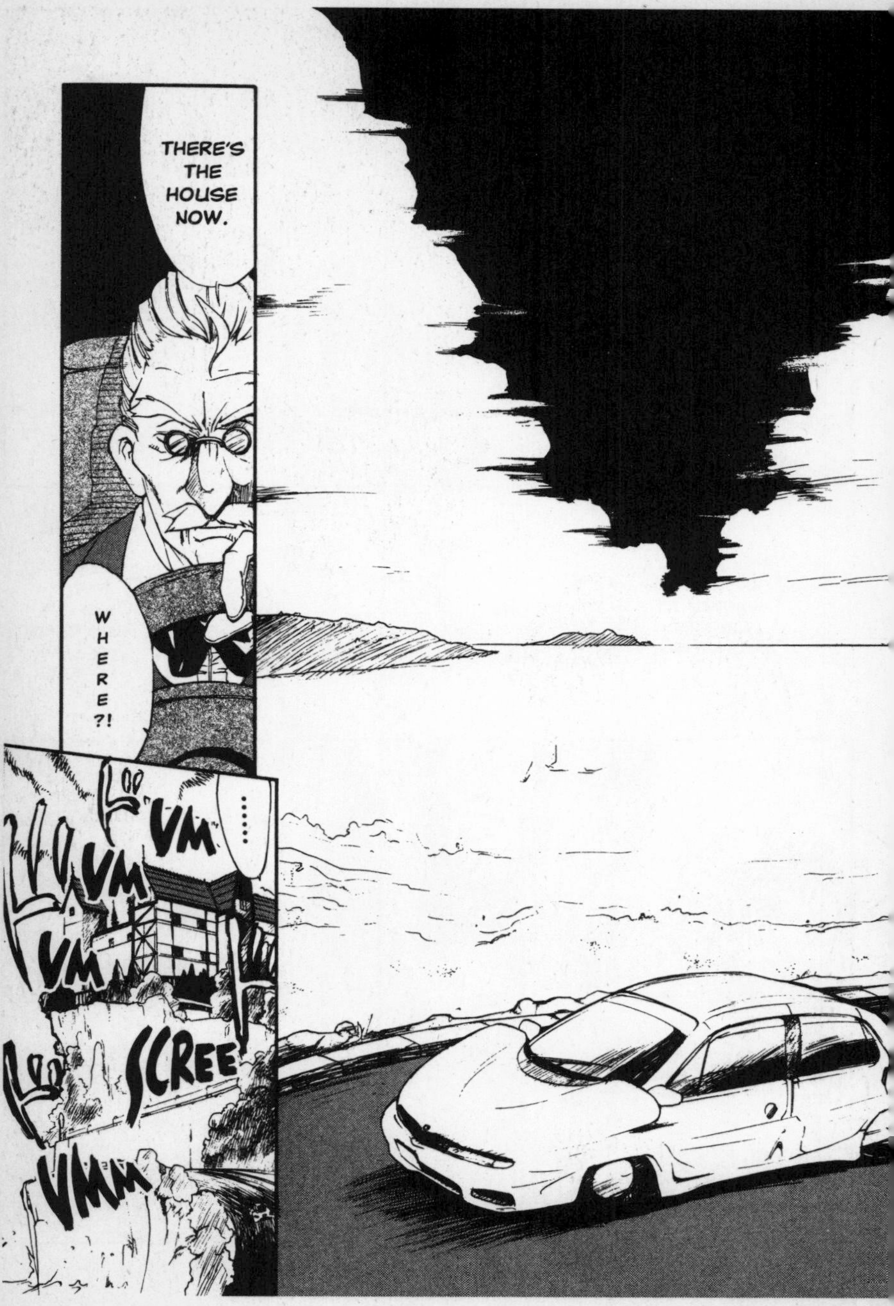
THERE'S THE HOUSE NOW.
WHERE?!
......
VM
VM
VM
SCREE
VMM

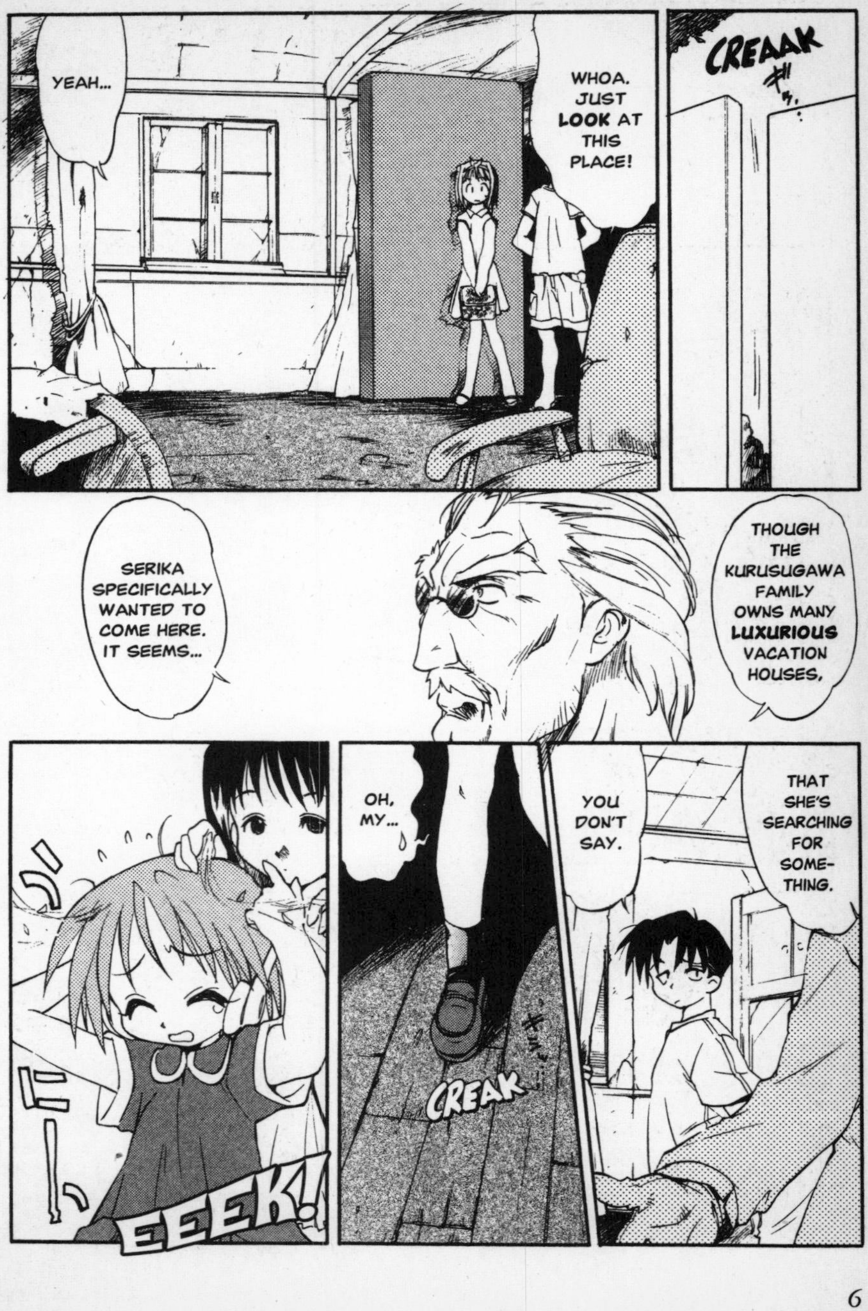
CREAAK
WHOA. JUST **LOOK** AT THIS PLACE!
YEAH...
THOUGH THE KURUSUGAWA FAMILY OWNS MANY **LUXURIOUS** VACATION HOUSES,
SERIKA SPECIFICALLY WANTED TO COME HERE. IT SEEMS...
THAT SHE'S SEARCHING FOR SOME-THING.
YOU DON'T SAY.
CREAK
OH, MY...
EEEK!

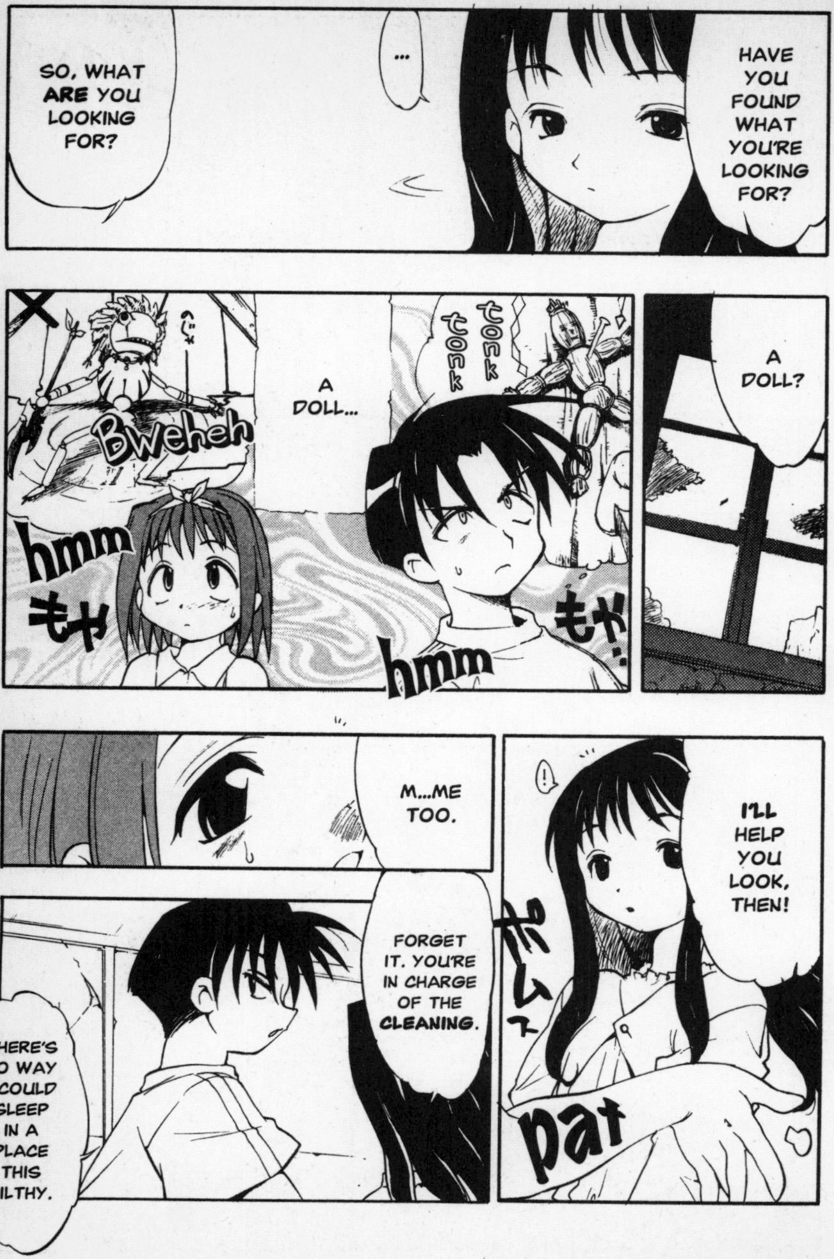
HAVE YOU FOUND WHAT YOU'RE LOOKING FOR?
...
SO, WHAT **ARE** YOU LOOKING FOR?
A DOLL?
tonk tonk
A DOLL...
Bweheh
hmm
もや
hmm
もや
!
I'LL HELP YOU LOOK, THEN!
pat
M...ME TOO.
FORGET IT. YOU'RE IN CHARGE OF THE **CLEANING**.
THERE'S NO WAY I COULD SLEEP IN A PLACE THIS FILTHY.

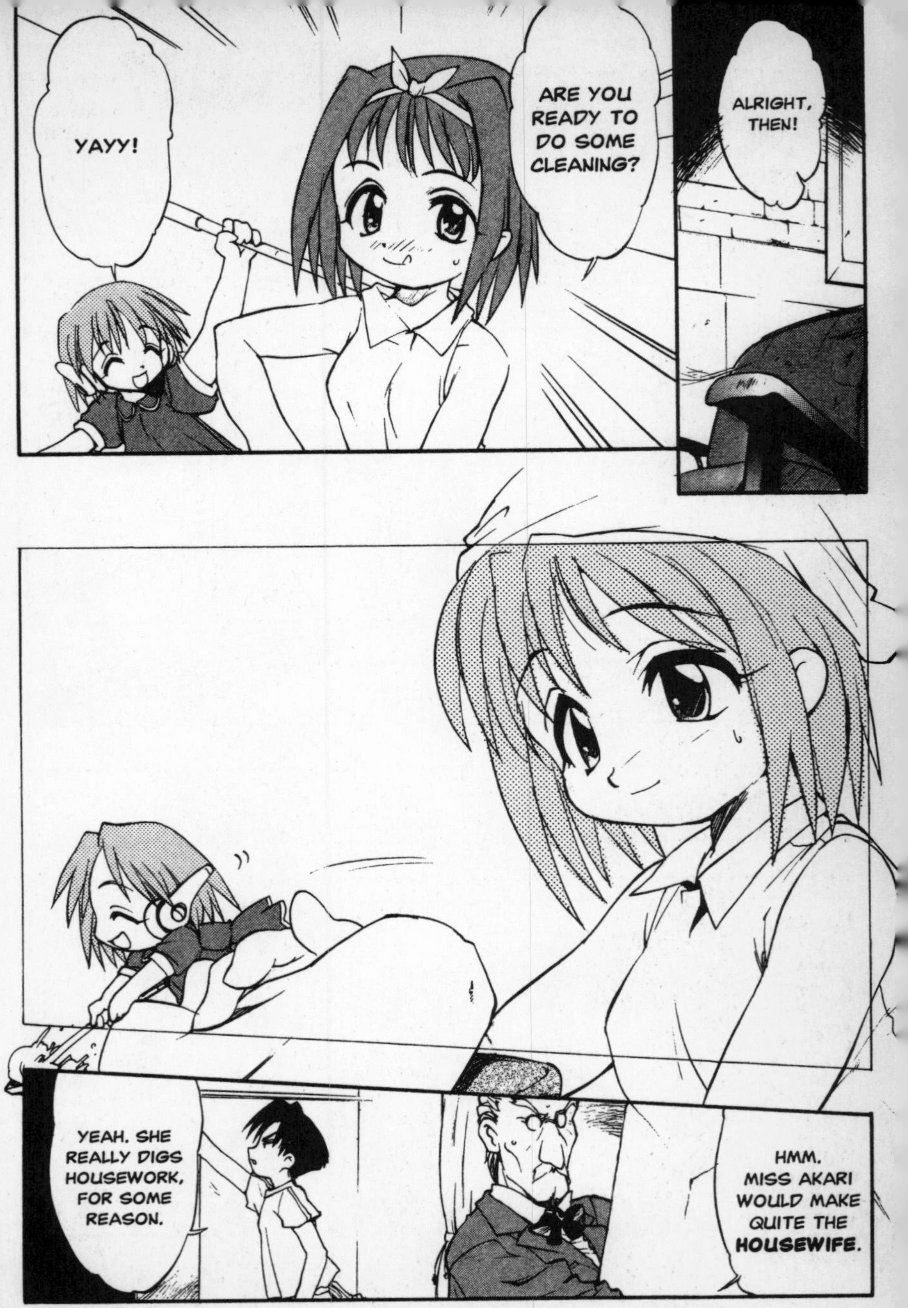
ALRIGHT, THEN!
ARE YOU READY TO DO SOME CLEANING?
YAYY!
HMM. MISS AKARI WOULD MAKE QUITE THE **HOUSEWIFE.**
YEAH. SHE REALLY DIGS HOUSEWORK, FOR SOME REASON.

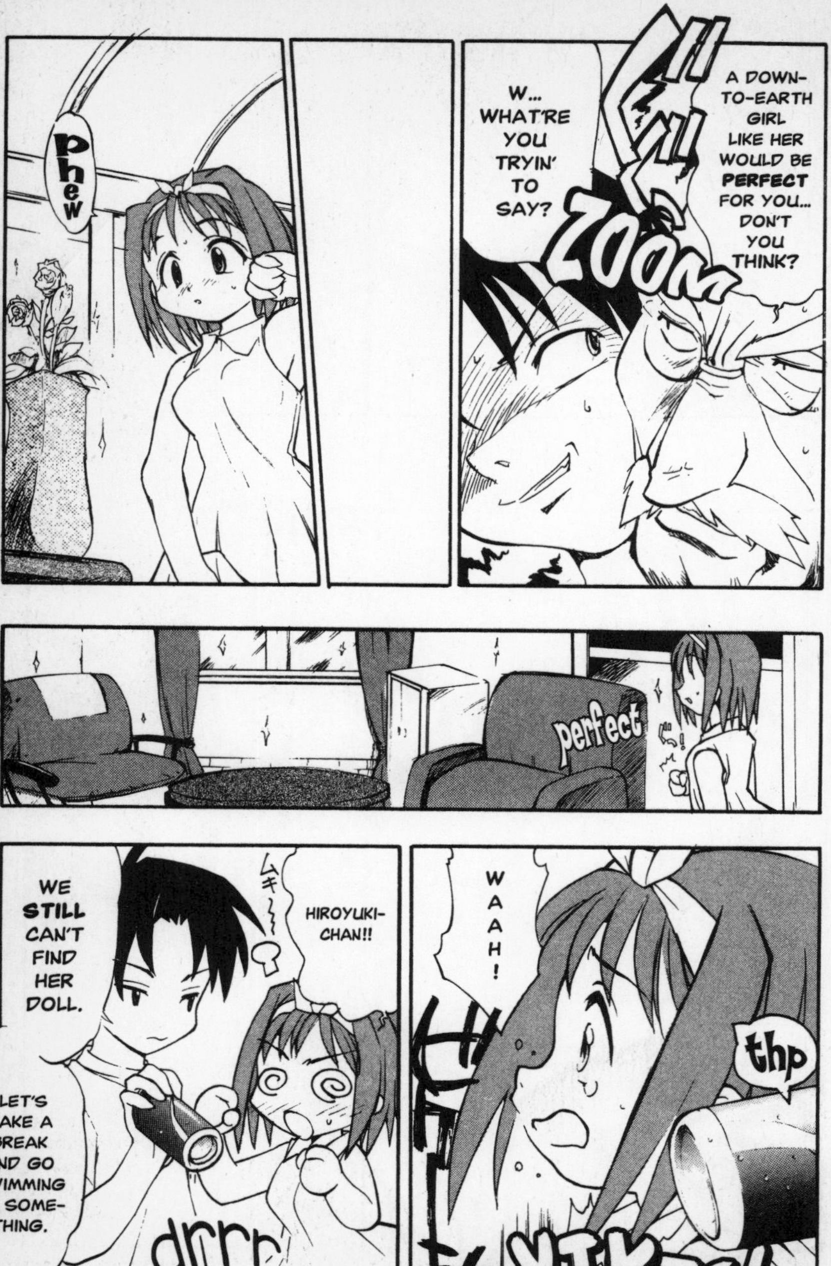
A DOWN-TO-EARTH GIRL LIKE HER WOULD BE PERFECT FOR YOU... DON'T YOU THINK?
ZOOM
W... WHAT'RE YOU TRYIN' TO SAY?
phew
perfect
HIROYUKI-CHAN!!
WE STILL CAN'T FIND HER DOLL.
LET'S TAKE A BREAK AND GO SWIMMING OR SOME-THING.
grrr
WAAH!
thp
YIKES!

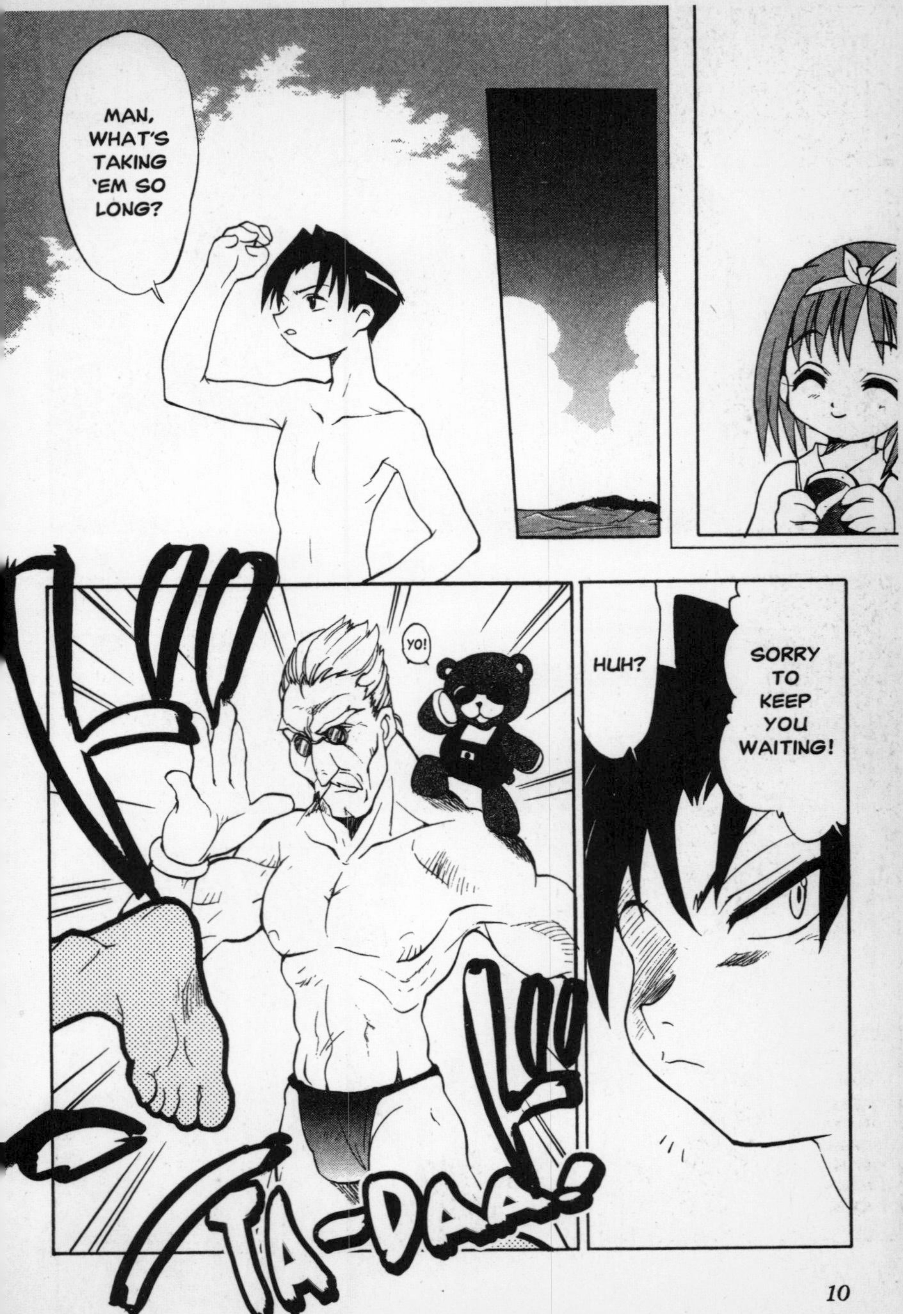
MAN, WHAT'S TAKING 'EM SO LONG?
SORRY TO KEEP YOU WAITING!
HUH?
YO!
TA-DAA!

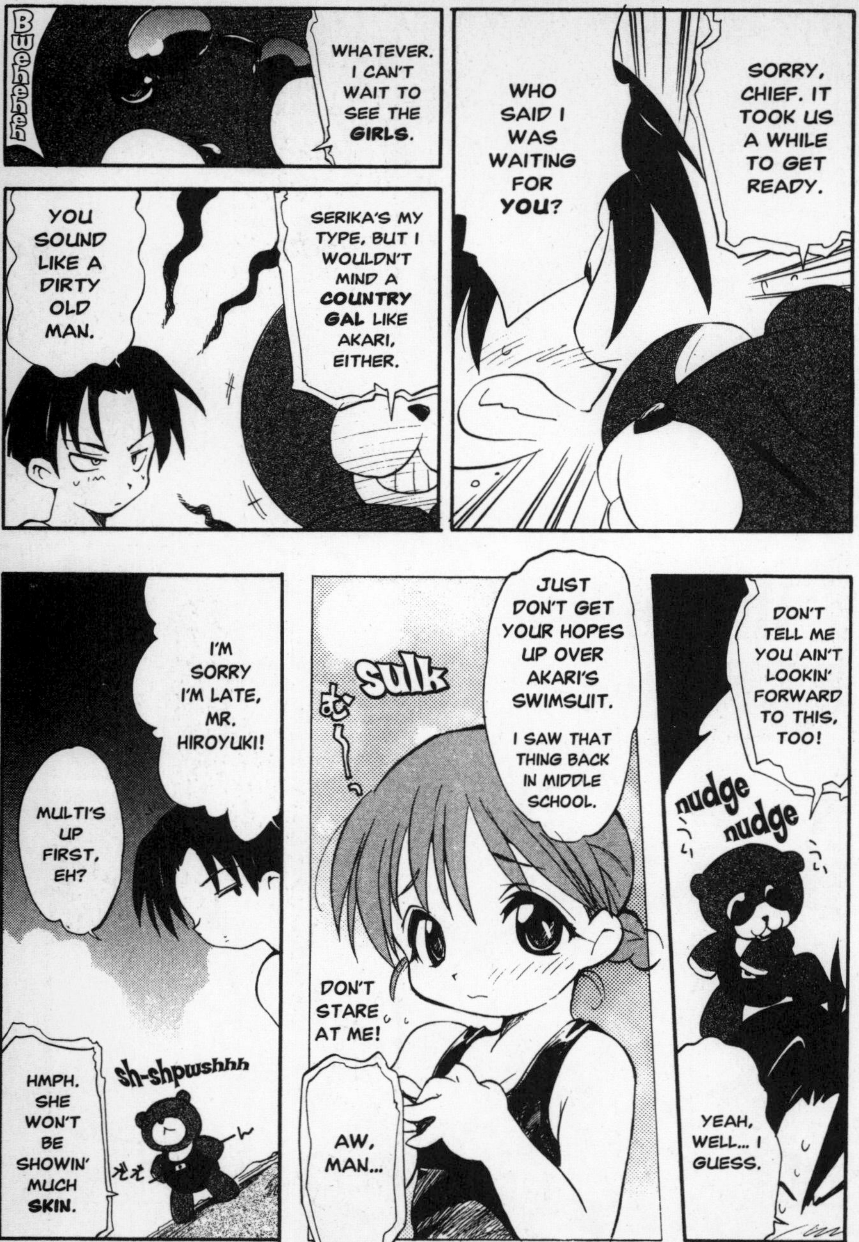
SORRY, CHIEF. IT TOOK US A WHILE TO GET READY.
WHO SAID I WAS WAITING FOR **YOU**?
WHATEVER. I CAN'T WAIT TO SEE THE **GIRLS**.
Bwehehe
SERIKA'S MY TYPE, BUT I WOULDN'T MIND A **COUNTRY GAL** LIKE AKARI, EITHER.
YOU SOUND LIKE A DIRTY OLD MAN.
DON'T TELL ME YOU AIN'T LOOKIN' FORWARD TO THIS, TOO!
nudge nudge
YEAH, WELL... I GUESS.
JUST DON'T GET YOUR HOPES UP OVER AKARI'S SWIMSUIT.
I SAW THAT THING BACK IN MIDDLE SCHOOL.
sulk
DON'T STARE AT ME!
AW, MAN...
I'M SORRY I'M LATE, MR. HIROYUKI!
MULTI'S UP FIRST, EH?
sh-shpwshhh
HMPH. SHE WON'T BE SHOWIN' MUCH **SKIN**.

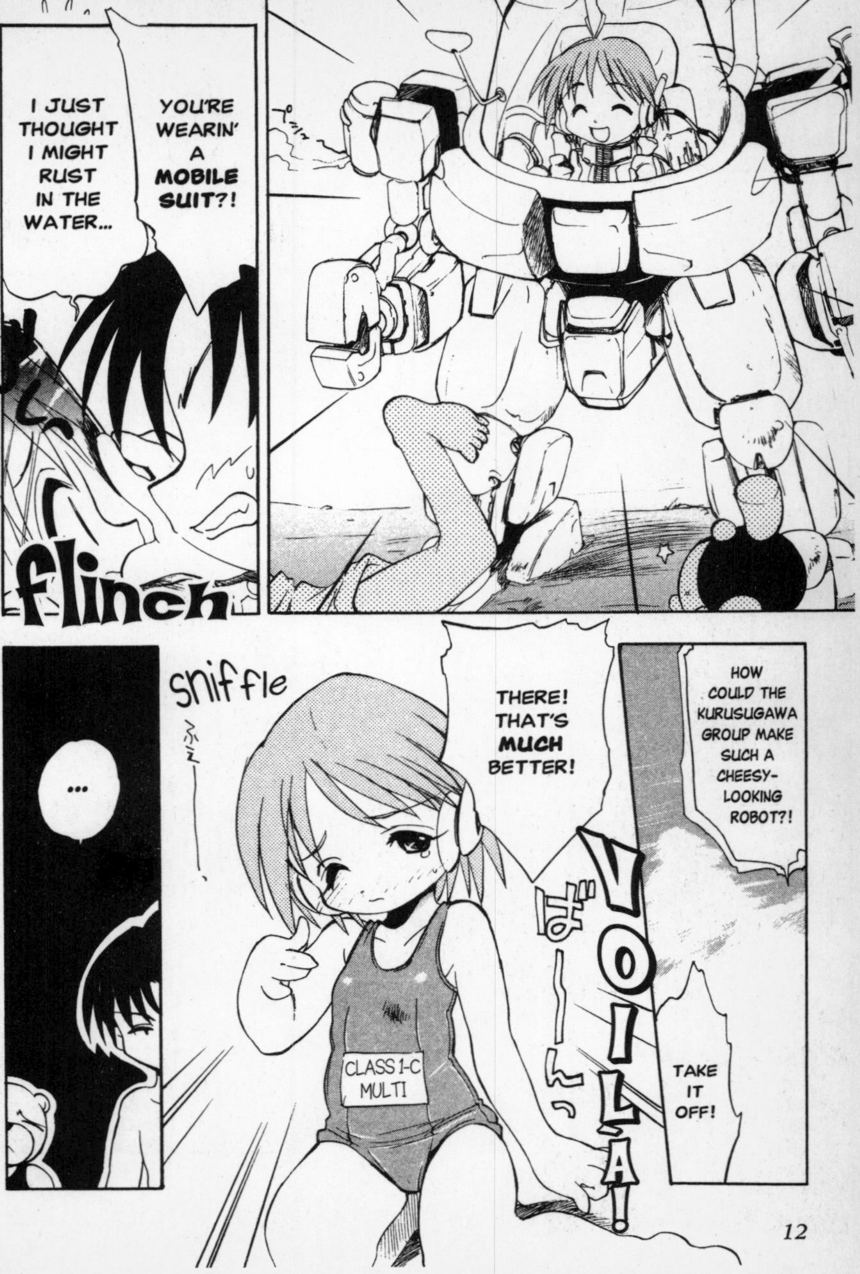
YOU'RE WEARIN' A MOBILE SUIT?!
I JUST THOUGHT I MIGHT RUST IN THE WATER...
flinch
HOW COULD THE KURUSUGAWA GROUP MAKE SUCH A CHEESY-LOOKING ROBOT?!
TAKE IT OFF!
THERE! THAT'S MUCH BETTER!
VOILA!
CLASS 1-C MULTI
sniffle
...

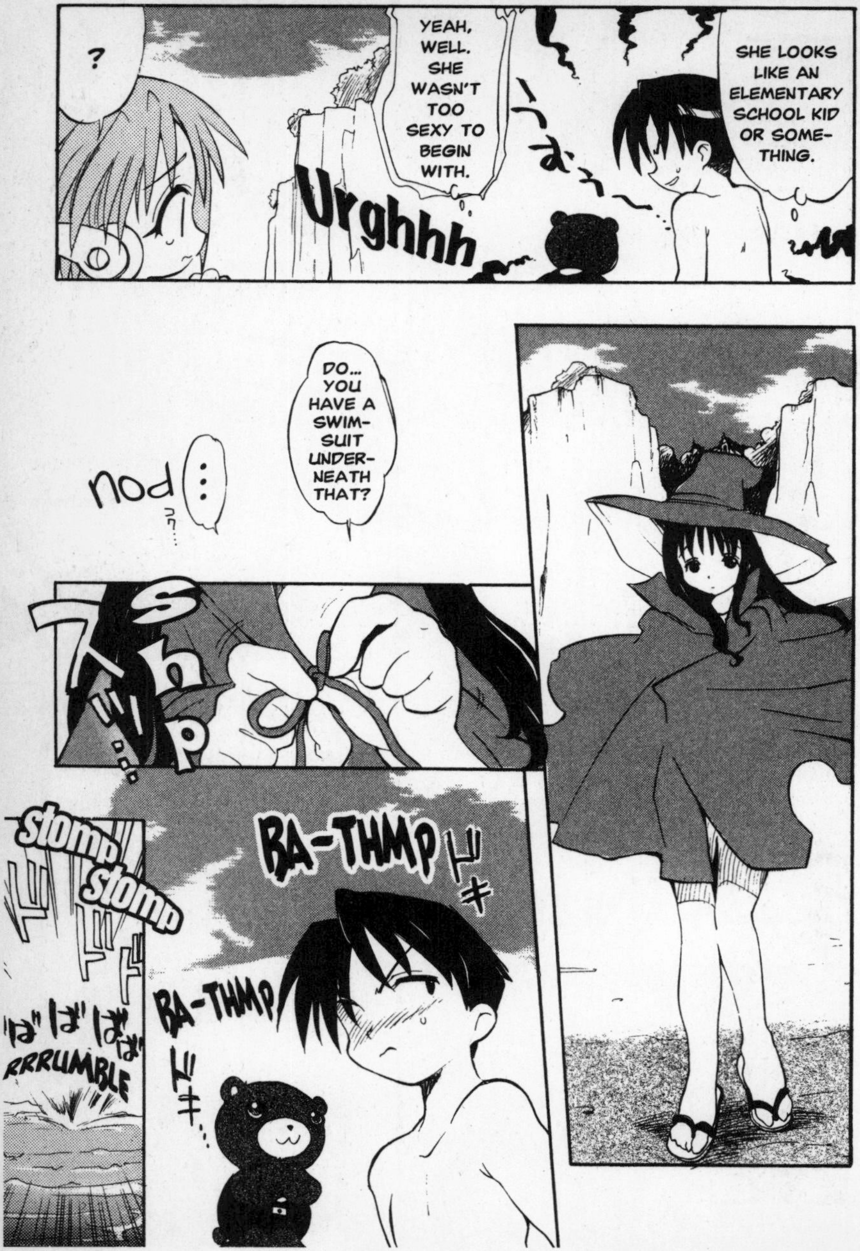

SHE LOOKS LIKE AN ELEMENTARY SCHOOL KID OR SOME-THING.
Urghhh
YEAH, WELL. SHE WASN'T TOO SEXY TO BEGIN WITH.
?
DO... YOU HAVE A SWIM-SUIT UNDER-NEATH THAT?
...
nod
Shp
BA-THMP
ドキ
BA-THMP
ドキ...
stomp stomp
ばばばば
RRRUMBLE

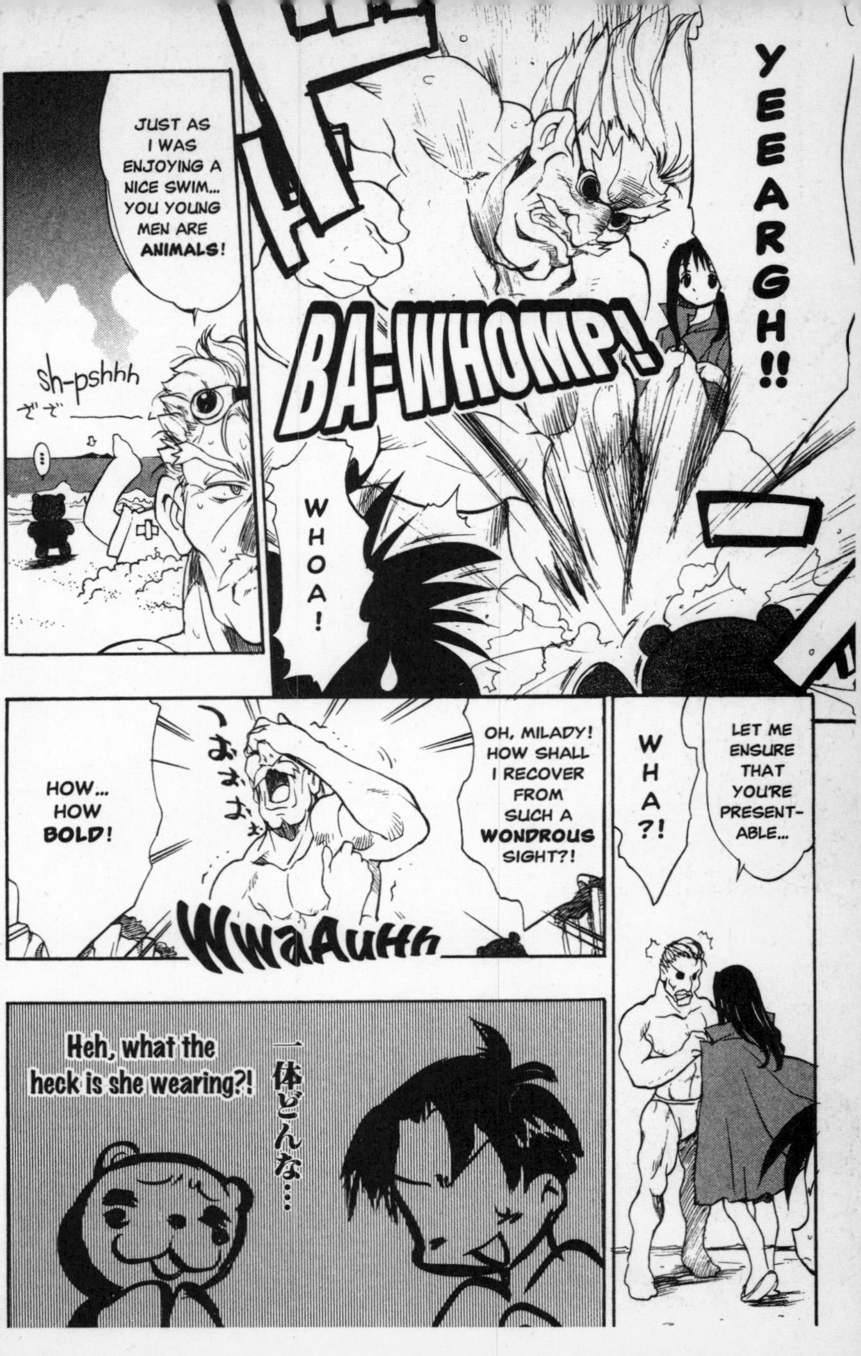
YEEARGH!!
BA-WHOMP!
WHOA!
JUST AS I WAS ENJOYING A NICE SWIM... YOU YOUNG MEN ARE ANIMALS!
sh-pshhh
ずで
...
LET ME ENSURE THAT YOU'RE PRESENT-ABLE...
WHA?!
OH, MILADY! HOW SHALL I RECOVER FROM SUCH A WONDROUS SIGHT?!
HOW... HOW BOLD!
WwaAuHh
Heh, what the heck is she wearing?!
一体どんな…

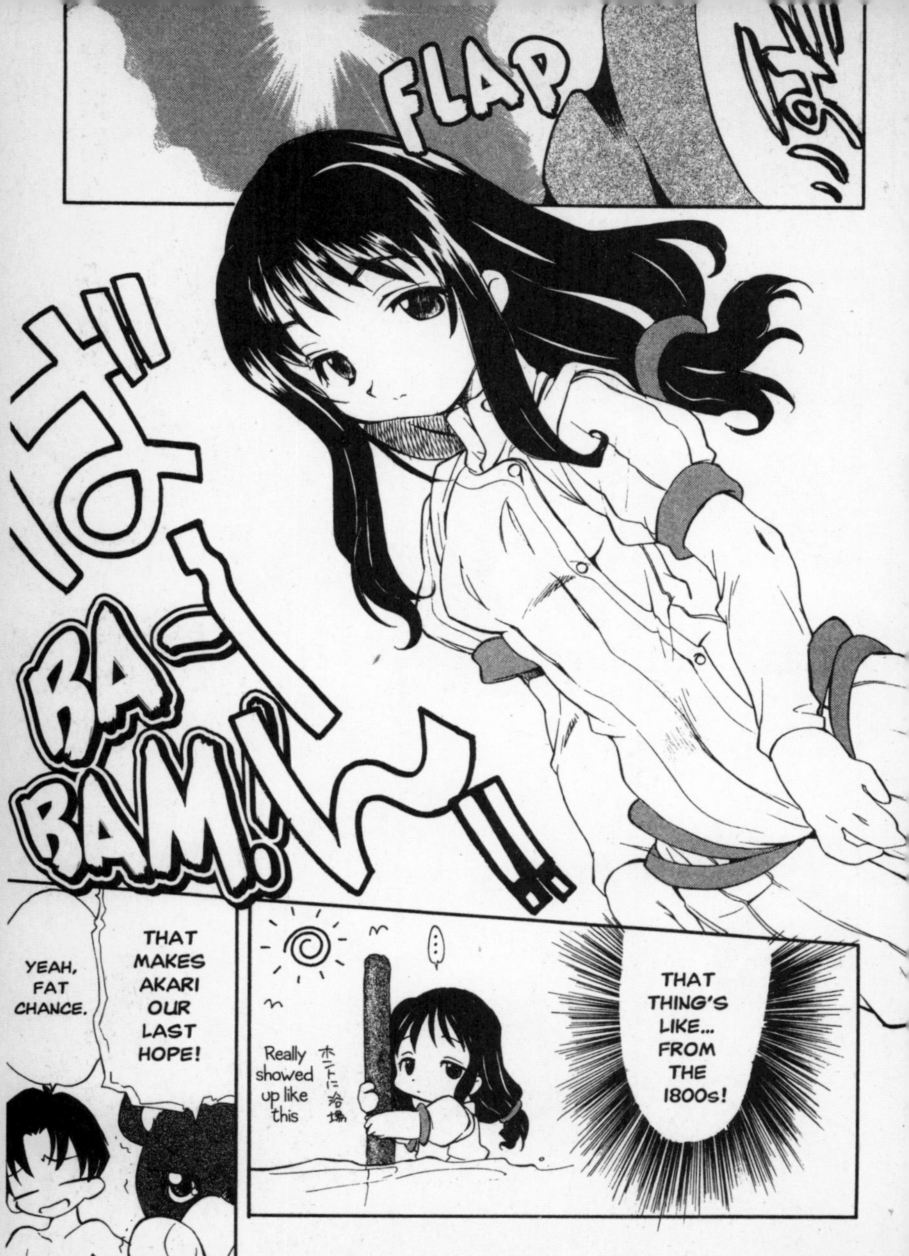

FLAP
ばっ
ばっ
BA-BAM!
THAT THING'S LIKE... FROM THE 1800s!
Really showed up like this
ホントに洛場
THAT MAKES AKARI OUR LAST HOPE!
YEAH, FAT CHANCE.

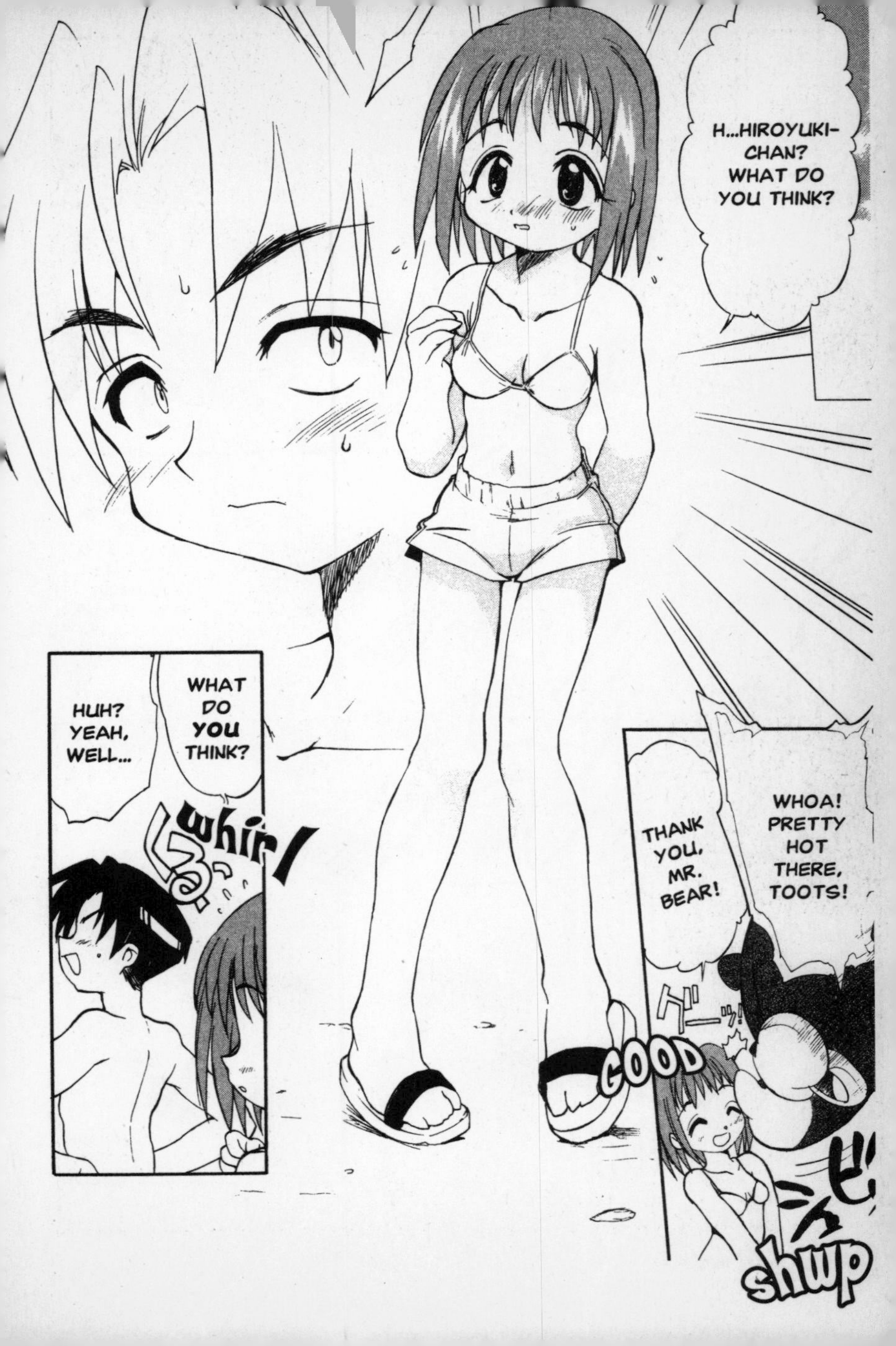
H...HIROYUKI-CHAN? WHAT DO YOU THINK?
WHOA! PRETTY HOT THERE, TOOTS!
THANK YOU, MR. BEAR!
GOOD
shwp
WHAT DO YOU THINK?
HUH? YEAH, WELL...
whirl

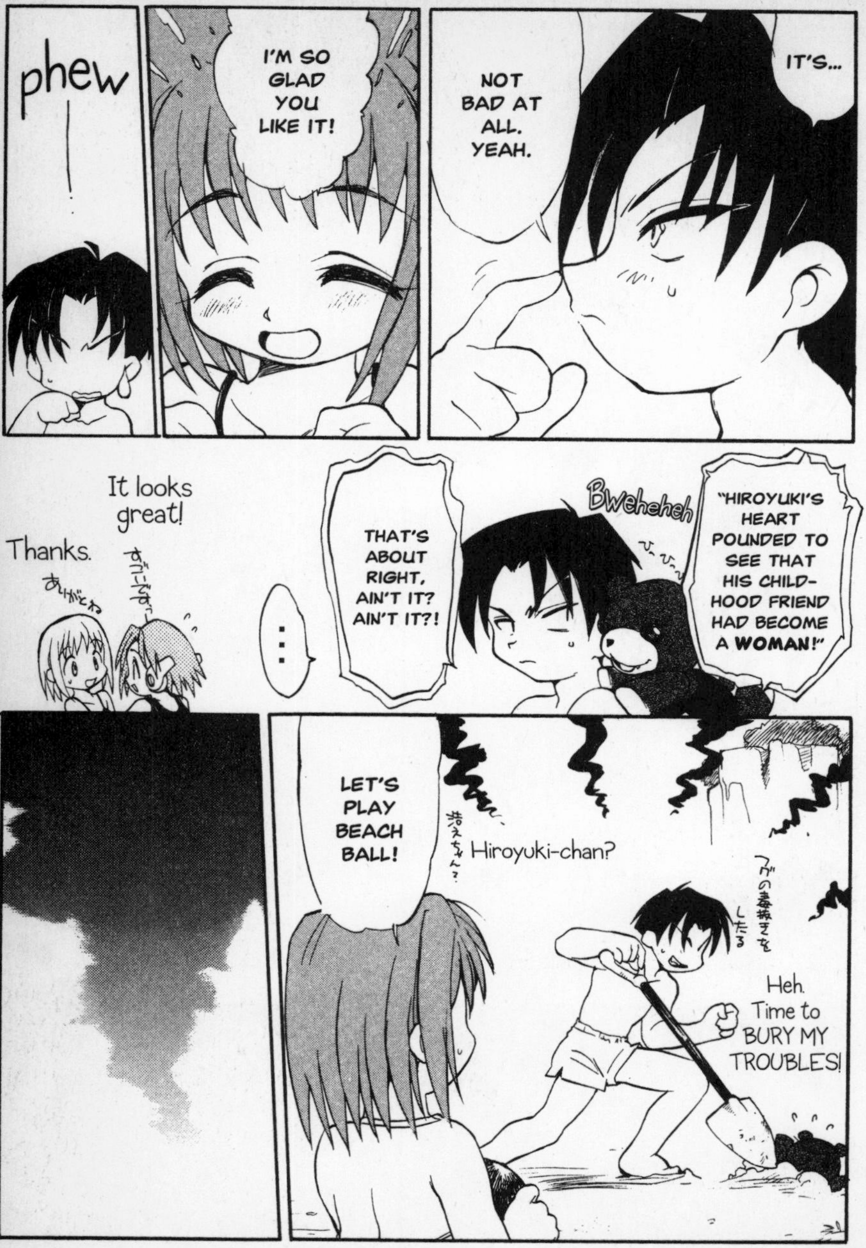
IT'S...
NOT BAD AT ALL. YEAH.
I'M SO GLAD YOU LIKE IT!
phew
"HIROYUKI'S HEART POUNDED TO SEE THAT HIS CHILD-HOOD FRIEND HAD BECOME A **WOMAN!**"
Bweheheh
THAT'S ABOUT RIGHT, AIN'T IT? AIN'T IT?!
...
It looks great!
Thanks.
LET'S PLAY BEACH BALL!
Hiroyuki-chan?
Heh. Time to BURY MY TROUBLES!

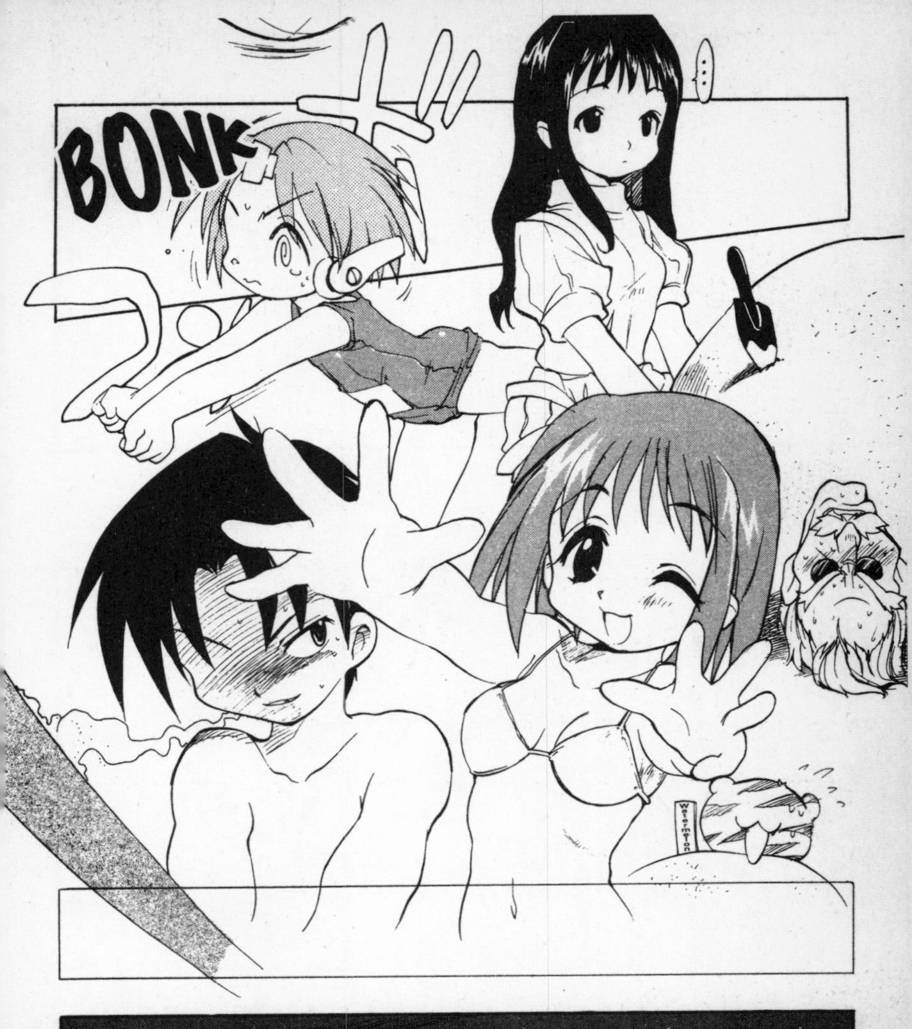
BONK
...
Watermelon
shpshhhh

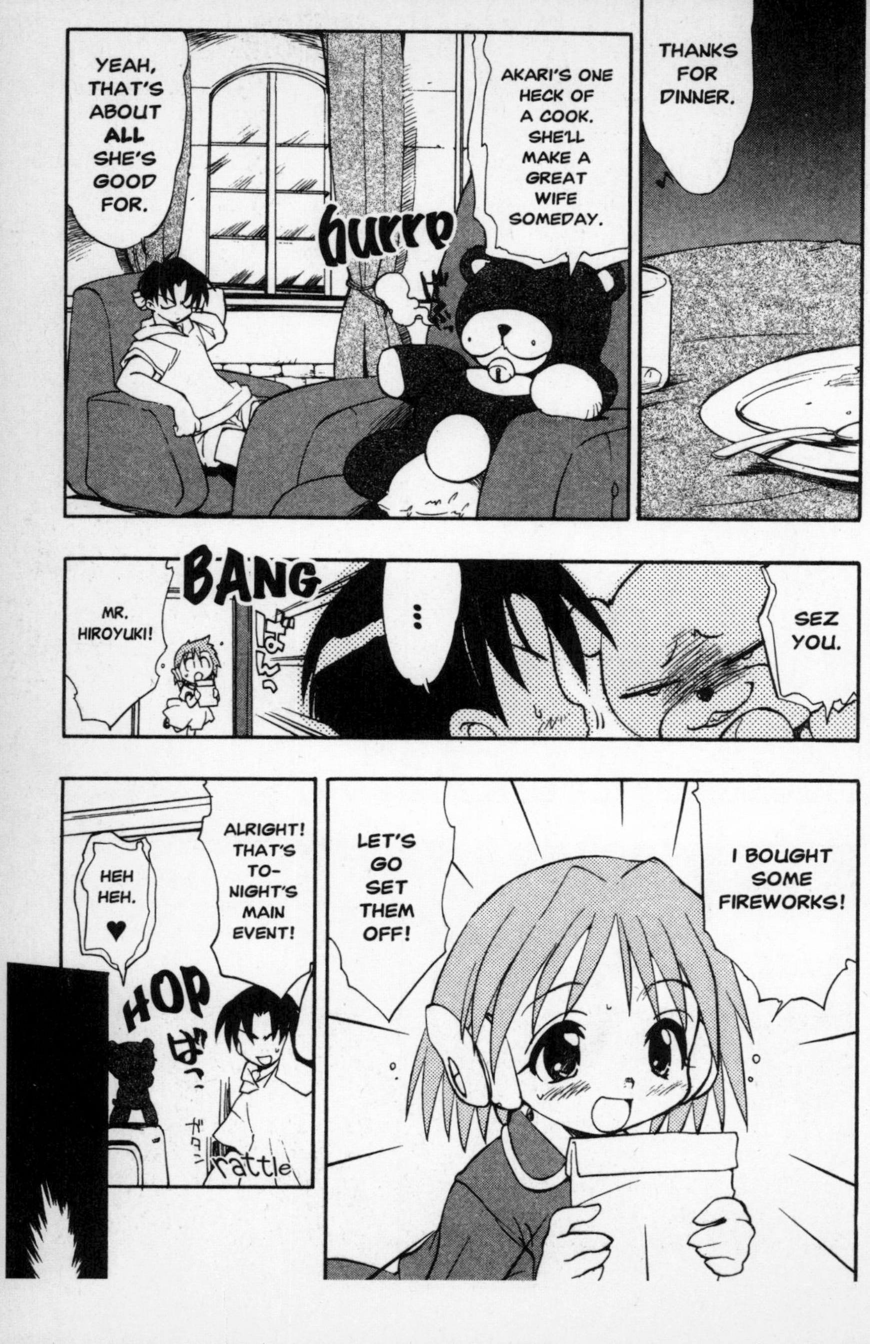
THANKS FOR DINNER.
AKARI'S ONE HECK OF A COOK. SHE'LL MAKE A GREAT WIFE SOMEDAY.
burrp
YEAH, THAT'S ABOUT ALL SHE'S GOOD FOR.
SEZ YOU.
...
BANG
MR. HIROYUKI!
I BOUGHT SOME FIREWORKS!
LET'S GO SET THEM OFF!
ALRIGHT! THAT'S TO-NIGHT'S MAIN EVENT!
HEH HEH. ♥
HOP
rattle

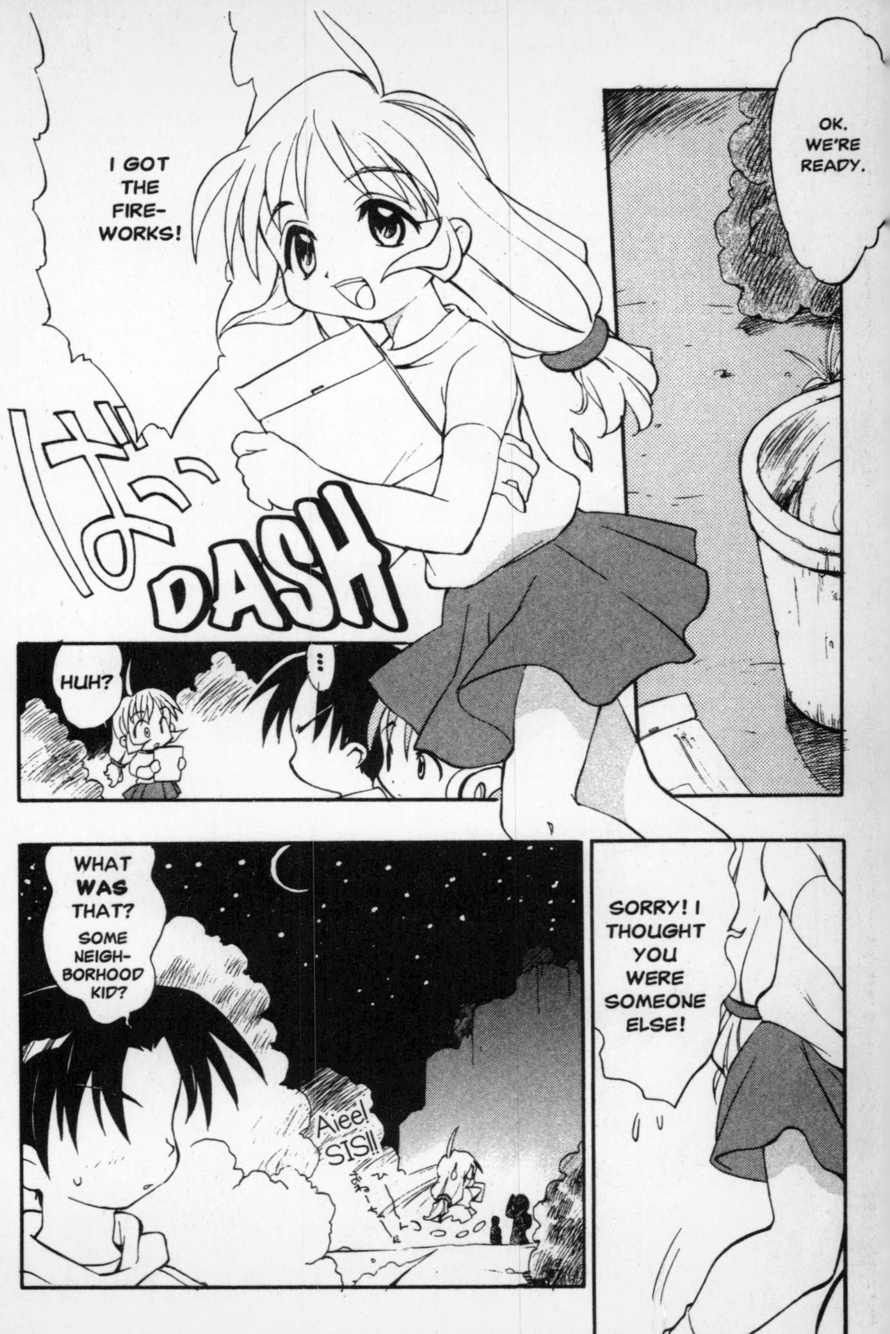
OK. WE'RE READY.
I GOT THE FIRE-WORKS!
ばっ
DASH
...
HUH?
SORRY! I THOUGHT YOU WERE SOMEONE ELSE!
WHAT WAS THAT? SOME NEIGHBORHOOD KID?
Aiee! SIS!!

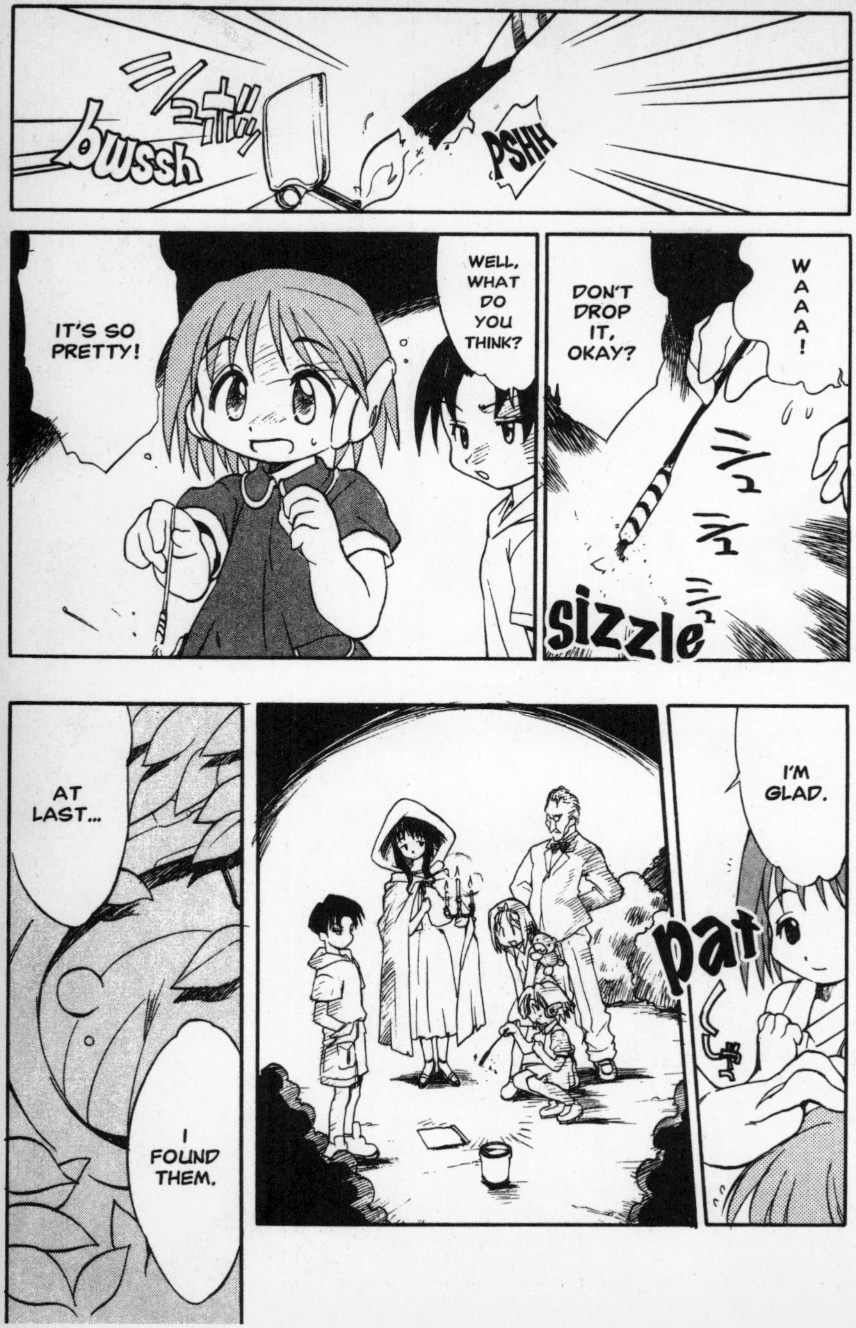

bwssh
PSHH
IT'S SO PRETTY!
WELL, WHAT DO YOU THINK?
DON'T DROP IT, OKAY?
WAAAA!
sizzle
AT LAST...
I FOUND THEM.
I'M GLAD.
pat

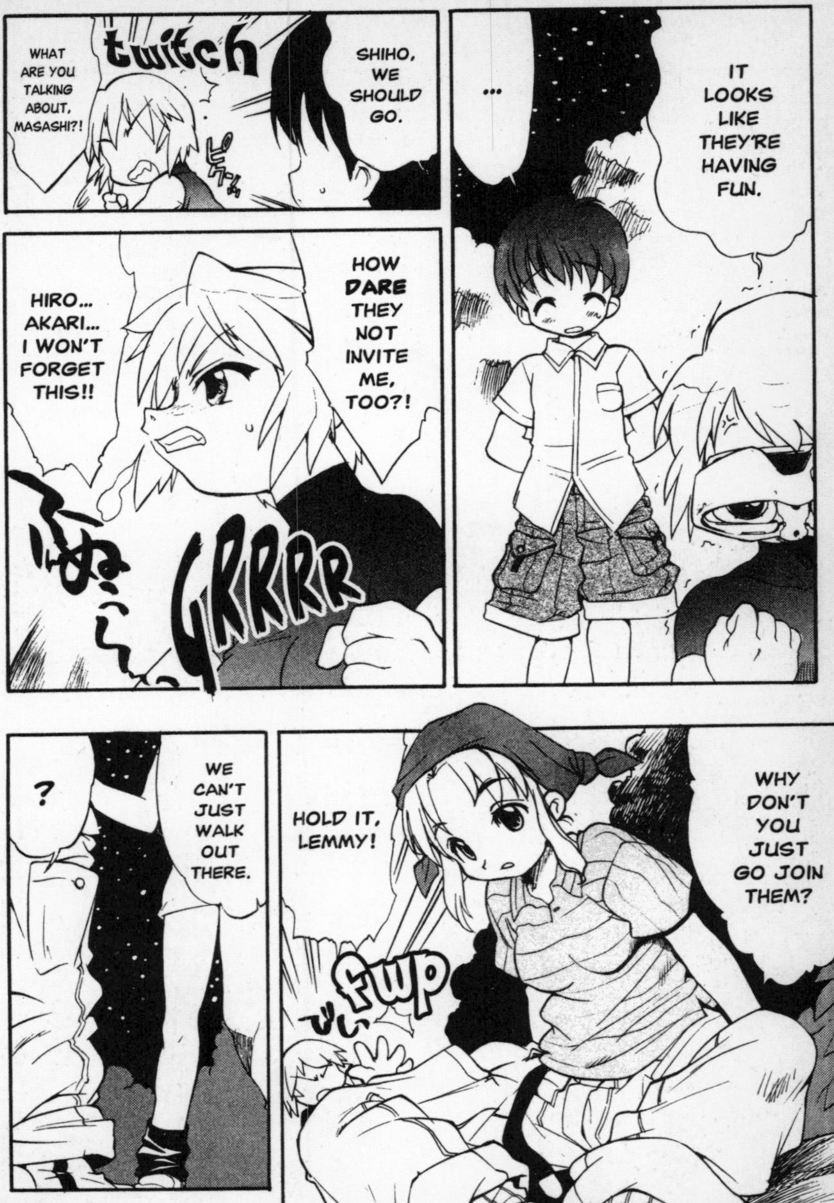
IT LOOKS LIKE THEY'RE HAVING FUN.
...
SHIHO, WE SHOULD GO.
twitch
WHAT ARE YOU TALKING ABOUT, MASASHI?!
HOW DARE THEY NOT INVITE ME, TOO?!
HIRO... AKARI... I WON'T FORGET THIS!!
GRRRR
WHY DON'T YOU JUST GO JOIN THEM?
HOLD IT, LEMMY!
fwp
WE CAN'T JUST WALK OUT THERE.
?

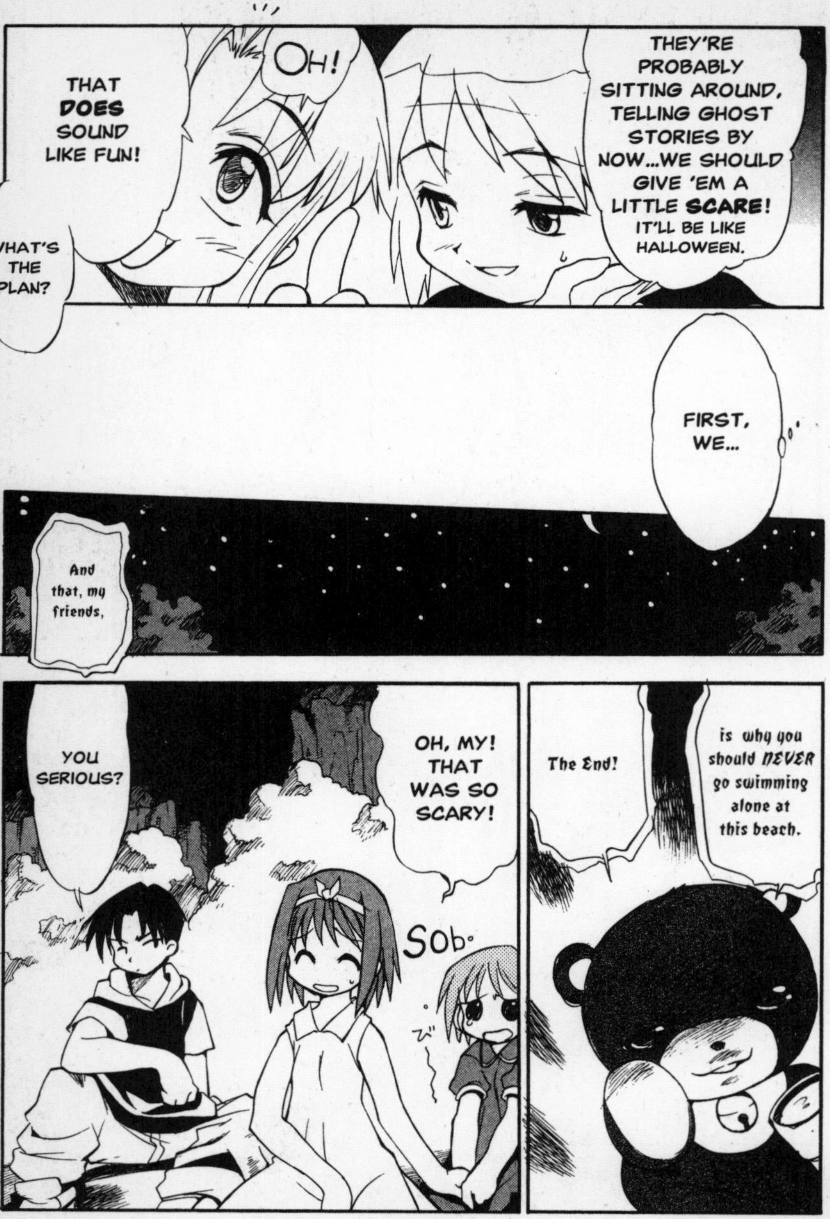
THEY'RE PROBABLY SITTING AROUND, TELLING GHOST STORIES BY NOW...WE SHOULD GIVE 'EM A LITTLE SCARE! IT'LL BE LIKE HALLOWEEN.
OH!
THAT DOES SOUND LIKE FUN!
WHAT'S THE PLAN?
FIRST, WE...
And that, my friends,
is why you should NEVER go swimming alone at this beach.
The End!
OH, MY! THAT WAS SO SCARY!
Sob
YOU SERIOUS?

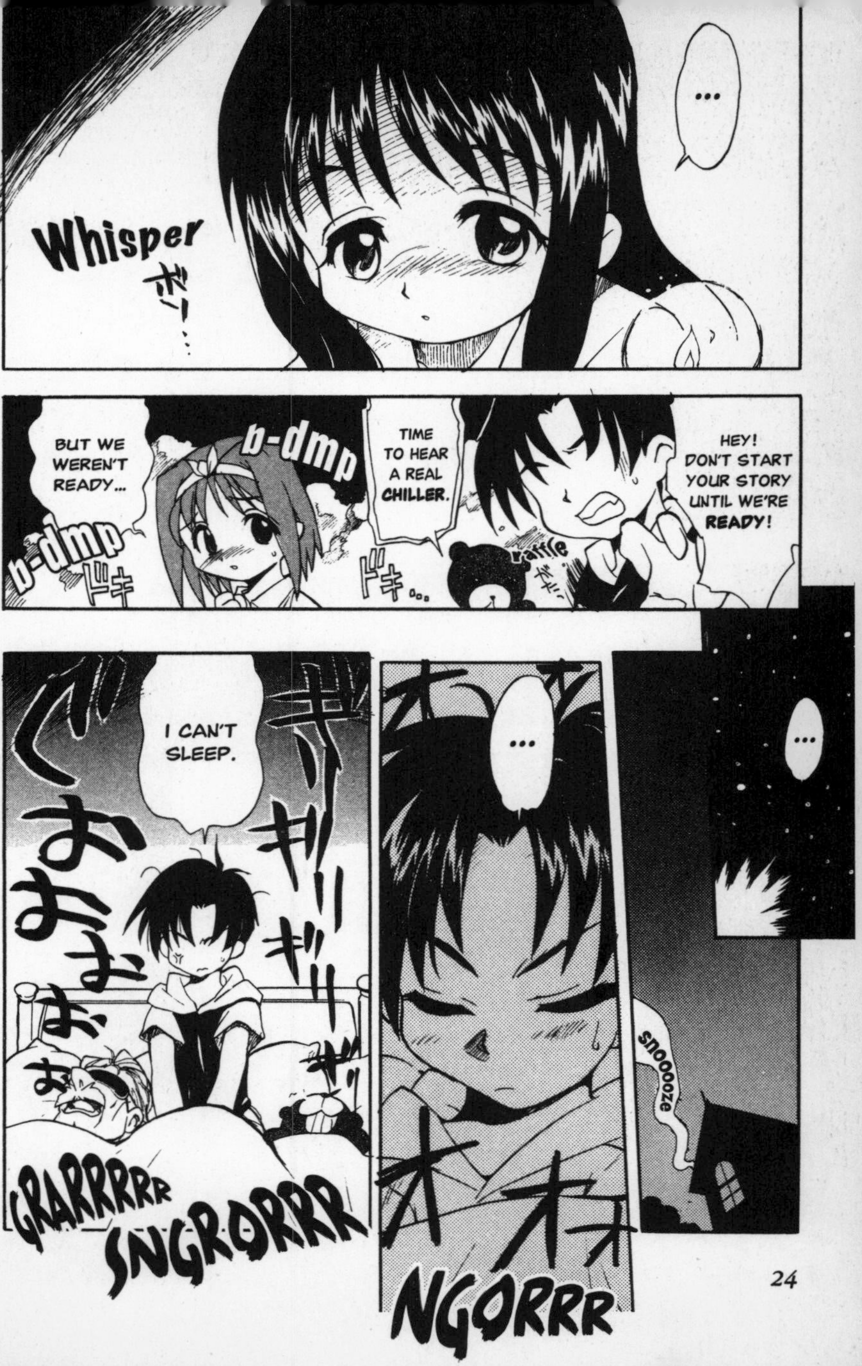
...
Whisper
HEY! DON'T START YOUR STORY UNTIL WE'RE READY!
rattle
TIME TO HEAR A REAL CHILLER.
ドキ
b-dmp
BUT WE WEREN'T READY...
b-dmp
ドキ
...
...
snoooze
NGORRR
I CAN'T SLEEP.
GRARRRRR
SNGRORRR

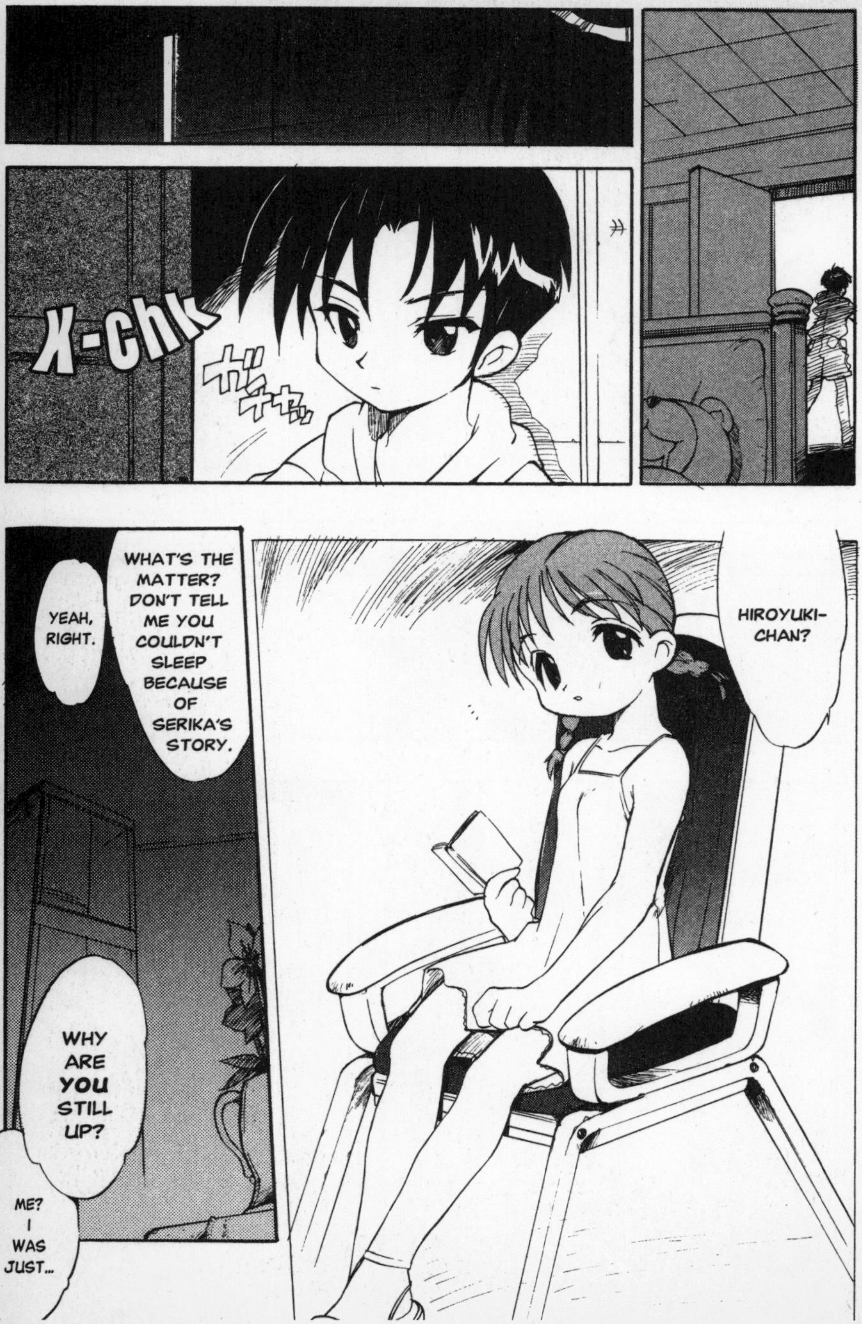
X-Chk
ガチャッ
HIROYUKI-CHAN?
WHAT'S THE MATTER? DON'T TELL ME YOU COULDN'T SLEEP BECAUSE OF SERIKA'S STORY.
YEAH, RIGHT.
WHY ARE YOU STILL UP?
ME? I WAS JUST...

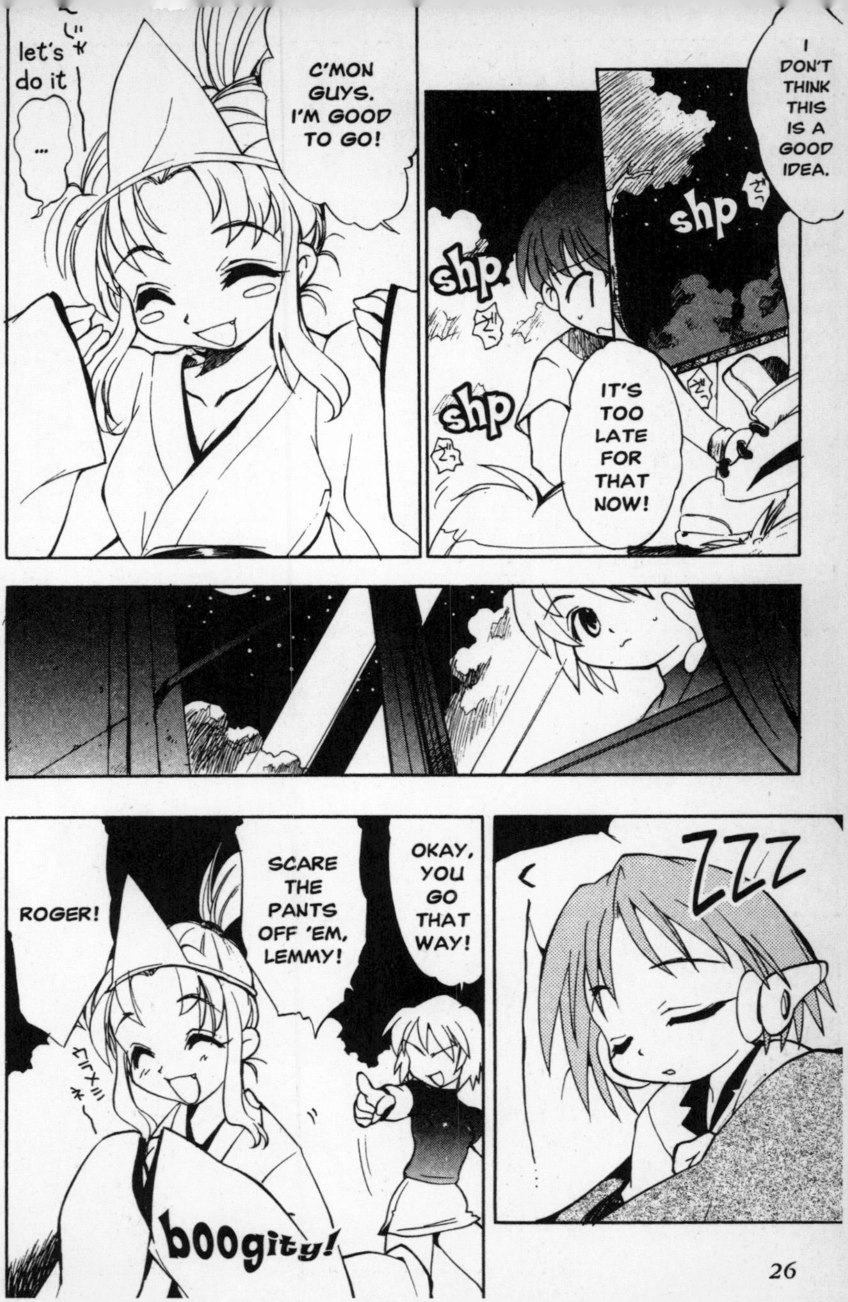
I DON'T THINK THIS IS A GOOD IDEA.
shp
shp
shp
IT'S TOO LATE FOR THAT NOW!
C'MON GUYS. I'M GOOD TO GO!
let's do it
...
ZZZ
OKAY, YOU GO THAT WAY!
SCARE THE PANTS OFF 'EM, LEMMY!
ROGER!
boogity!

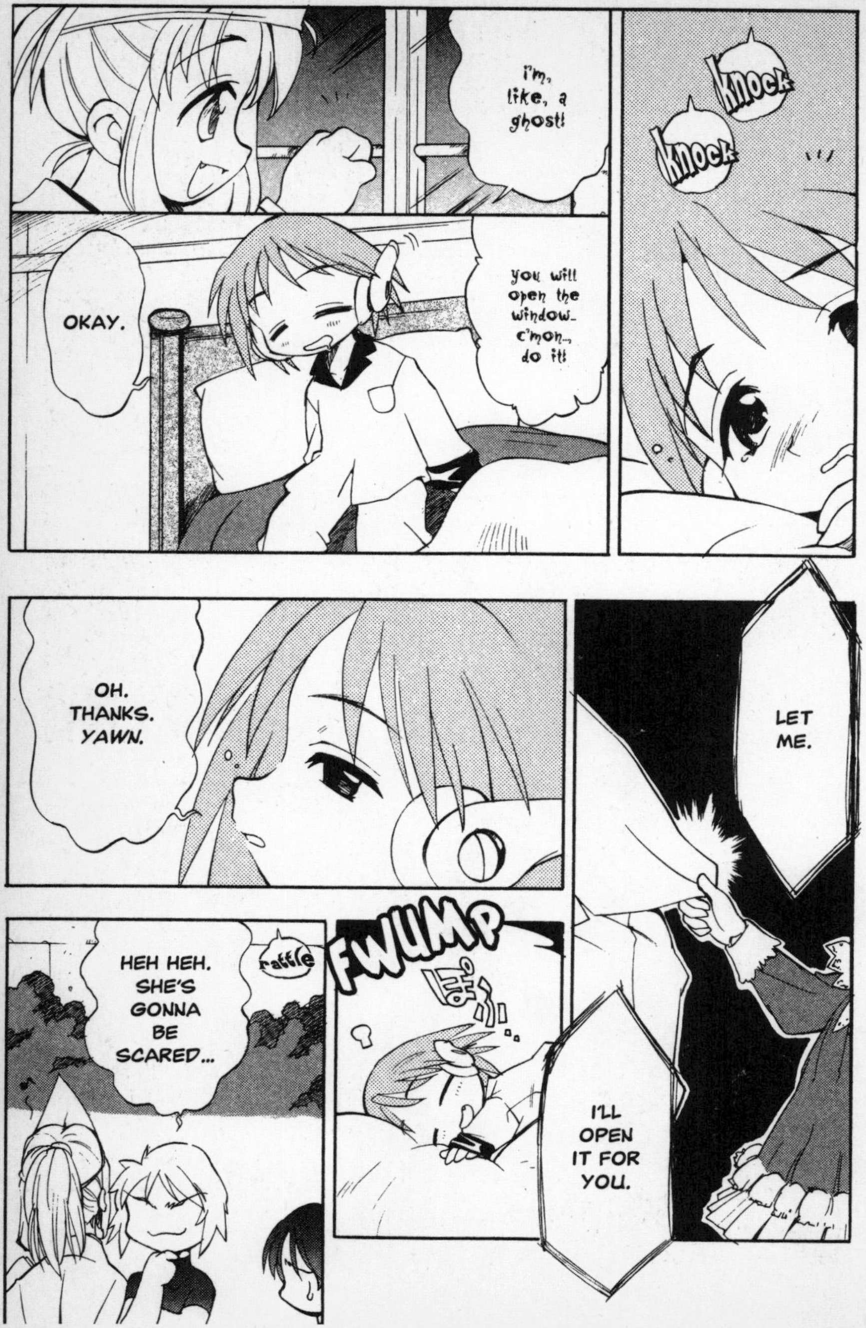
Knock
Knock
i'm, like, a ghost!
you will open the window... c'mon... do it!
OKAY.
LET ME.
OH. THANKS. YAWN.
I'LL OPEN IT FOR YOU.
FWUMP
ぽふ
rattle
HEH HEH. SHE'S GONNA BE SCARED...

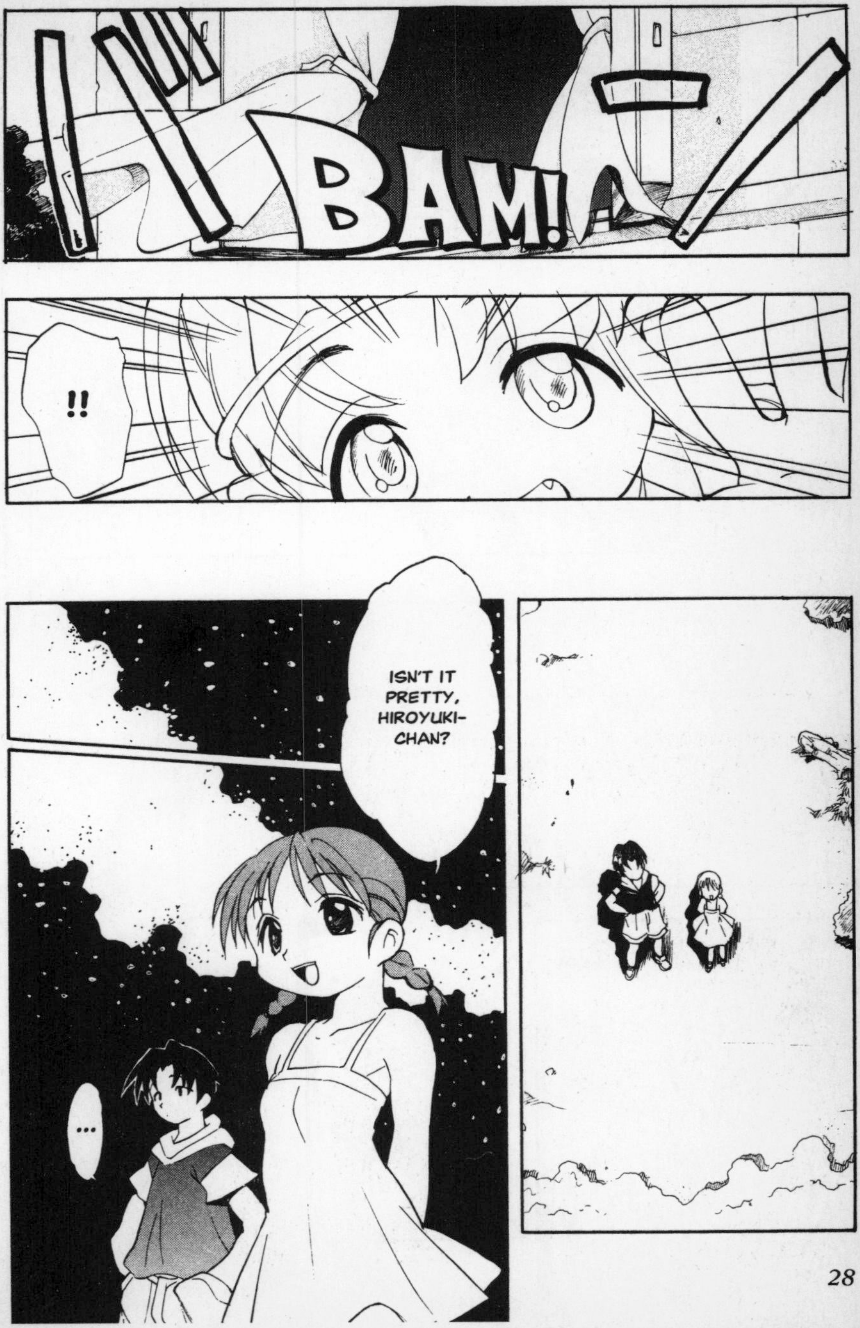
BAM!
!!
ISN'T IT PRETTY, HIROYUKI-CHAN?
...

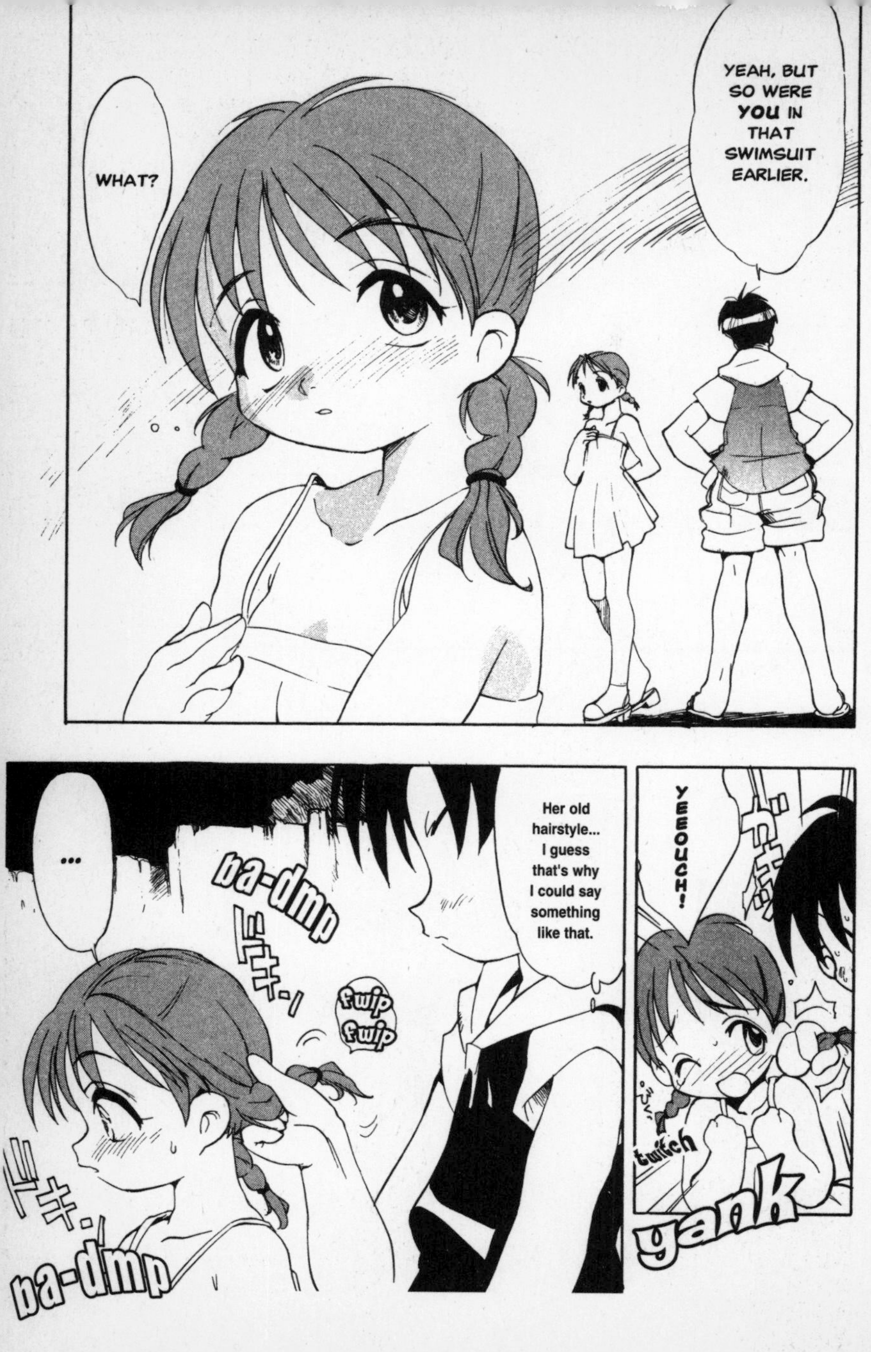
WHAT?
YEAH, BUT SO WERE YOU IN THAT SWIMSUIT EARLIER.
...
ba-dmp
Her old hairstyle... I guess that's why I could say something like that.
fwip fwip
ba-dmp
YEEOUCH!
twitch
yank

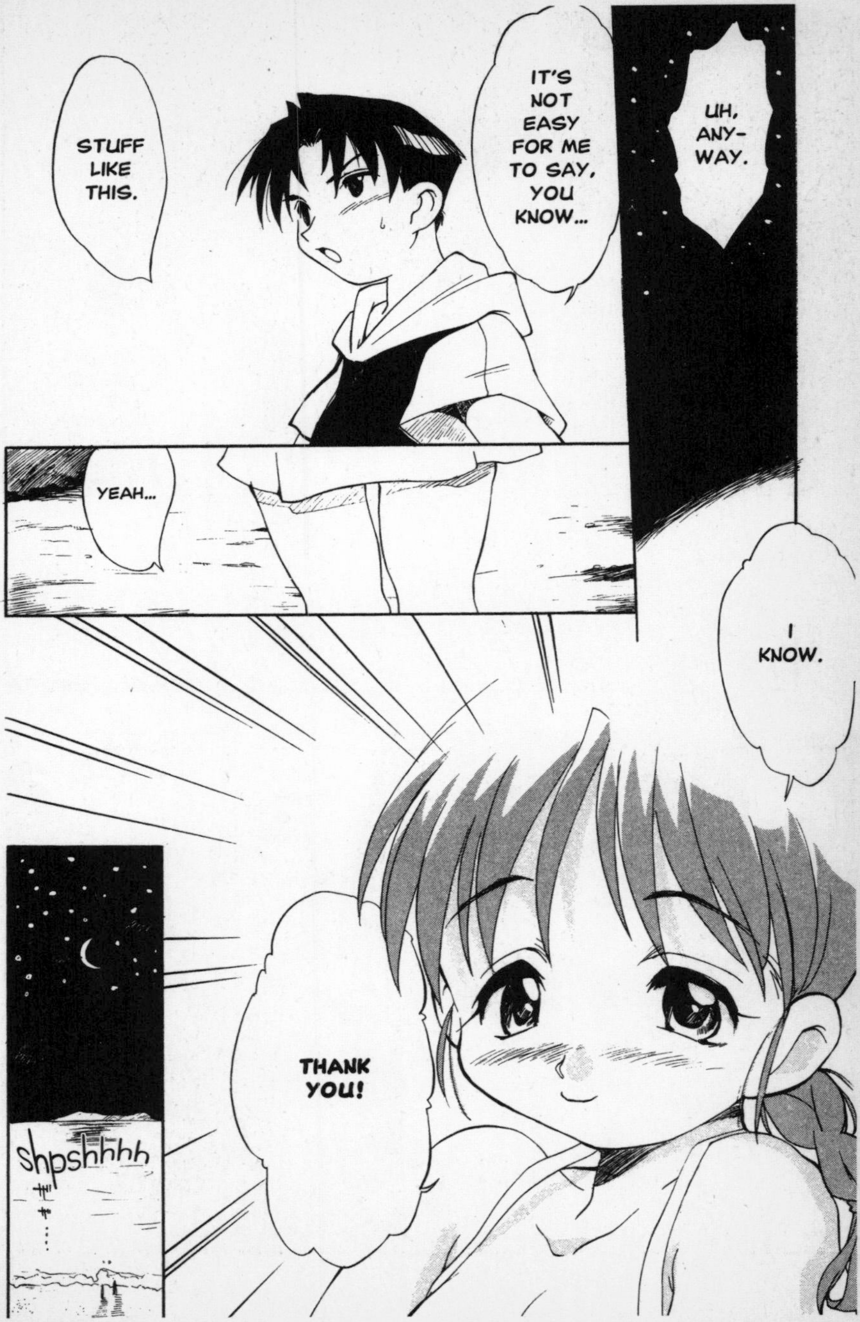
UH, ANYWAY.
IT'S NOT EASY FOR ME TO SAY, YOU KNOW...
STUFF LIKE THIS.
YEAH...
I KNOW.
THANK YOU!
shpshhhh

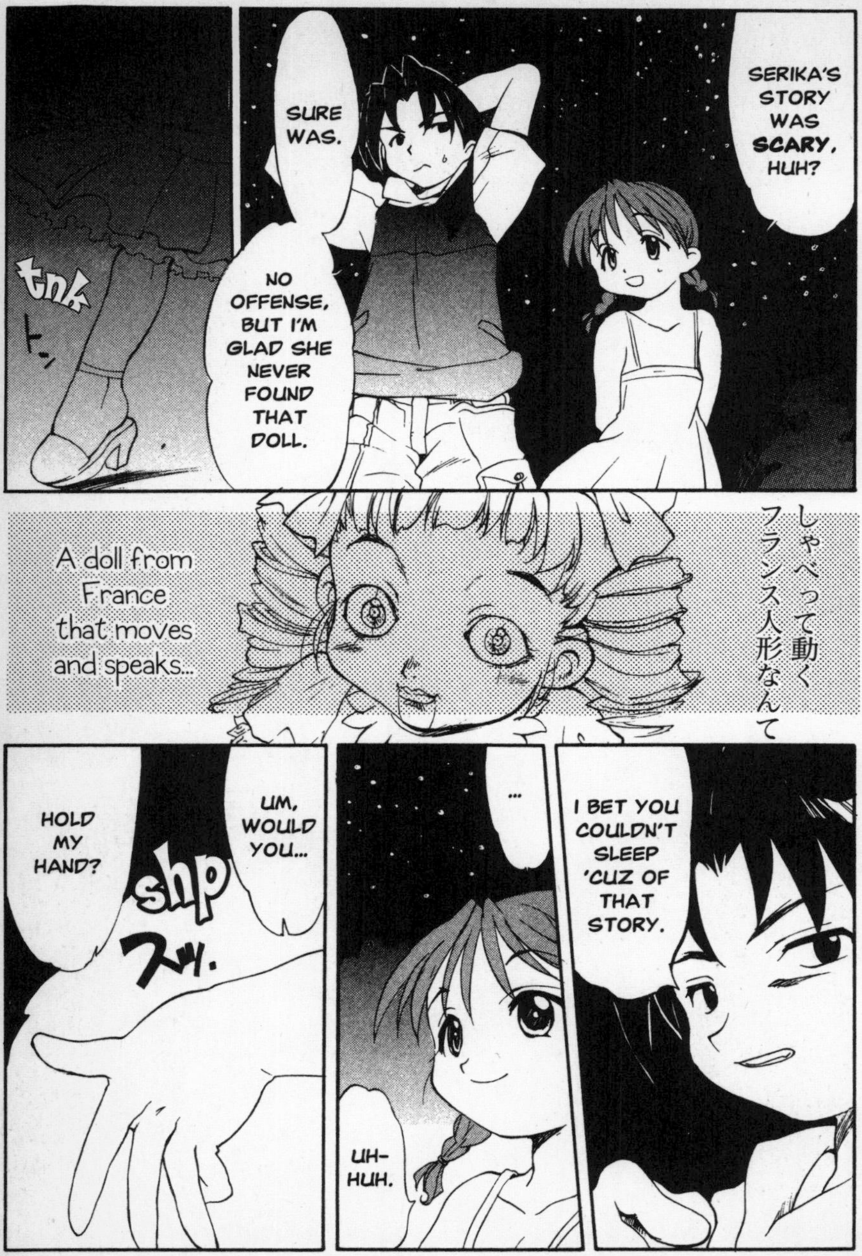

SERIKA'S STORY WAS SCARY, HUH?
SURE WAS.
NO OFFENSE, BUT I'M GLAD SHE NEVER FOUND THAT DOLL.
tnk
トッ
しゃべって動くフランス人形なんて
A doll from France that moves and speaks...
I BET YOU COULDN'T SLEEP 'CUZ OF THAT STORY.
...
UH-HUH.
UM, WOULD YOU...
HOLD MY HAND?
shp
スッ.

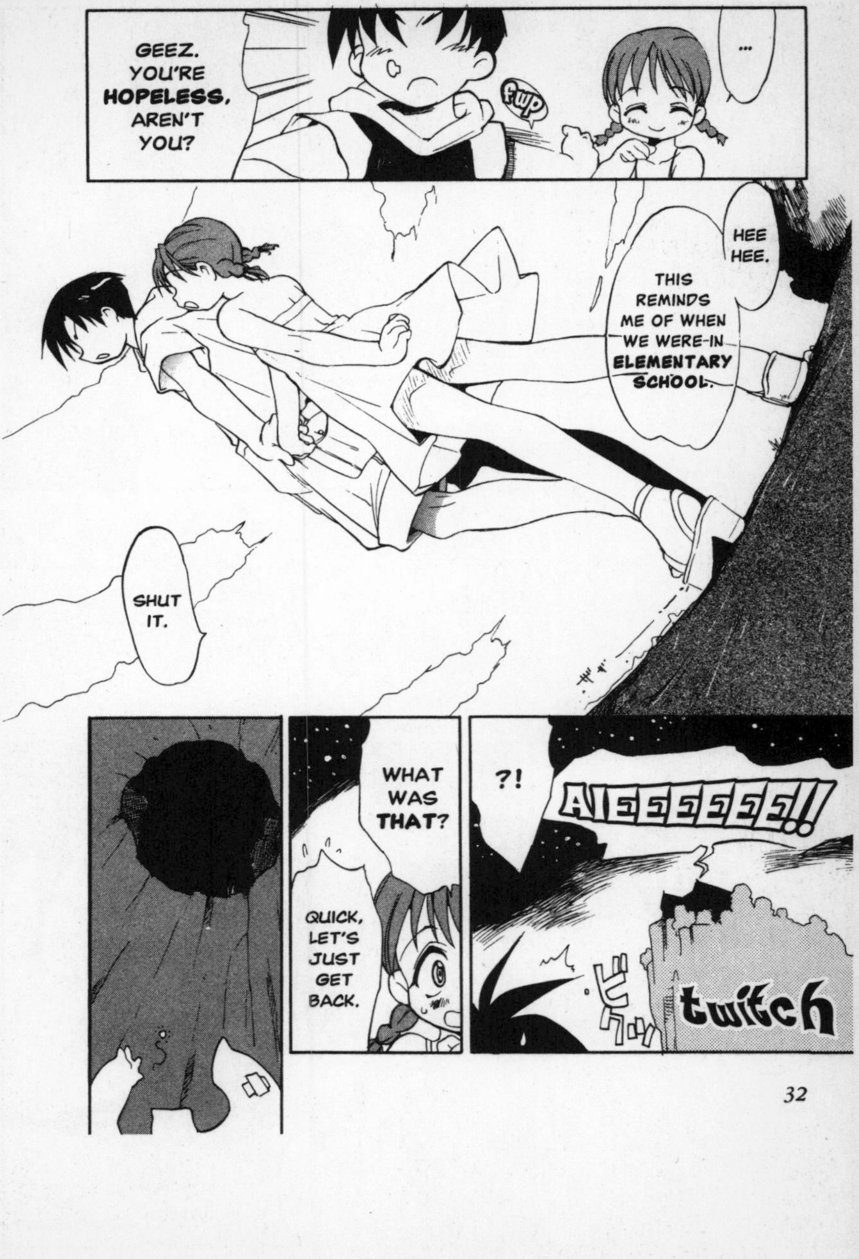
...
GEEZ. YOU'RE HOPELESS, AREN'T YOU?
fwp
HEE HEE.
THIS REMINDS ME OF WHEN WE WERE IN ELEMENTARY SCHOOL.
SHUT IT.
?!
AIEEEEEEE!!
twitch
WHAT WAS THAT?
QUICK, LET'S JUST GET BACK.

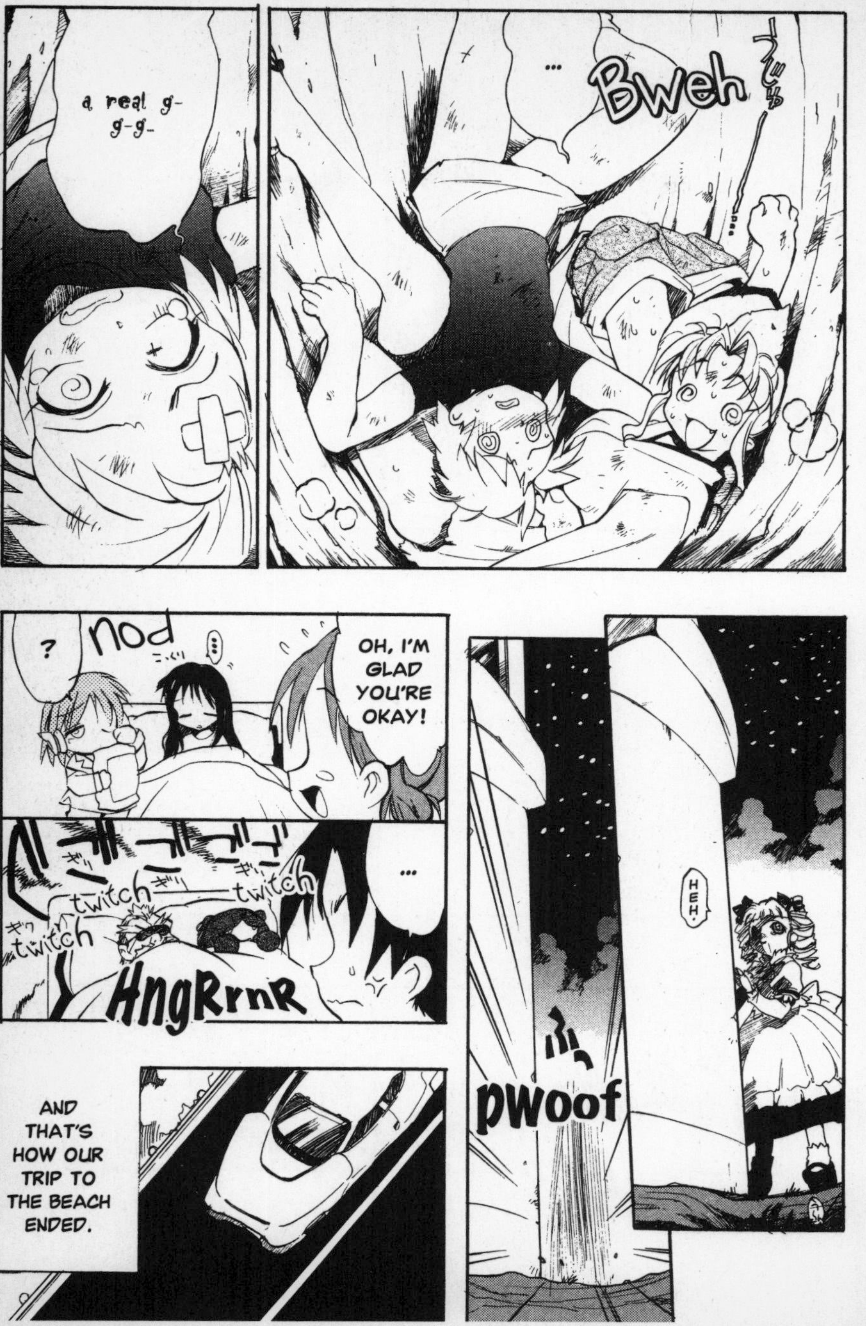

...
Bweh
a real g-
g-g-
HEH.
ふっ
pwoof
OH, I'M GLAD YOU'RE OKAY!
...
nod
?
...
twitch
twitch
twitch
HngRrnR
AND THAT'S HOW OUR TRIP TO THE BEACH ENDED.

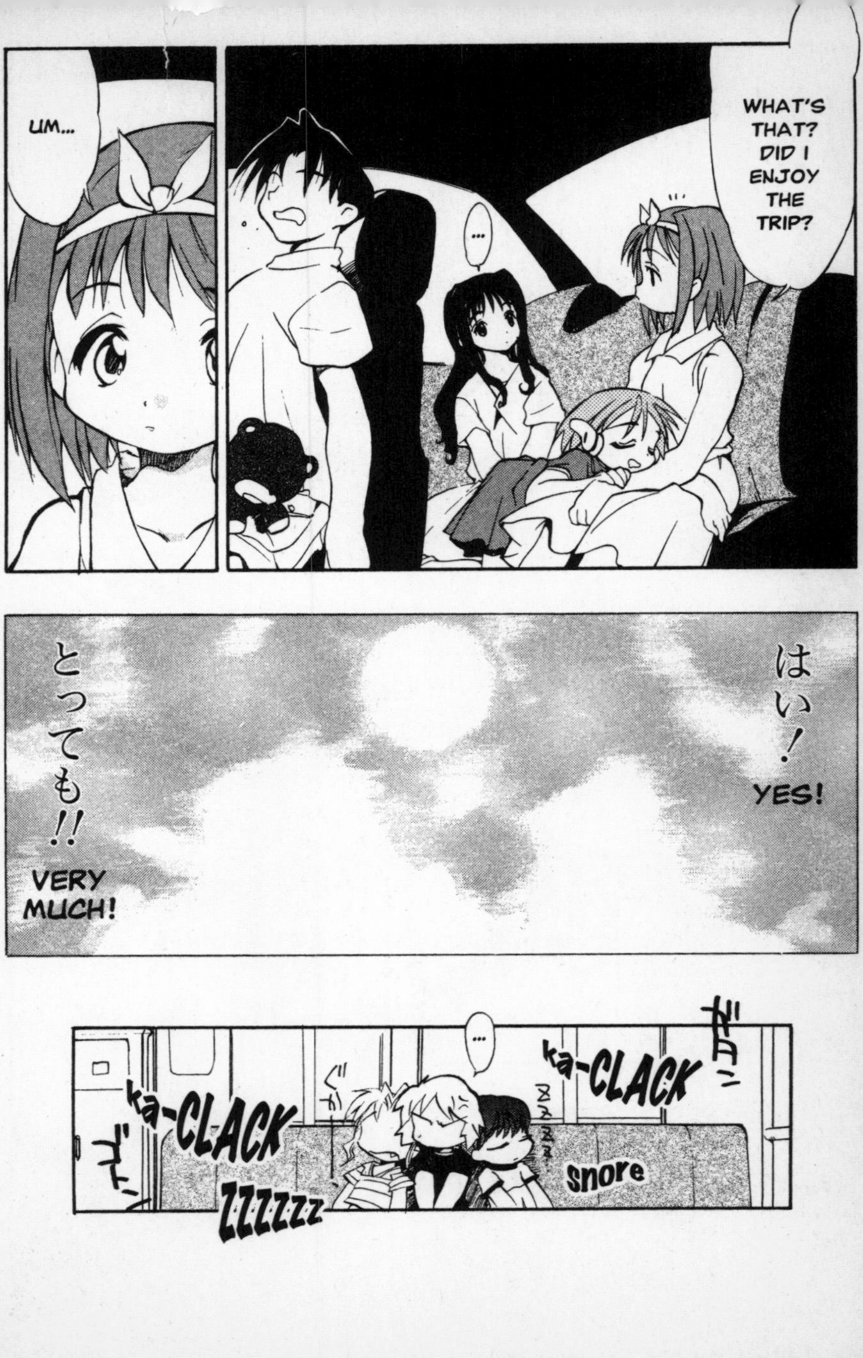

WHAT'S THAT? DID I ENJOY THE TRIP?
...
UM...
はい！
YES!
とっても!!
VERY MUCH!
...
ka-CLACK
snore
ka-CLACK
ZZZZZZ

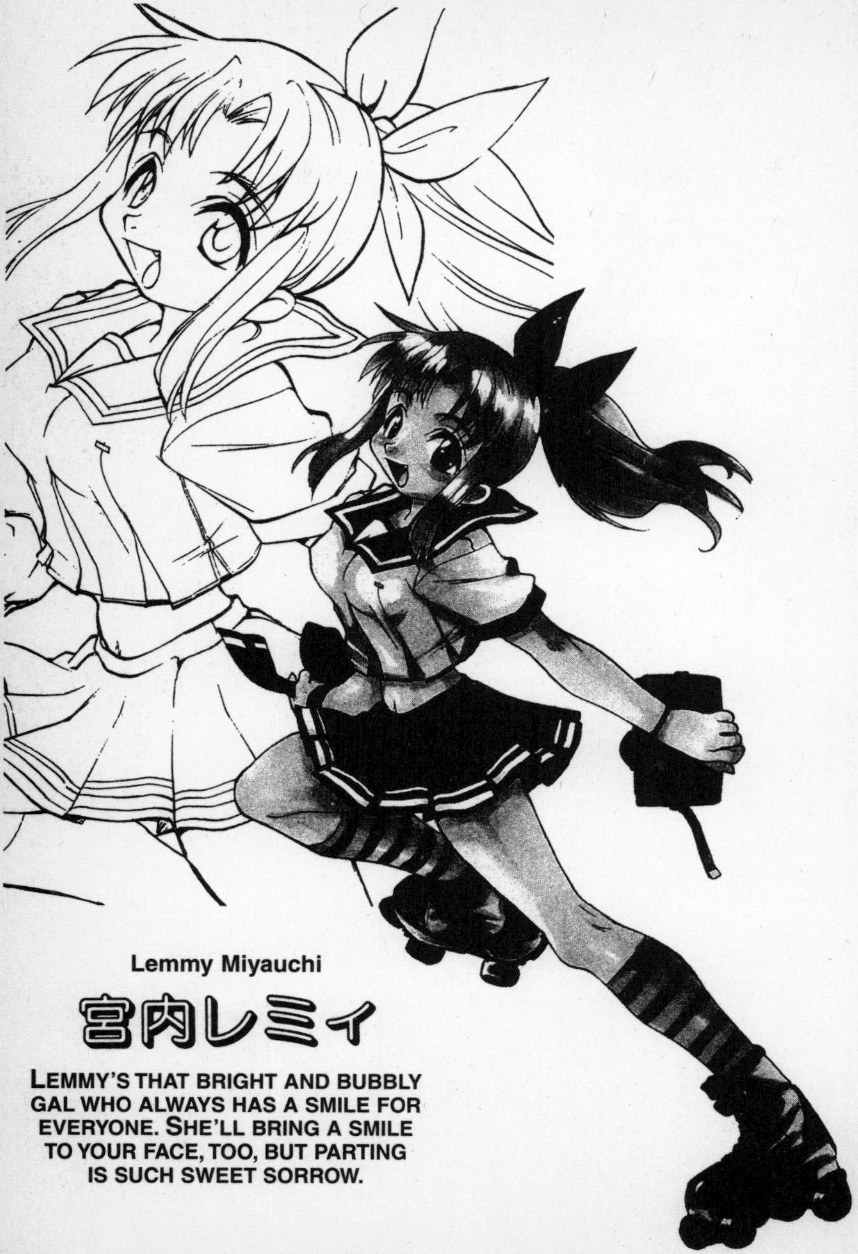

Lemmy Miyauchi

宮内レミィ

LEMMY'S THAT BRIGHT AND BUBBLY GAL WHO ALWAYS HAS A SMILE FOR EVERYONE. SHE'LL BRING A SMILE TO YOUR FACE, TOO, BUT PARTING IS SUCH SWEET SORROW.

Episode 5
『The Girl Who Fights』
~ Aoi Matsubara ~

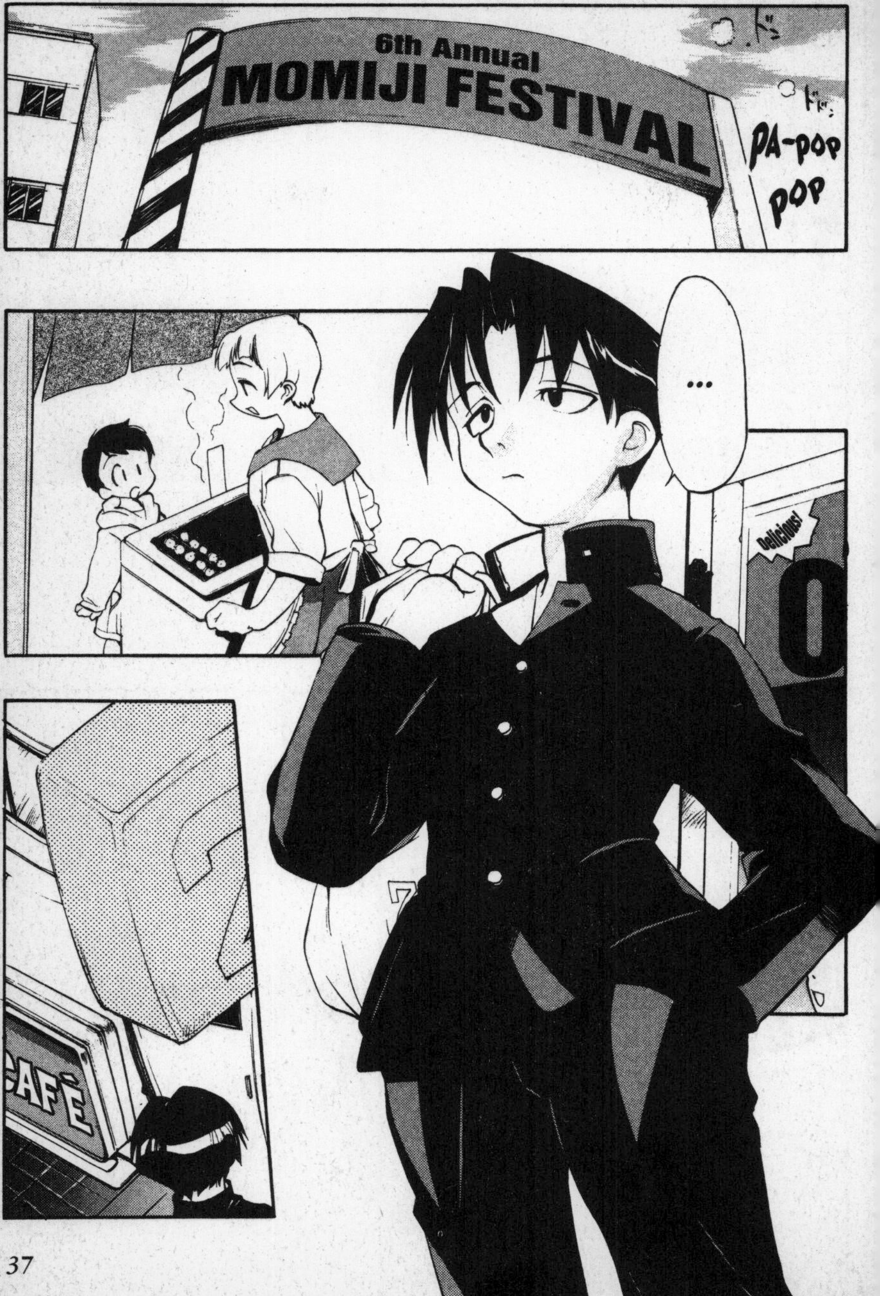
6th Annual
MOMIJI FESTIVAL
PA-POP
POP
...
Delicious!
CAFÉ

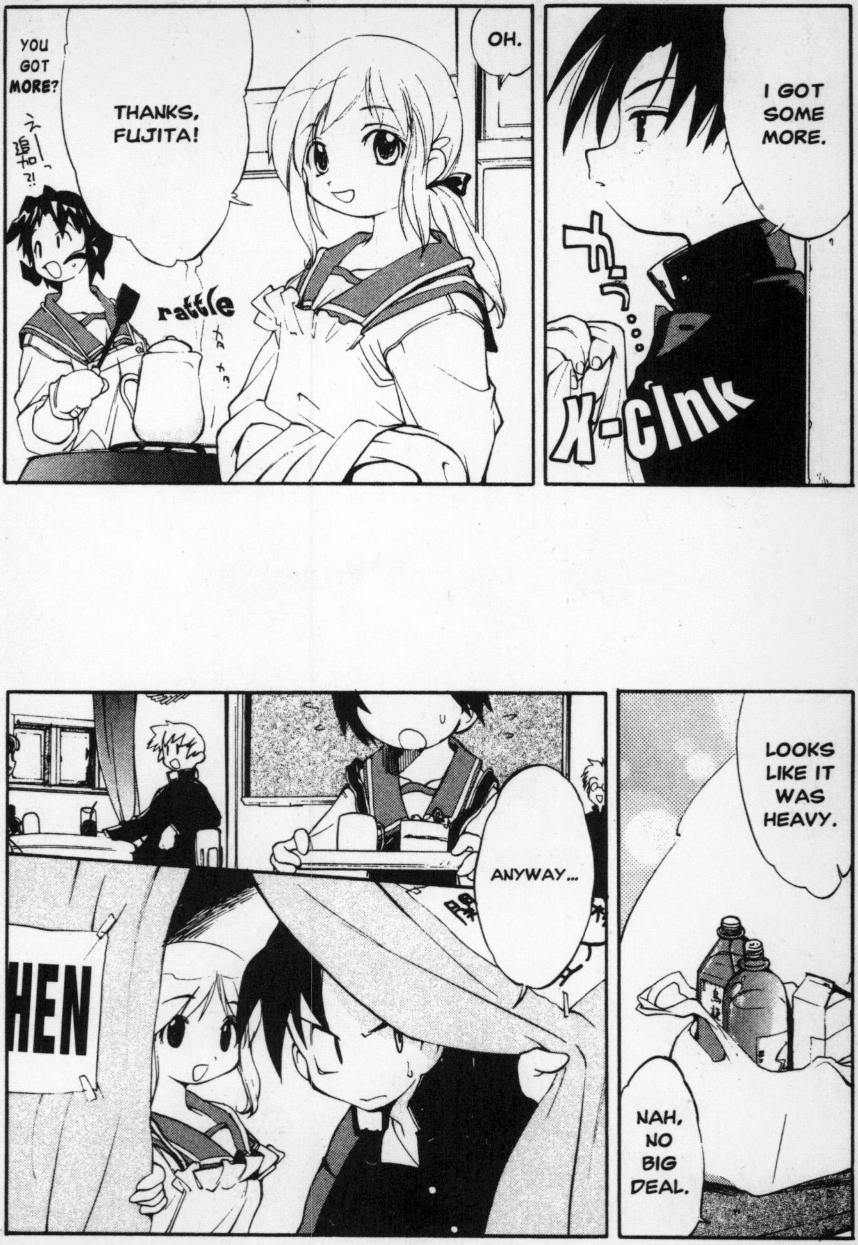
I GOT SOME MORE.
X-clnk
OH.
THANKS, FUJITA!
YOU GOT MORE?
rattle
LOOKS LIKE IT WAS HEAVY.
NAH, NO BIG DEAL.
ANYWAY...
HEN

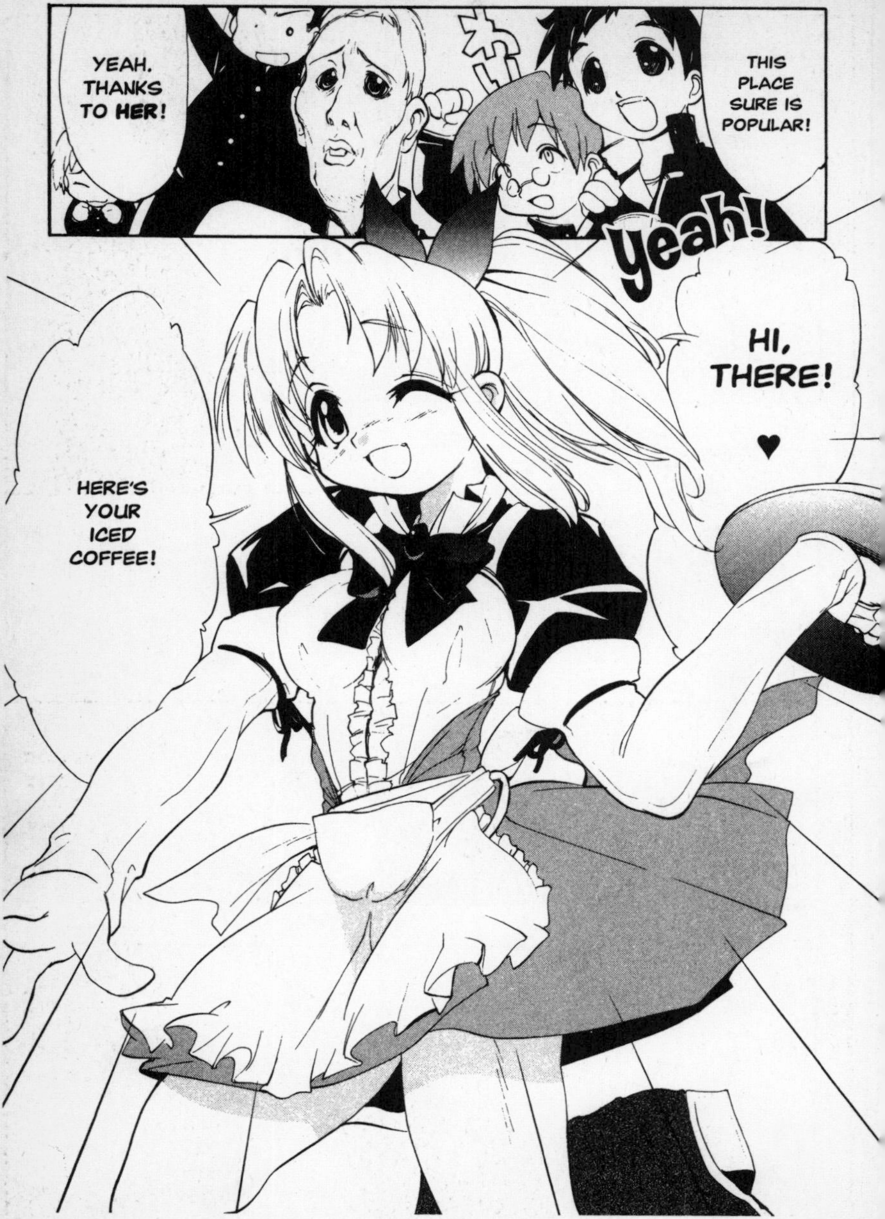
THIS PLACE SURE IS POPULAR!
YEAH. THANKS TO **HER**!
yeah!
HI, THERE! ♥
HERE'S YOUR ICED COFFEE!

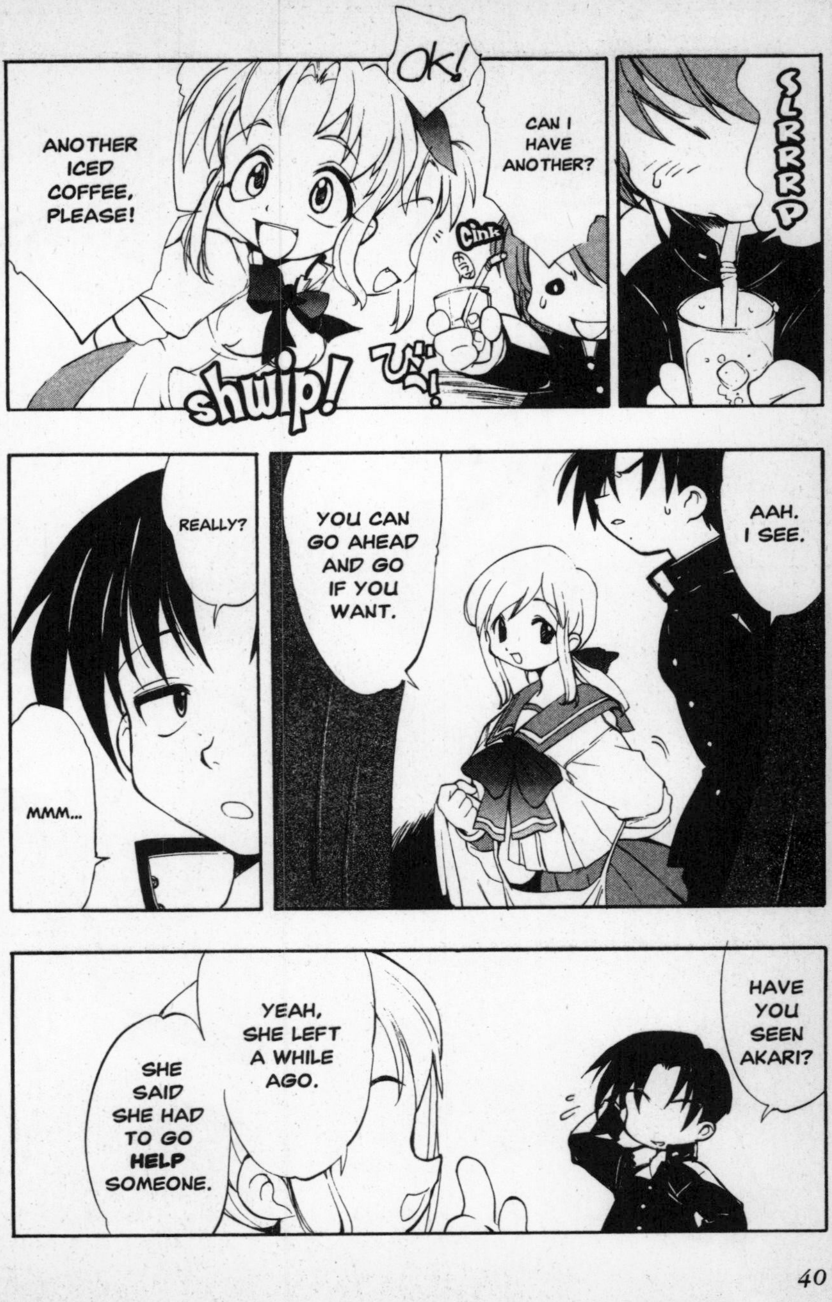

SLRRRP
CAN I HAVE ANOTHER?
OK!
Cink
ANOTHER ICED COFFEE, PLEASE!
shwip!
AAH. I SEE.
YOU CAN GO AHEAD AND GO IF YOU WANT.
REALLY?
MMM...
HAVE YOU SEEN AKARI?
YEAH, SHE LEFT A WHILE AGO.
SHE SAID SHE HAD TO GO **HELP** SOMEONE.

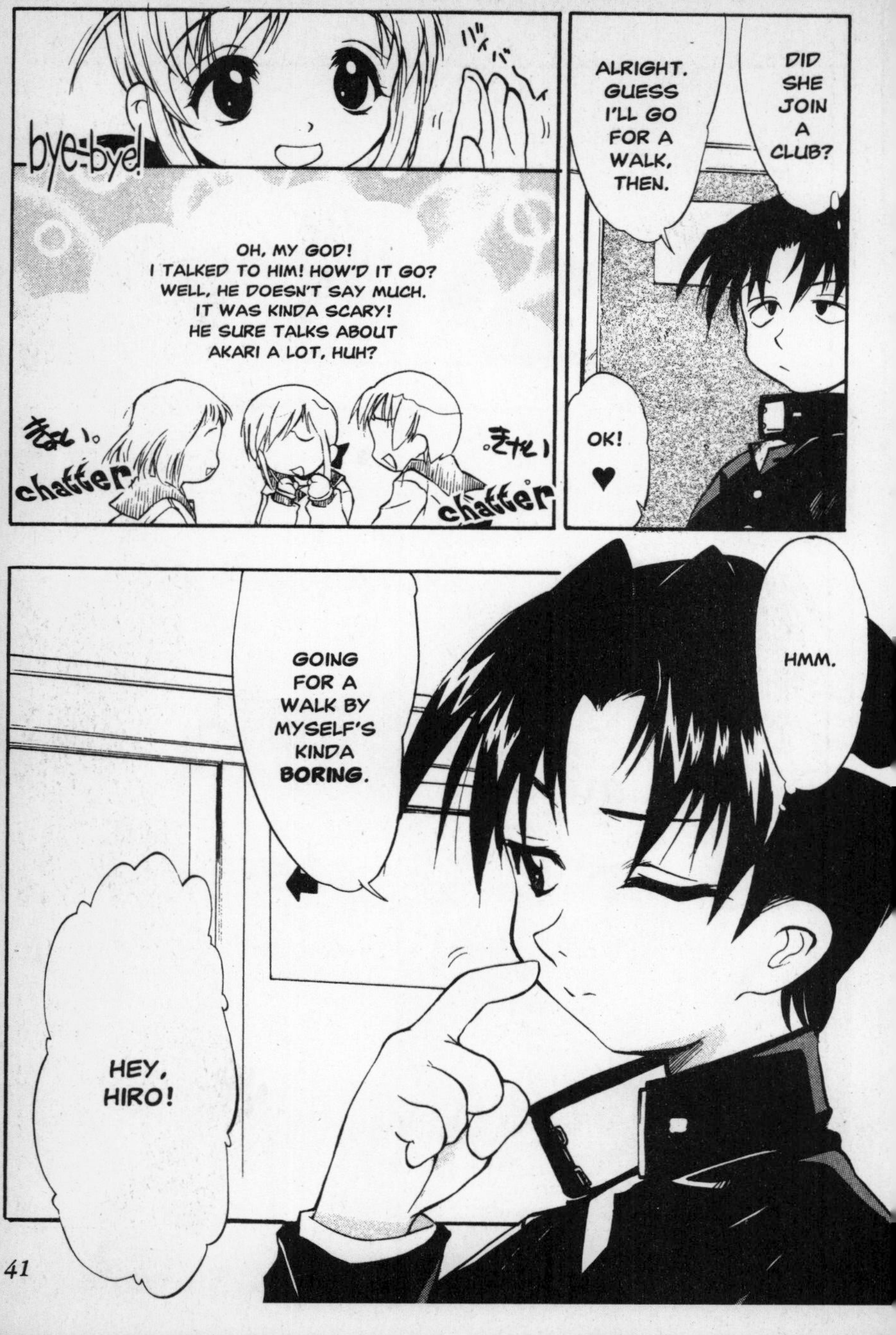
DID SHE JOIN A CLUB?
ALRIGHT. GUESS I'LL GO FOR A WALK, THEN.
OK! ♥
bye-bye!
OH, MY GOD! I TALKED TO HIM! HOW'D IT GO? WELL, HE DOESN'T SAY MUCH. IT WAS KINDA SCARY! HE SURE TALKS ABOUT AKARI A LOT, HUH?
chatter
chatter
HMM.
GOING FOR A WALK BY MYSELF'S KINDA BORING.
HEY, HIRO!

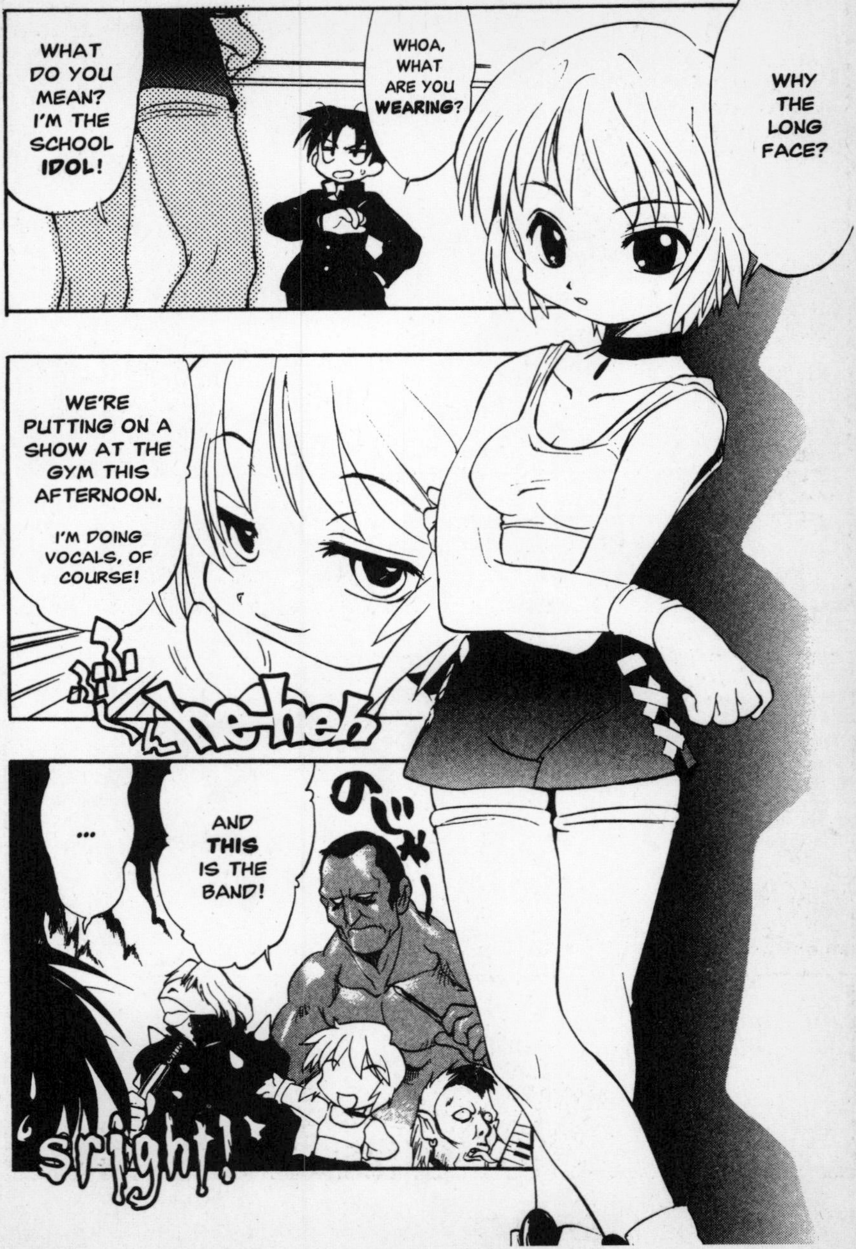
WHY THE LONG FACE?
WHOA, WHAT ARE YOU WEARING?
WHAT DO YOU MEAN? I'M THE SCHOOL IDOL!
WE'RE PUTTING ON A SHOW AT THE GYM THIS AFTERNOON.
I'M DOING VOCALS, OF COURSE!
he-heh
AND THIS IS THE BAND!
...
sright!

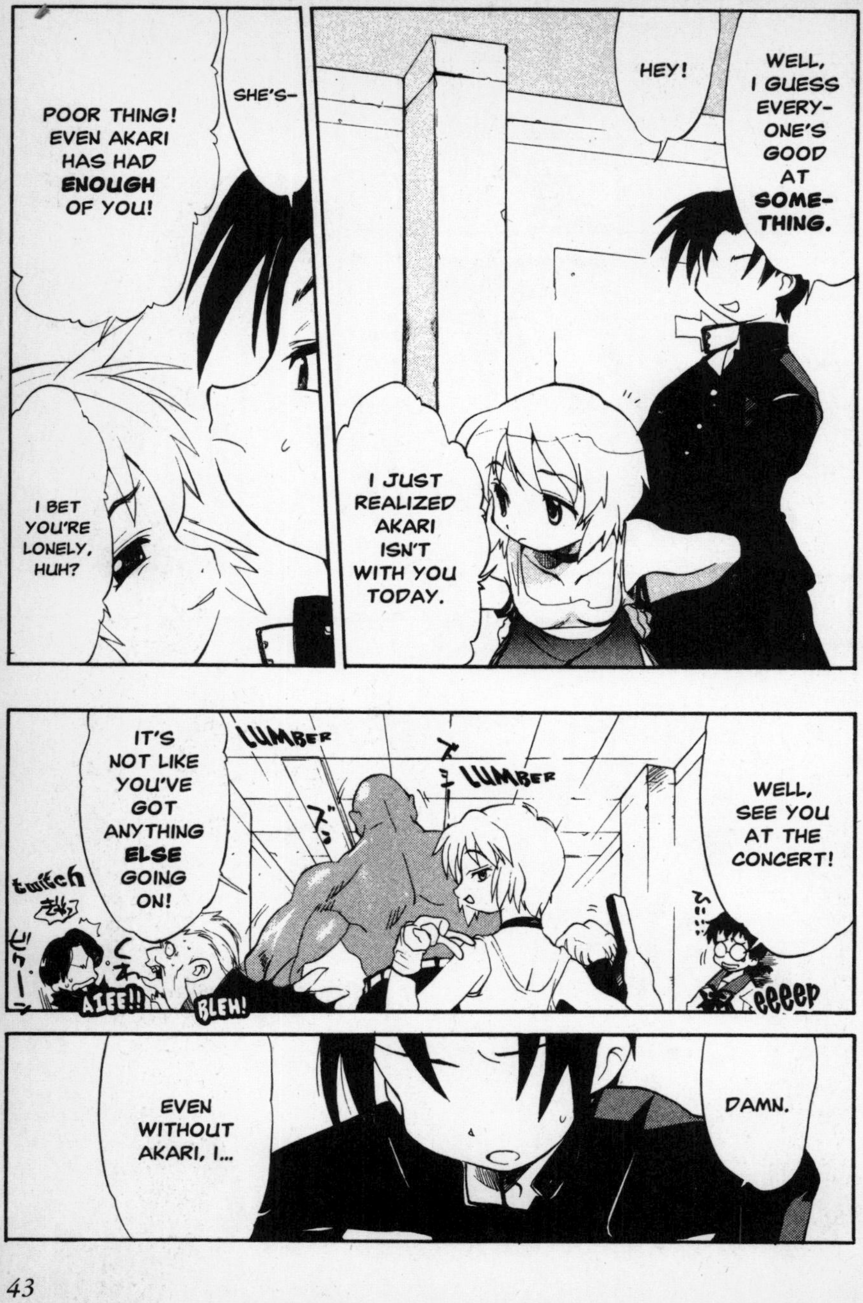
WELL, I GUESS EVERYONE'S GOOD AT SOMETHING.
HEY!
I JUST REALIZED AKARI ISN'T WITH YOU TODAY.
SHE'S-
POOR THING! EVEN AKARI HAS HAD ENOUGH OF YOU!
I BET YOU'RE LONELY, HUH?
WELL, SEE YOU AT THE CONCERT!
eeeep
LUMBER
LUMBER
IT'S NOT LIKE YOU'VE GOT ANYTHING ELSE GOING ON!
twitch
AIEE!!
BLEH!
DAMN.
EVEN WITHOUT AKARI, I...

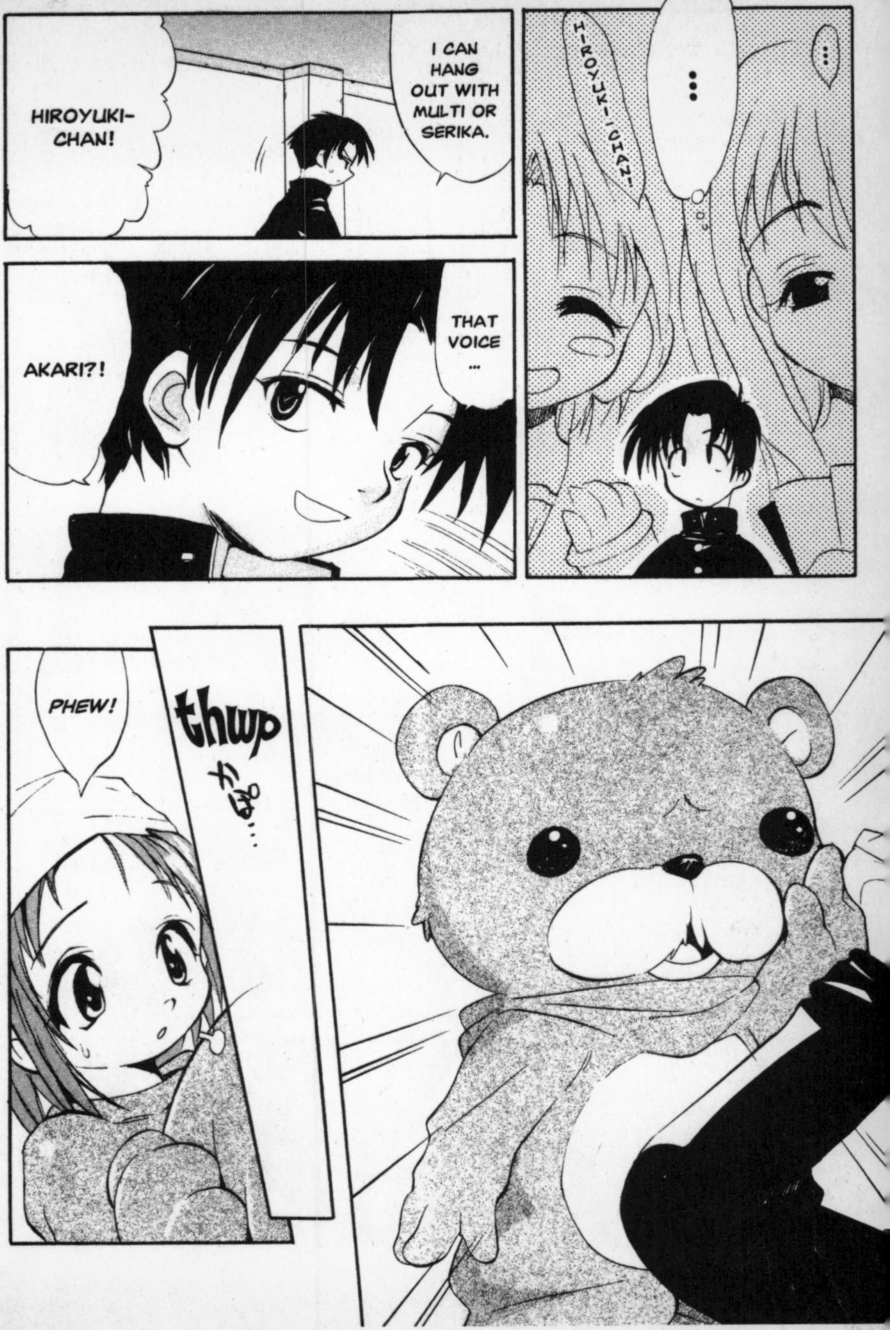
...
HIROYUKI-CHAN!
I CAN HANG OUT WITH MULTI OR SERIKA.
HIROYUKI-CHAN!
THAT VOICE ...
AKARI?!
thwp
PHEW!

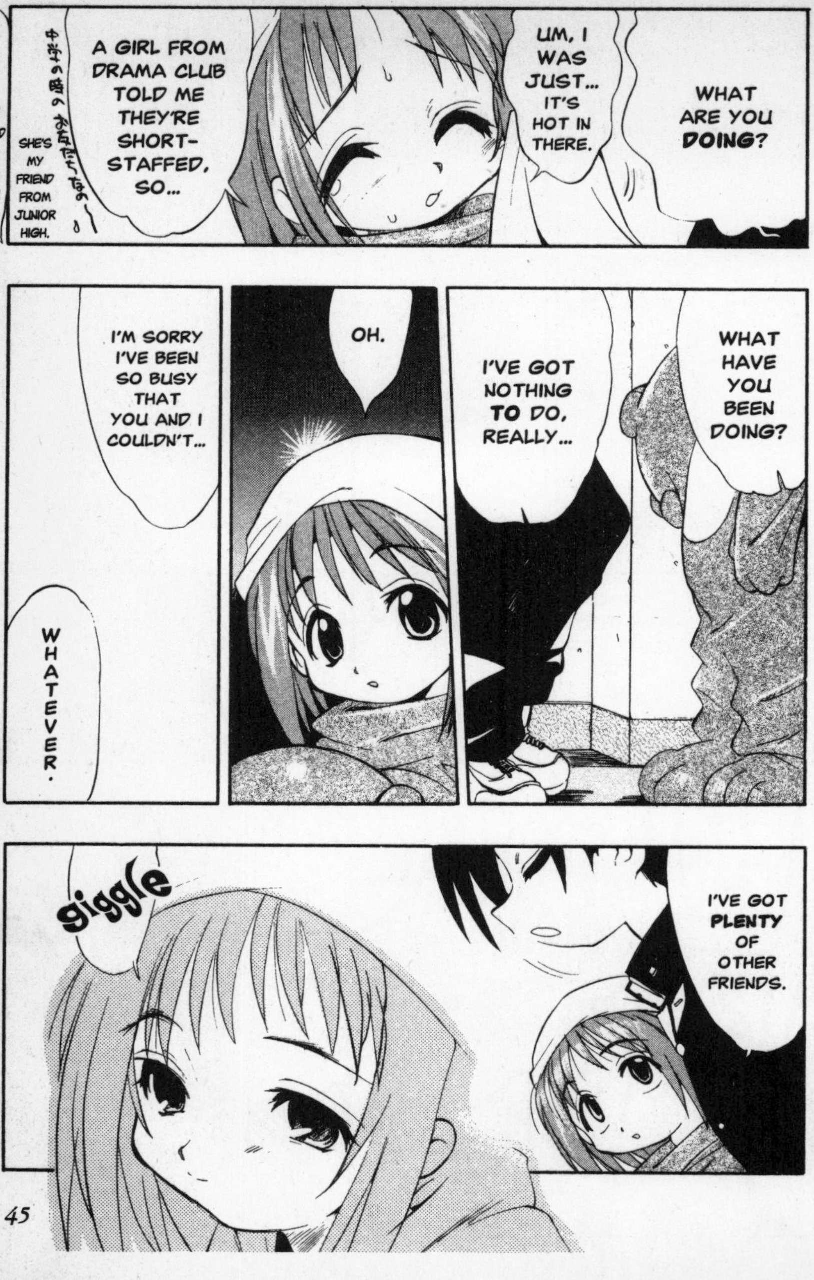
WHAT ARE YOU DOING?
UM, I WAS JUST... IT'S HOT IN THERE.
A GIRL FROM DRAMA CLUB TOLD ME THEY'RE SHORT-STAFFED, SO...
中学の時のお友だちなの〜♪
SHE'S MY FRIEND FROM JUNIOR HIGH.
I BET YOU JUST WANTED TO WEAR THAT!
WHAT HAVE YOU BEEN DOING?
I'VE GOT NOTHING TO DO, REALLY...
OH.
I'M SORRY I'VE BEEN SO BUSY THAT YOU AND I COULDN'T...
WHATEVER.
I'VE GOT PLENTY OF OTHER FRIENDS.
giggle

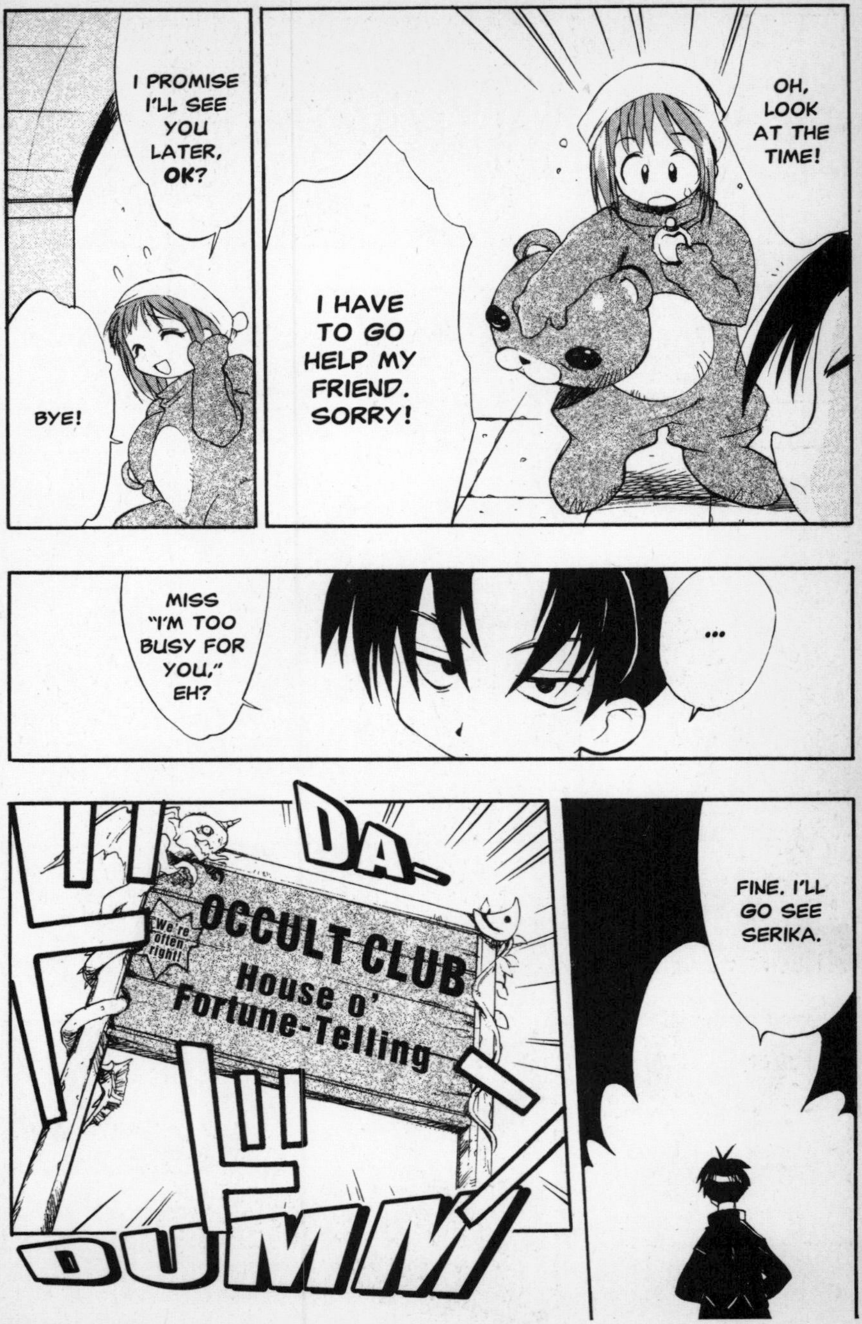
OH, LOOK AT THE TIME!
I HAVE TO GO HELP MY FRIEND. SORRY!
I PROMISE I'LL SEE YOU LATER, **OK**?
BYE!
...
MISS "I'M TOO BUSY FOR YOU," EH?
FINE. I'LL GO SEE SERIKA.
DA-
OCCULT CLUB
House o' Fortune-Telling
We're often right!
DUMM

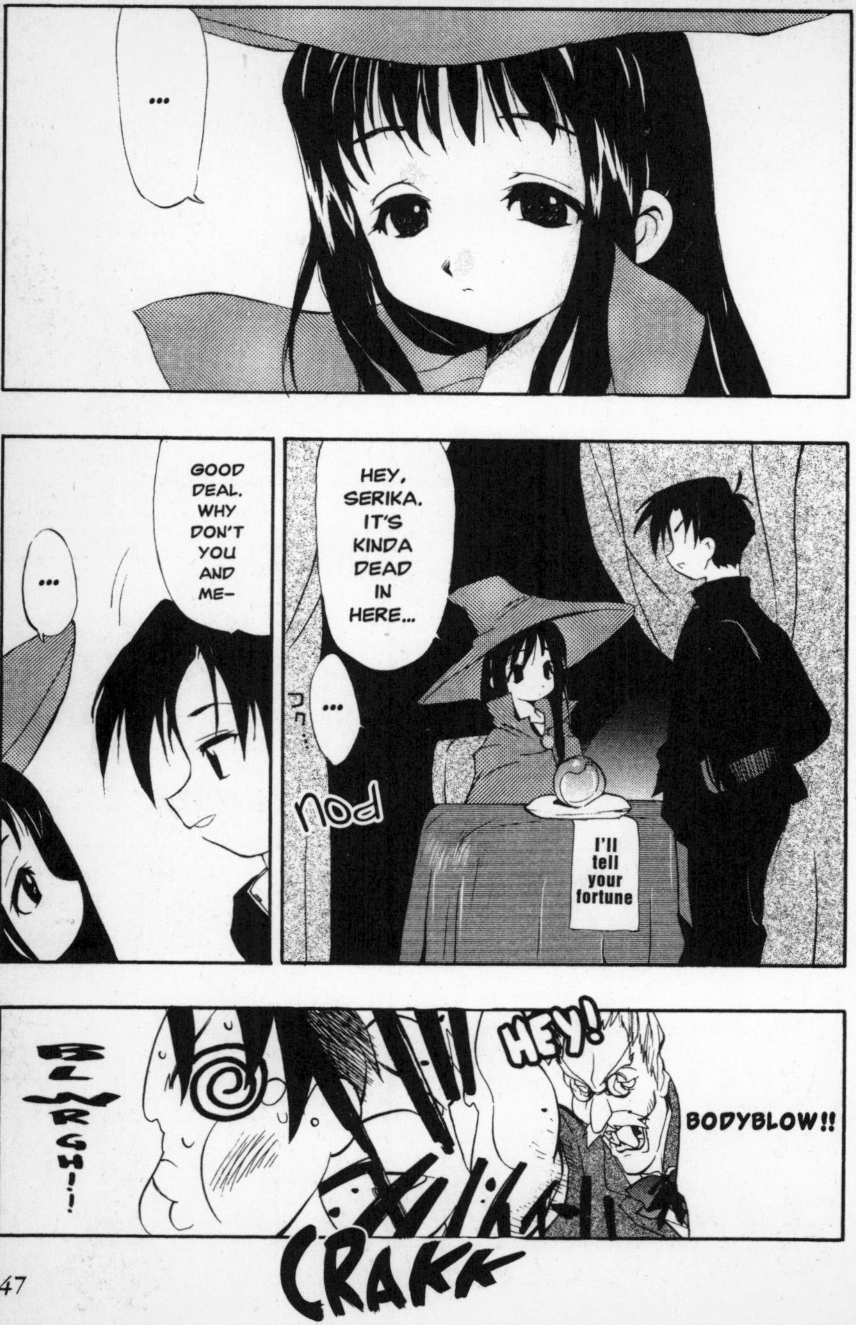
...
HEY, SERIKA. IT'S KINDA DEAD IN HERE...
...
nod
I'll tell your fortune
GOOD DEAL. WHY DON'T YOU AND ME–
...
HEY!
BODYBLOW!!
BLURGH!!
CRAKK

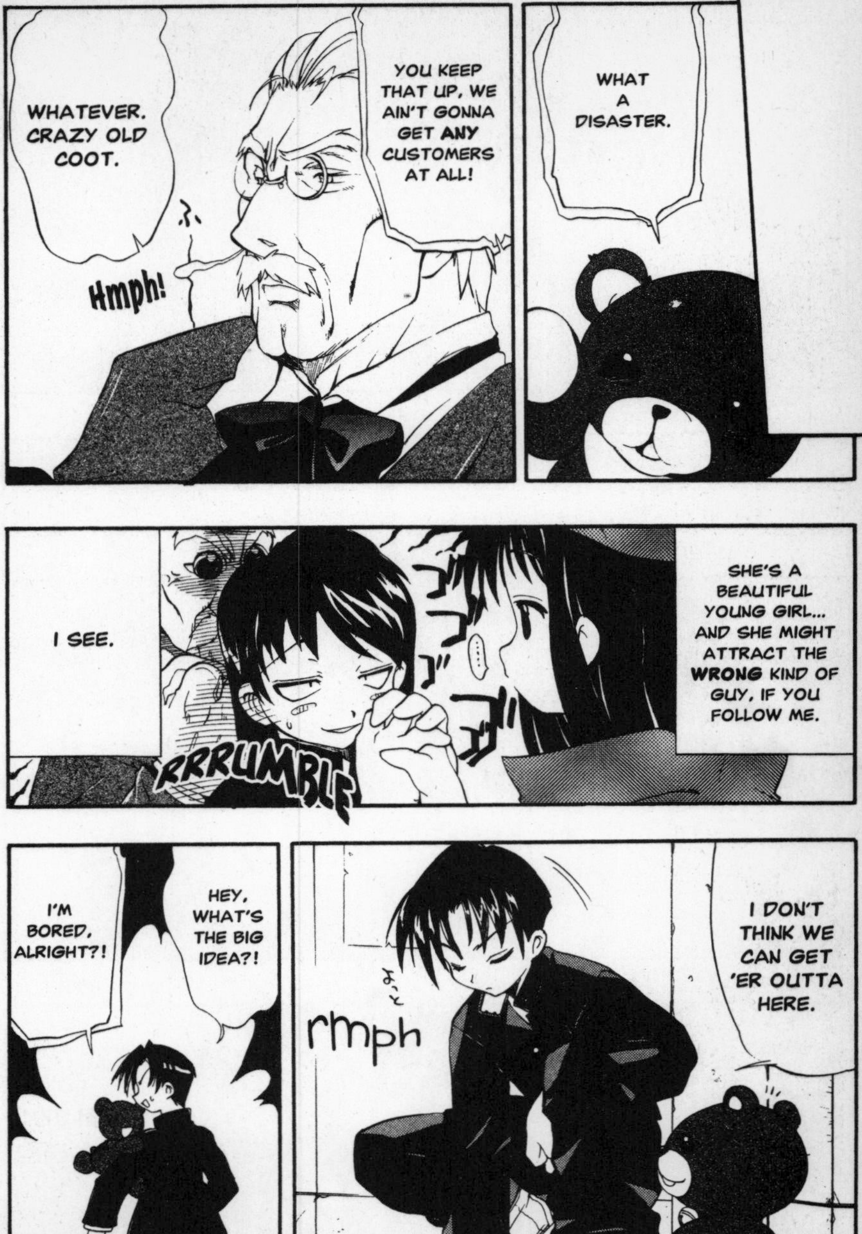
WHAT A DISASTER.
YOU KEEP THAT UP, WE AIN'T GONNA GET ANY CUSTOMERS AT ALL!
WHATEVER. CRAZY OLD COOT.
Hmph!
SHE'S A BEAUTIFUL YOUNG GIRL... AND SHE MIGHT ATTRACT THE WRONG KIND OF GUY, IF YOU FOLLOW ME.
I SEE.
RRRUMBLE
I DON'T THINK WE CAN GET 'ER OUTTA HERE.
rmph
HEY, WHAT'S THE BIG IDEA?!
I'M BORED, ALRIGHT?!

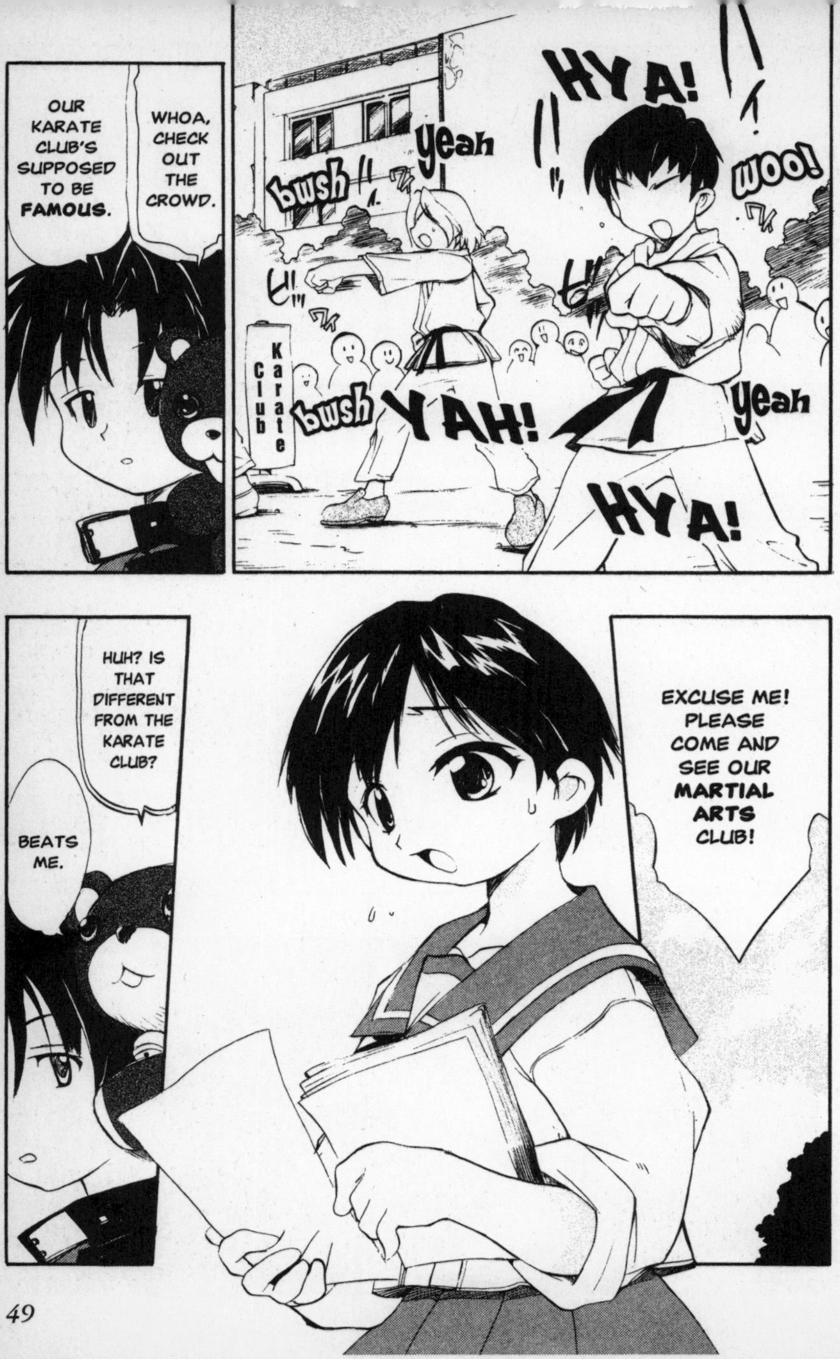
HYA!
WOO!
yeah
bwsh
Karate Club
bwsh
YAH!
yeah
HYA!
WHOA, CHECK OUT THE CROWD.
OUR KARATE CLUB'S SUPPOSED TO BE FAMOUS.
EXCUSE ME! PLEASE COME AND SEE OUR MARTIAL ARTS CLUB!
HUH? IS THAT DIFFERENT FROM THE KARATE CLUB?
BEATS ME.

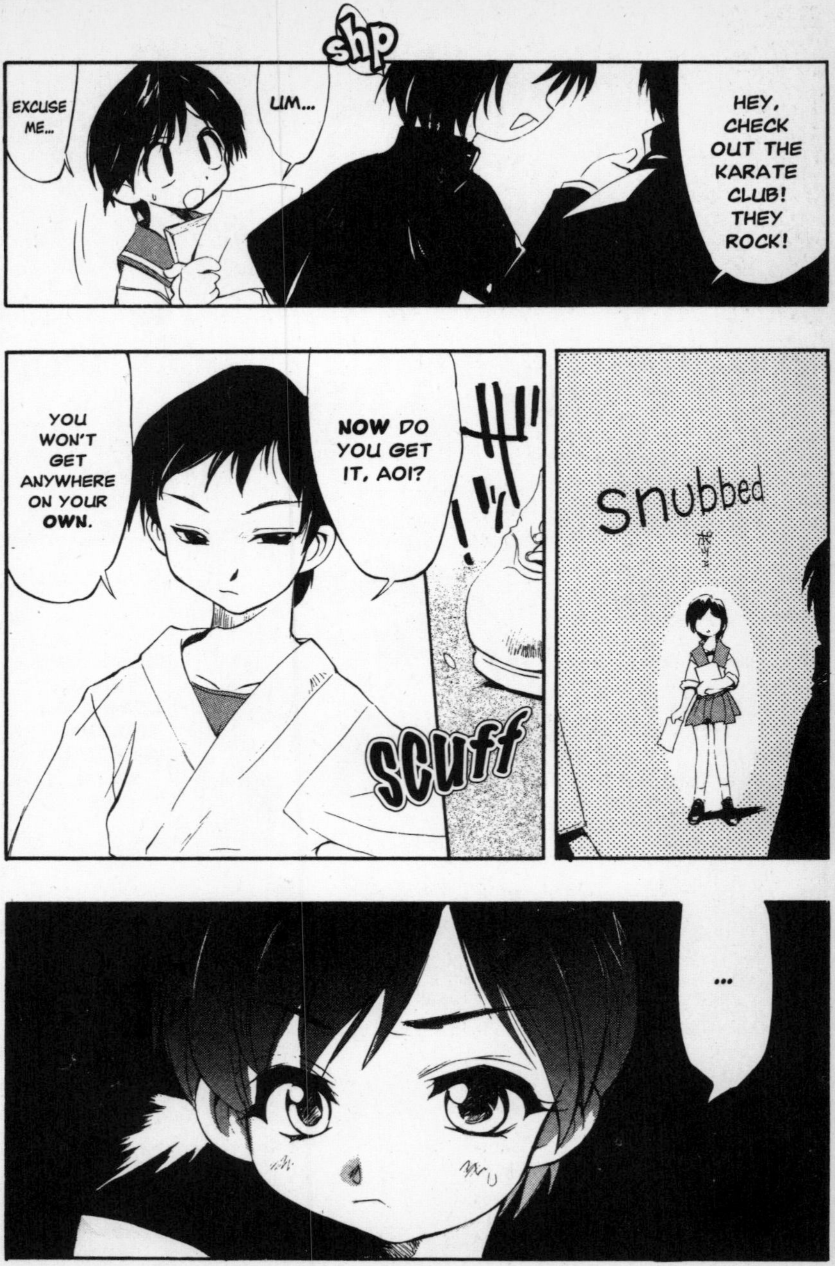
shp
HEY, CHECK OUT THE KARATE CLUB! THEY ROCK!
UM...
EXCUSE ME...
Snubbed
NOW DO YOU GET IT, AOI?
YOU WON'T GET ANYWHERE ON YOUR OWN.
scuff
...

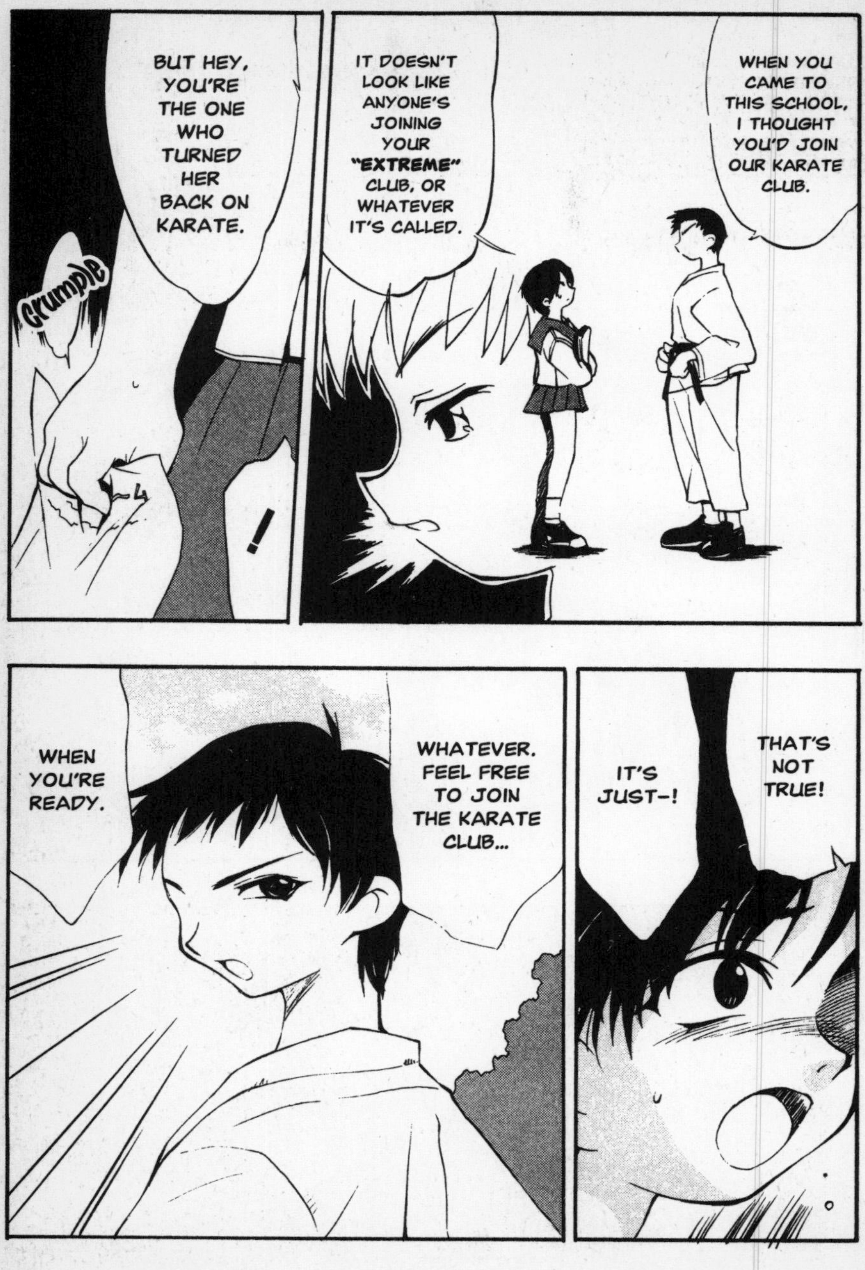
WHEN YOU CAME TO THIS SCHOOL, I THOUGHT YOU'D JOIN OUR KARATE CLUB.
IT DOESN'T LOOK LIKE ANYONE'S JOINING YOUR "EXTREME" CLUB, OR WHATEVER IT'S CALLED.
BUT HEY, YOU'RE THE ONE WHO TURNED HER BACK ON KARATE.
Crumple
!
THAT'S NOT TRUE!
IT'S JUST-!
WHATEVER. FEEL FREE TO JOIN THE KARATE CLUB...
WHEN YOU'RE READY.

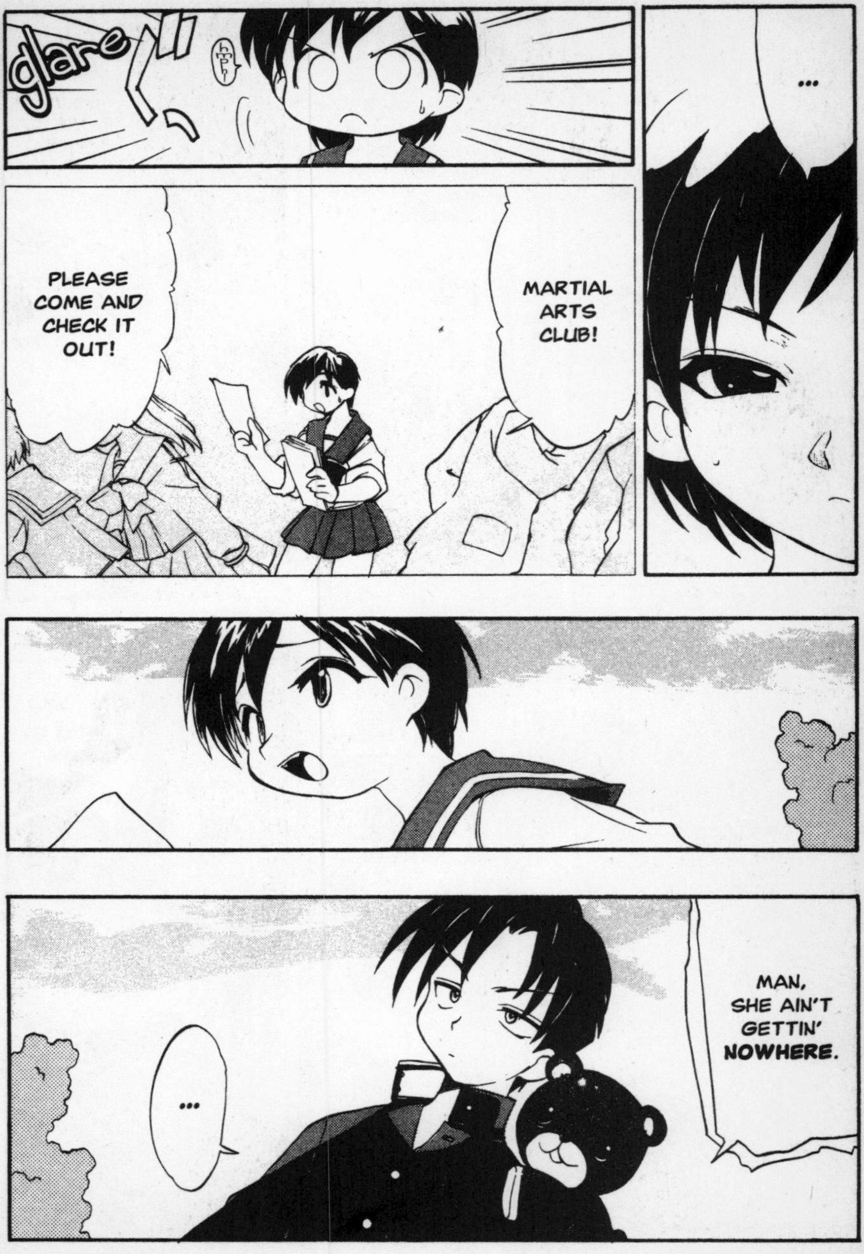
...
glare
MARTIAL ARTS CLUB!
PLEASE COME AND CHECK IT OUT!
MAN, SHE AIN'T GETTIN' **NOWHERE.**
...

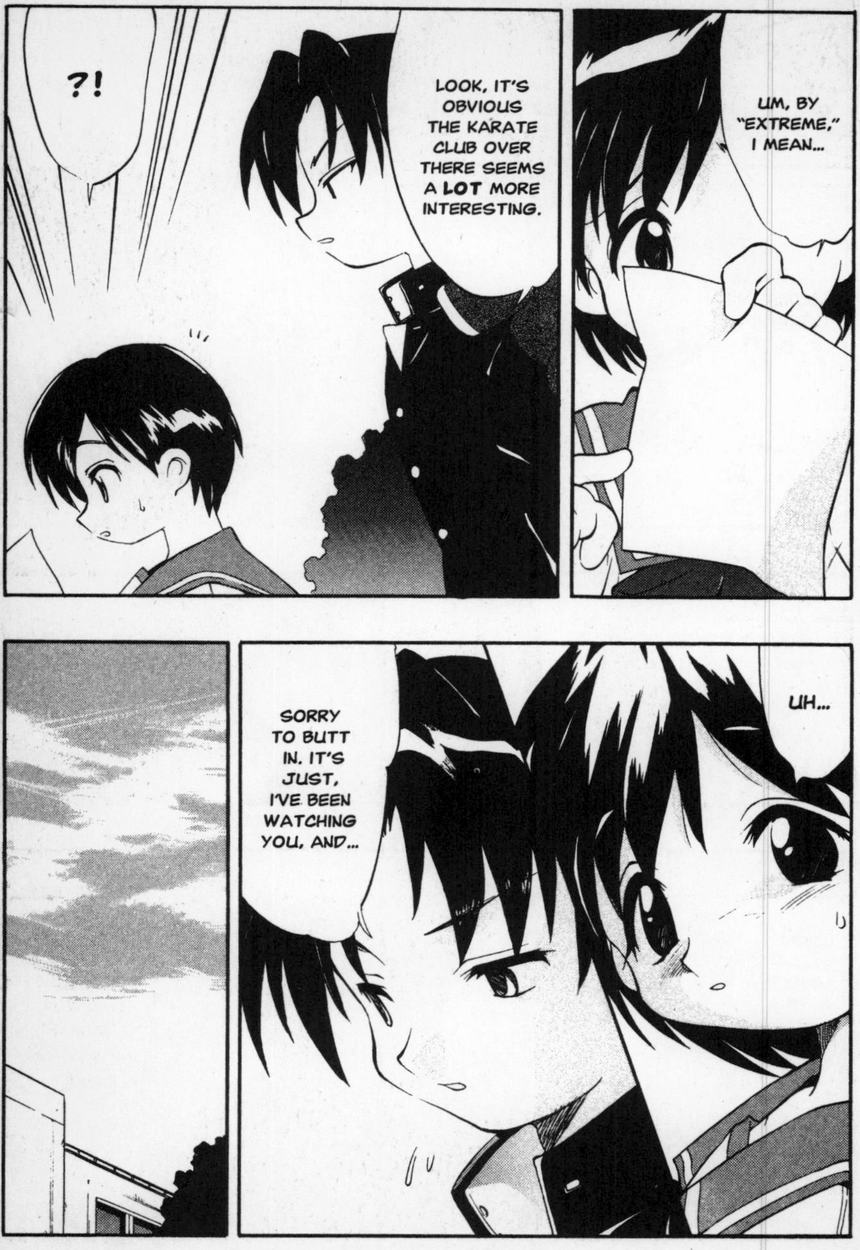
UM, BY "EXTREME," I MEAN...
LOOK, IT'S OBVIOUS THE KARATE CLUB OVER THERE SEEMS A **LOT** MORE INTERESTING.
?!
UH...
SORRY TO BUTT IN. IT'S JUST, I'VE BEEN WATCHING YOU, AND...

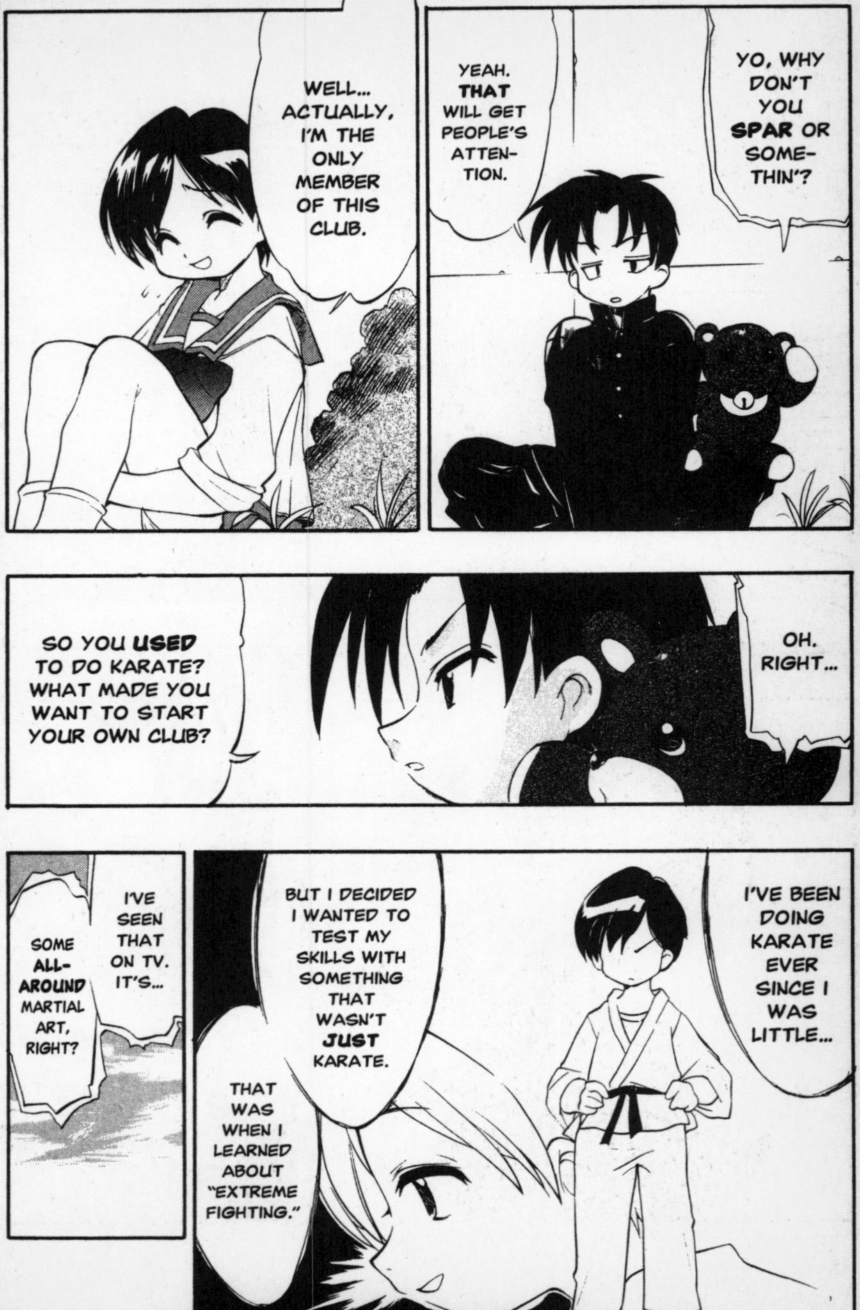
YO, WHY DON'T YOU SPAR OR SOME-THIN'?
YEAH. THAT WILL GET PEOPLE'S ATTEN-TION.
WELL... ACTUALLY, I'M THE ONLY MEMBER OF THIS CLUB.
OH. RIGHT...
SO YOU USED TO DO KARATE? WHAT MADE YOU WANT TO START YOUR OWN CLUB?
I'VE BEEN DOING KARATE EVER SINCE I WAS LITTLE...
BUT I DECIDED I WANTED TO TEST MY SKILLS WITH SOMETHING THAT WASN'T JUST KARATE.
THAT WAS WHEN I LEARNED ABOUT "EXTREME FIGHTING."
I'VE SEEN THAT ON TV. IT'S...
SOME ALL-AROUND MARTIAL ART, RIGHT?

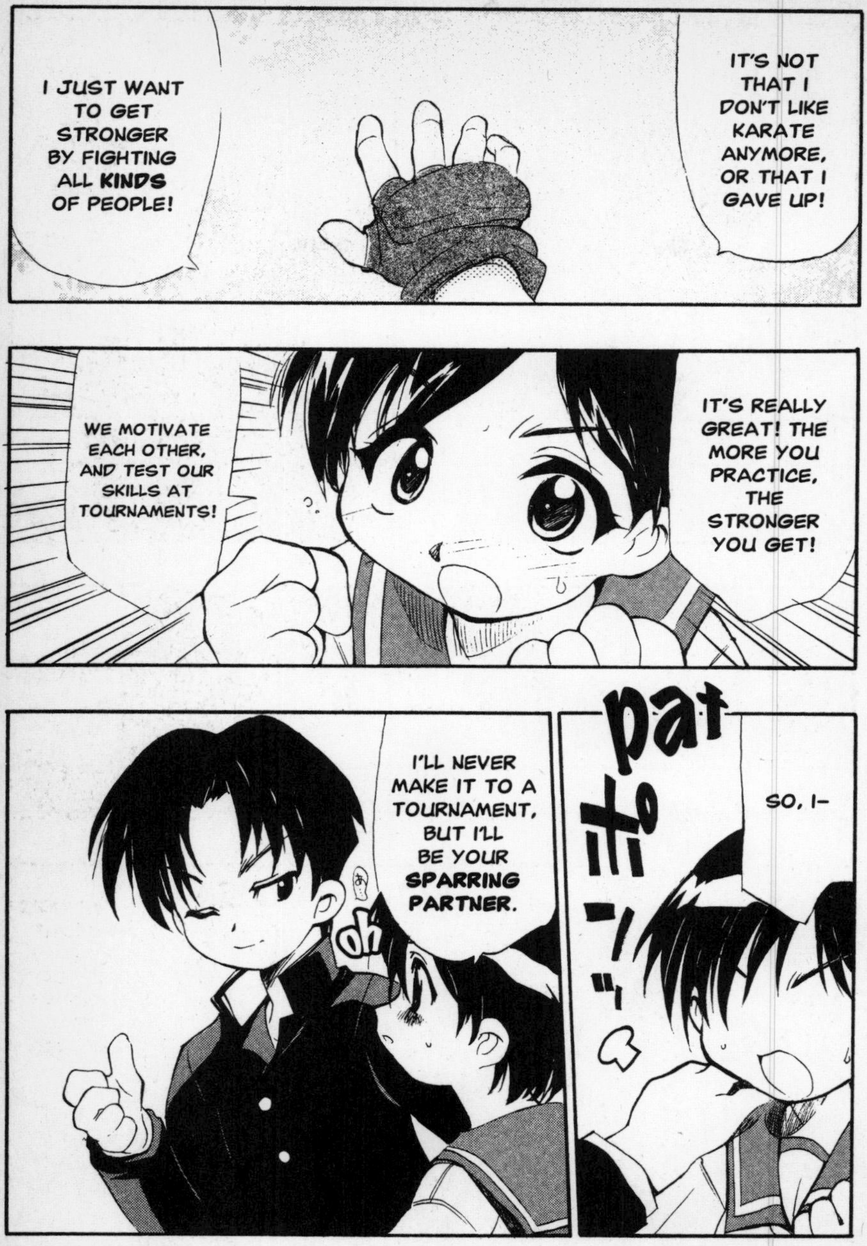
IT'S NOT THAT I DON'T LIKE KARATE ANYMORE, OR THAT I GAVE UP!
I JUST WANT TO GET STRONGER BY FIGHTING ALL **KINDS** OF PEOPLE!
IT'S REALLY GREAT! THE MORE YOU PRACTICE, THE STRONGER YOU GET!
WE MOTIVATE EACH OTHER, AND TEST OUR SKILLS AT TOURNAMENTS!
SO, I-
pat
I'LL NEVER MAKE IT TO A TOURNAMENT, BUT I'LL BE YOUR **SPARRING PARTNER.**
oh

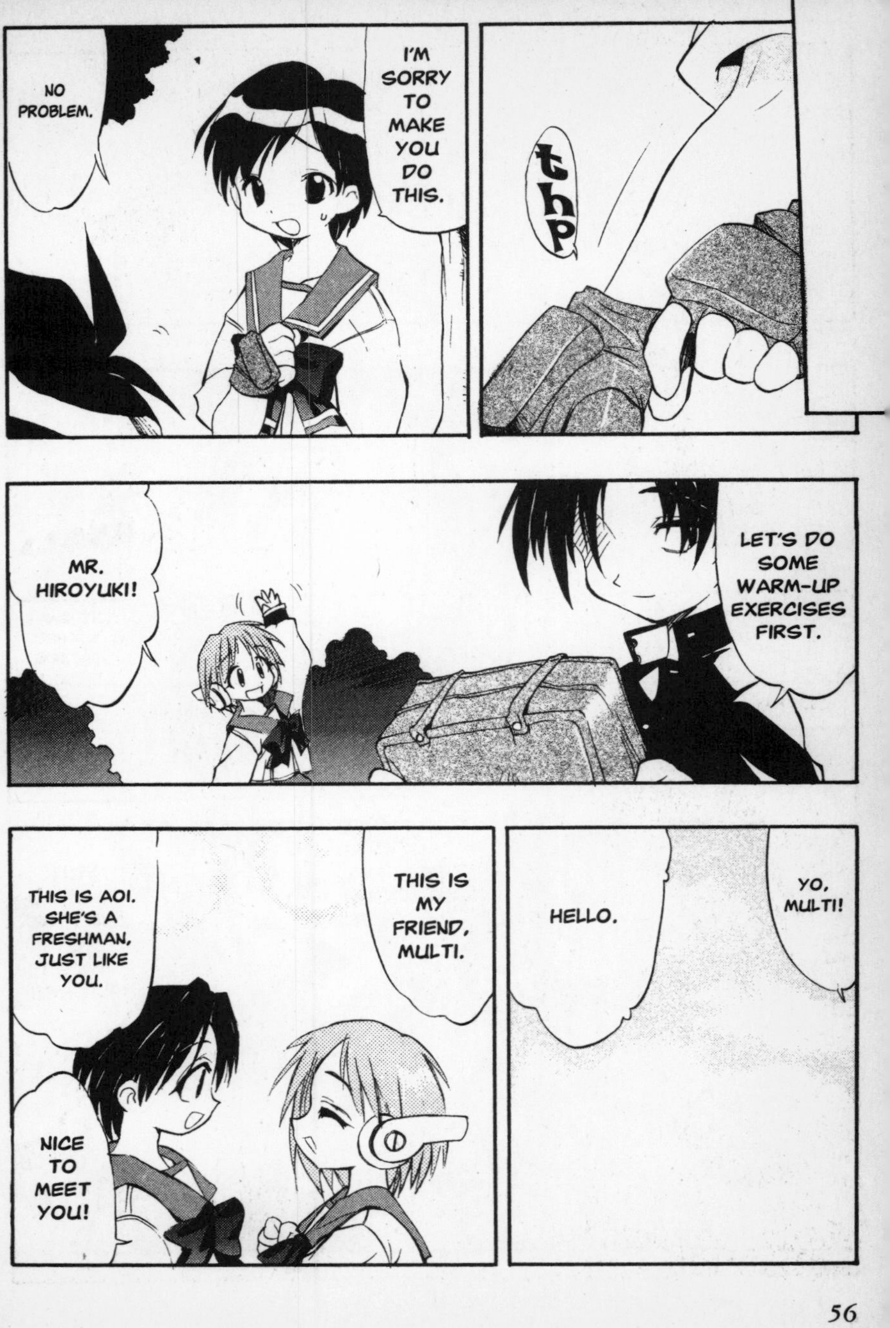
thp
I'M SORRY TO MAKE YOU DO THIS.
NO PROBLEM.
LET'S DO SOME WARM-UP EXERCISES FIRST.
MR. HIROYUKI!
YO, MULTI!
HELLO.
THIS IS MY FRIEND, MULTI.
THIS IS AOI. SHE'S A FRESHMAN, JUST LIKE YOU.
NICE TO MEET YOU!

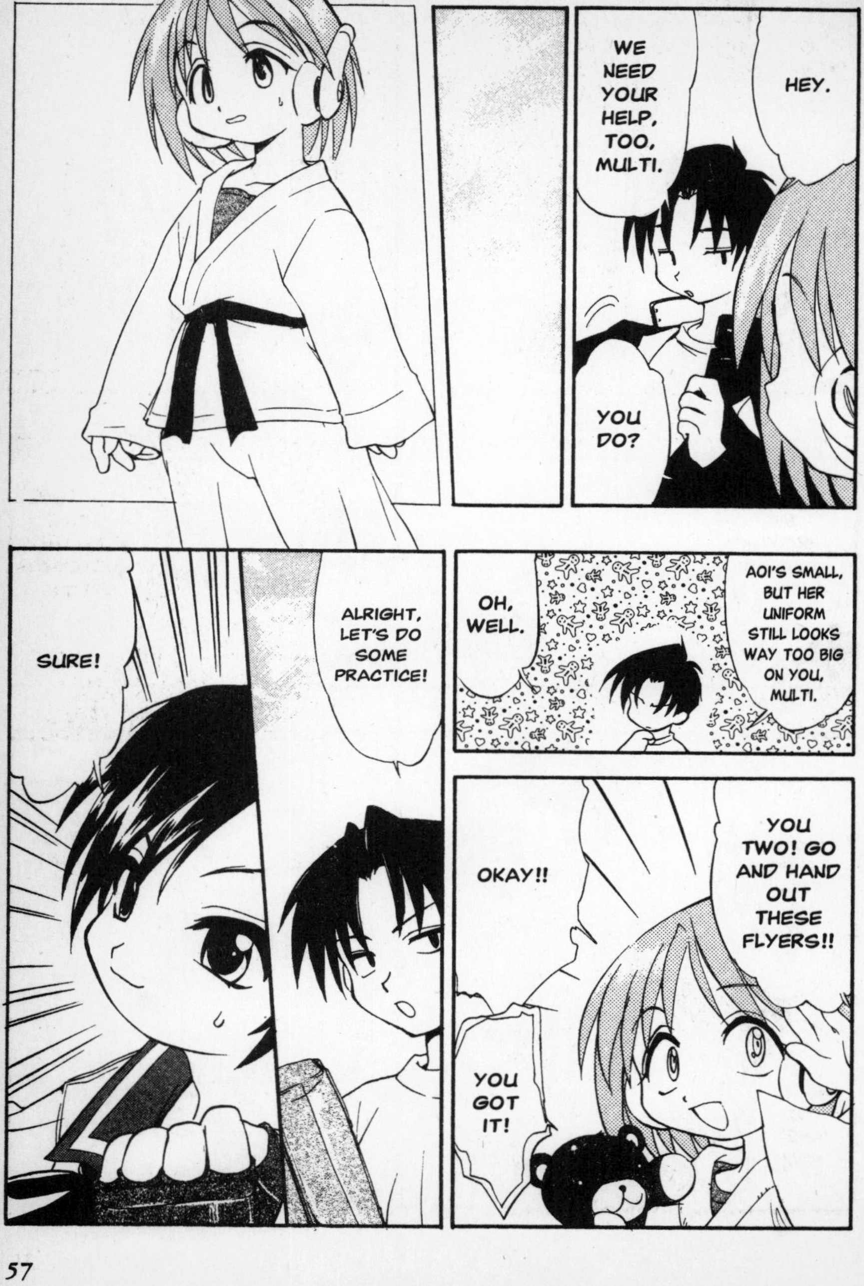
HEY.
WE NEED YOUR HELP, TOO, MULTI.
YOU DO?
AOI'S SMALL, BUT HER UNIFORM STILL LOOKS WAY TOO BIG ON YOU, MULTI.
OH, WELL.
YOU TWO! GO AND HAND OUT THESE FLYERS!!
OKAY!!
YOU GOT IT!
ALRIGHT, LET'S DO SOME PRACTICE!
SURE!

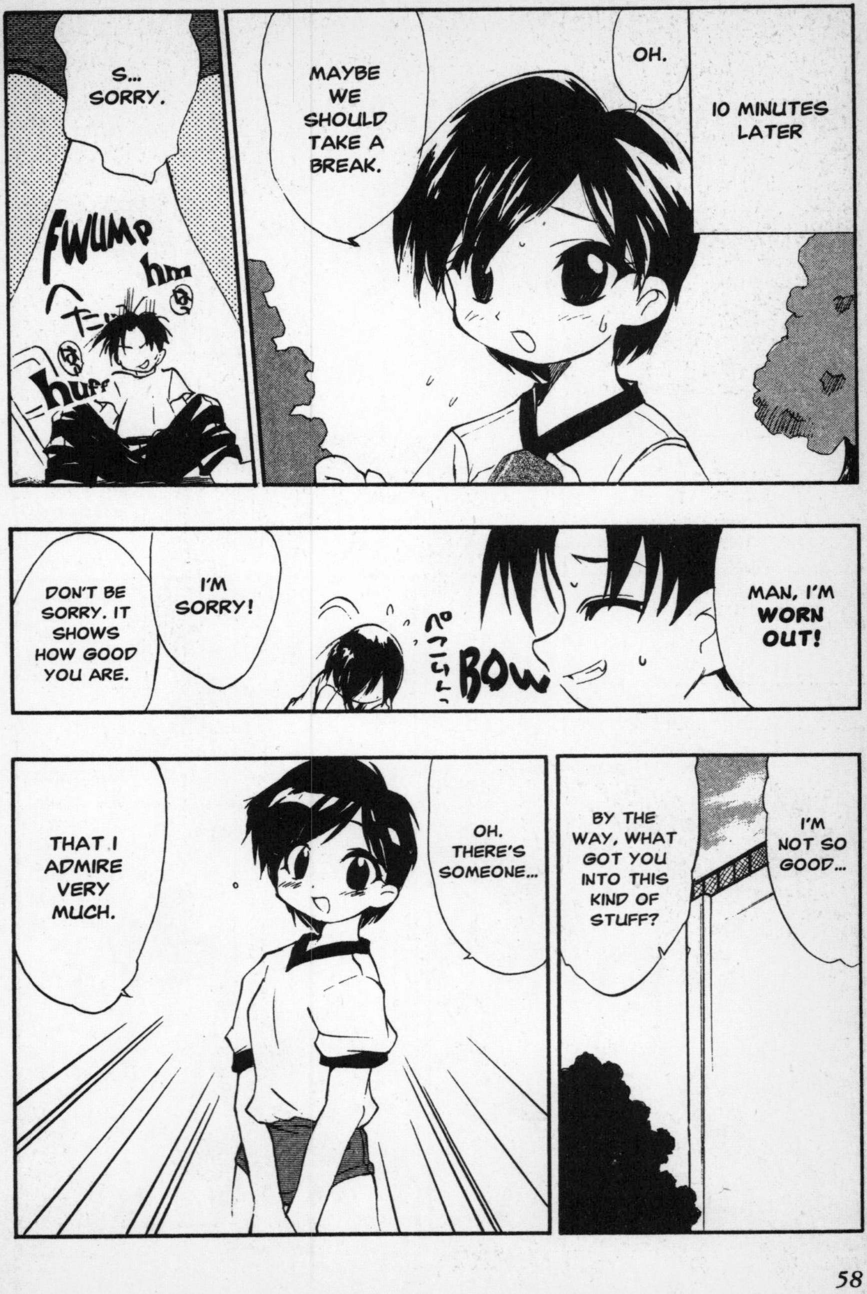

10 MINUTES LATER
OH.
MAYBE WE SHOULD TAKE A BREAK.
S... SORRY.
FWUMP
hm
huff
MAN, I'M WORN OUT!
BOW
I'M SORRY!
DON'T BE SORRY. IT SHOWS HOW GOOD YOU ARE.
I'M NOT SO GOOD...
BY THE WAY, WHAT GOT YOU INTO THIS KIND OF STUFF?
OH. THERE'S SOMEONE...
THAT I ADMIRE VERY MUCH.

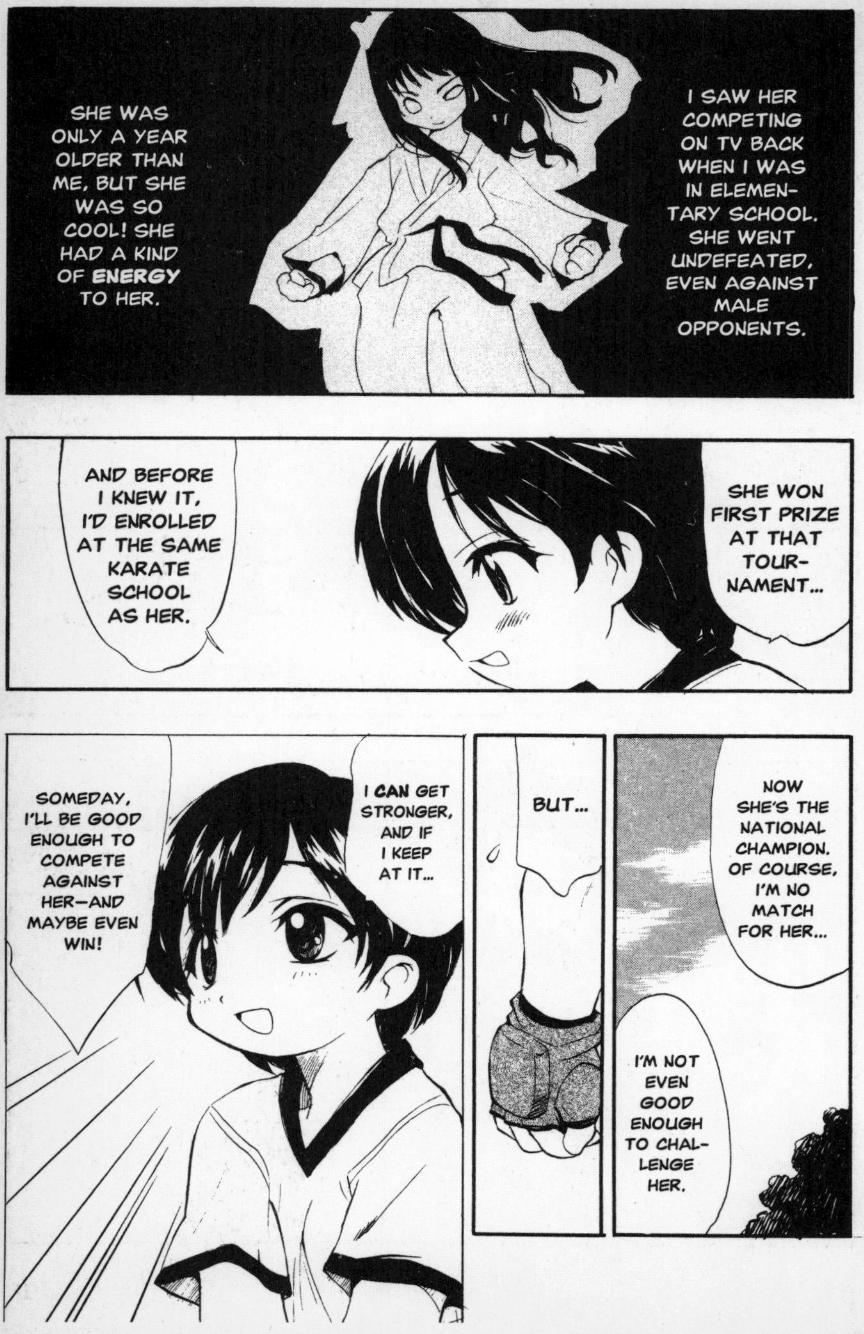
I SAW HER COMPETING ON TV BACK WHEN I WAS IN ELEMENTARY SCHOOL. SHE WENT UNDEFEATED, EVEN AGAINST MALE OPPONENTS.
SHE WAS ONLY A YEAR OLDER THAN ME, BUT SHE WAS SO COOL! SHE HAD A KIND OF **ENERGY** TO HER.
SHE WON FIRST PRIZE AT THAT TOURNAMENT...
AND BEFORE I KNEW IT, I'D ENROLLED AT THE SAME KARATE SCHOOL AS HER.
NOW SHE'S THE NATIONAL CHAMPION. OF COURSE, I'M NO MATCH FOR HER...
I'M NOT EVEN GOOD ENOUGH TO CHALLENGE HER.
BUT...
I **CAN** GET STRONGER, AND IF I KEEP AT IT...
SOMEDAY, I'LL BE GOOD ENOUGH TO COMPETE AGAINST HER—AND MAYBE EVEN WIN!

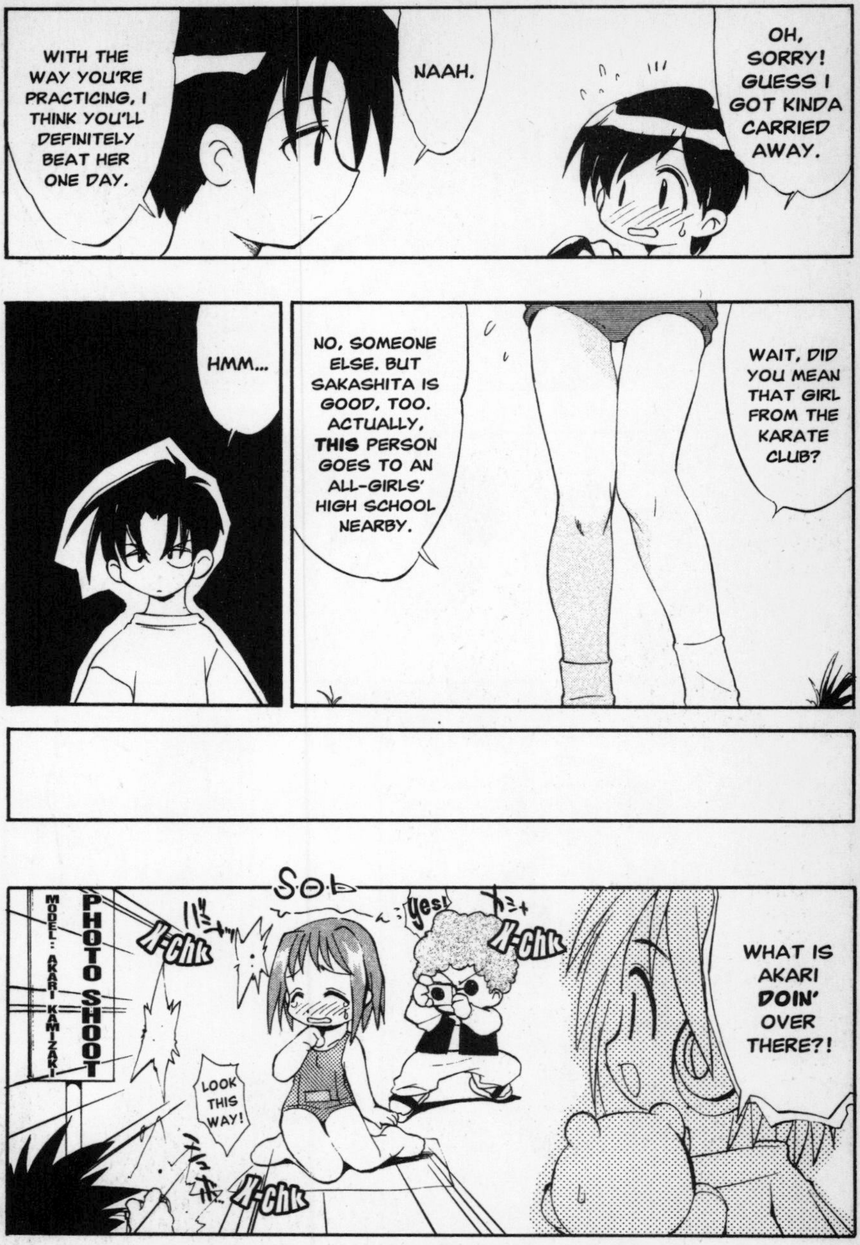

OH, SORRY! GUESS I GOT KINDA CARRIED AWAY.
NAAH.
WITH THE WAY YOU'RE PRACTICING, I THINK YOU'LL DEFINITELY BEAT HER ONE DAY.
WAIT, DID YOU MEAN THAT GIRL FROM THE KARATE CLUB?
NO, SOMEONE ELSE. BUT SAKASHITA IS GOOD, TOO. ACTUALLY, THIS PERSON GOES TO AN ALL-GIRLS' HIGH SCHOOL NEARBY.
HMM...
WHAT IS AKARI DOIN' OVER THERE?!
X-Chk
Yes!
SOB
X-Chk
PHOTO SHOOT
MODEL: AKARI KAMIZAKI
LOOK THIS WAY!
X-Chk

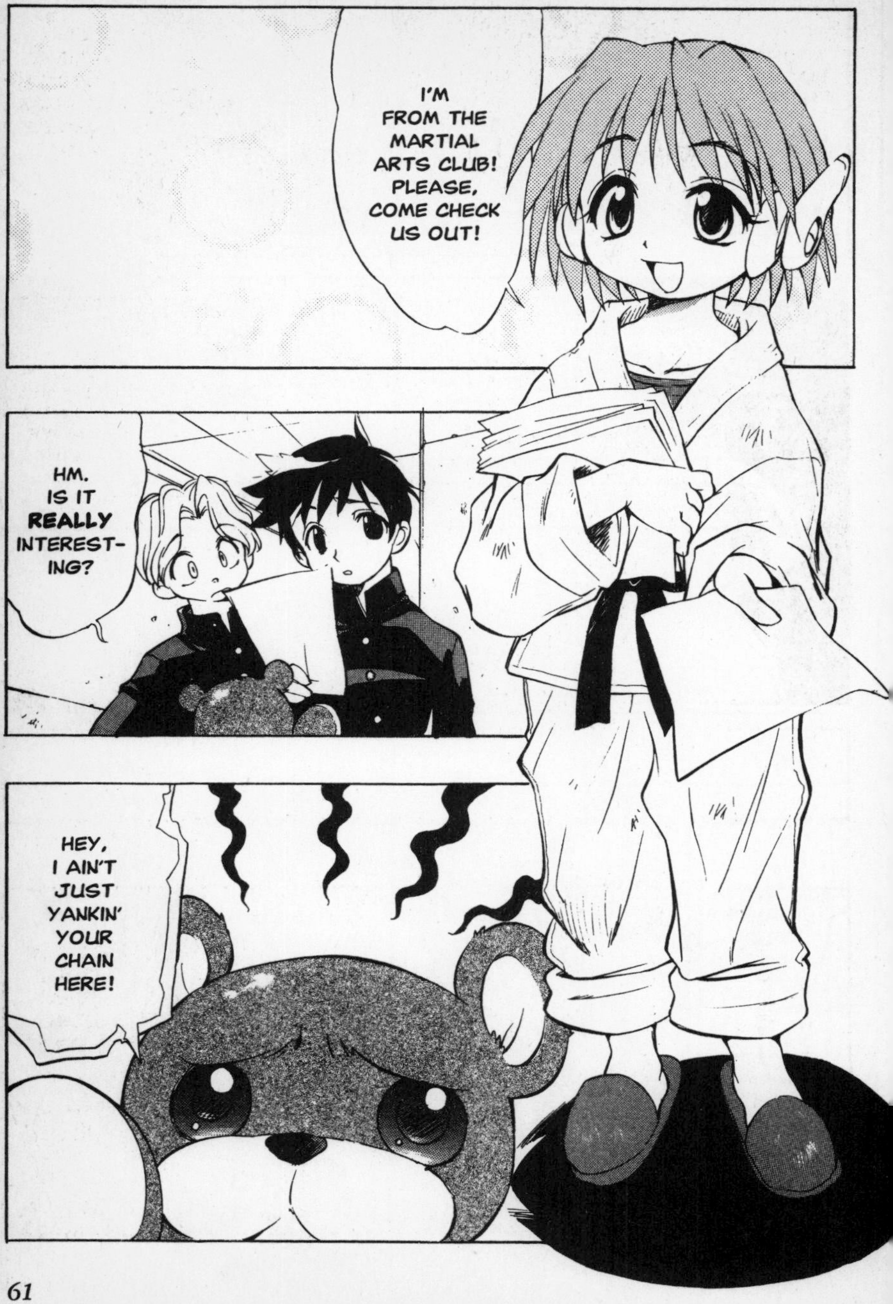
I'M FROM THE MARTIAL ARTS CLUB! PLEASE, COME CHECK US OUT!
HM. IS IT REALLY INTEREST-ING?
HEY, I AIN'T JUST YANKIN' YOUR CHAIN HERE!

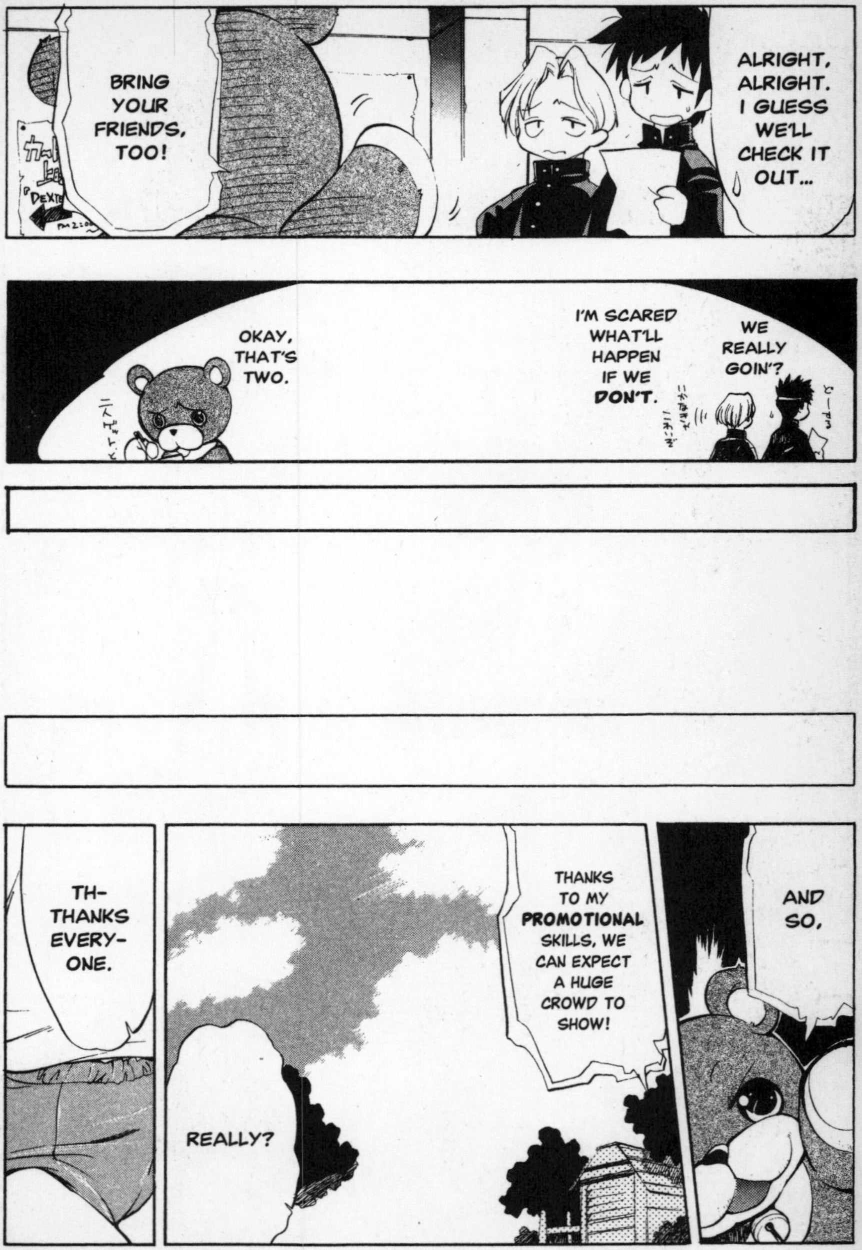
ALRIGHT, ALRIGHT. I GUESS WE'LL CHECK IT OUT...
BRING YOUR FRIENDS, TOO!
WE REALLY GOIN'?
I'M SCARED WHAT'LL HAPPEN IF WE **DON'T**.
OKAY, THAT'S TWO.
AND SO,
THANKS TO MY **PROMOTIONAL** SKILLS, WE CAN EXPECT A HUGE CROWD TO SHOW!
REALLY?
TH-THANKS EVERY-ONE.

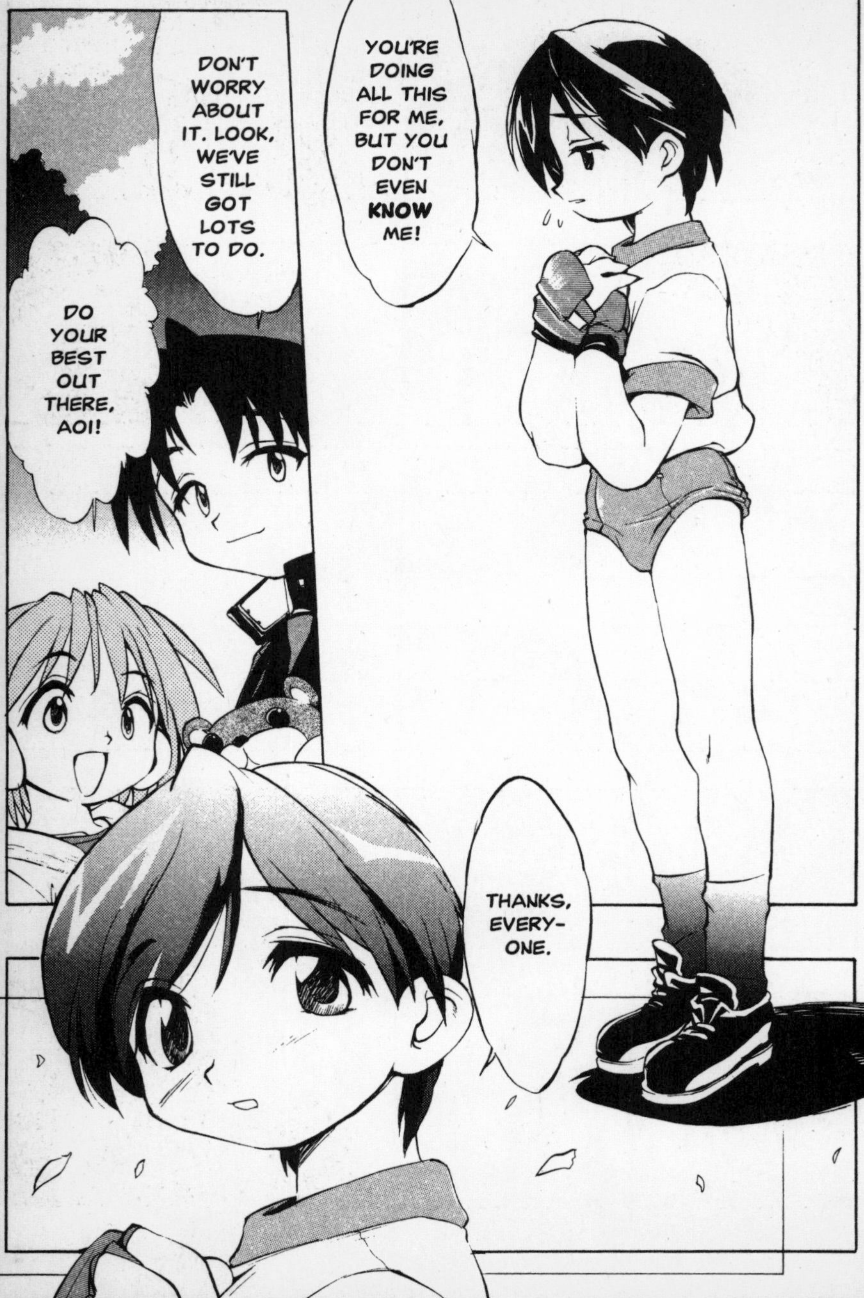
YOU'RE DOING ALL THIS FOR ME, BUT YOU DON'T EVEN KNOW ME!
DON'T WORRY ABOUT IT. LOOK, WE'VE STILL GOT LOTS TO DO.
DO YOUR BEST OUT THERE, AOI!
THANKS, EVERY-ONE.

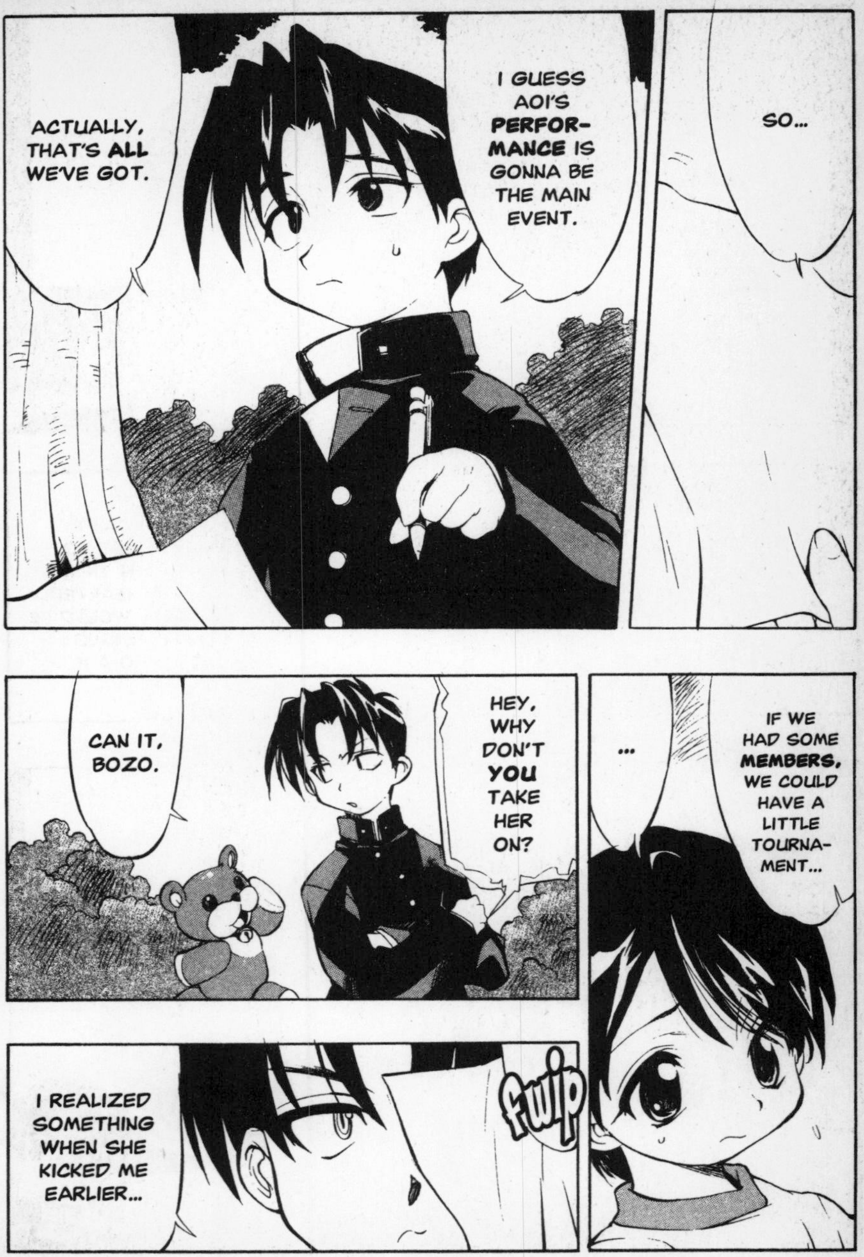
SO...
I GUESS AOI'S PERFORMANCE IS GONNA BE THE MAIN EVENT.
ACTUALLY, THAT'S ALL WE'VE GOT.
IF WE HAD SOME MEMBERS, WE COULD HAVE A LITTLE TOURNAMENT...
...
HEY, WHY DON'T YOU TAKE HER ON?
CAN IT, BOZO.
fwip
I REALIZED SOMETHING WHEN SHE KICKED ME EARLIER...

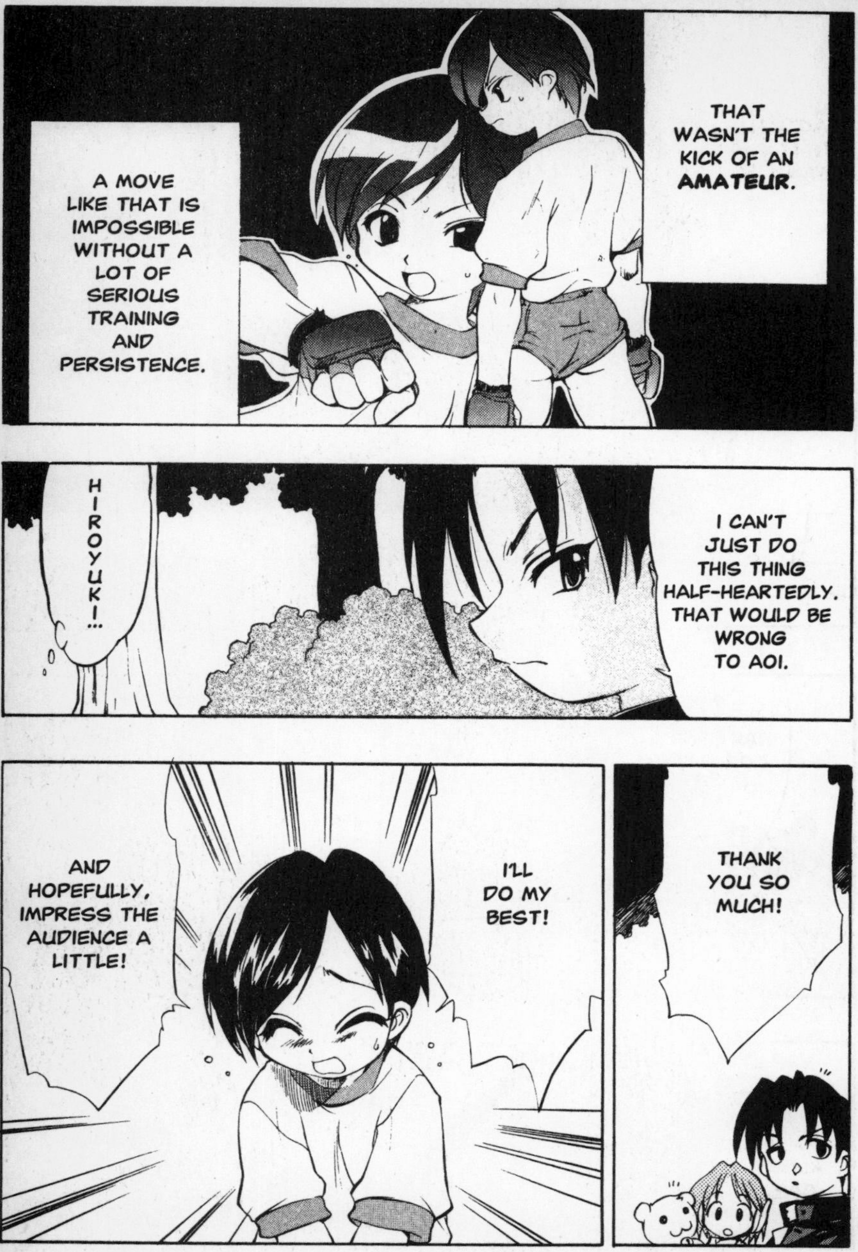
THAT WASN'T THE KICK OF AN AMATEUR.
A MOVE LIKE THAT IS IMPOSSIBLE WITHOUT A LOT OF SERIOUS TRAINING AND PERSISTENCE.
I CAN'T JUST DO THIS THING HALF-HEARTEDLY. THAT WOULD BE WRONG TO AOI.
HIROYUKI!...
THANK YOU SO MUCH!
I'LL DO MY BEST!
AND HOPEFULLY, IMPRESS THE AUDIENCE A LITTLE!

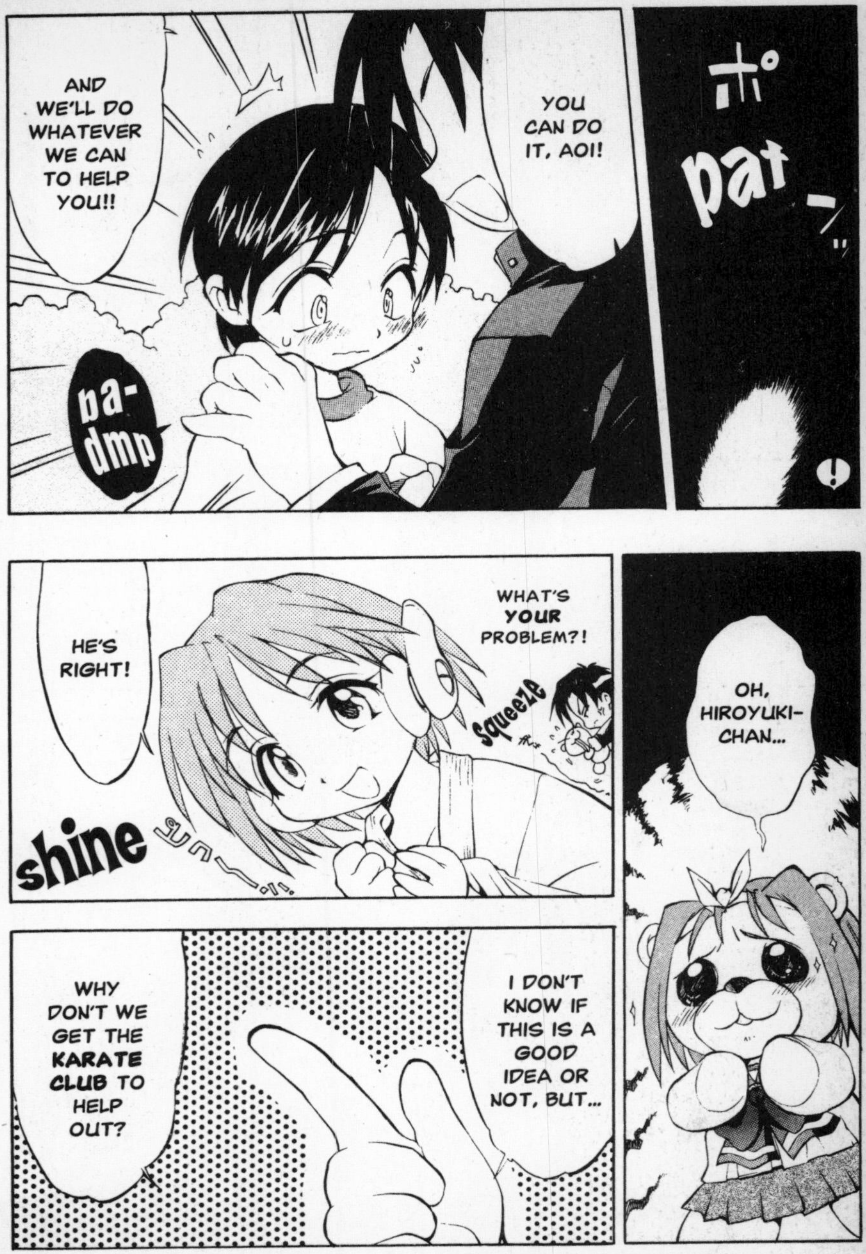
pat
!
YOU CAN DO IT, AOI!
AND WE'LL DO WHATEVER WE CAN TO HELP YOU!!
pa-dmp
OH, HIROYUKI-CHAN...
WHAT'S **YOUR** PROBLEM?!
squeeze
HE'S RIGHT!
shine
I DON'T KNOW IF THIS IS A GOOD IDEA OR NOT, BUT...
WHY DON'T WE GET THE **KARATE CLUB** TO HELP OUT?

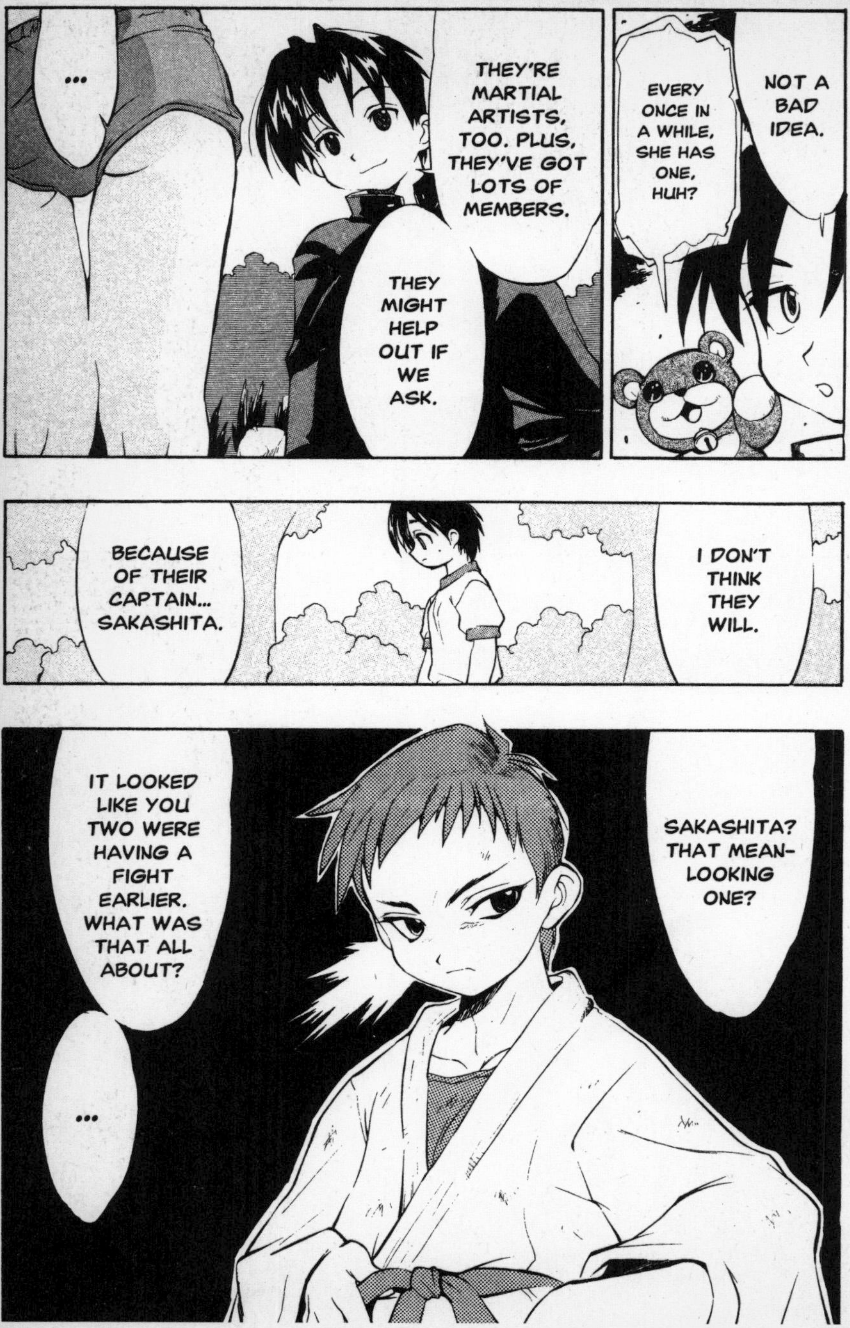
NOT A BAD IDEA.
EVERY ONCE IN A WHILE, SHE HAS ONE, HUH?
THEY'RE MARTIAL ARTISTS, TOO. PLUS, THEY'VE GOT LOTS OF MEMBERS.
THEY MIGHT HELP OUT IF WE ASK.
...
I DON'T THINK THEY WILL.
BECAUSE OF THEIR CAPTAIN... SAKASHITA.
SAKASHITA? THAT MEAN-LOOKING ONE?
IT LOOKED LIKE YOU TWO WERE HAVING A FIGHT EARLIER. WHAT WAS THAT ALL ABOUT?
...

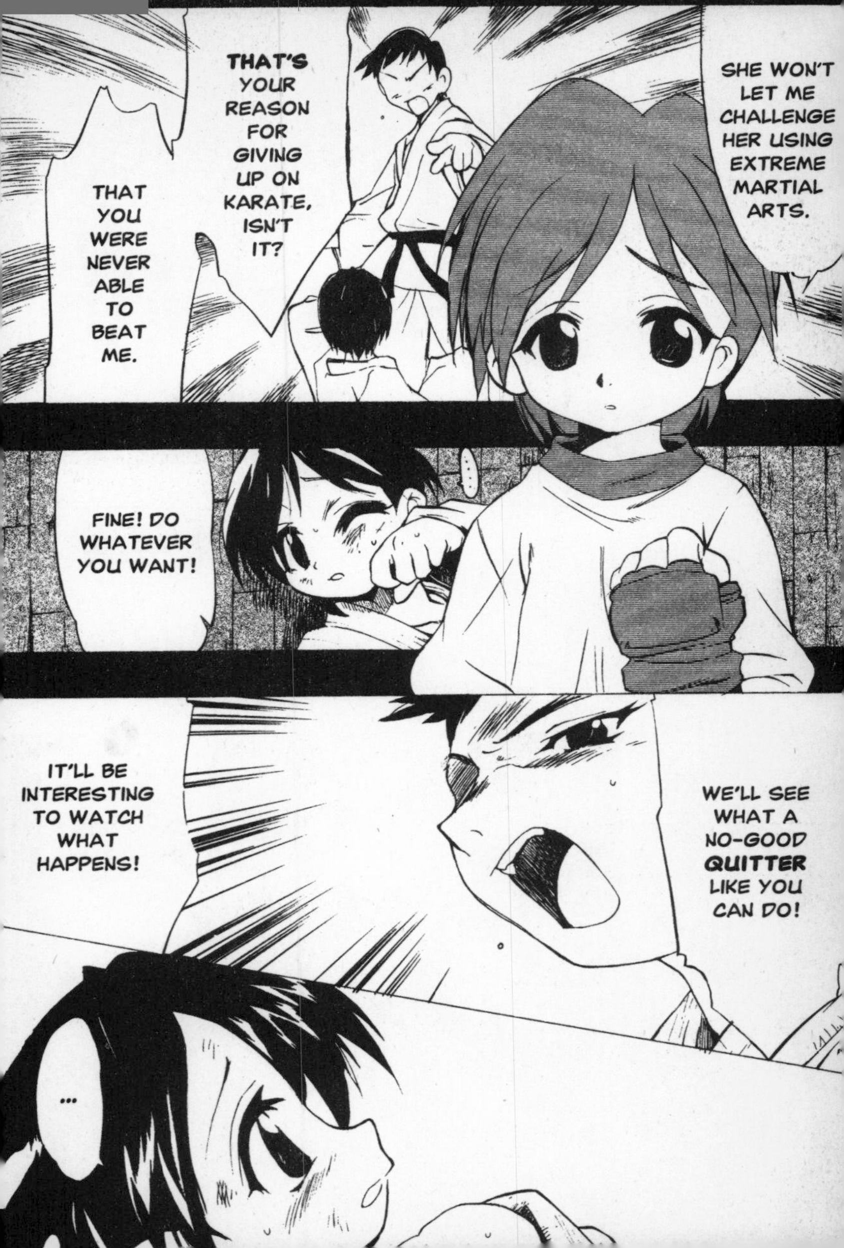
SHE WON'T LET ME CHALLENGE HER USING EXTREME MARTIAL ARTS.
THAT'S YOUR REASON FOR GIVING UP ON KARATE, ISN'T IT?
THAT YOU WERE NEVER ABLE TO BEAT ME.
FINE! DO WHATEVER YOU WANT!
WE'LL SEE WHAT A NO-GOOD QUITTER LIKE YOU CAN DO!
IT'LL BE INTERESTING TO WATCH WHAT HAPPENS!
...

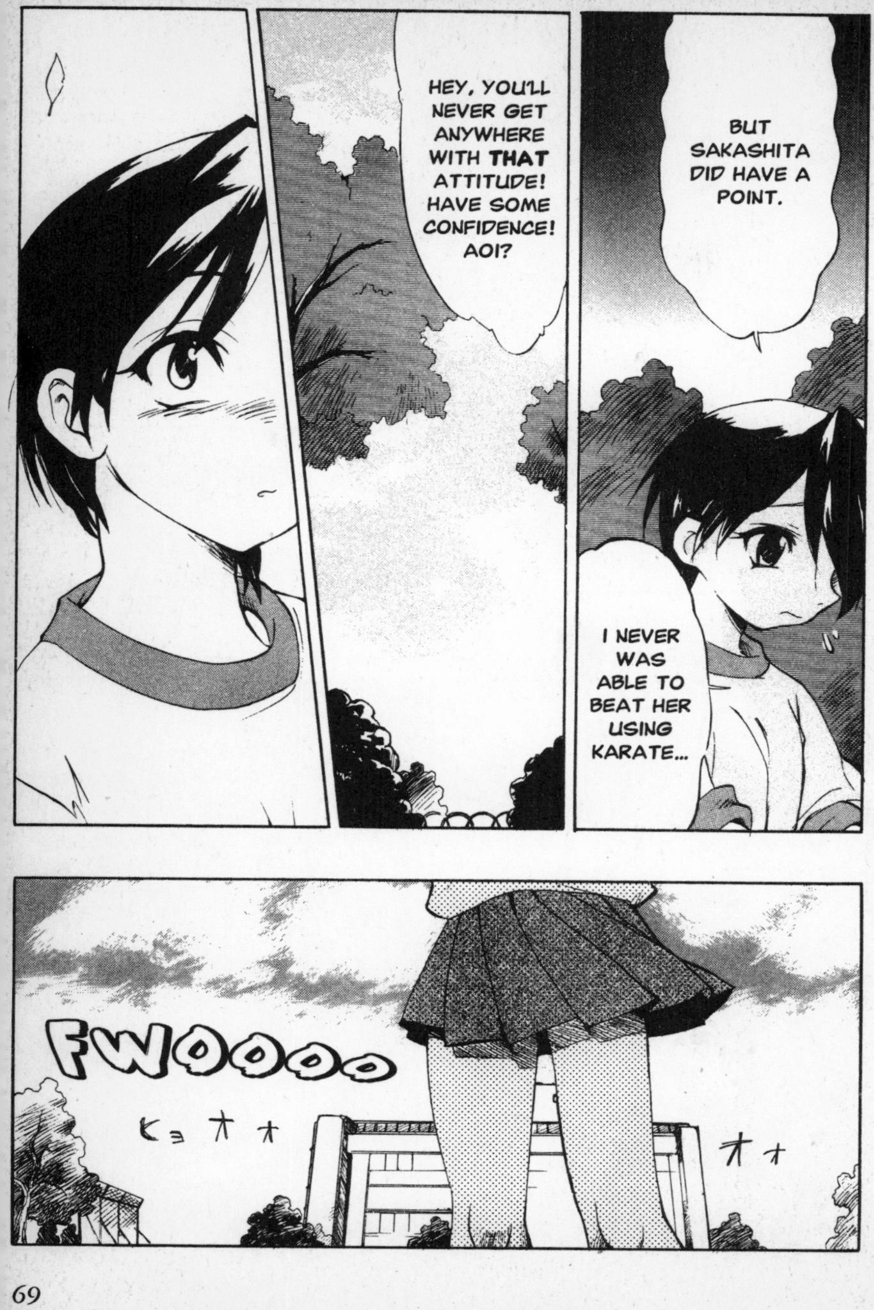
BUT SAKASHITA DID HAVE A POINT.
I NEVER WAS ABLE TO BEAT HER USING KARATE...
HEY, YOU'LL NEVER GET ANYWHERE WITH **THAT** ATTITUDE! HAVE SOME CONFIDENCE! AOI?
FWOOOO
ヒョオオ
オオ

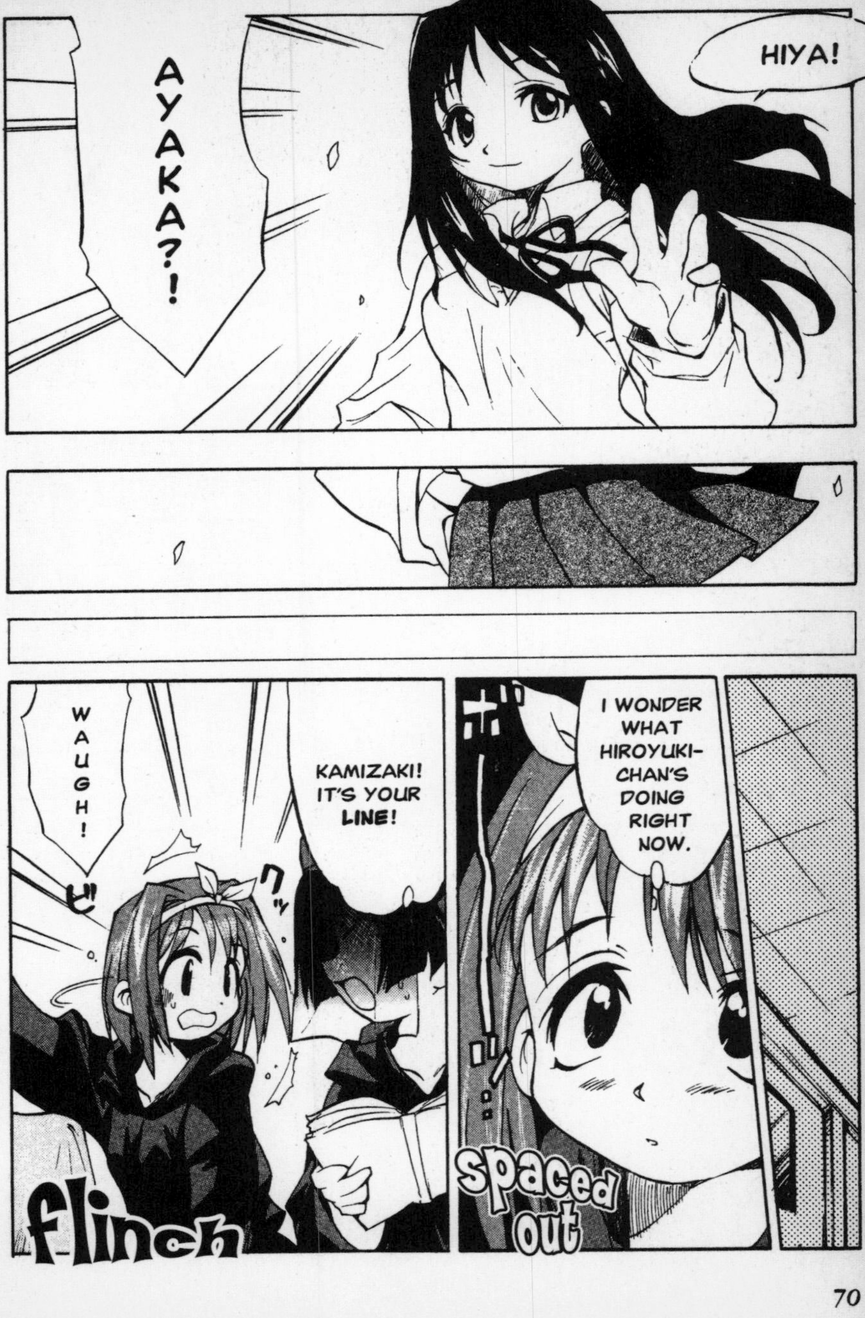
HIYA!
AYAKA?!
I WONDER WHAT HIROYUKI-CHAN'S DOING RIGHT NOW.
spaced out
KAMIZAKI! IT'S YOUR LINE!
WAUGH!
flinch

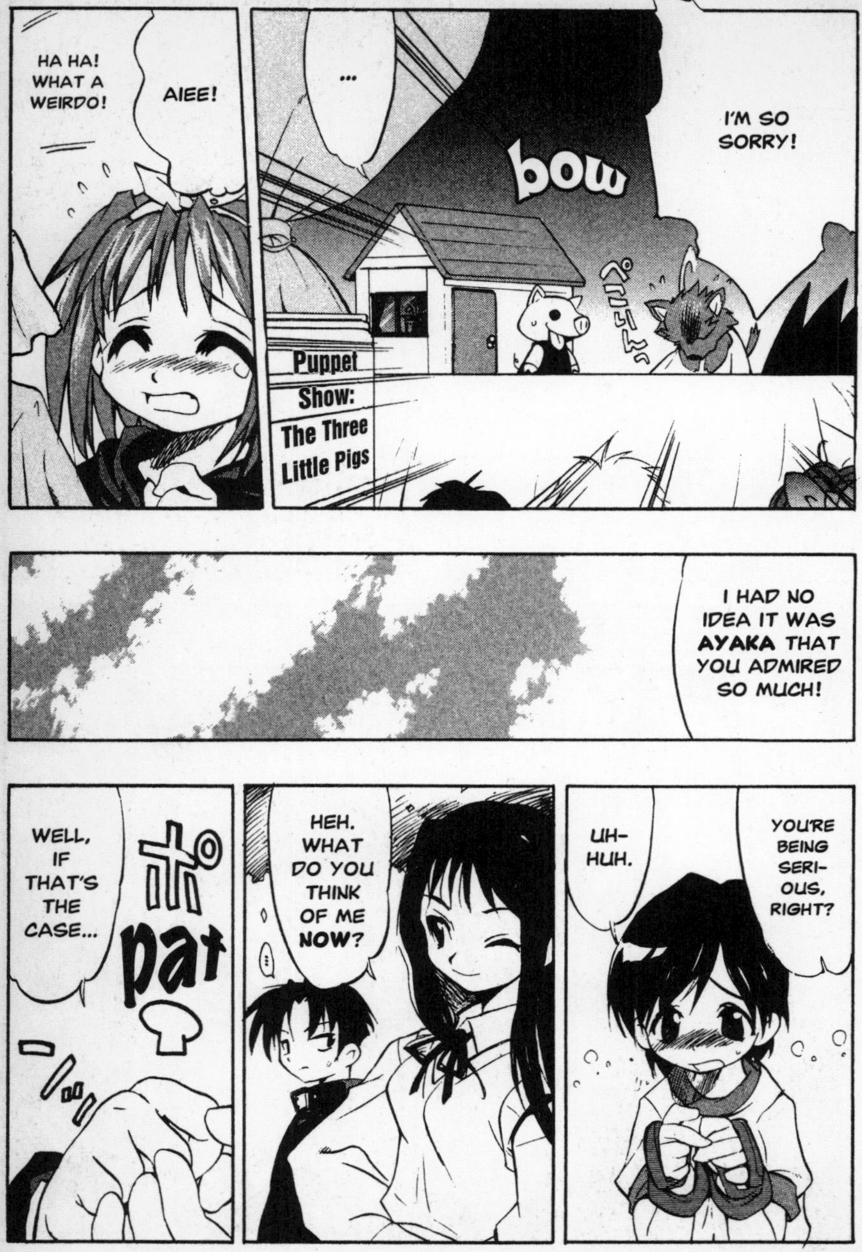
I'M SO SORRY!
bow
...
Puppet Show: The Three Little Pigs
AIEE!
HA HA! WHAT A WEIRDO!
I HAD NO IDEA IT WAS AYAKA THAT YOU ADMIRED SO MUCH!
YOU'RE BEING SERI-OUS, RIGHT?
UH-HUH.
HEH. WHAT DO YOU THINK OF ME NOW?
pat
WELL, IF THAT'S THE CASE...

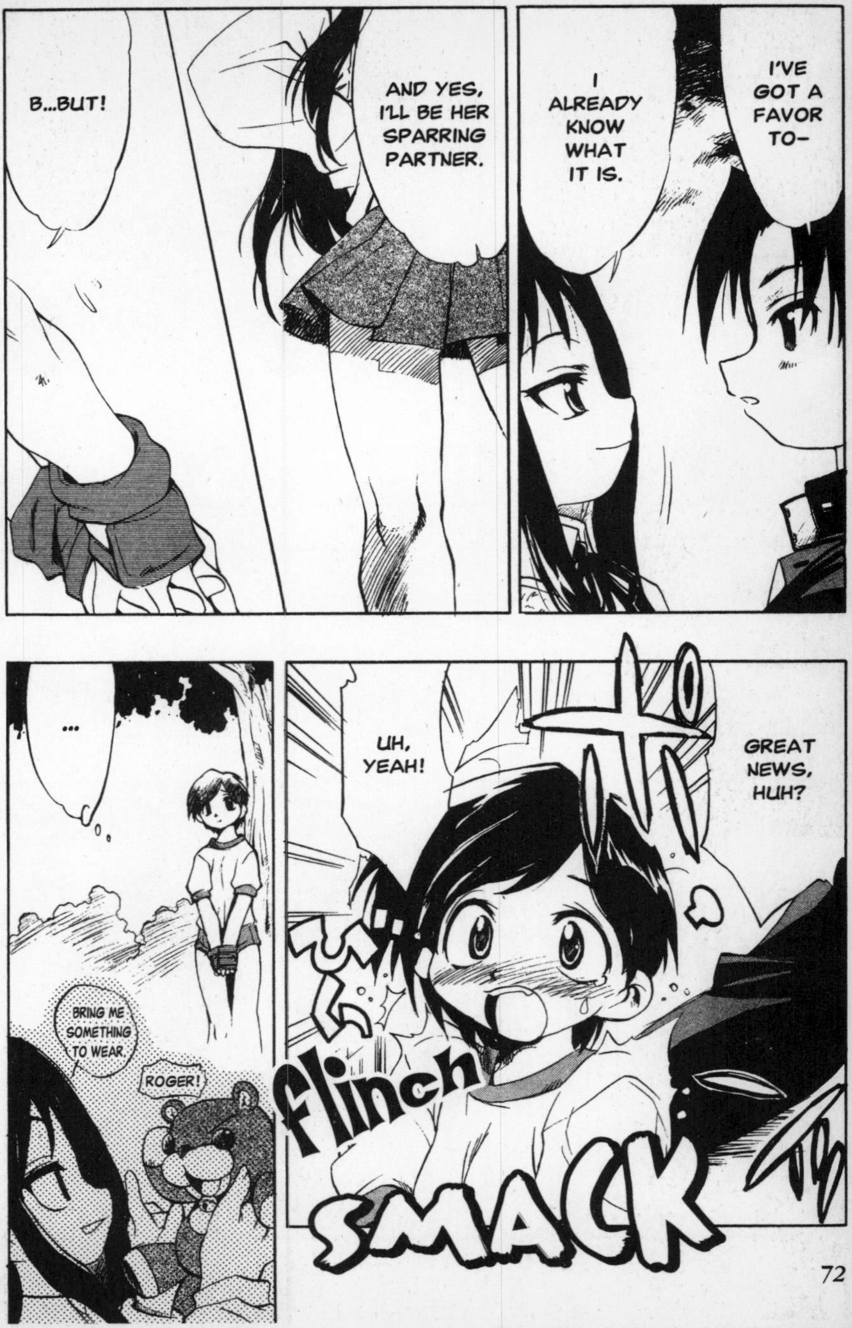
I'VE GOT A FAVOR TO–
I ALREADY KNOW WHAT IT IS.
AND YES, I'LL BE HER SPARRING PARTNER.
B...BUT!
GREAT NEWS, HUH?
UH, YEAH!
flinch
SMACK
...
BRING ME SOMETHING TO WEAR.
ROGER!

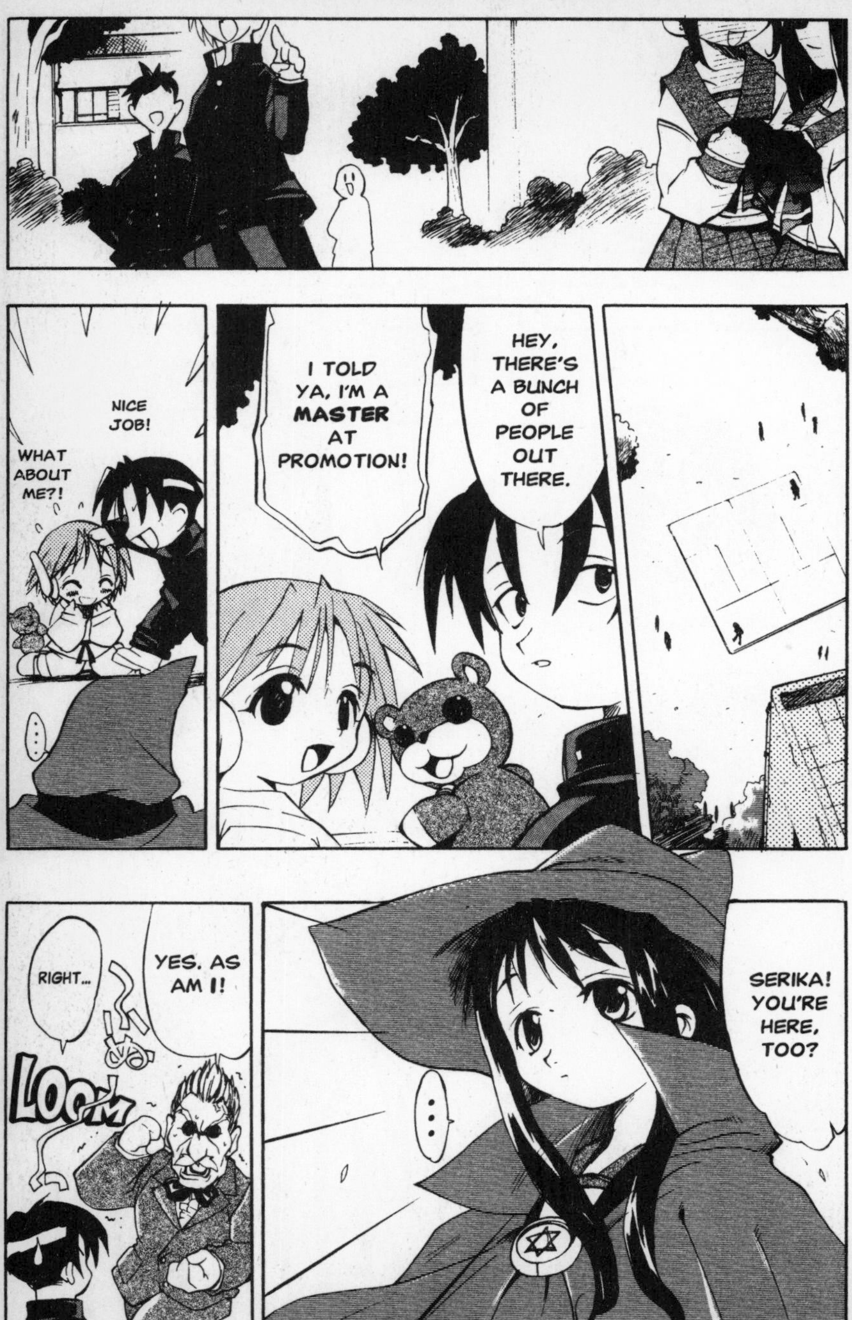
HEY, THERE'S A BUNCH OF PEOPLE OUT THERE.
I TOLD YA, I'M A MASTER AT PROMOTION!
NICE JOB!
WHAT ABOUT ME?!
...
SERIKA! YOU'RE HERE, TOO?
...
YES. AS AM I!
RIGHT...
LOOM

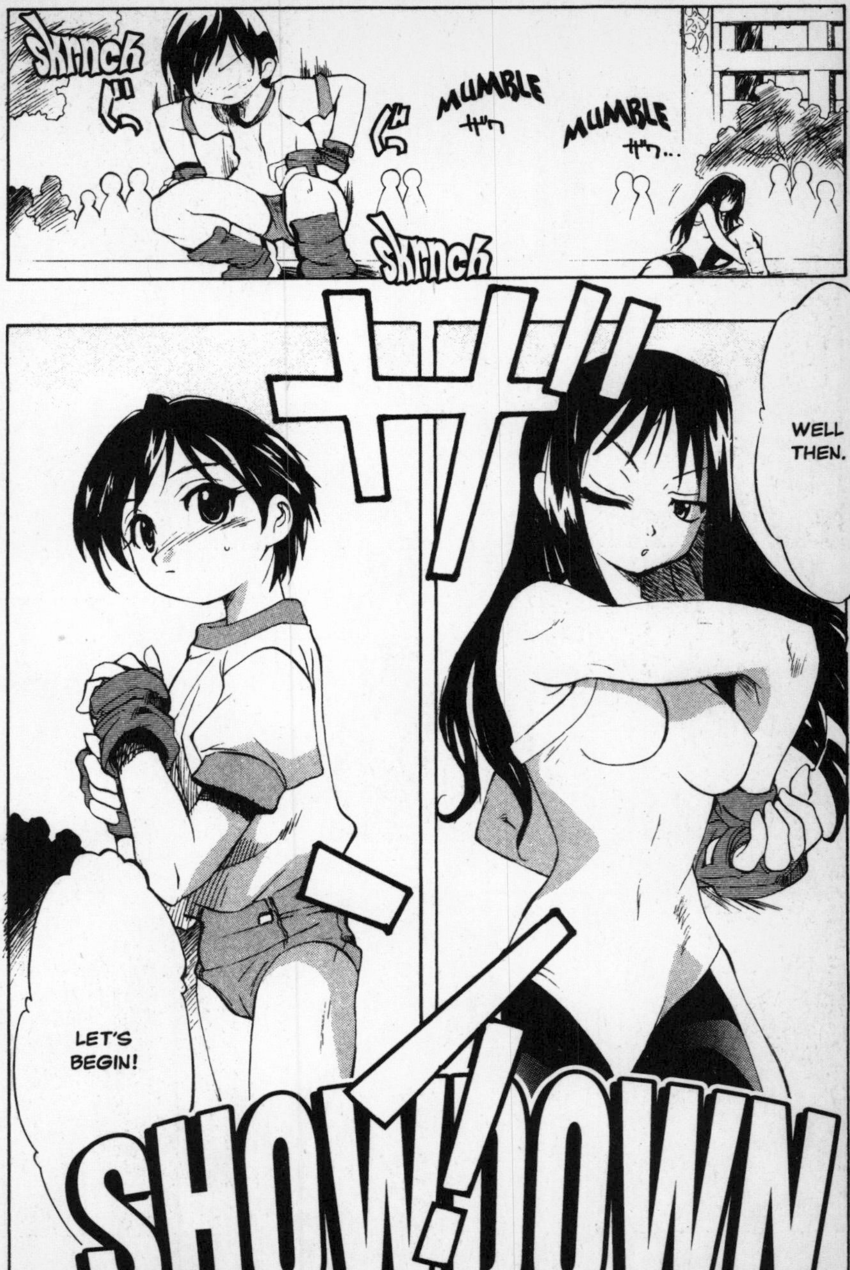
MUMBLE
ザワ…
MUMBLE
ザワ
skrnch
ぐ
skrnch
ぐ
WELL THEN.
LET'S BEGIN!
SHOWDOWN

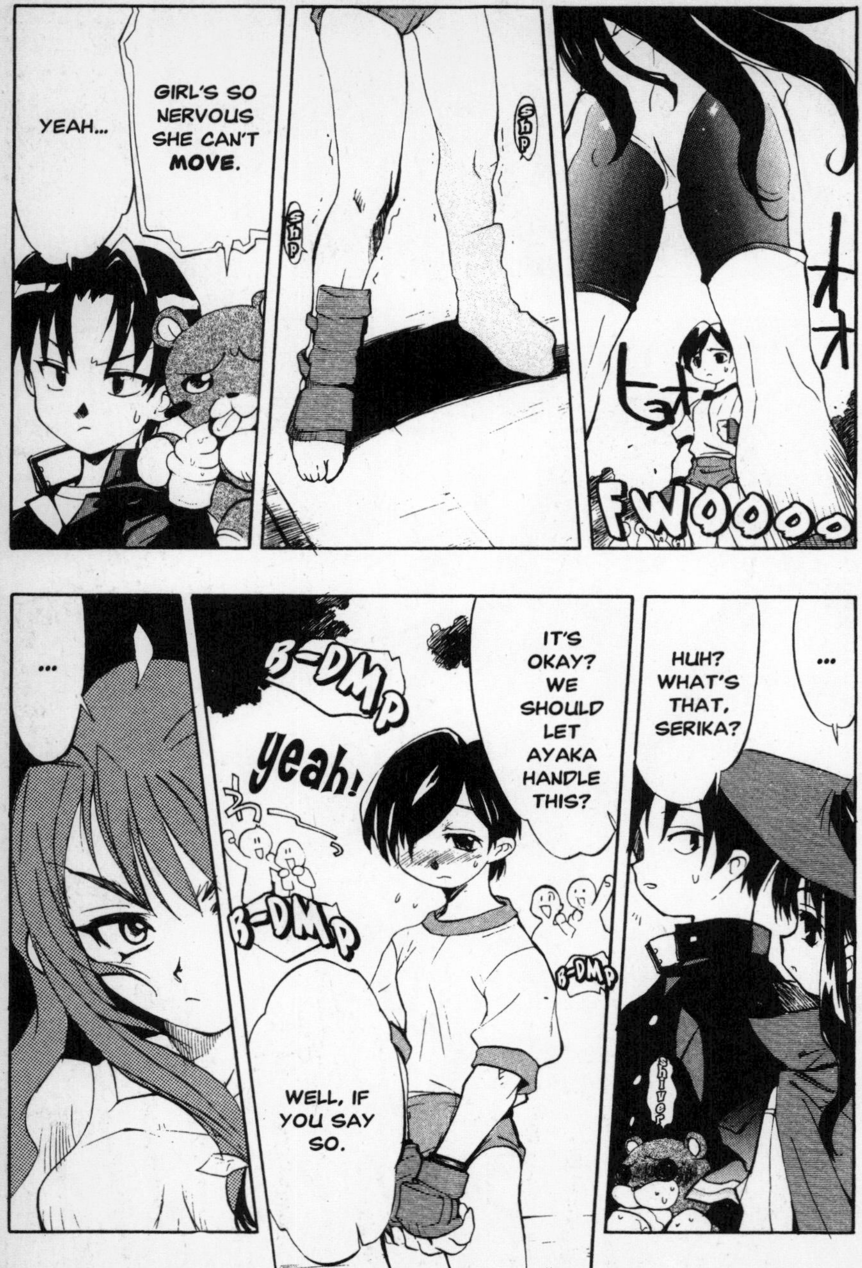
FWOOOO
shp
shp
GIRL'S SO NERVOUS SHE CAN'T MOVE.
YEAH...
...
HUH? WHAT'S THAT, SERIKA?
shiver
IT'S OKAY? WE SHOULD LET AYAKA HANDLE THIS?
B-DMP
yeah!
B-DMP
B-DMP
WELL, IF YOU SAY SO.
...

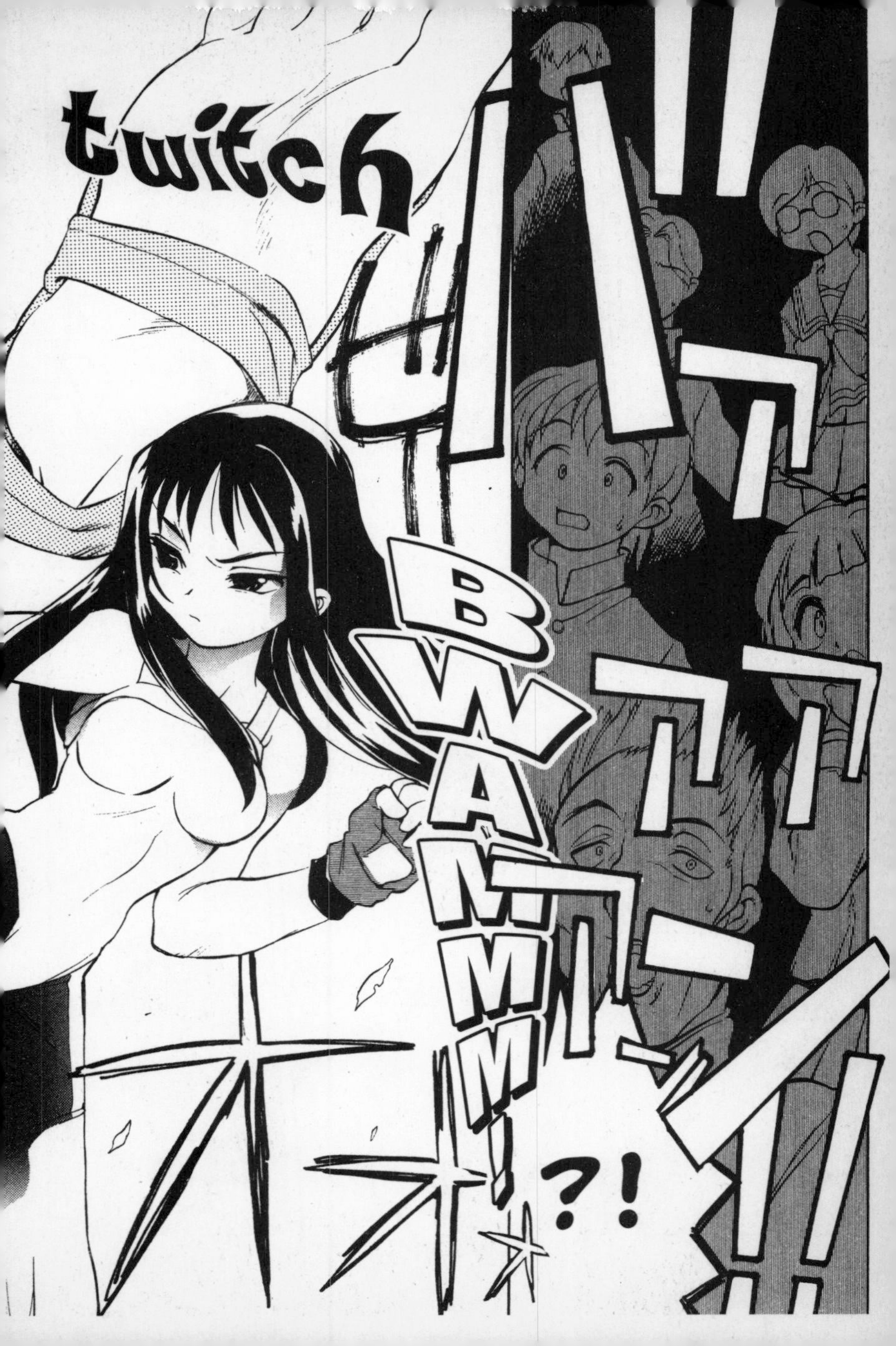
twitch
BWAMMM!
?!

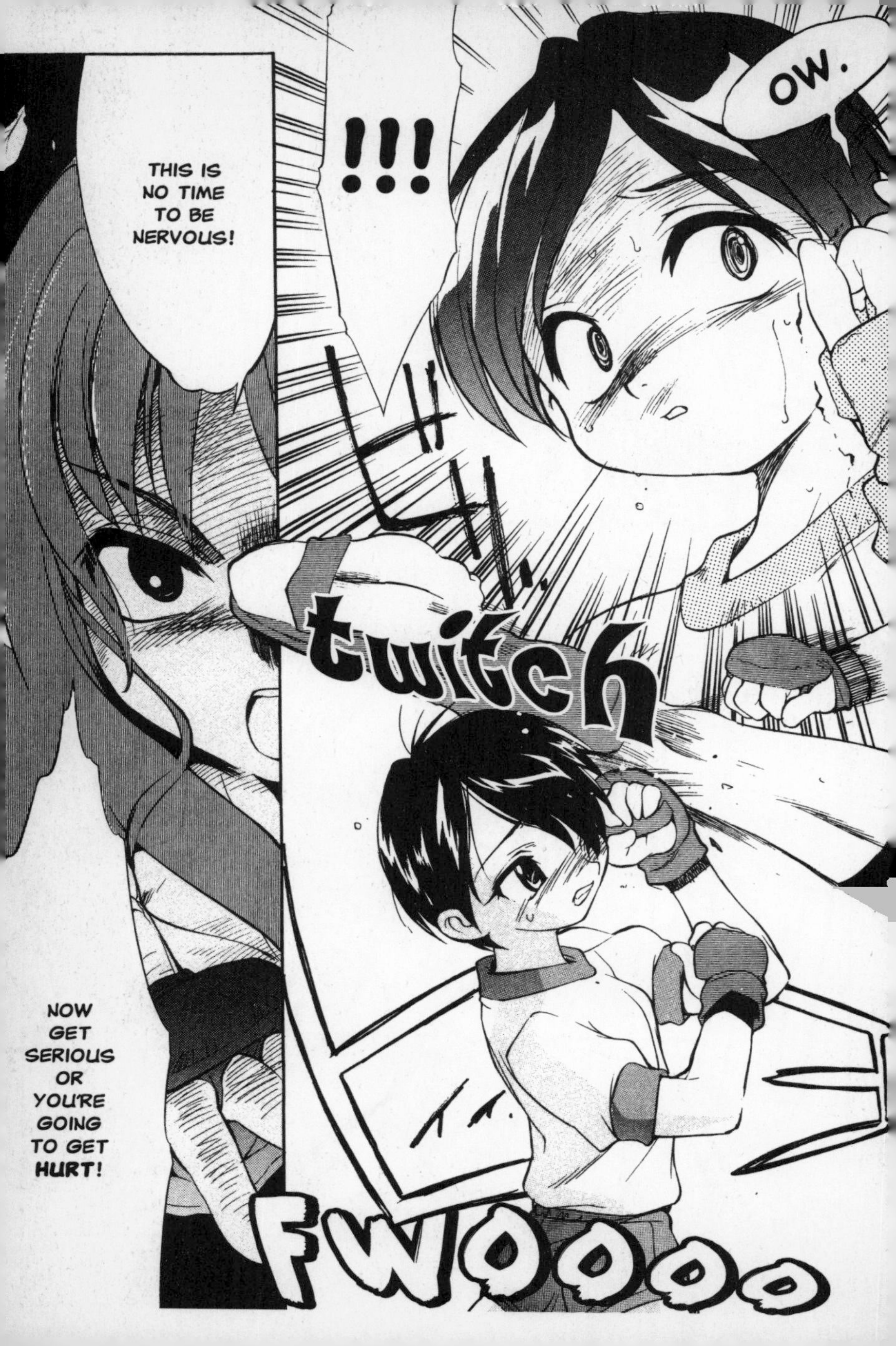
OW.
!!!
THIS IS NO TIME TO BE NERVOUS!
twitch
NOW GET SERIOUS OR YOU'RE GOING TO GET HURT!
FWOOOO

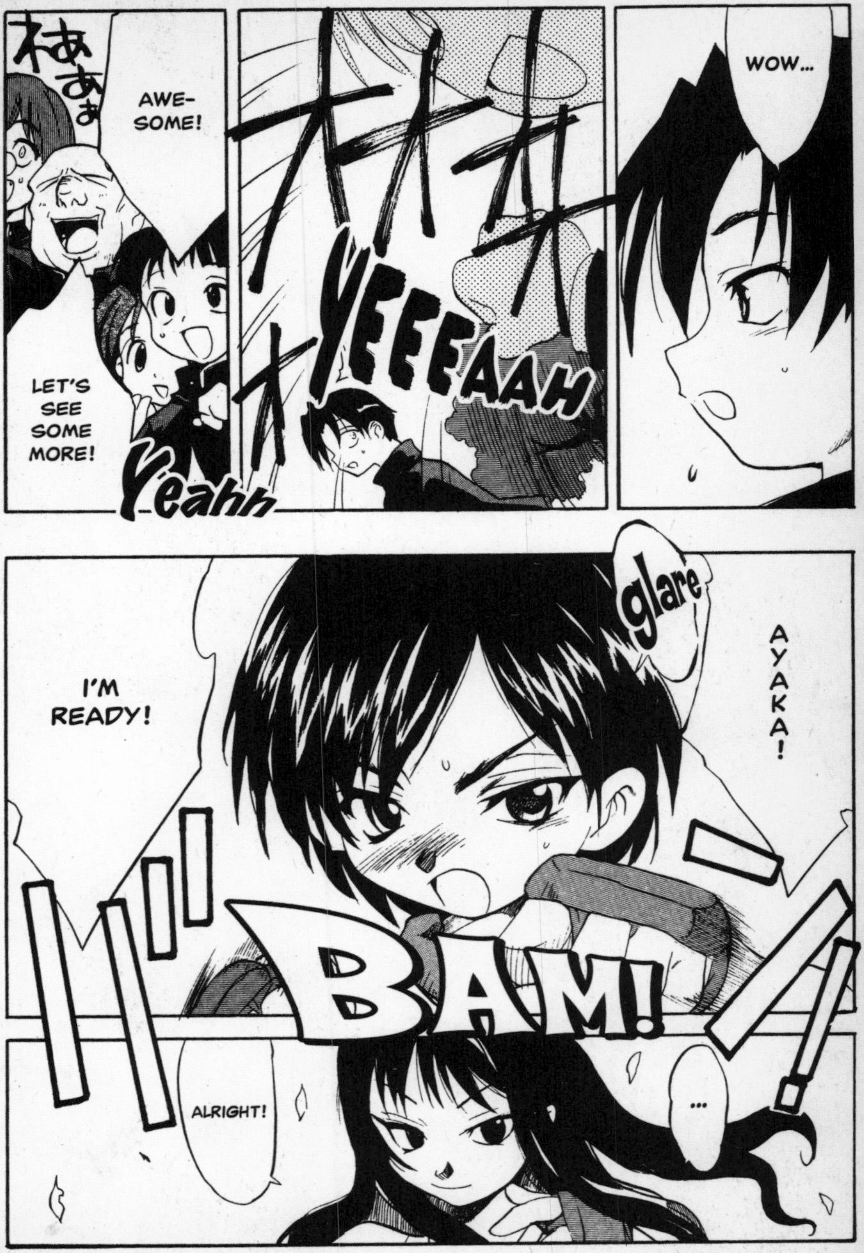
WOW...
YEEEAAAH
AWE-SOME!
LET'S SEE SOME MORE!
Yeahh
glare
AYAKA!
I'M READY!
BAM!
...
ALRIGHT!

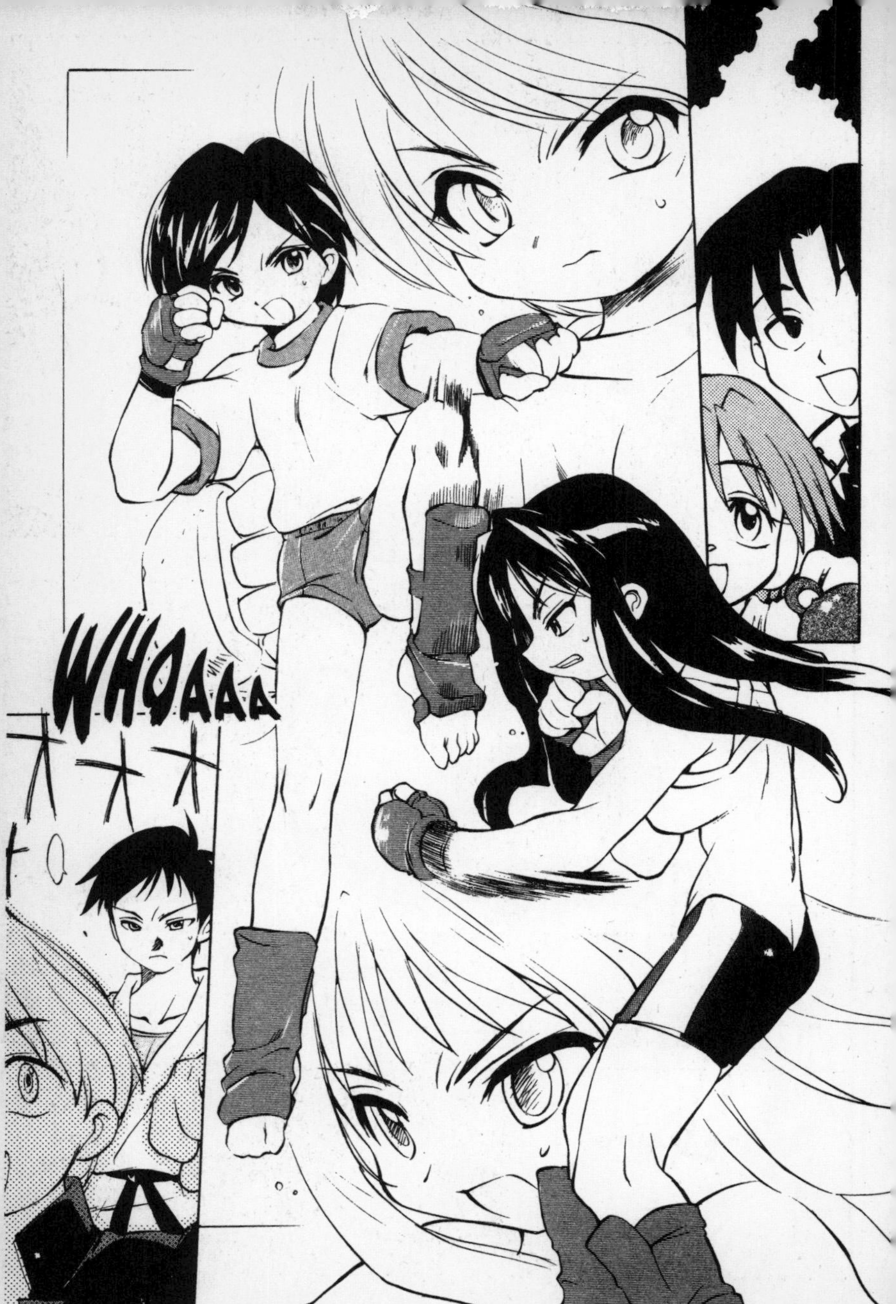
WHOAAA

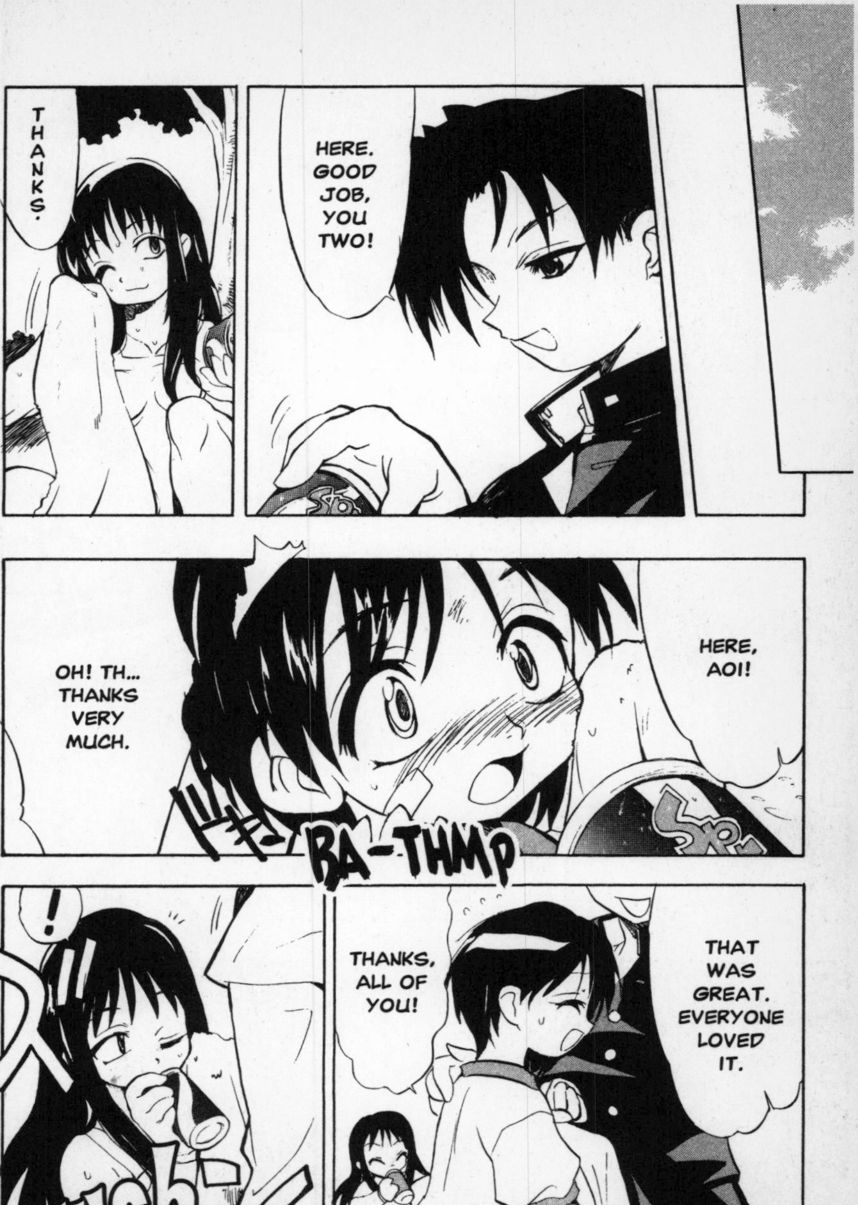
HERE. GOOD JOB, YOU TWO!
THANKS.
HERE, AOI!
OH! TH... THANKS VERY MUCH.
BA-THMP
THAT WAS GREAT. EVERYONE LOVED IT.
THANKS, ALL OF YOU!
!
SUSH

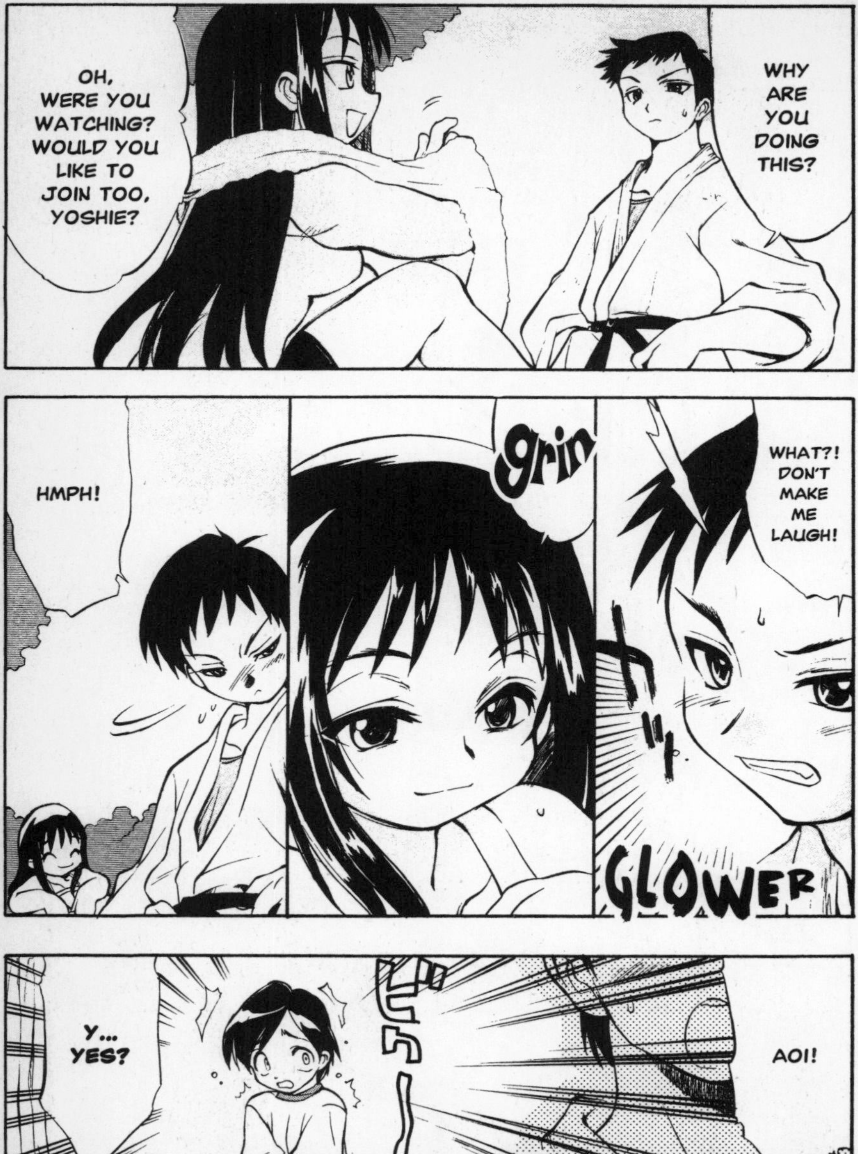
WHY ARE YOU DOING THIS?
OH, WERE YOU WATCHING? WOULD YOU LIKE TO JOIN TOO, YOSHIE?
WHAT?! DON'T MAKE ME LAUGH!
GLOWER
grin
HMPH!
AOI!
flinch
Y... YES?

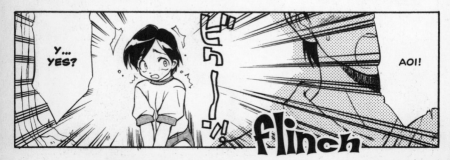

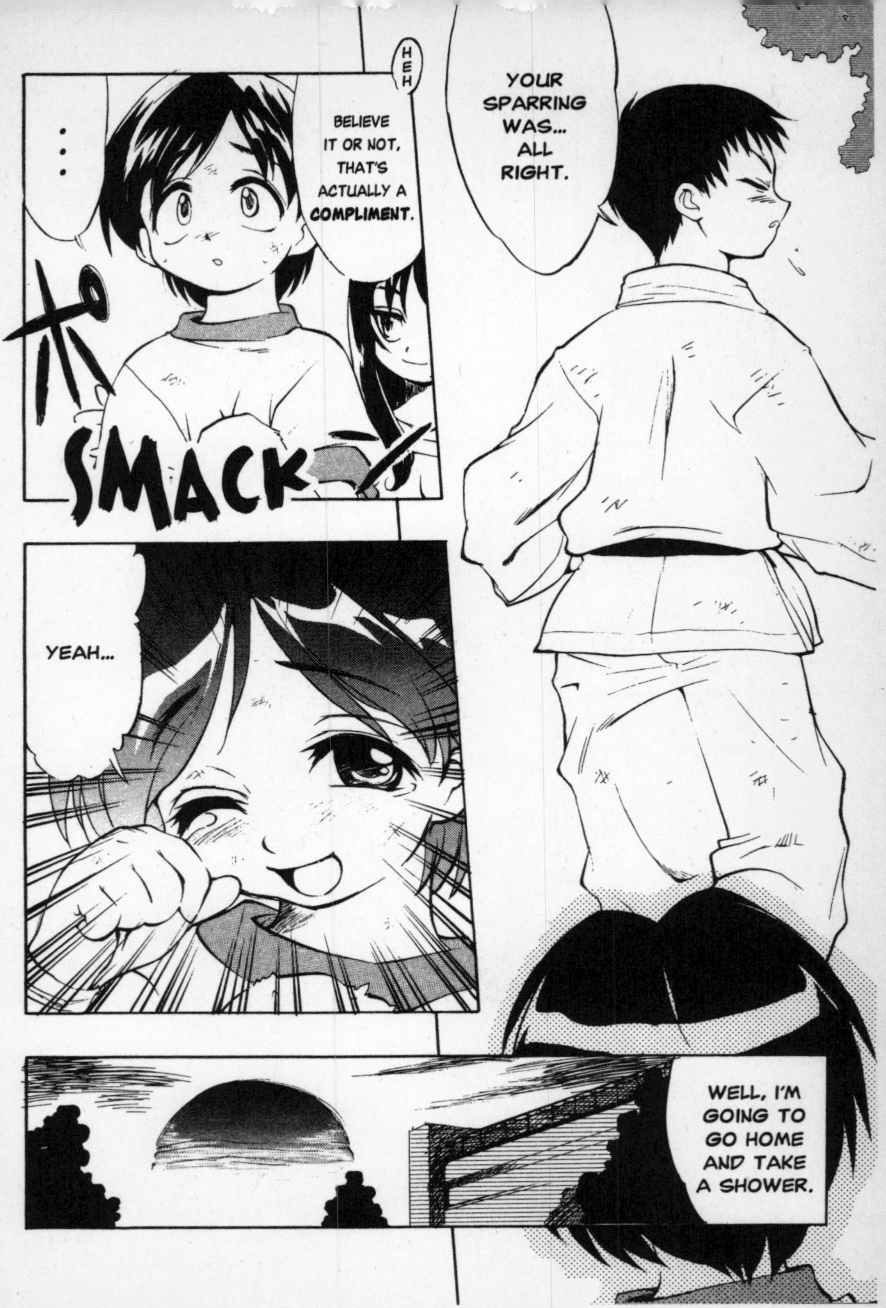
YOUR SPARRING WAS... ALL RIGHT.
HEH
BELIEVE IT OR NOT, THAT'S ACTUALLY A COMPLIMENT.
...
SMACK
YEAH...
WELL, I'M GOING TO GO HOME AND TAKE A SHOWER.

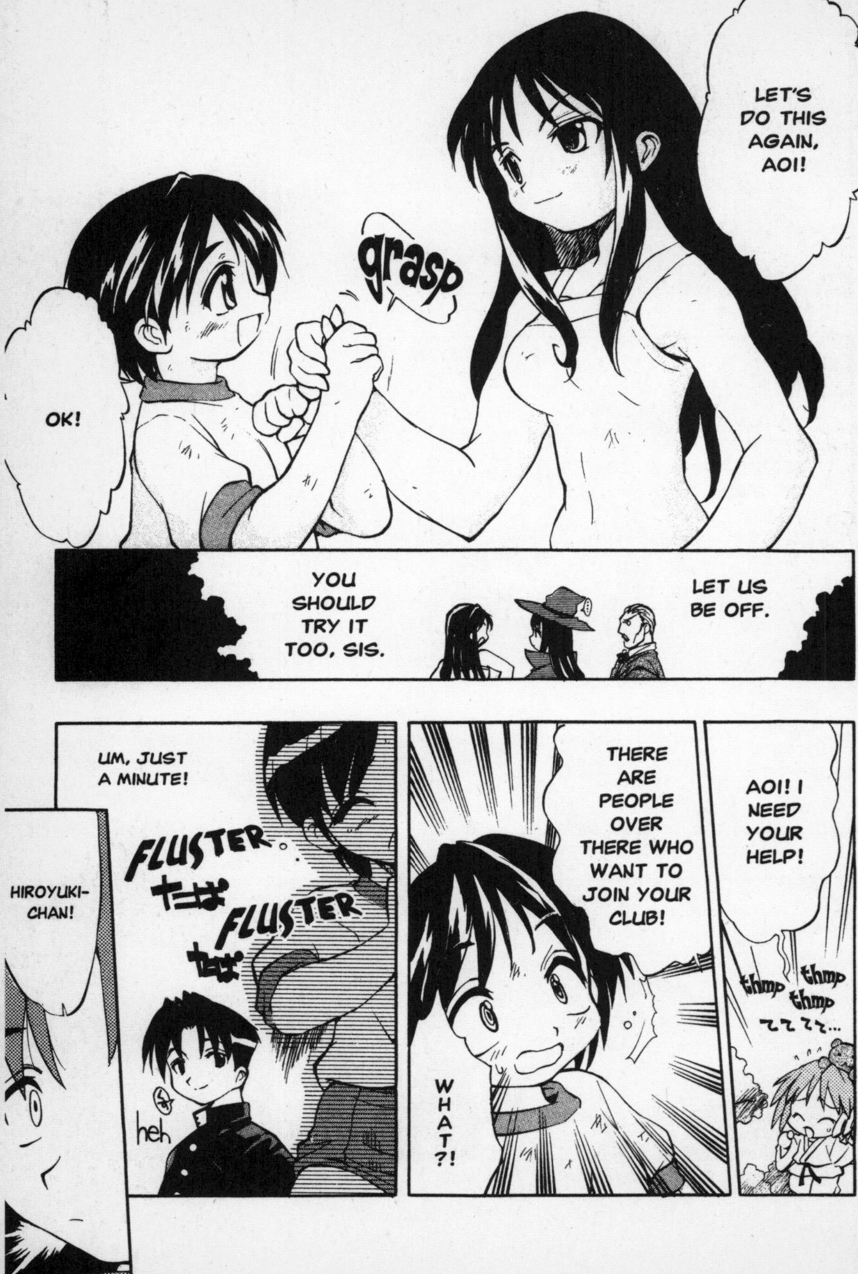
LET'S DO THIS AGAIN, AOI!
grasp
OK!
LET US BE OFF.
YOU SHOULD TRY IT TOO, SIS.
AOI! I NEED YOUR HELP!
thmp thmp thmp
THERE ARE PEOPLE OVER THERE WHO WANT TO JOIN YOUR CLUB!
WHAT?!
UM, JUST A MINUTE!
FLUSTER
FLUSTER
heh
HIROYUKI-CHAN!

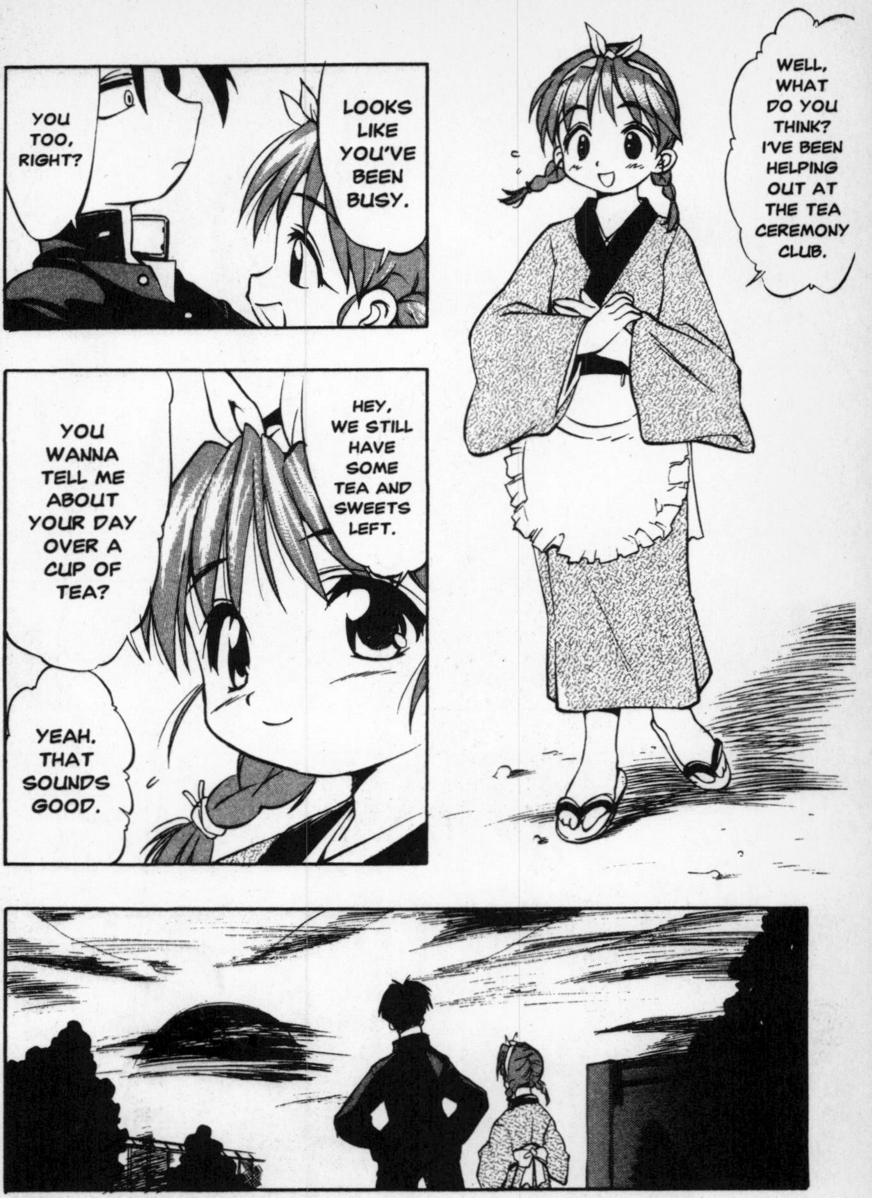
WELL, WHAT DO YOU THINK? I'VE BEEN HELPING OUT AT THE TEA CEREMONY CLUB.
LOOKS LIKE YOU'VE BEEN BUSY.
YOU TOO, RIGHT?
HEY, WE STILL HAVE SOME TEA AND SWEETS LEFT.
YOU WANNA TELL ME ABOUT YOUR DAY OVER A CUP OF TEA?
YEAH. THAT SOUNDS GOOD.

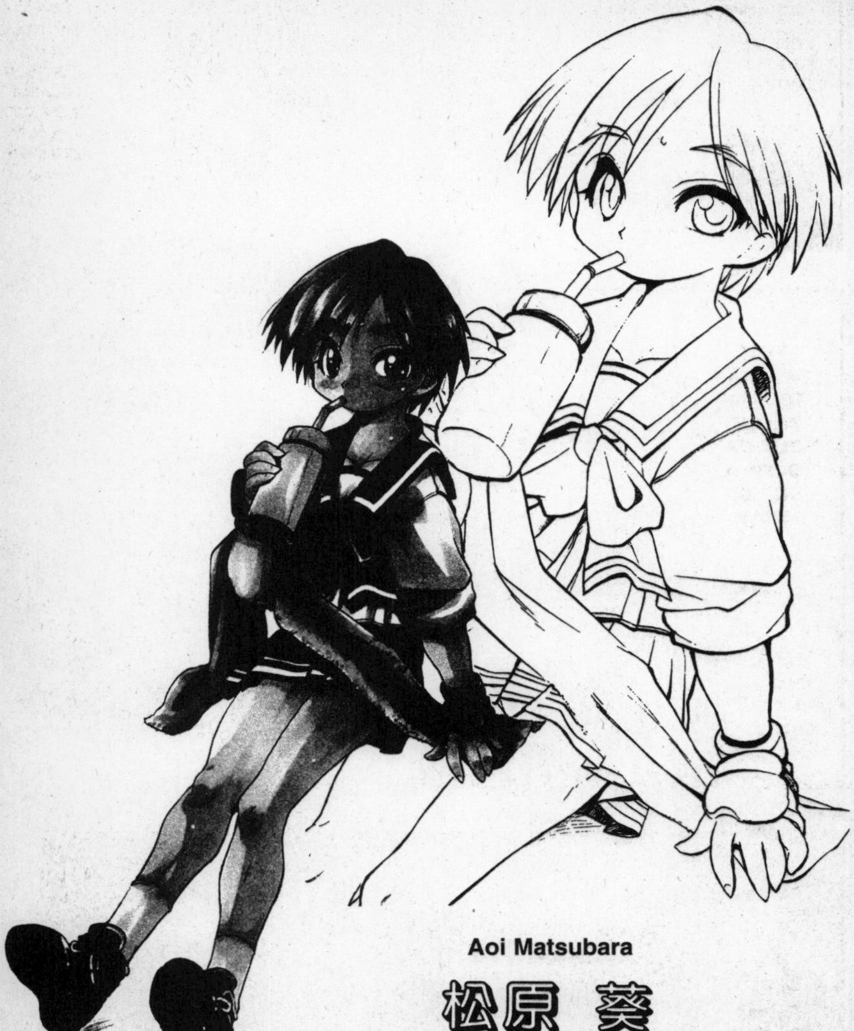

Aoi Matsubara

松原 葵

HANG IN THERE, AOI!
SHE'LL DO WHATEVER IT TAKES
TO CATCH UP WITH THAT CERTAIN
PERSON SHE ADMIRES SO MUCH!

Episode 6
『Special Xmas』

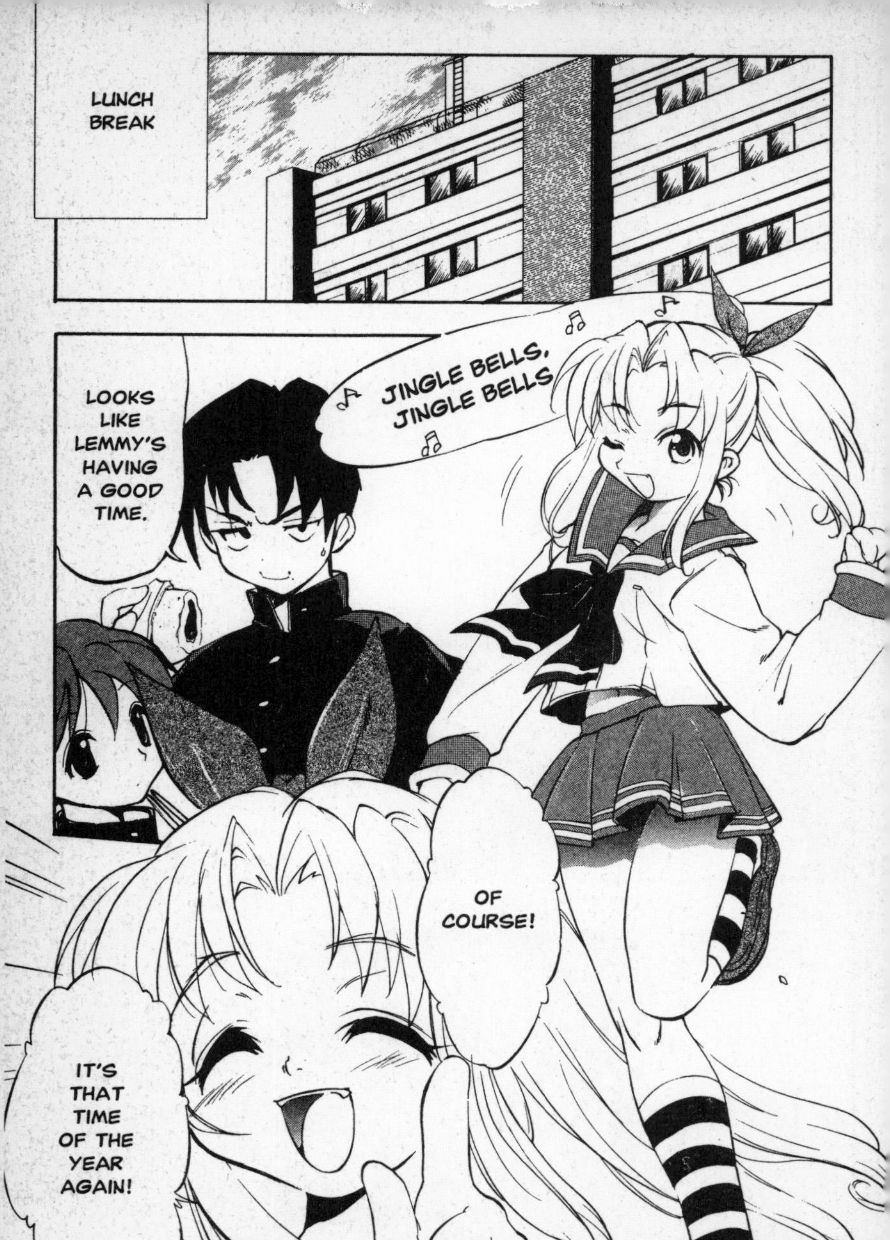
LUNCH BREAK
JINGLE BELLS, JINGLE BELLS
LOOKS LIKE LEMMY'S HAVING A GOOD TIME.
OF COURSE!
IT'S THAT TIME OF THE YEAR AGAIN!

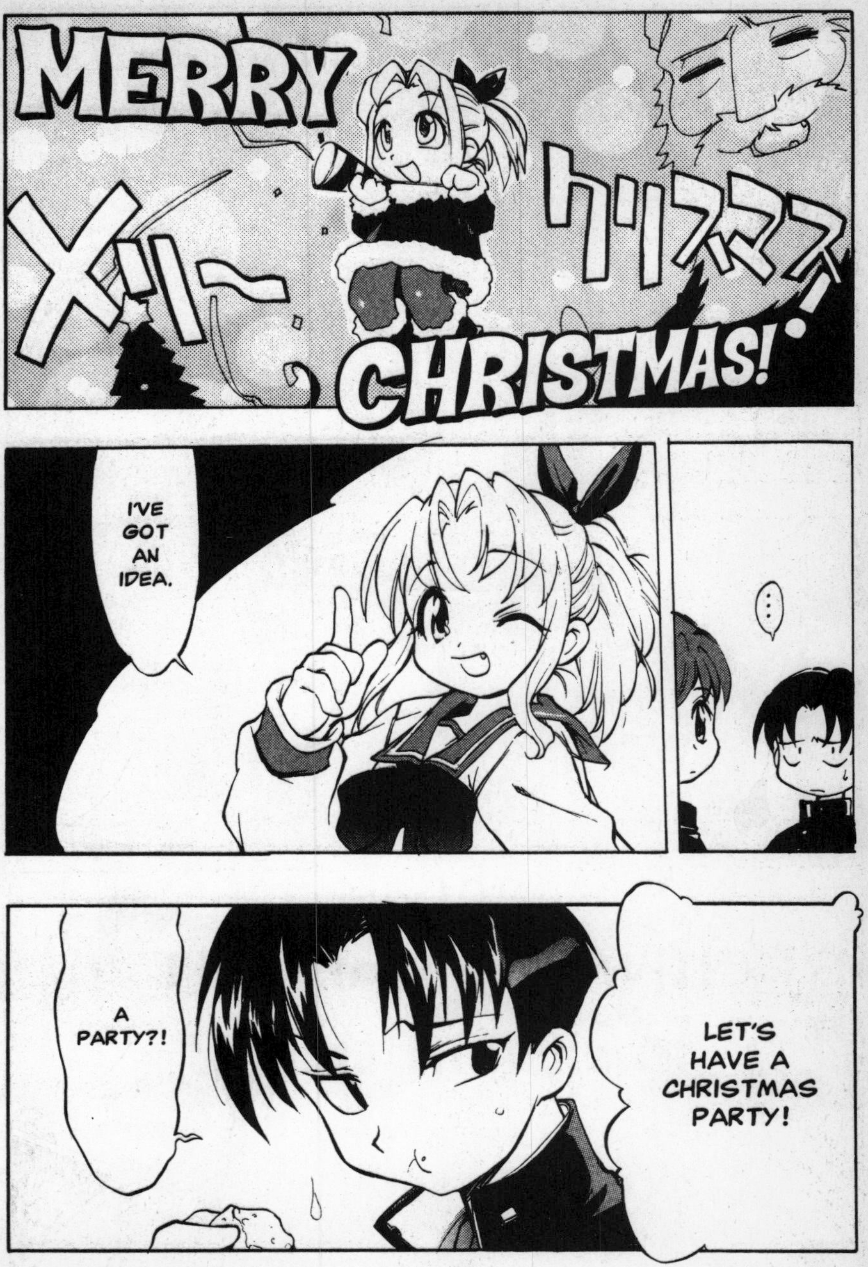
MERRY
メリ〜
クリスマス!
CHRISTMAS!
. . .
I'VE GOT AN IDEA.
LET'S HAVE A CHRISTMAS PARTY!
A PARTY?!

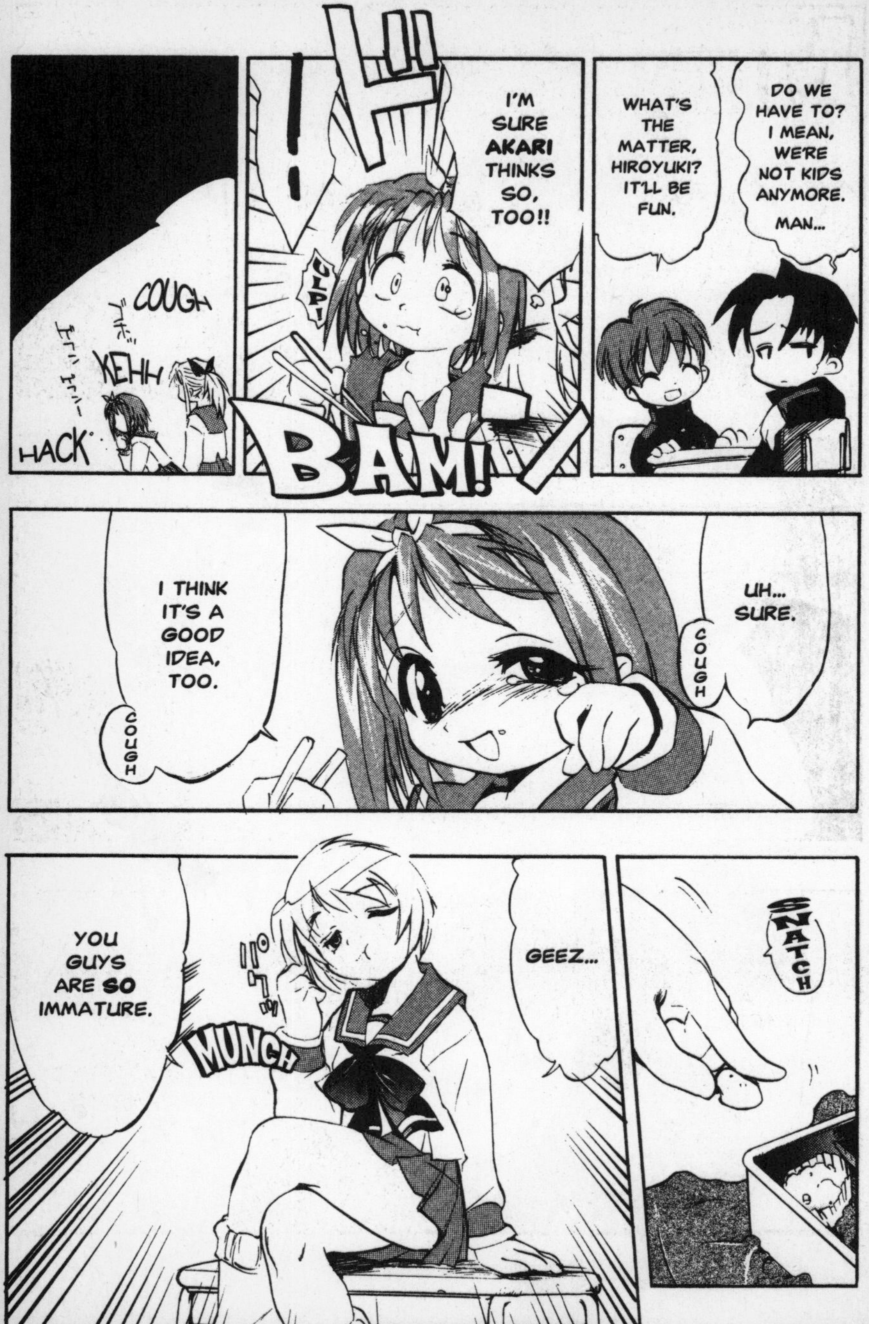
DO WE HAVE TO? I MEAN, WE'RE NOT KIDS ANYMORE.
MAN...
WHAT'S THE MATTER, HIROYUKI? IT'LL BE FUN.
I'M SURE AKARI THINKS SO, TOO!!
ULP!
BAM!
COUGH
KEHH
HACK
UH... SURE.
COUGH
I THINK IT'S A GOOD IDEA, TOO.
COUGH
SNATCH
GEEZ...
YOU GUYS ARE SO IMMATURE.
MUNCH

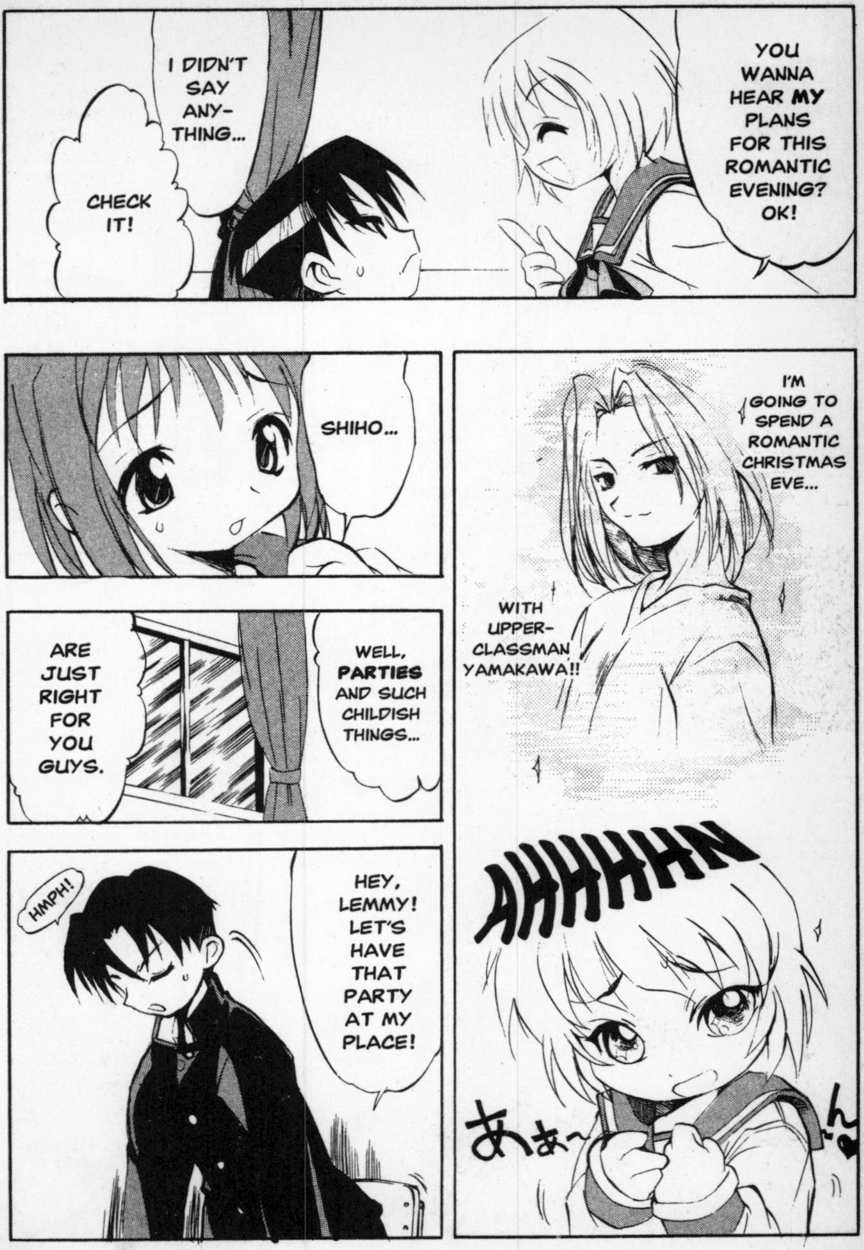
YOU WANNA HEAR MY PLANS FOR THIS ROMANTIC EVENING? OK!
I DIDN'T SAY ANY-THING...
CHECK IT!
I'M GOING TO SPEND A ROMANTIC CHRISTMAS EVE...
WITH UPPER-CLASSMAN YAMAKAWA!!
SHIHO...
WELL, PARTIES AND SUCH CHILDISH THINGS...
ARE JUST RIGHT FOR YOU GUYS.
AHHHHN
あぁ~
ん
HEY, LEMMY! LET'S HAVE THAT PARTY AT MY PLACE!
HMPH!

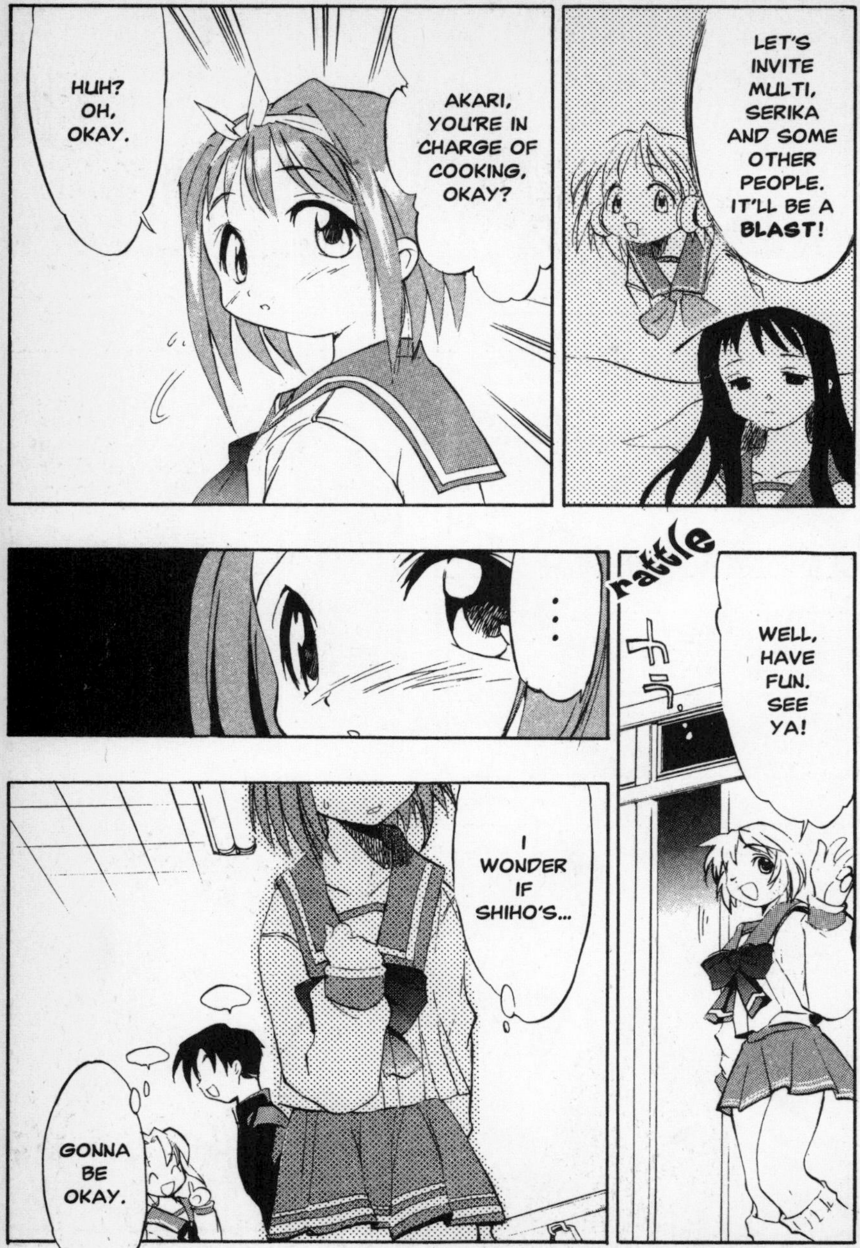
LET'S INVITE MULTI, SERIKA AND SOME OTHER PEOPLE. IT'LL BE A **BLAST**!
AKARI, YOU'RE IN CHARGE OF COOKING, OKAY?
HUH? OH, OKAY.
rattle
WELL, HAVE FUN. SEE YA!
...
I WONDER IF SHIHO'S...
GONNA BE OKAY.

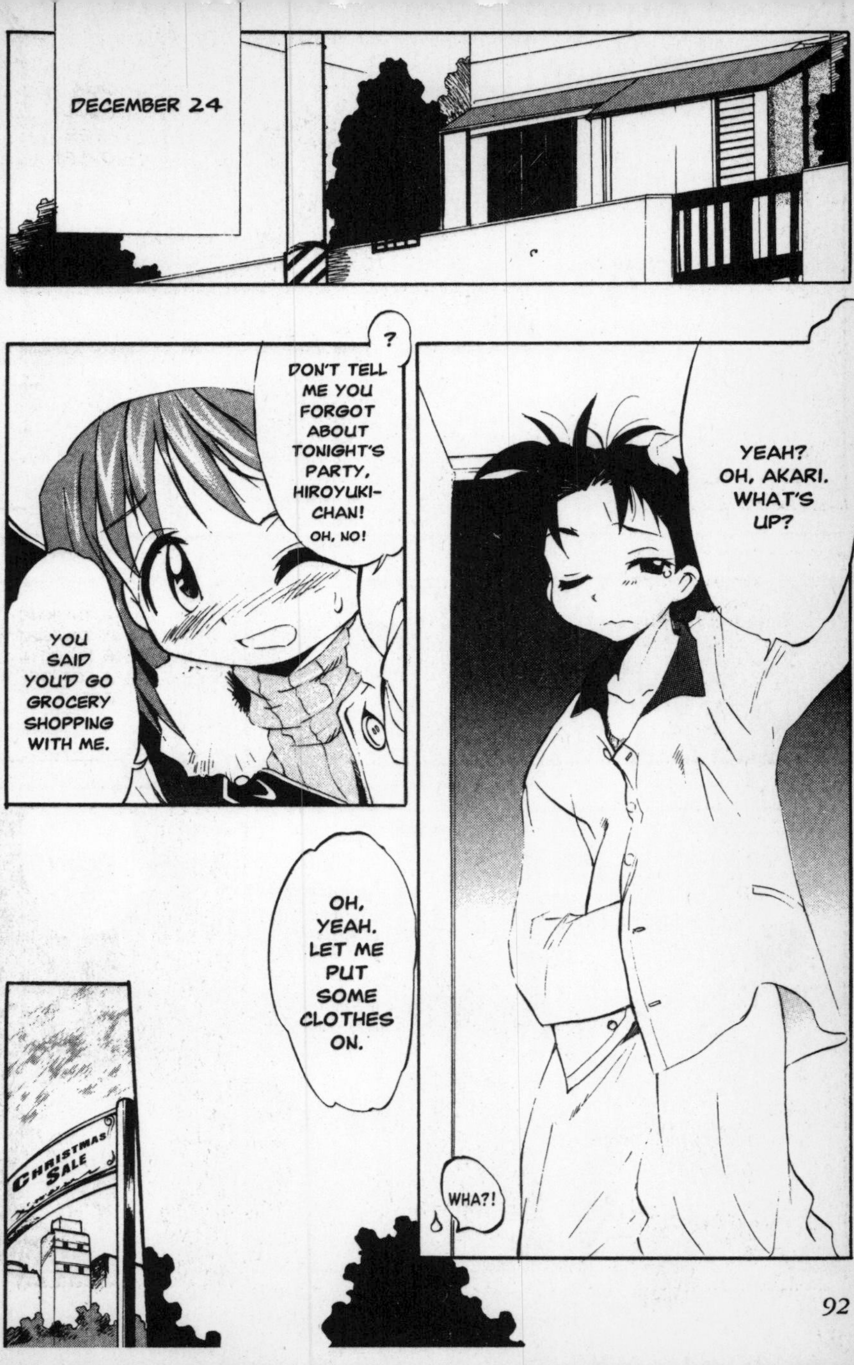
DECEMBER 24
YEAH? OH, AKARI. WHAT'S UP?
YOU SAID YOU'D GO GROCERY SHOPPING WITH ME.
?
DON'T TELL ME YOU FORGOT ABOUT TONIGHT'S PARTY, HIROYUKI-CHAN!
OH, NO!
WHA?!
OH, YEAH. LET ME PUT SOME CLOTHES ON.
CHRISTMAS SALE

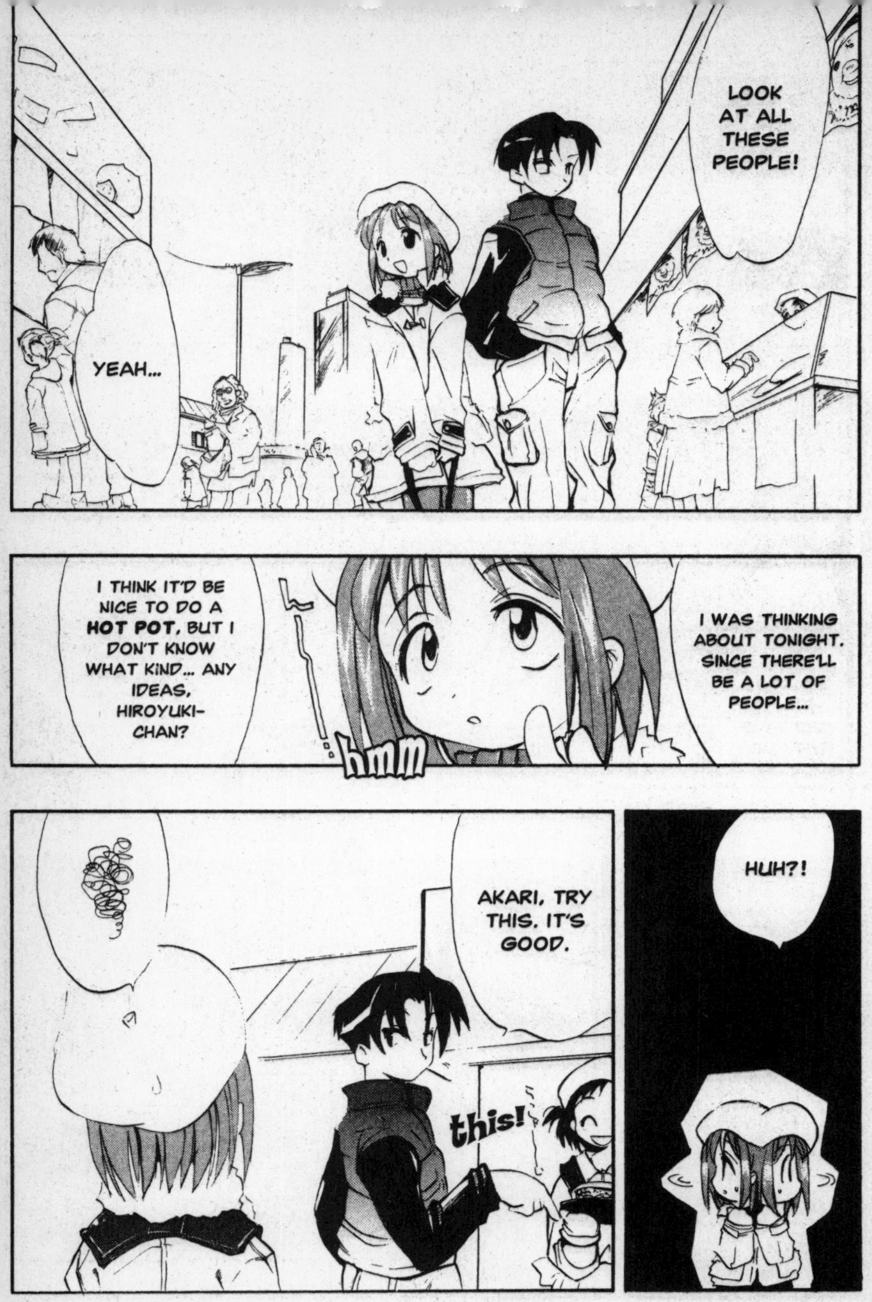

LOOK AT ALL THESE PEOPLE!
YEAH...
I WAS THINKING ABOUT TONIGHT. SINCE THERE'LL BE A LOT OF PEOPLE...
I THINK IT'D BE NICE TO DO A **HOT POT**, BUT I DON'T KNOW WHAT KIND... ANY IDEAS, HIROYUKI-CHAN?
hmm
HUH?!
AKARI, TRY THIS. IT'S GOOD.
this!

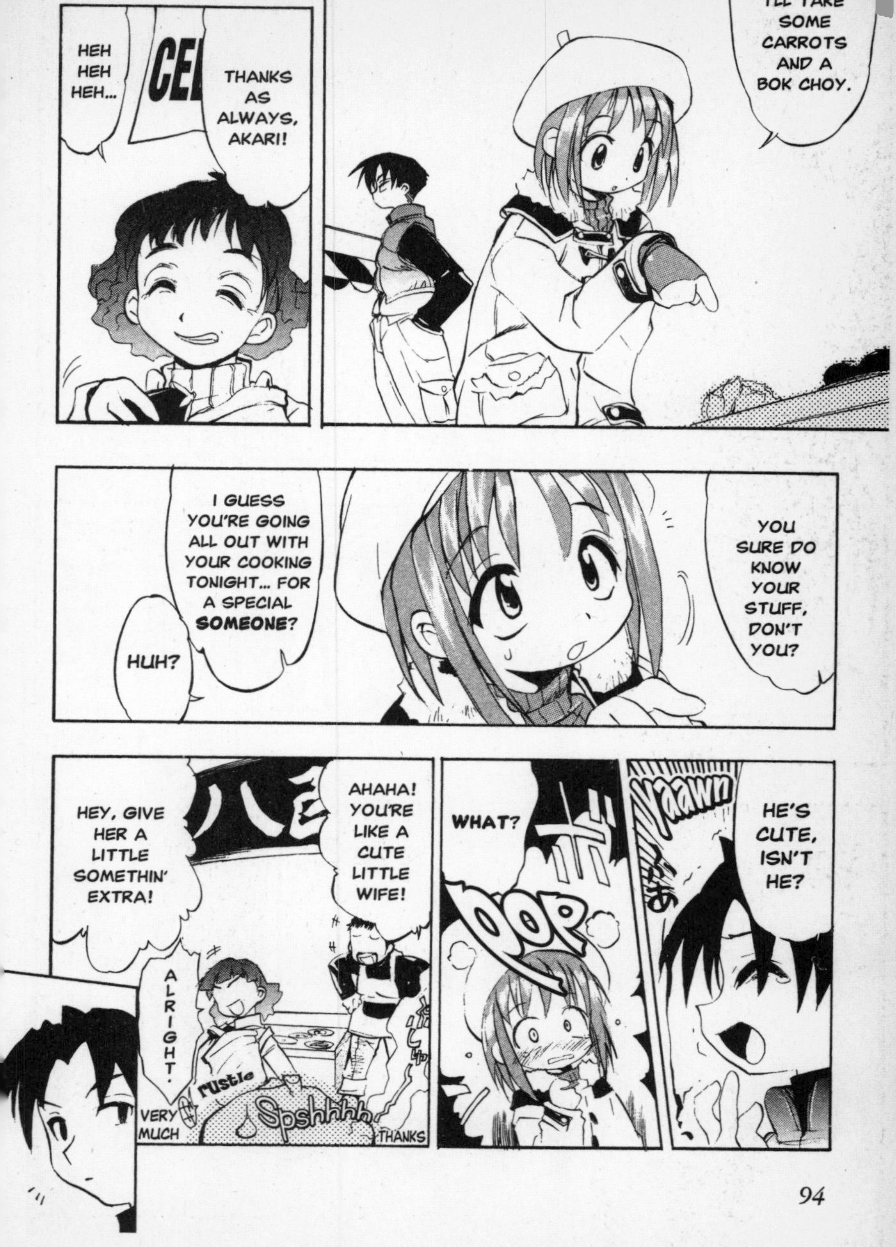
I'LL TAKE SOME CARROTS AND A BOK CHOY.
THANKS AS ALWAYS, AKARI!
CEL
HEH HEH HEH...
YOU SURE DO KNOW YOUR STUFF, DON'T YOU?
I GUESS YOU'RE GOING ALL OUT WITH YOUR COOKING TONIGHT... FOR A SPECIAL SOMEONE?
HUH?
HE'S CUTE, ISN'T HE?
Yaawn
WHAT?
OOP
AHAHA! YOU'RE LIKE A CUTE LITTLE WIFE!
HEY, GIVE HER A LITTLE SOMETHIN' EXTRA!
ALRIGHT.
THANKS
VERY MUCH
rustle
Spshhhh

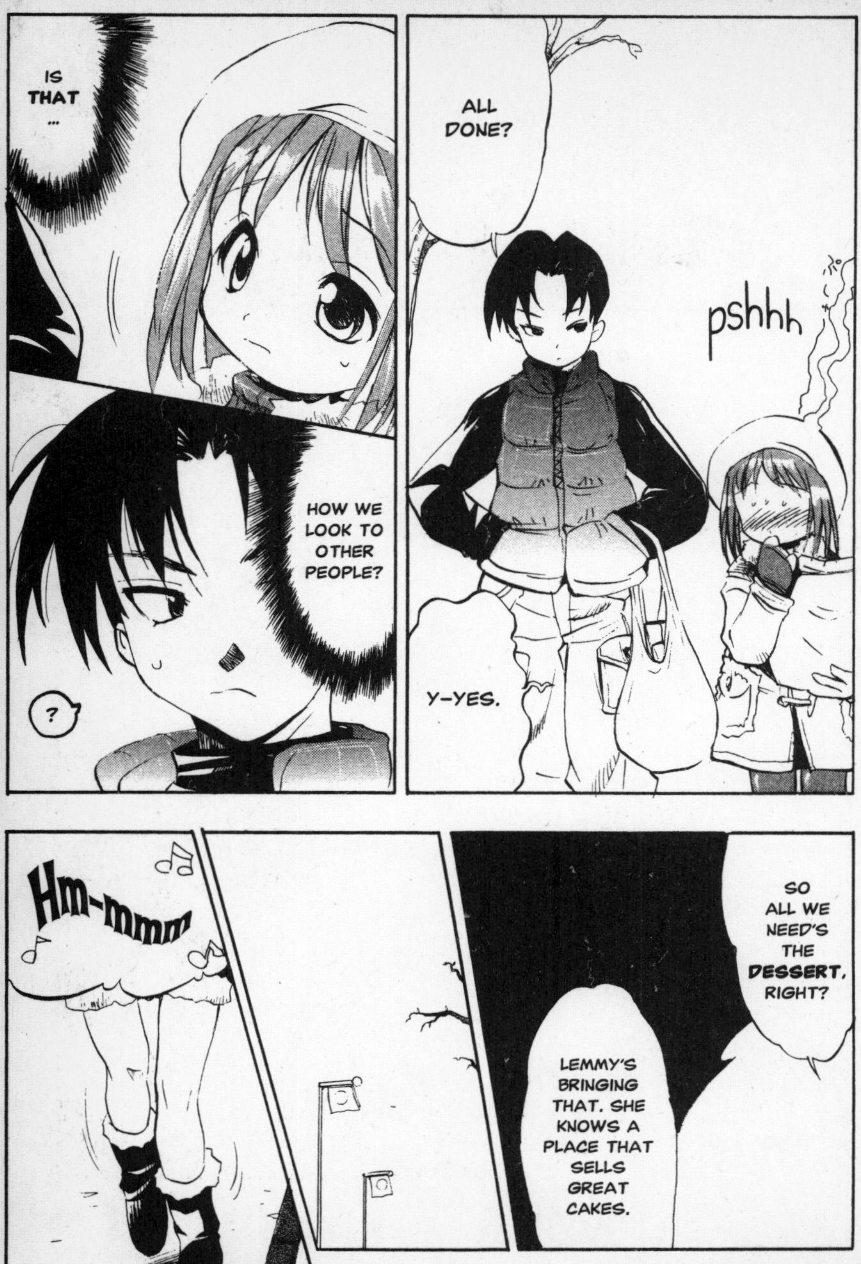
ALL DONE?
pshhh
Y-YES.
IS THAT ...
HOW WE LOOK TO OTHER PEOPLE?
?
SO ALL WE NEED'S THE **DESSERT**, RIGHT?
LEMMY'S BRINGING THAT. SHE KNOWS A PLACE THAT SELLS GREAT CAKES.
Hm-mmm

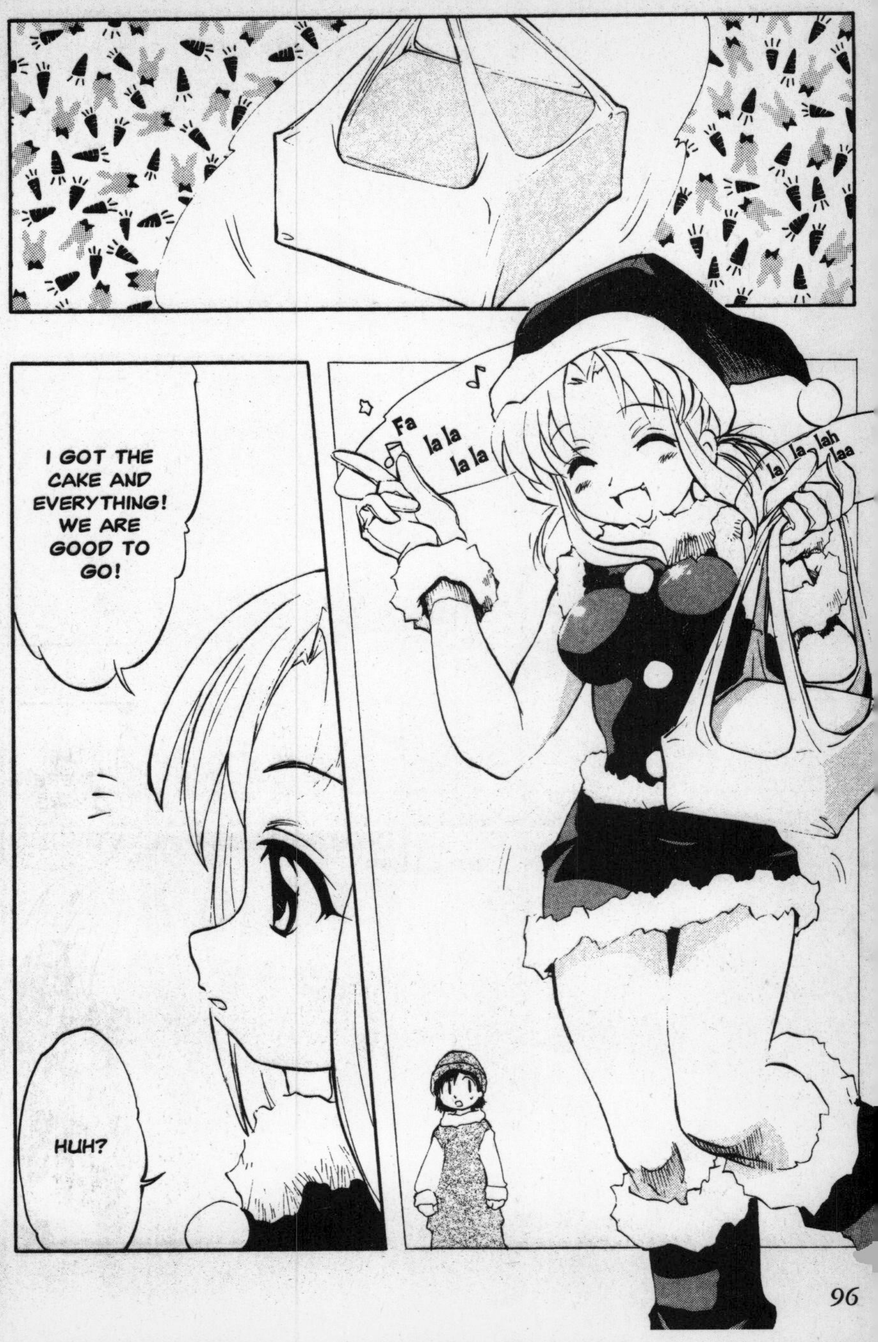
Fa
la la
la la
la
la
lah
laa
I GOT THE CAKE AND EVERYTHING! WE ARE GOOD TO GO!
HUH?

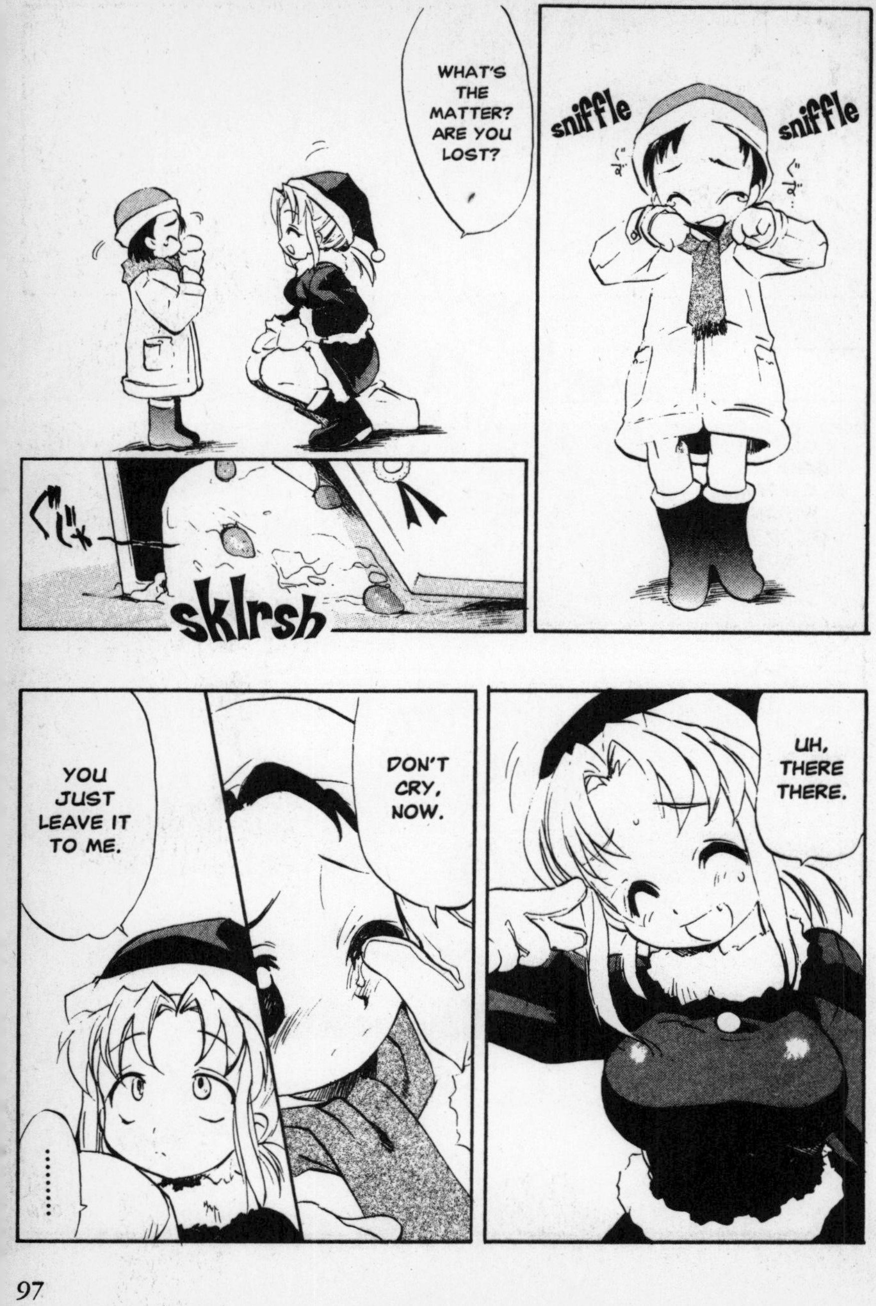
sniffle
sniffle
WHAT'S THE MATTER? ARE YOU LOST?
sklrsh
UH, THERE THERE.
DON'T CRY, NOW.
YOU JUST LEAVE IT TO ME.
......

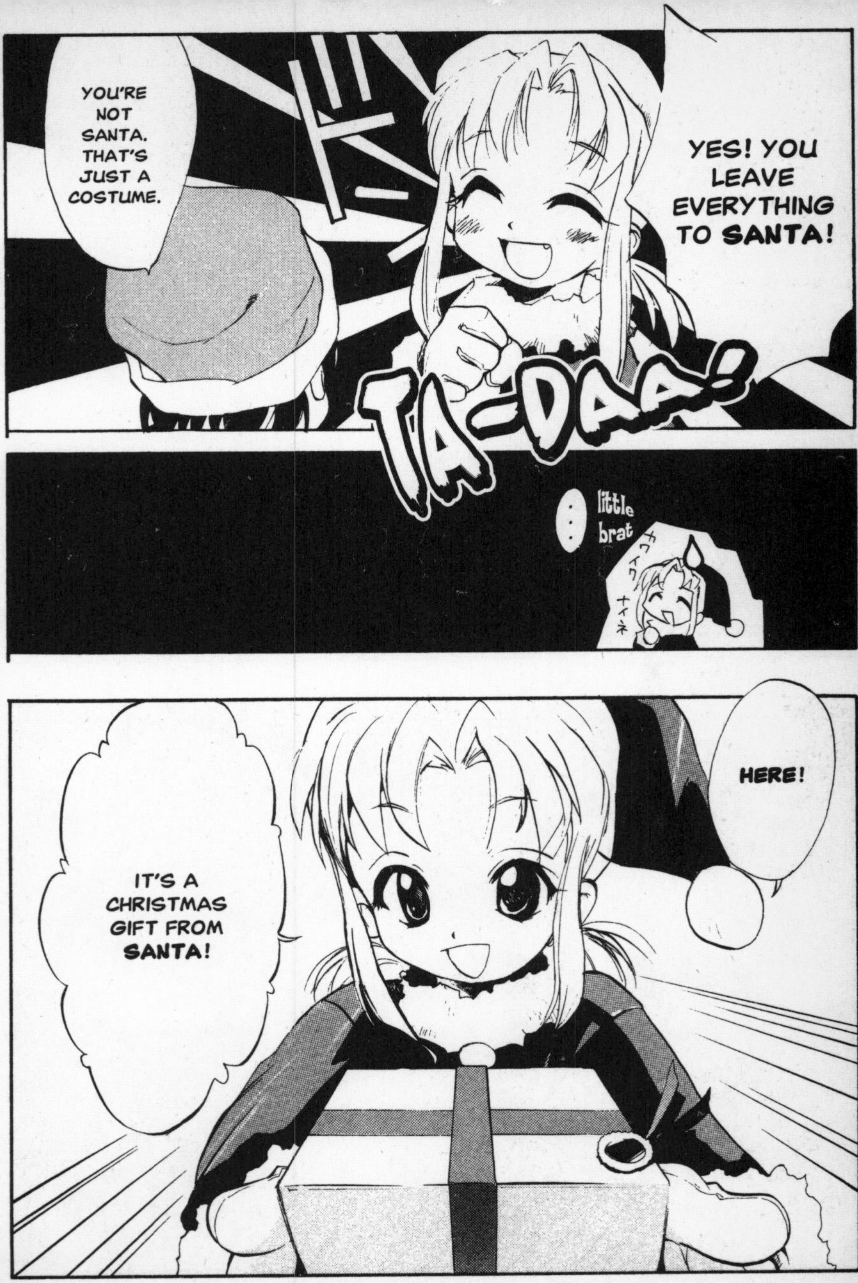
YES! YOU LEAVE EVERYTHING TO SANTA!
YOU'RE NOT SANTA. THAT'S JUST A COSTUME.
TA-DAA!
...
little brat
HERE!
IT'S A CHRISTMAS GIFT FROM SANTA!

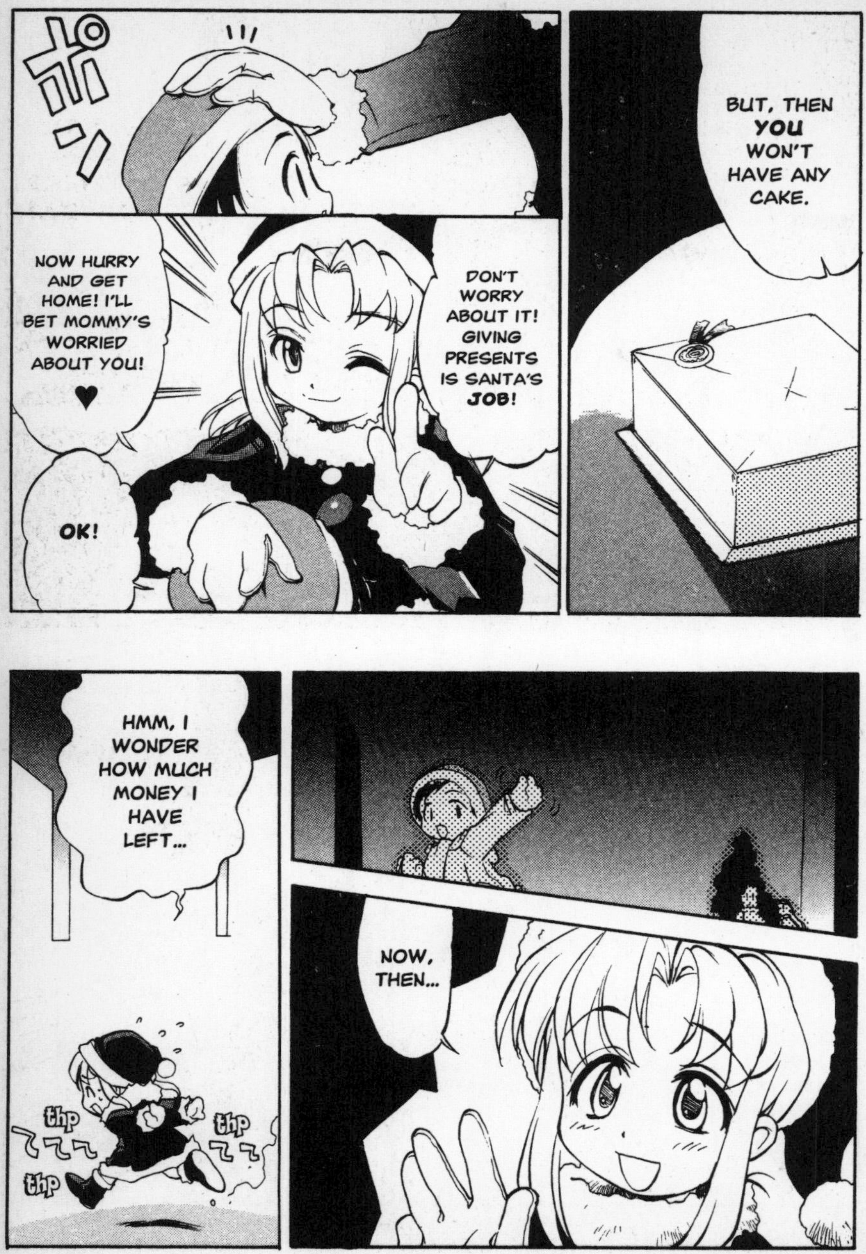
BUT, THEN YOU WON'T HAVE ANY CAKE.
DON'T WORRY ABOUT IT! GIVING PRESENTS IS SANTA'S JOB!
NOW HURRY AND GET HOME! I'LL BET MOMMY'S WORRIED ABOUT YOU! ♥
OK!
NOW, THEN...
HMM, I WONDER HOW MUCH MONEY I HAVE LEFT...
thp
thp
thp

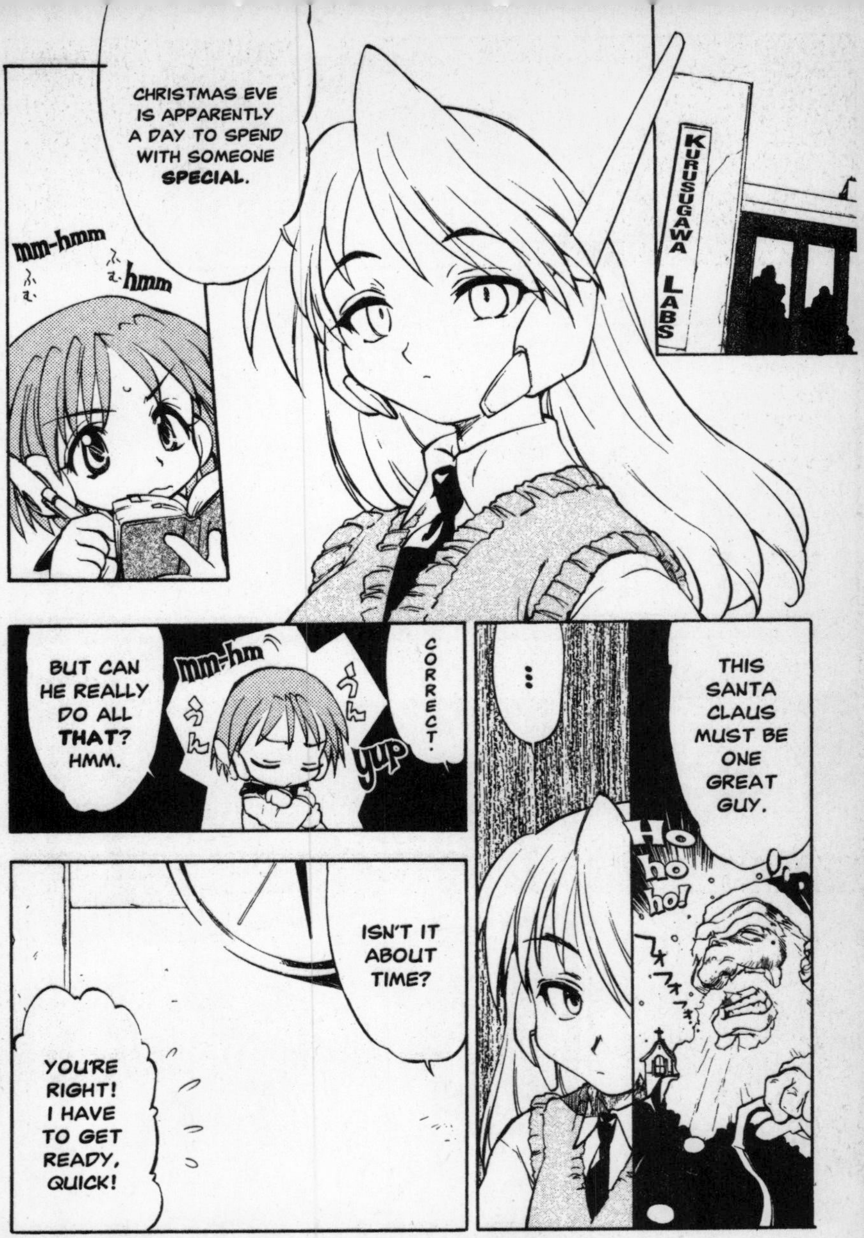
KURUSUGAWA LABS
CHRISTMAS EVE IS APPARENTLY A DAY TO SPEND WITH SOMEONE **SPECIAL**.
mm-hmm ふむ
ふむ hmm
THIS SANTA CLAUS MUST BE ONE GREAT GUY.
Ho ho ho!
...
CORRECT.
yup うん
うん mm-hm
BUT CAN HE REALLY DO ALL **THAT**? HMM.
ISN'T IT ABOUT TIME?
YOU'RE RIGHT! I HAVE TO GET READY, QUICK!

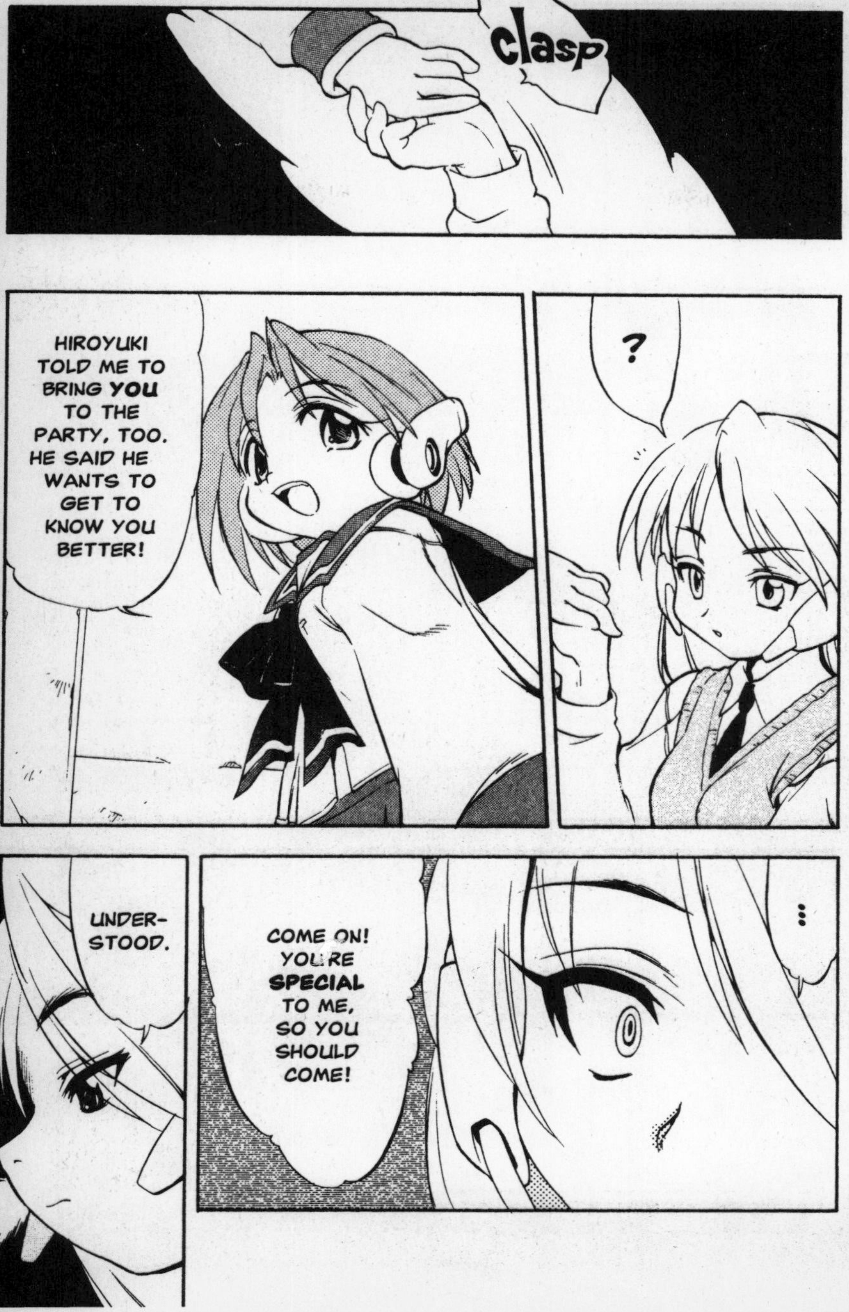
clasp
?
HIROYUKI TOLD ME TO BRING YOU TO THE PARTY, TOO. HE SAID HE WANTS TO GET TO KNOW YOU BETTER!
...
COME ON! YOU'RE SPECIAL TO ME, SO YOU SHOULD COME!
UNDER-STOOD.

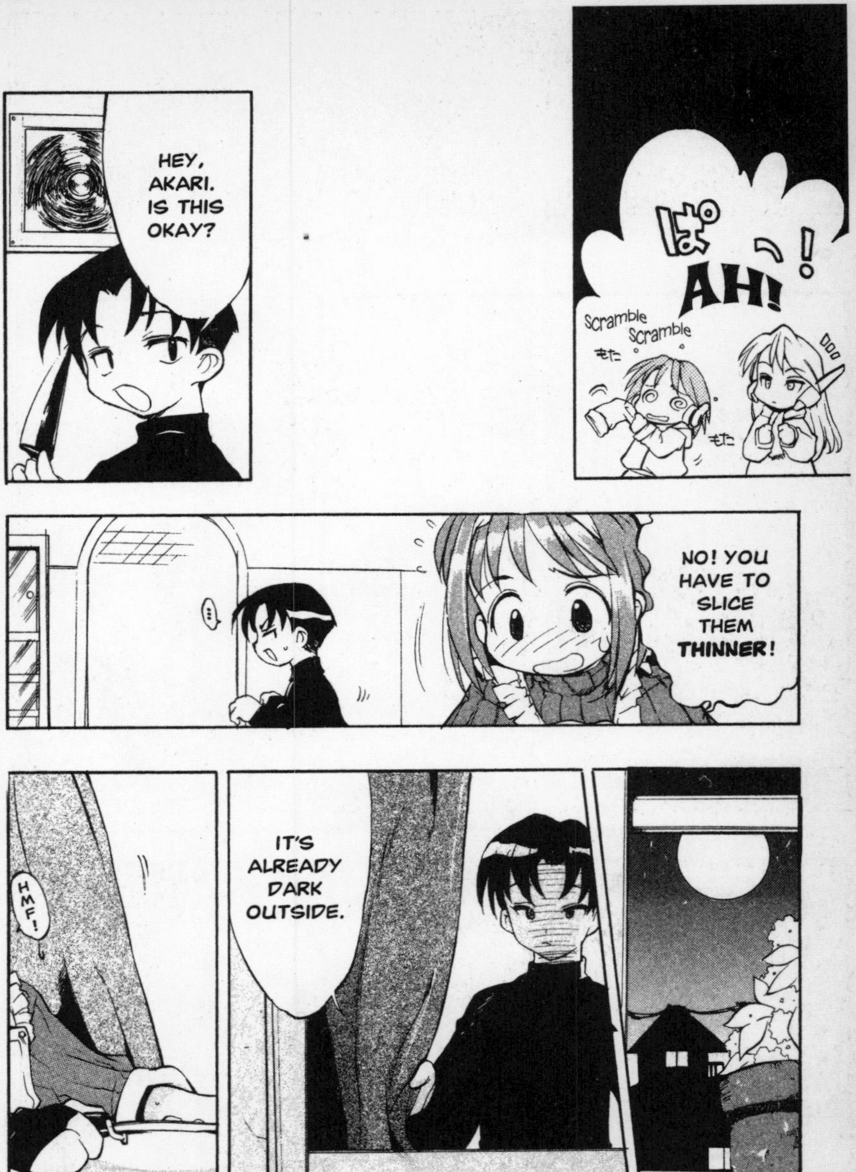

ぱ〜!
AH!
Scramble Scramble
もた
もた
HEY, AKARI. IS THIS OKAY?
...
NO! YOU HAVE TO SLICE THEM THINNER!
IT'S ALREADY DARK OUTSIDE.
HMF!

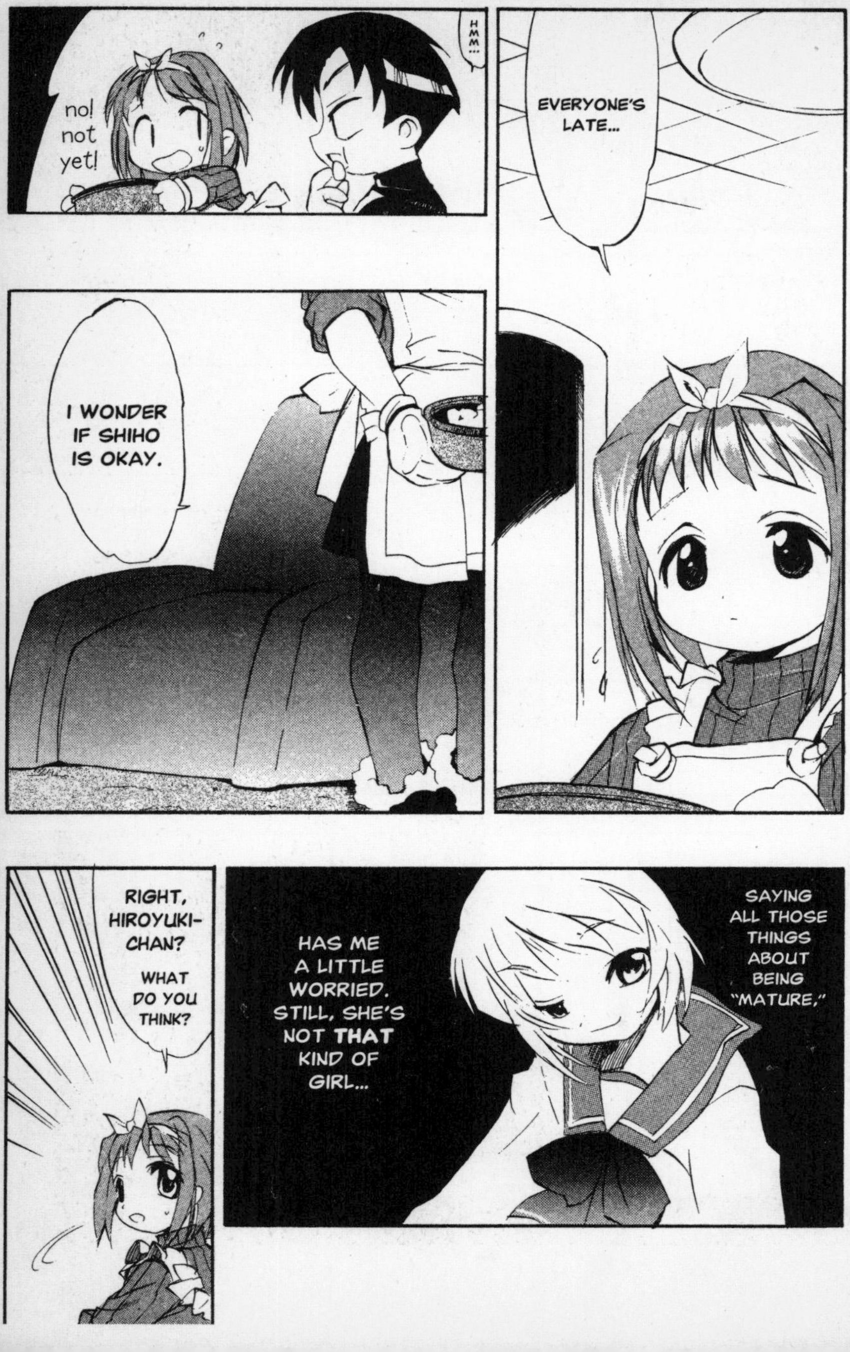
EVERYONE'S LATE...
HMM...
no! not yet!
I WONDER IF SHIHO IS OKAY.
SAYING ALL THOSE THINGS ABOUT BEING "MATURE,"
HAS ME A LITTLE WORRIED. STILL, SHE'S NOT THAT KIND OF GIRL...
RIGHT, HIROYUKI-CHAN?
WHAT DO YOU THINK?

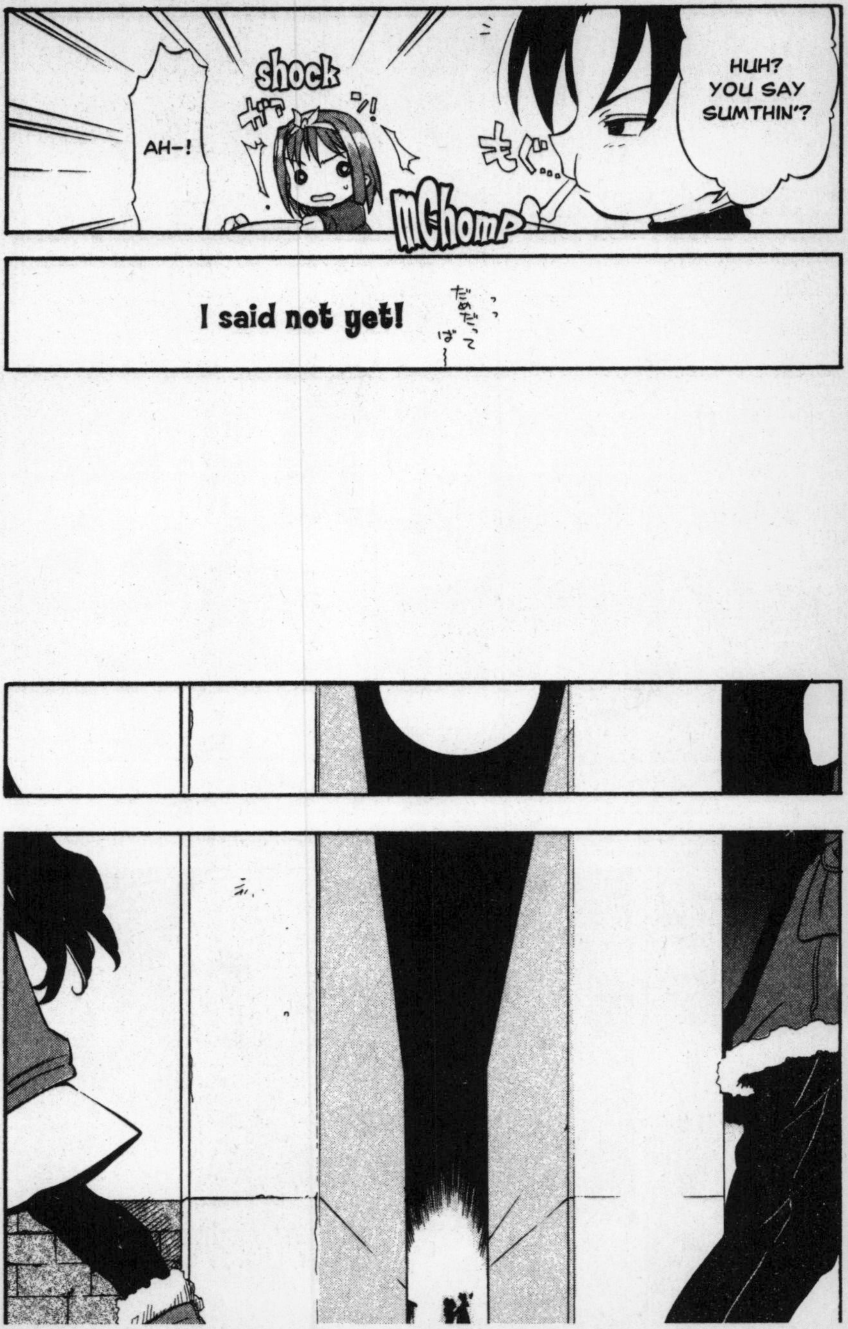
HUH? YOU SAY SUMTHIN'?
もぐ…
mChomp
shock
AH-!
I said not yet!
だめだってばっ~

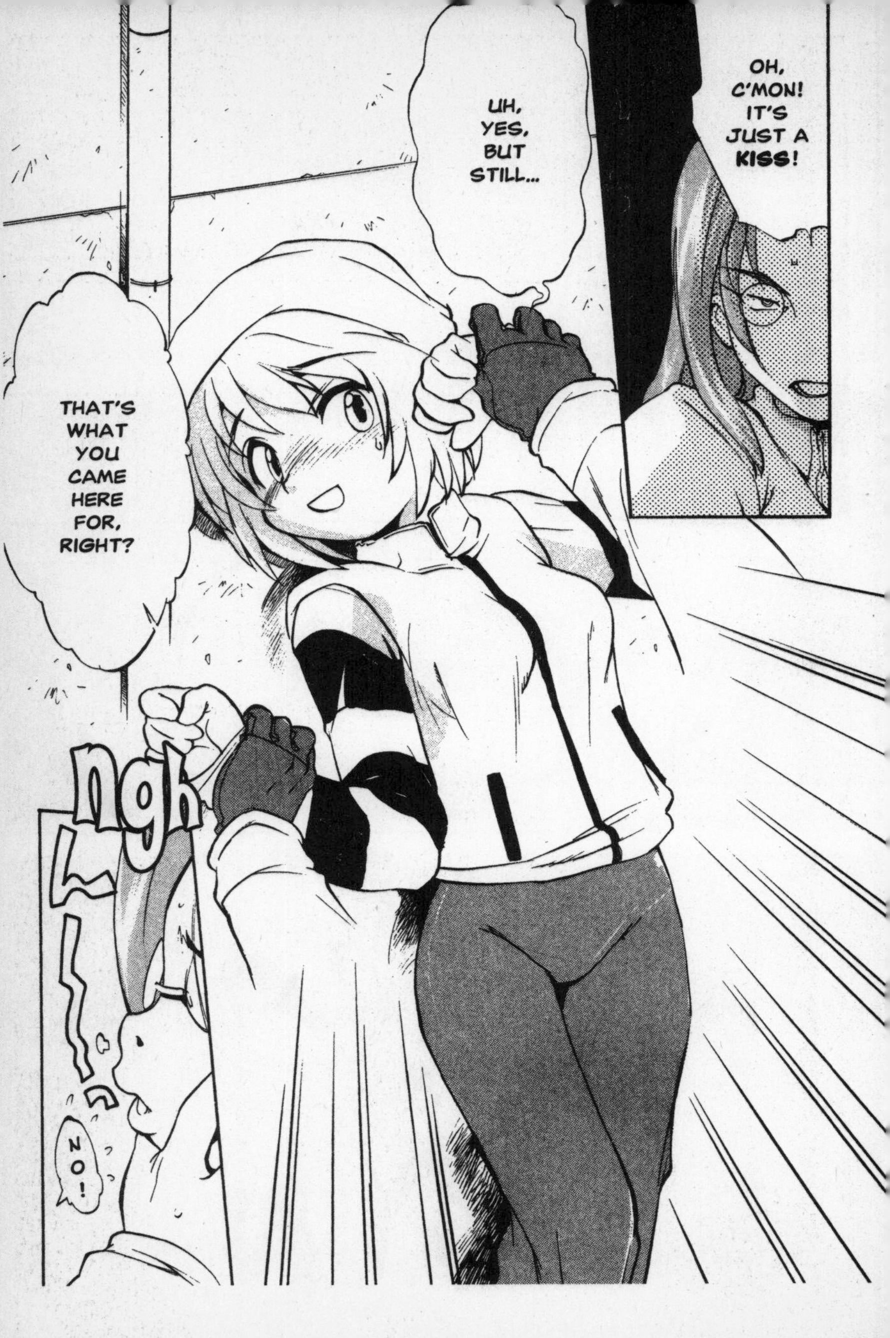
OH, C'MON! IT'S JUST A KISS!
UH, YES, BUT STILL...
THAT'S WHAT YOU CAME HERE FOR, RIGHT?
ngh
NO!

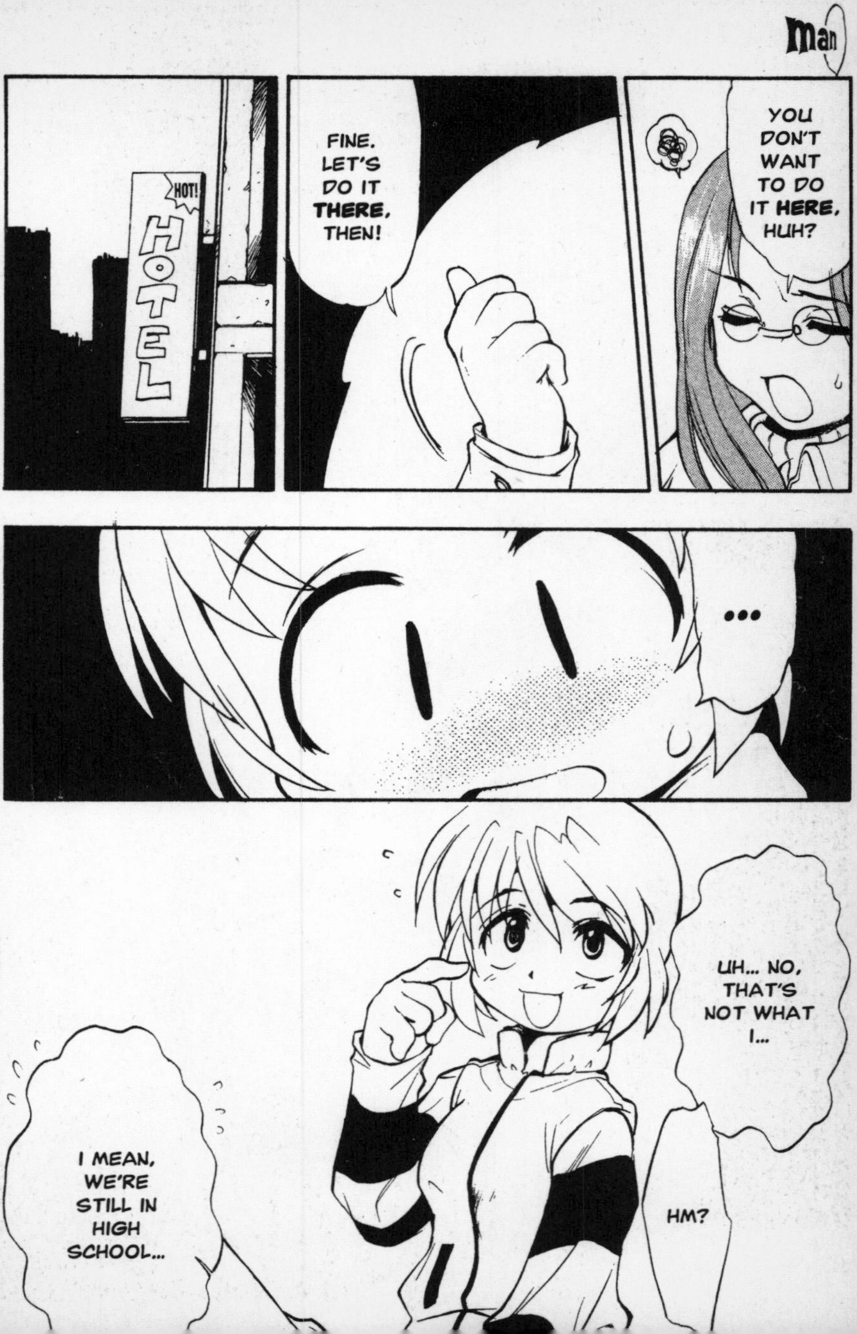
man
YOU DON'T WANT TO DO IT HERE, HUH?
FINE. LET'S DO IT THERE, THEN!
HOT!
HOTEL
...
UH... NO, THAT'S NOT WHAT I...
HM?
I MEAN, WE'RE STILL IN HIGH SCHOOL...

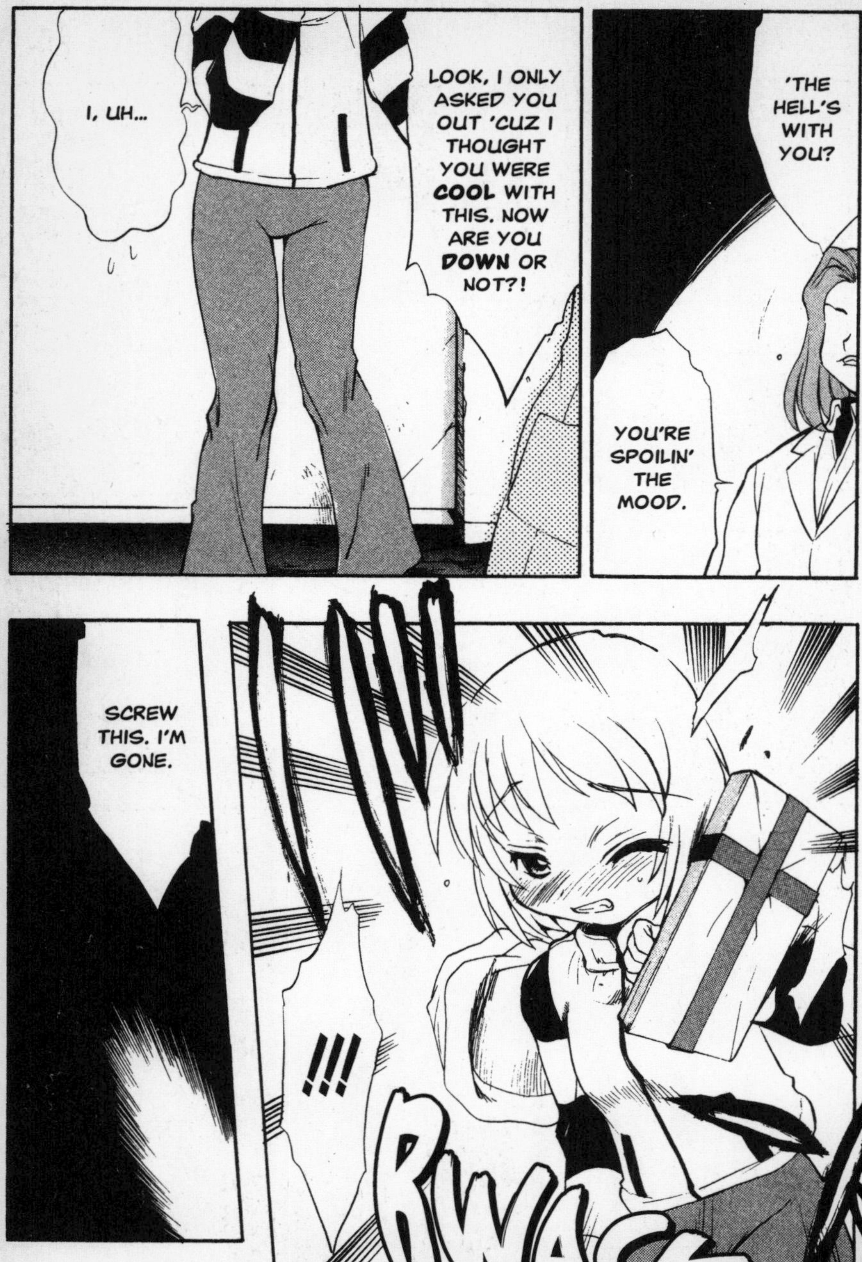
'THE HELL'S WITH YOU?
YOU'RE SPOILIN' THE MOOD.
LOOK, I ONLY ASKED YOU OUT 'CUZ I THOUGHT YOU WERE COOL WITH THIS. NOW ARE YOU DOWN OR NOT?!
I, UH...
SCREW THIS. I'M GONE.
!!!!
BWACK!

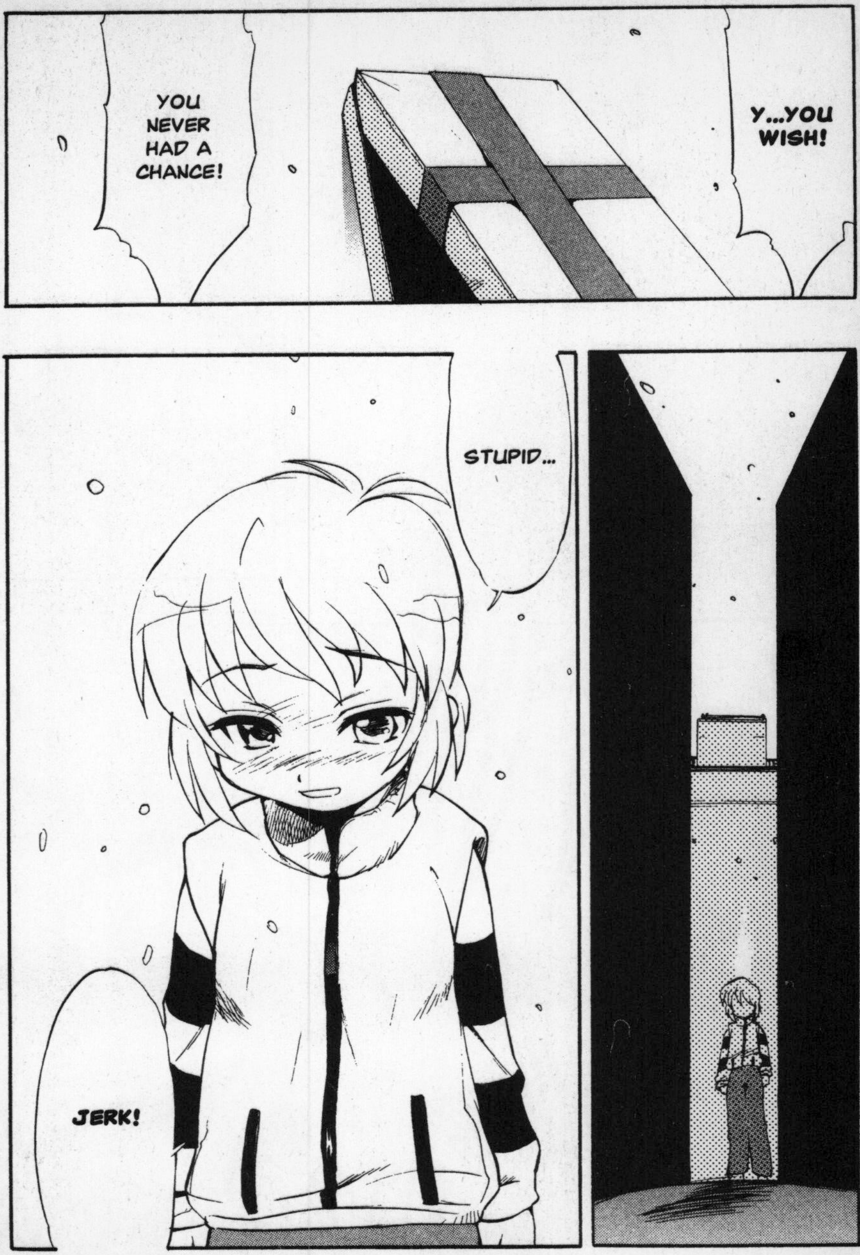
Y...YOU WISH!
YOU NEVER HAD A CHANCE!
STUPID...
JERK!

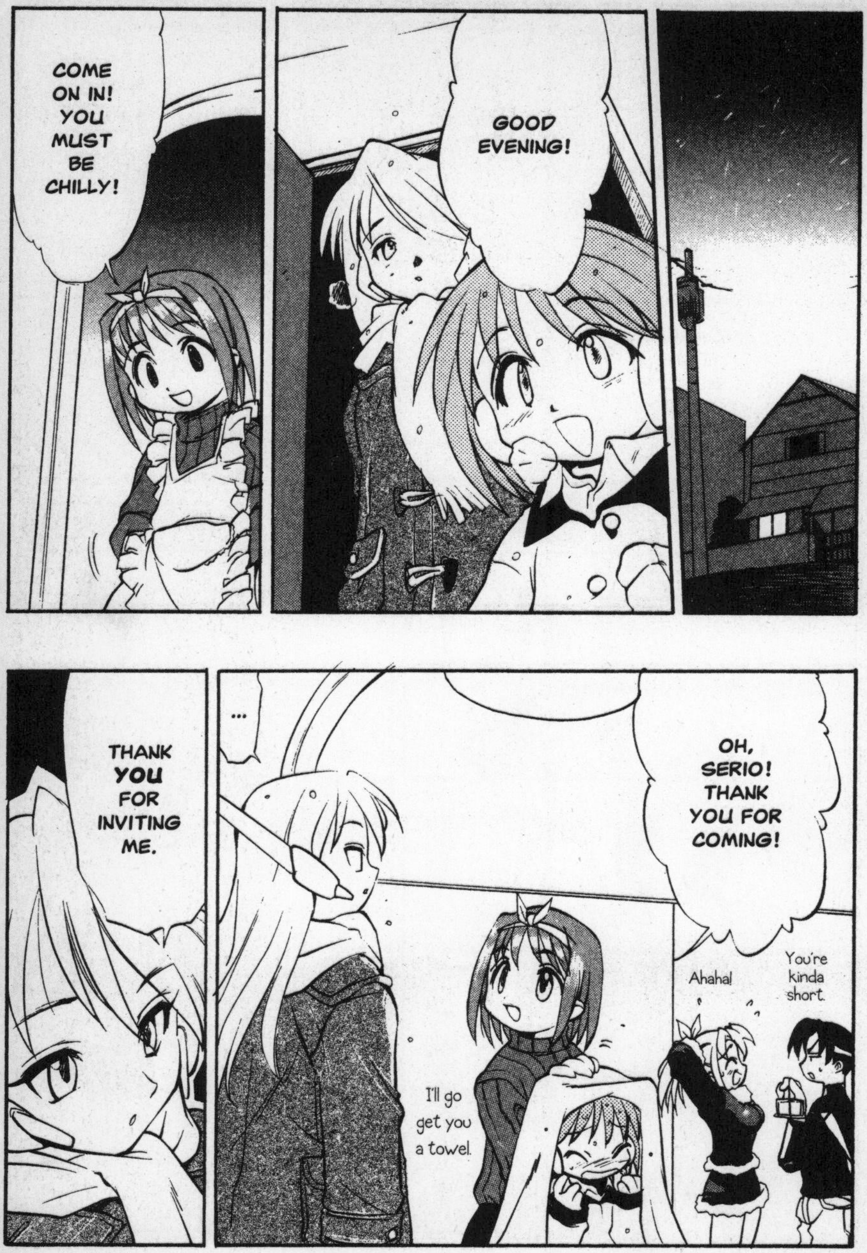
GOOD EVENING!
COME ON IN! YOU MUST BE CHILLY!
OH, SERIO! THANK YOU FOR COMING!
You're kinda short.
Ahaha!
I'll go get you a towel.
...
THANK YOU FOR INVITING ME.

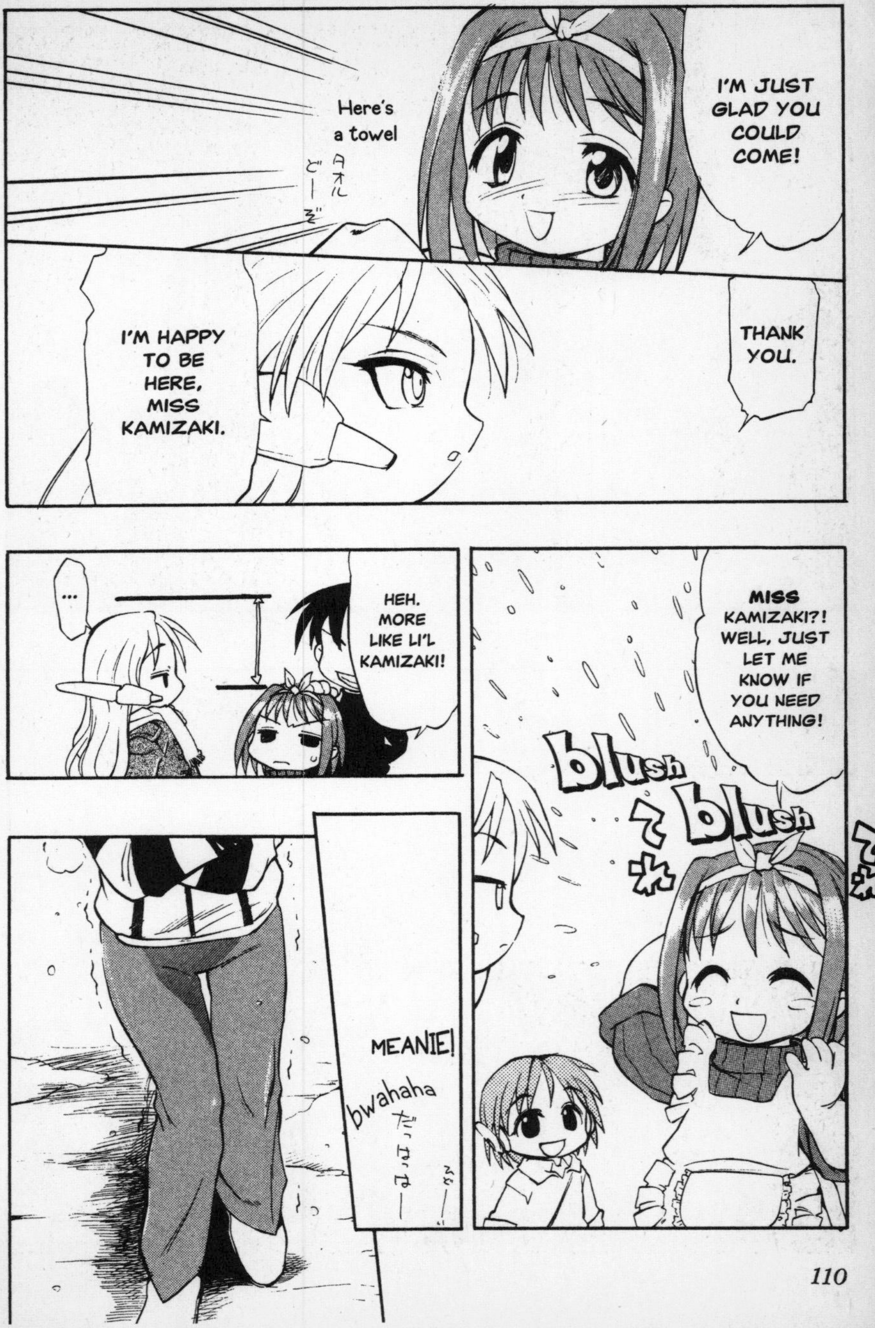
I'M JUST GLAD YOU COULD COME!
Here's a towel
タオルどーぞ
THANK YOU.
I'M HAPPY TO BE HERE, MISS KAMIZAKI.
MISS KAMIZAKI?! WELL, JUST LET ME KNOW IF YOU NEED ANYTHING!
blush
blush
HEH. MORE LIKE LI'L KAMIZAKI!
...
MEANIE!
bwahaha

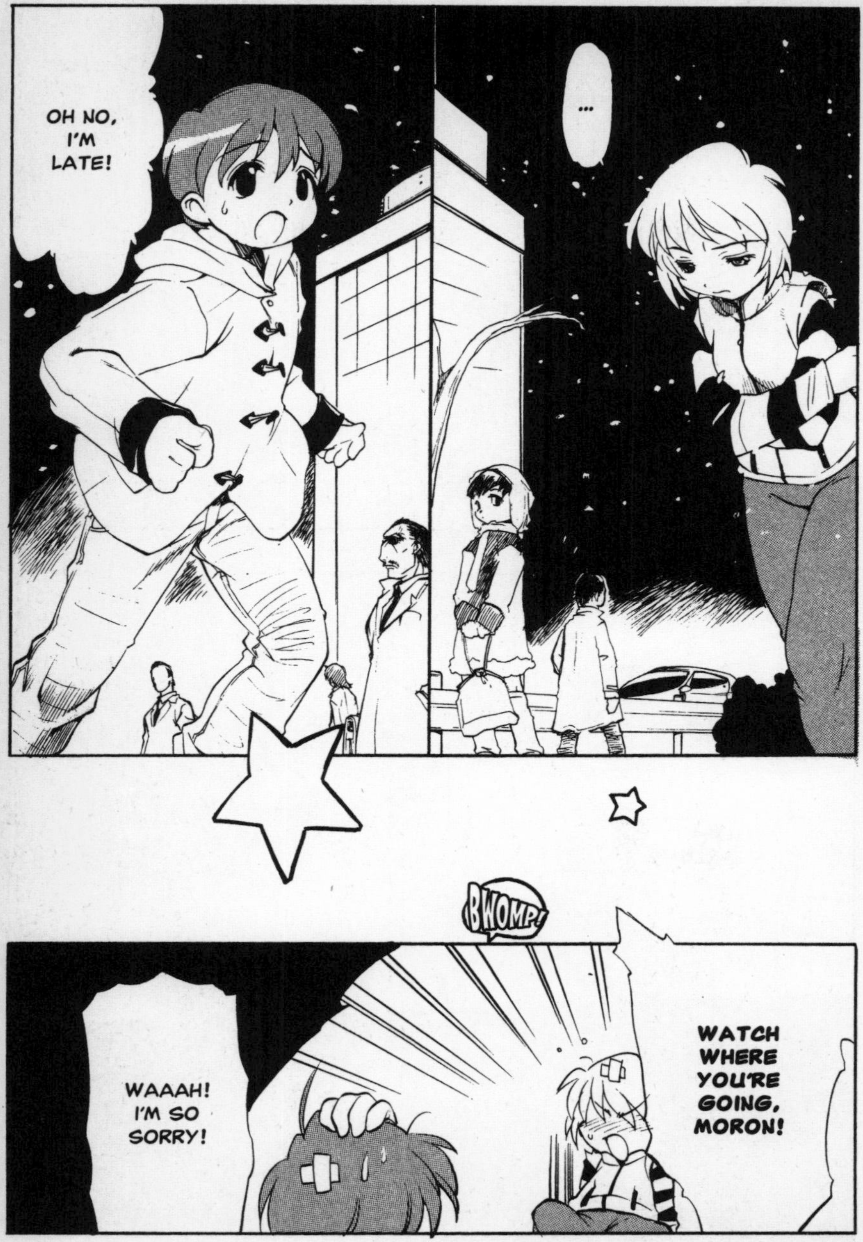
OH NO, I'M LATE!
...
BWOMP!
WATCH WHERE YOU'RE GOING, MORON!
WAAAH! I'M SO SORRY!

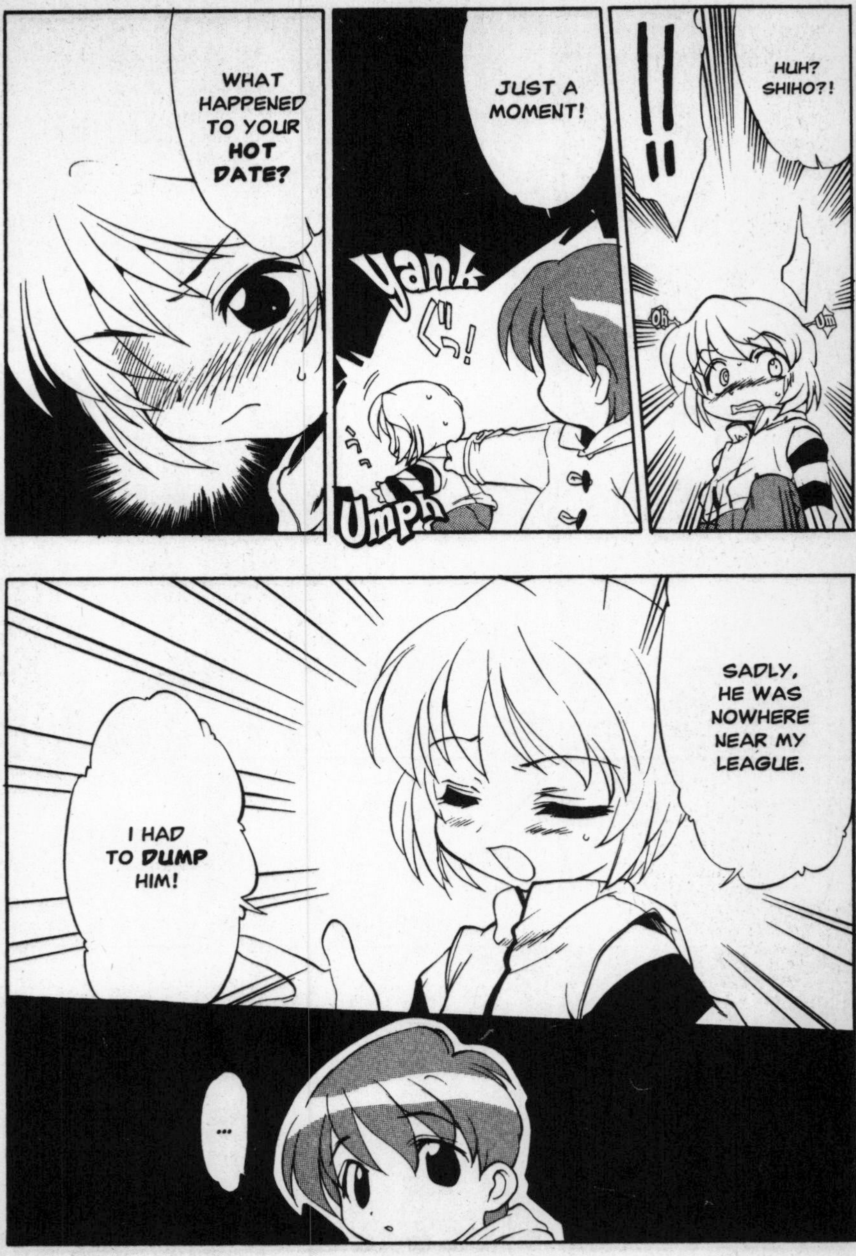

HUH? SHIHO?!
!!
Oh
Um
JUST A MOMENT!
yank
ぐっ!
Umph
WHAT HAPPENED TO YOUR HOT DATE?
SADLY, HE WAS NOWHERE NEAR MY LEAGUE.
I HAD TO DUMP HIM!
...

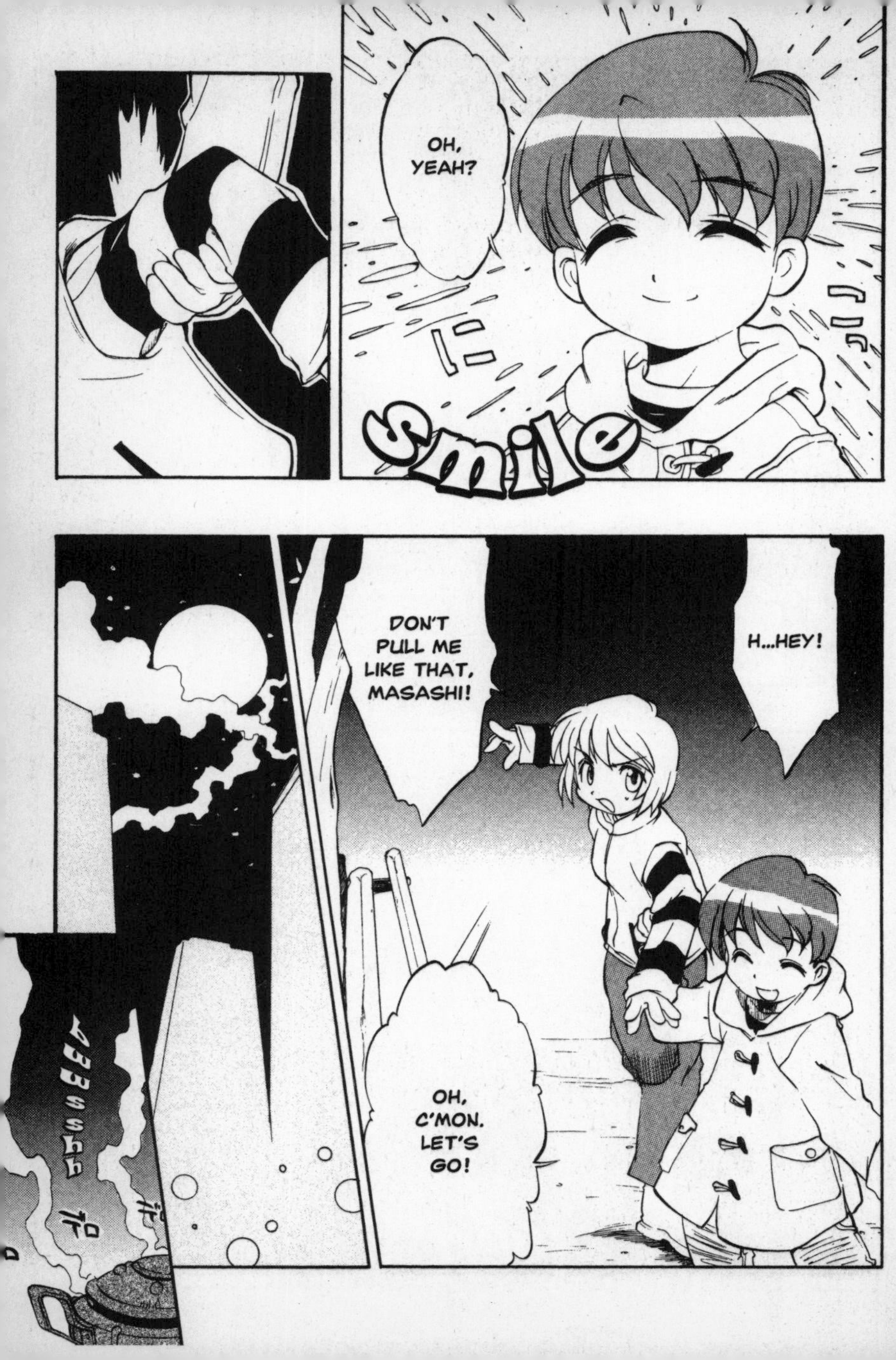
OH, YEAH?
smile
H...HEY!
DON'T PULL ME LIKE THAT, MASASHI!
OH, C'MON. LET'S GO!

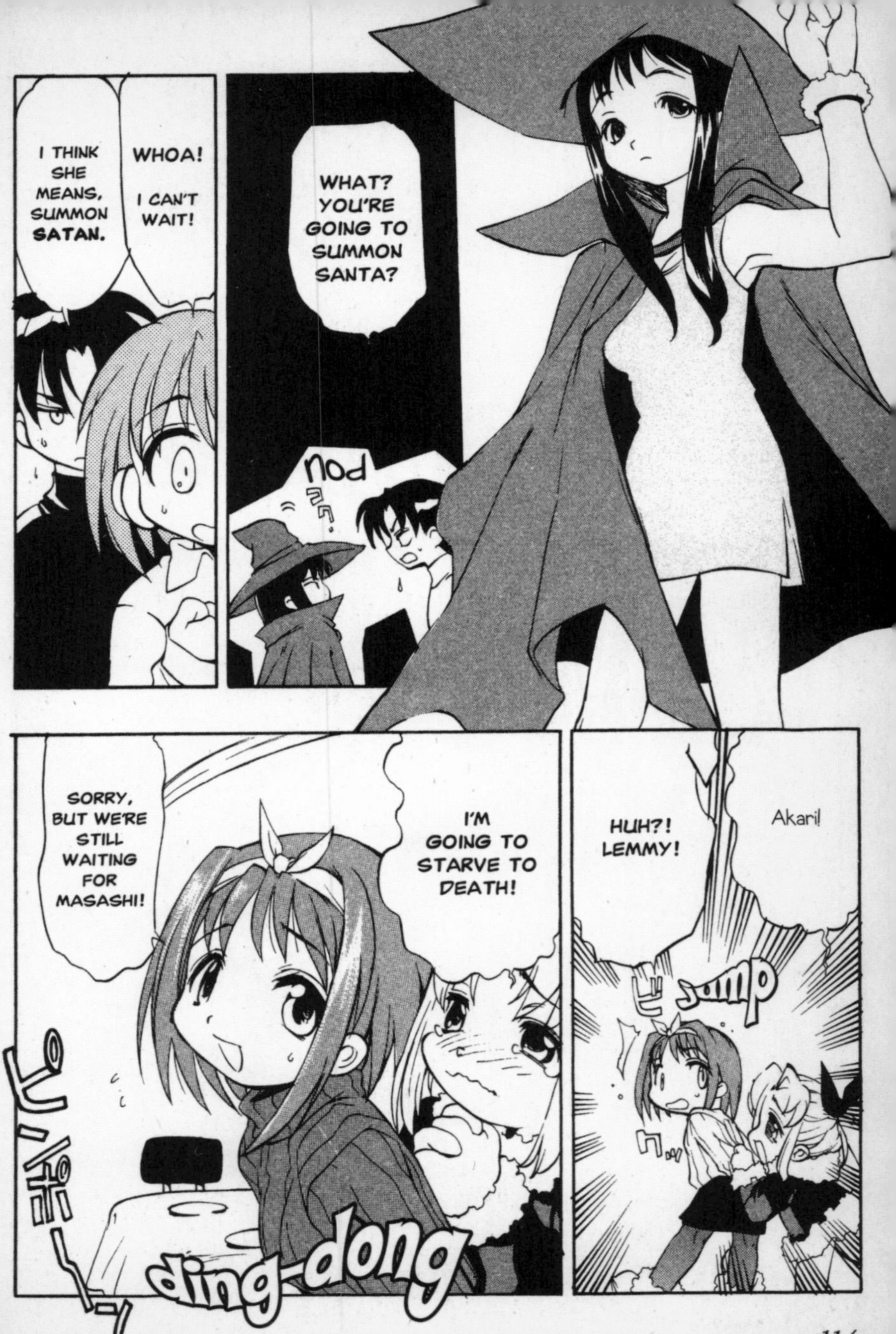
WHAT? YOU'RE GOING TO SUMMON SANTA?
nod
WHOA! I CAN'T WAIT!
I THINK SHE MEANS, SUMMON SATAN.
Akari!
HUH?! LEMMY!
jump
I'M GOING TO STARVE TO DEATH!
SORRY, BUT WE'RE STILL WAITING FOR MASASHI!
ding-dong

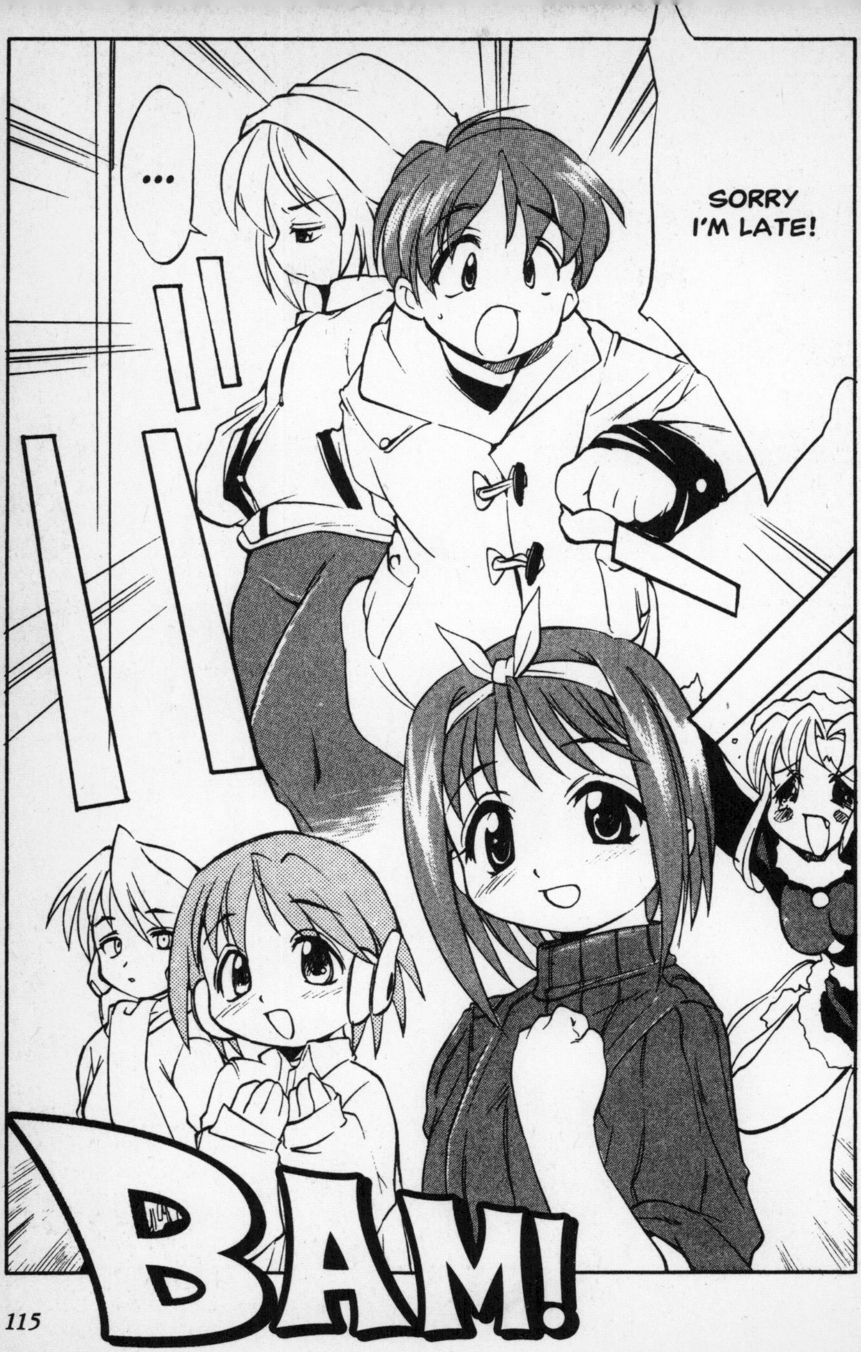
SORRY I'M LATE!
...
BAM!

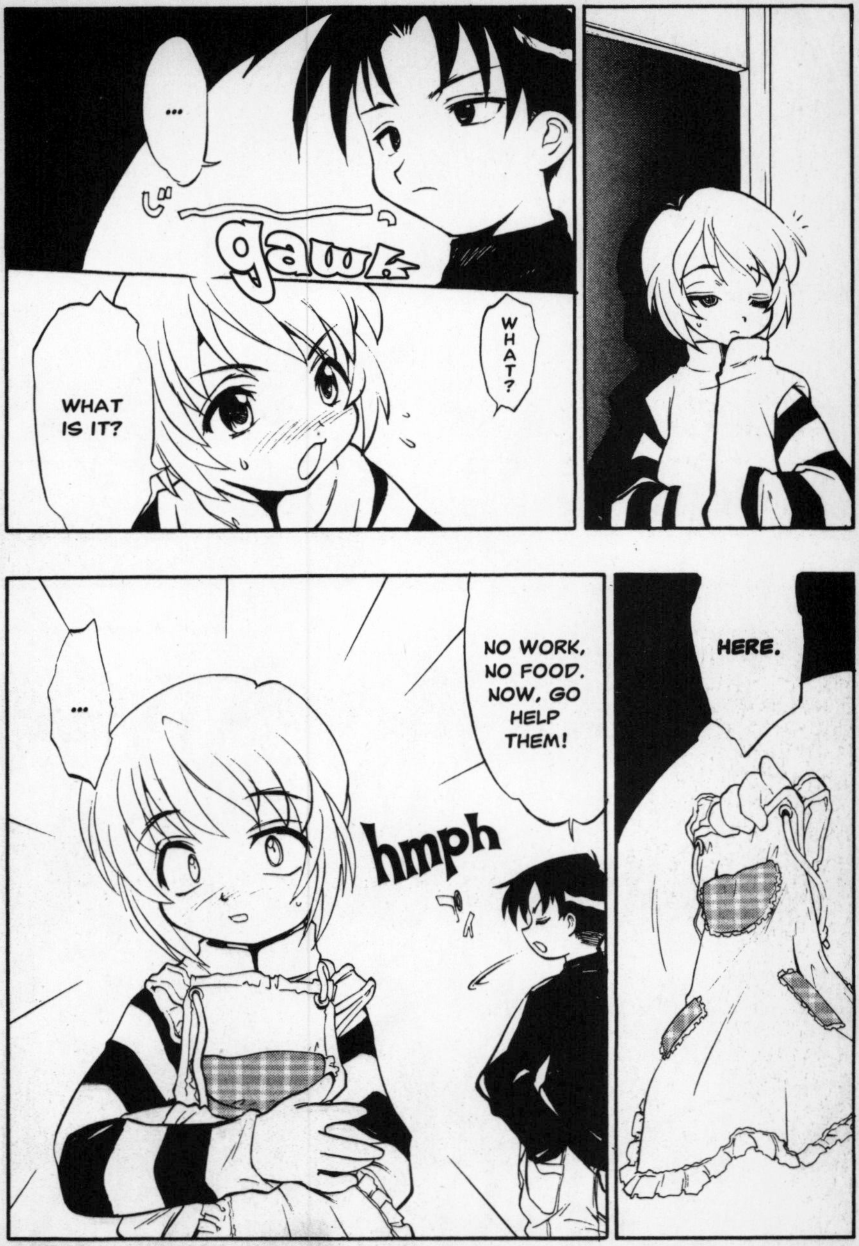
...
gawk
WHAT?
WHAT IS IT?
HERE.
NO WORK, NO FOOD. NOW, GO HELP THEM!
hmph
...

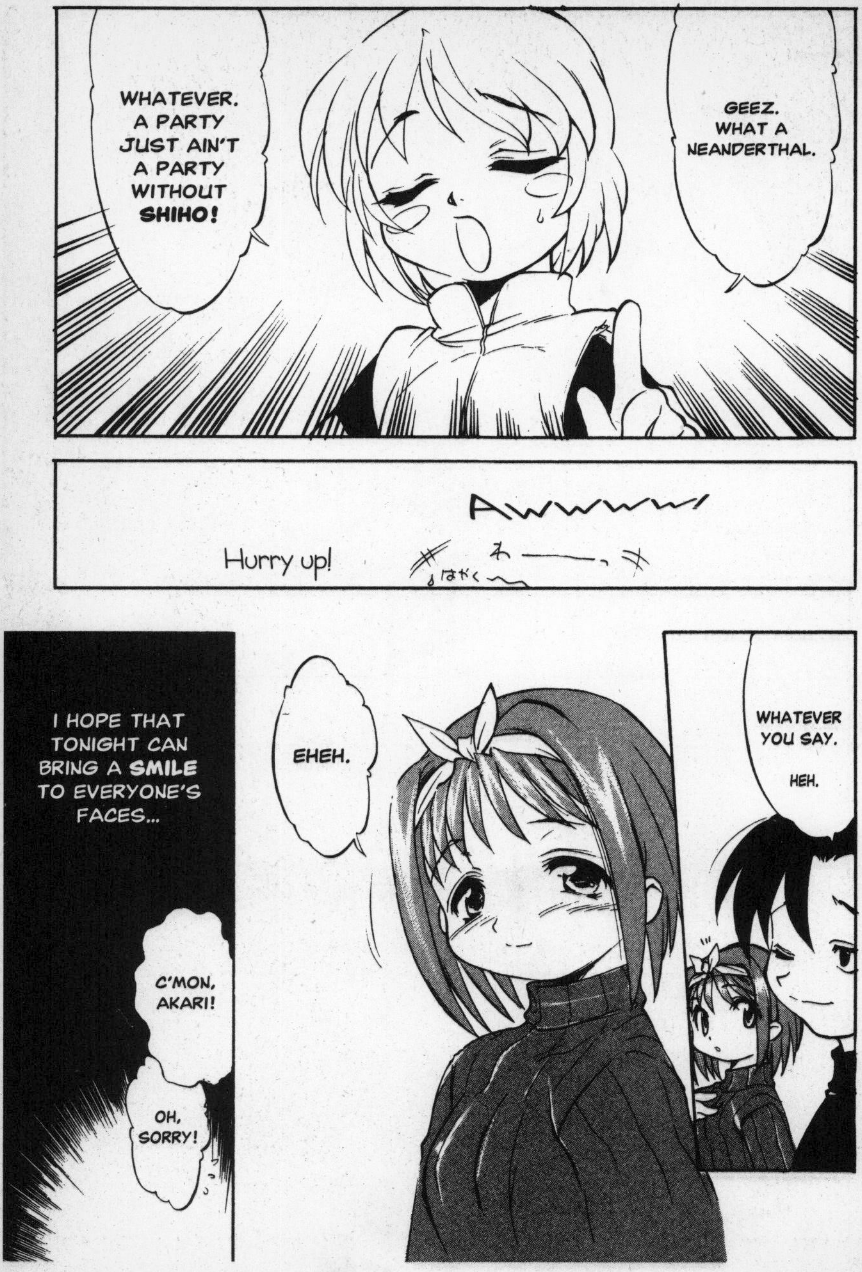
WHATEVER. A PARTY JUST AIN'T A PARTY WITHOUT **SHIHO!**
GEEZ. WHAT A NEANDERTHAL.
Awwww!
Hurry up!
I HOPE THAT TONIGHT CAN BRING A **SMILE** TO EVERYONE'S FACES...
C'MON, AKARI!
OH, SORRY!
EHEH.
WHATEVER YOU SAY.
HEH.

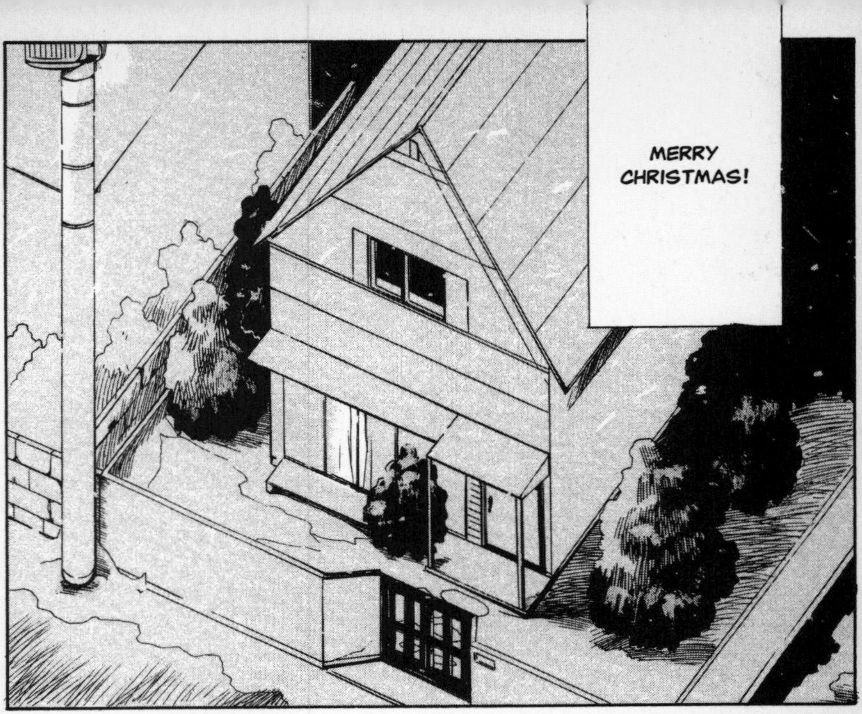
MERRY
CHRISTMAS!
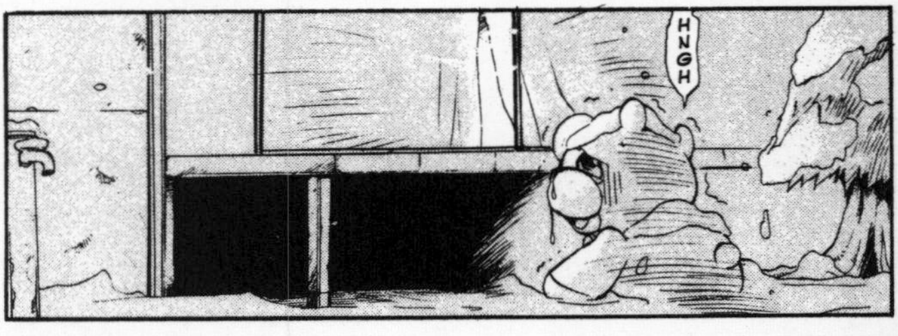
HNGH

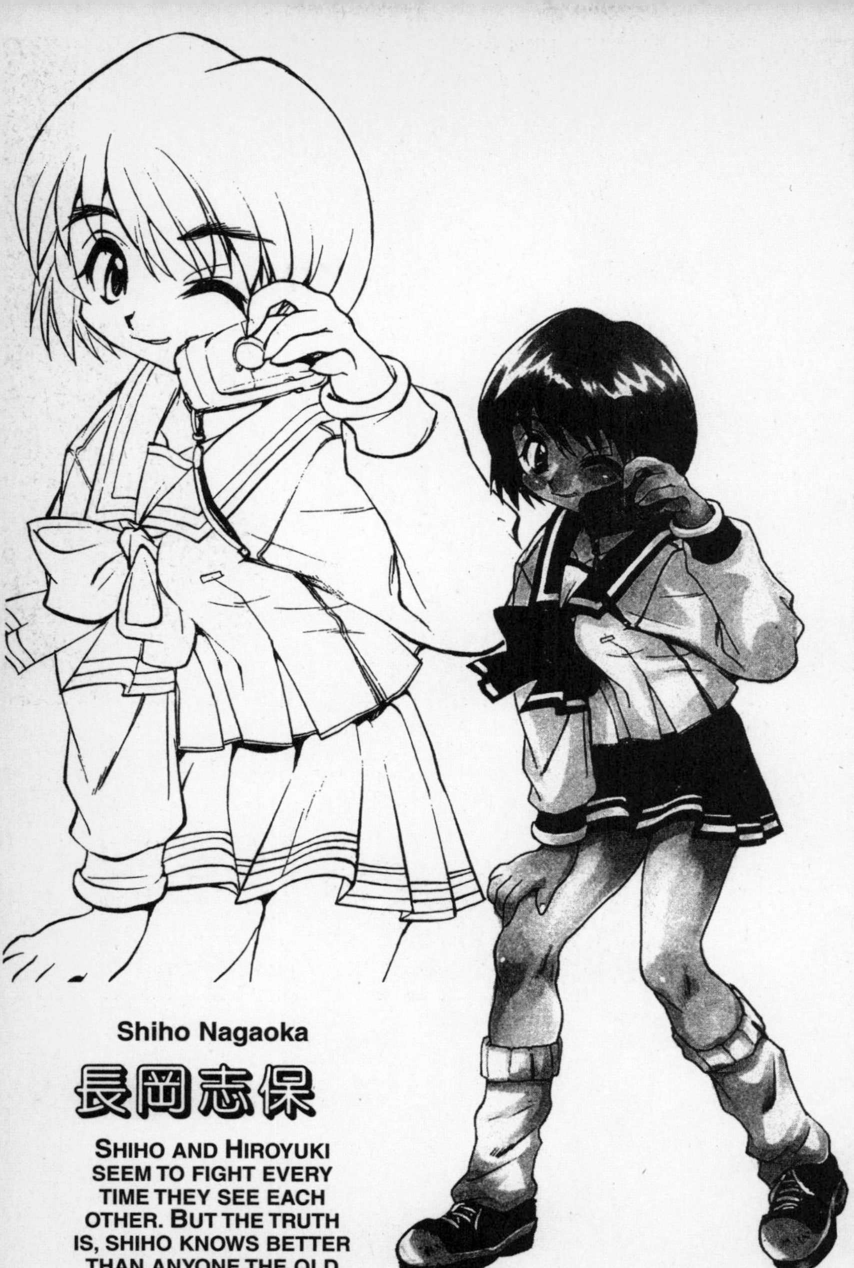

Shiho Nagaoka

長岡志保

SHIHO AND HIROYUKI SEEM TO FIGHT EVERY TIME THEY SEE EACH OTHER. BUT THE TRUTH IS, SHIHO KNOWS BETTER THAN ANYONE THE OLD SAYING, "FIGHTING LIKE OLD FRIENDS."

Episode 7
『The Power of Will』
~ Kotone Himekawa ~

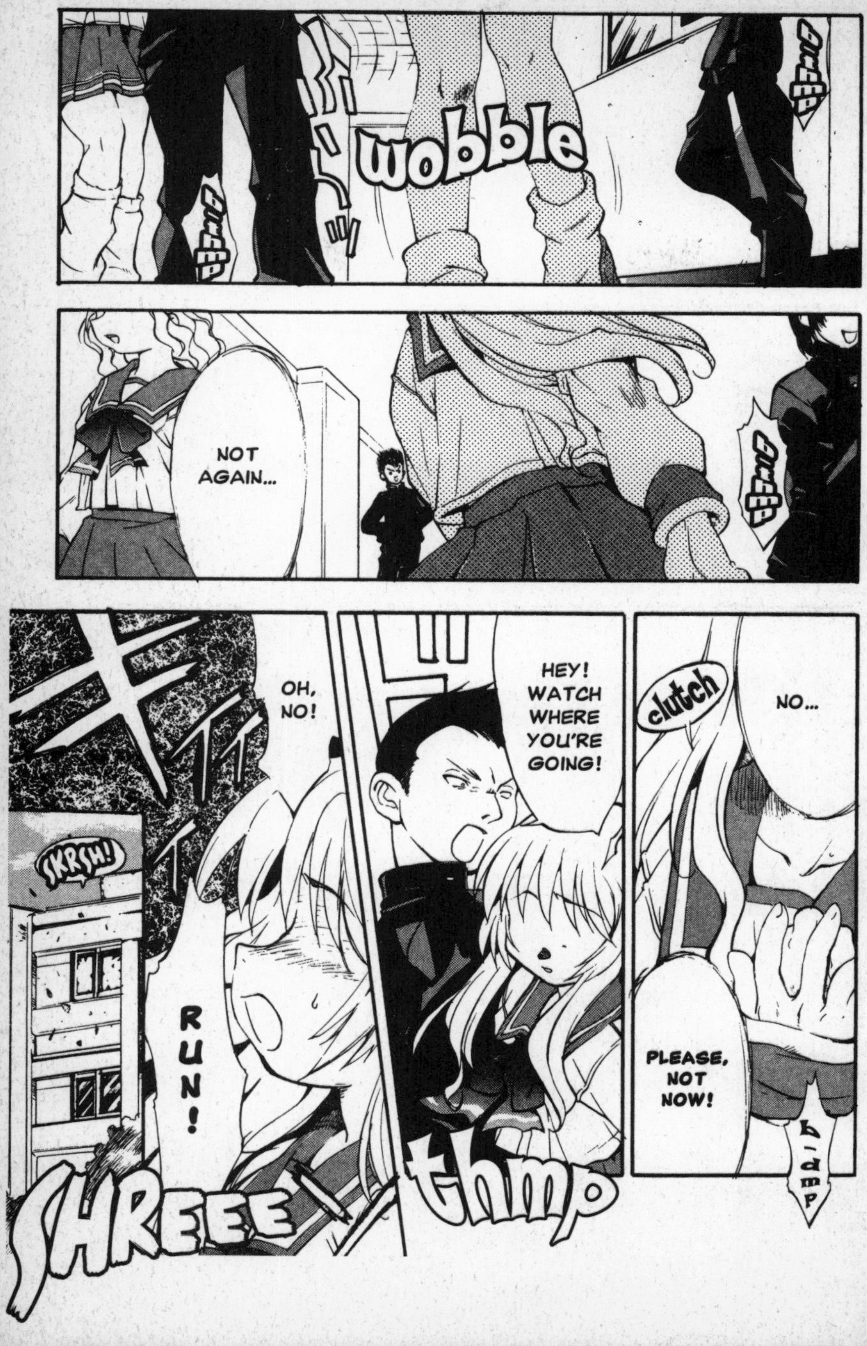
wobble
NOT AGAIN...
clutch
NO...
PLEASE, NOT NOW!
b-dmp
HEY! WATCH WHERE YOU'RE GOING!
thmp
OH, NO!
RUN!
SKRSH!
SHREEE

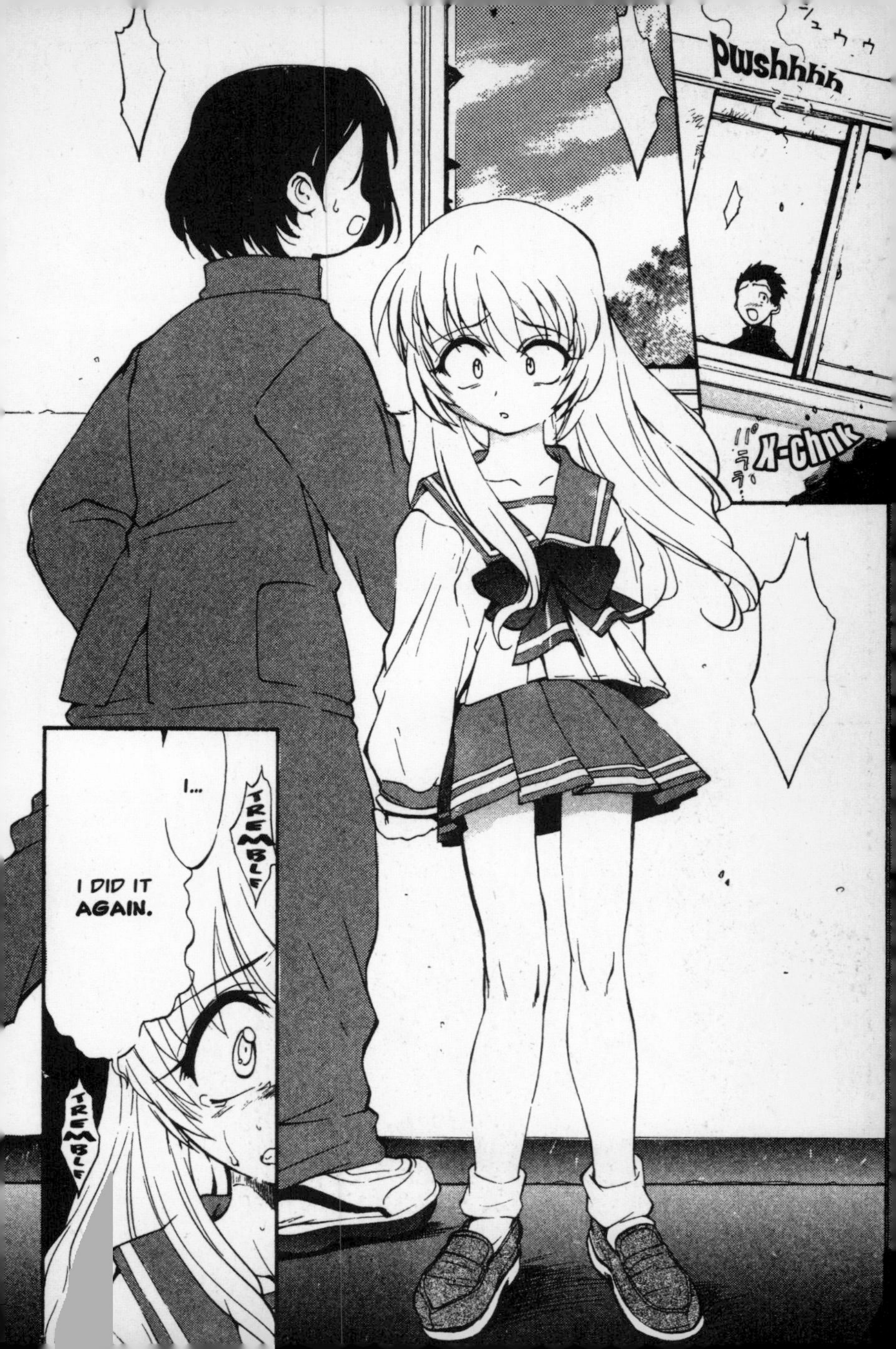
シュウウ
pwshhhh
X-chnk
I...
TREMBLE
I DID IT AGAIN.
TREMBLE

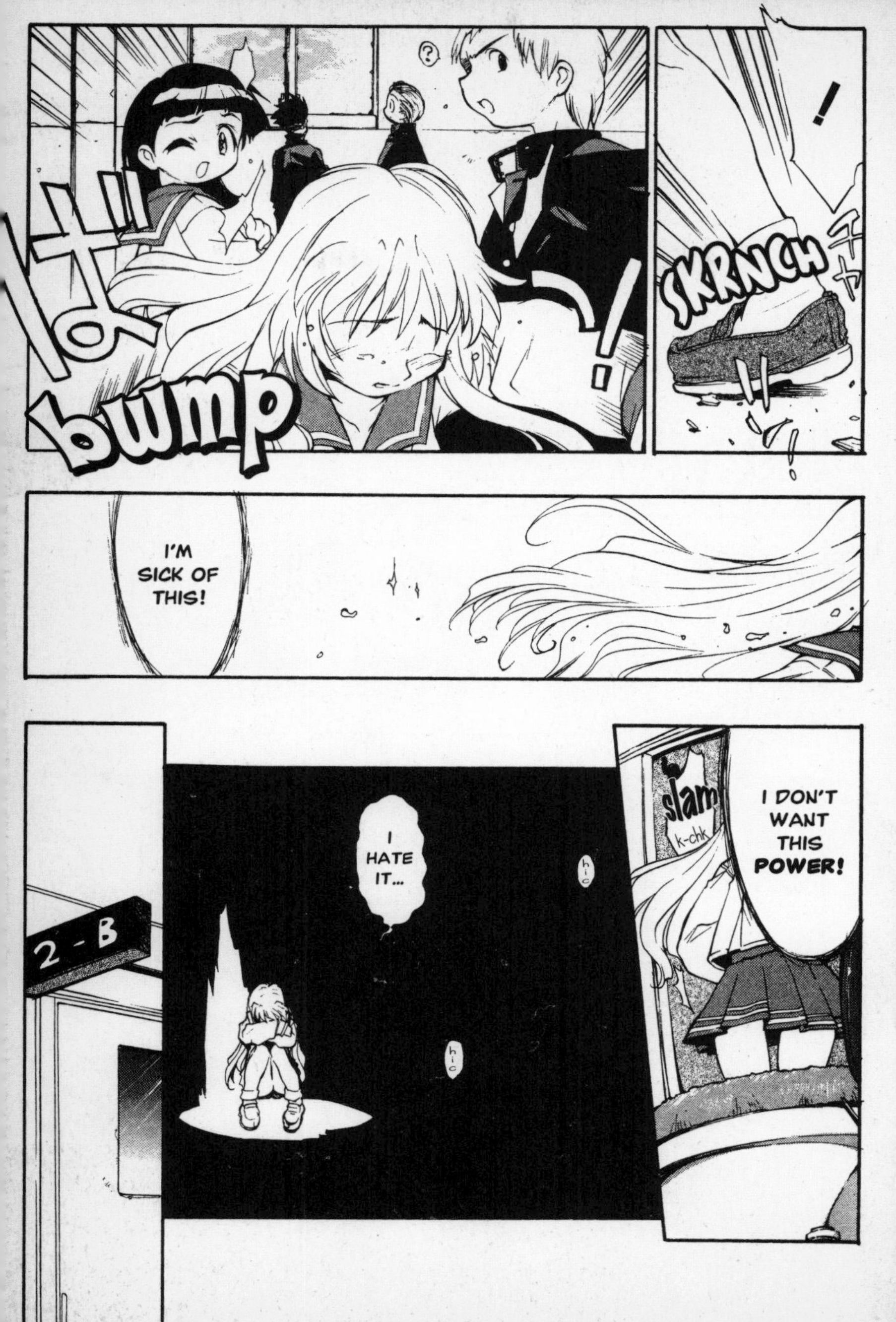

!
SKRNCH
bwump
I'M SICK OF THIS!
slam
k-chk
I DON'T WANT THIS POWER!
I HATE IT...
hic
hic
2 - B

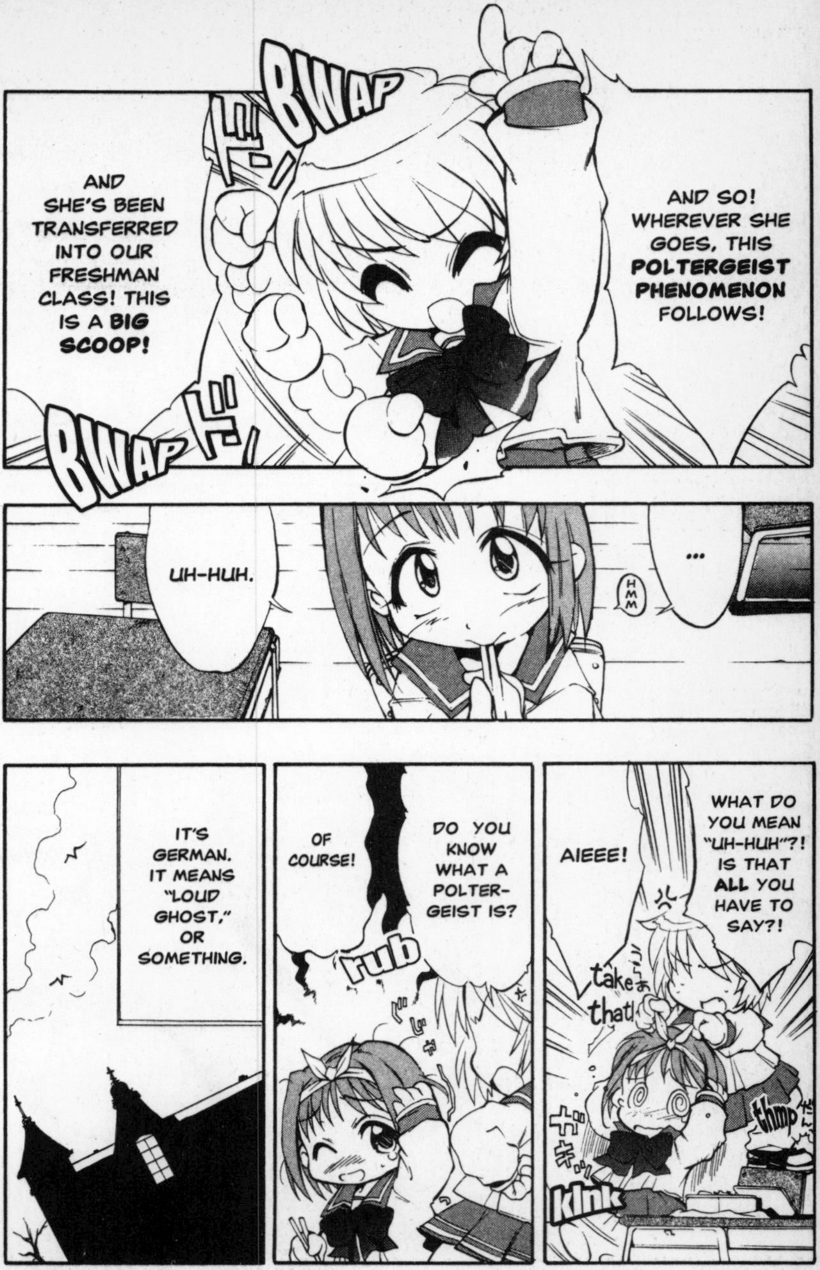
BWAP
AND SO! WHEREVER SHE GOES, THIS POLTERGEIST PHENOMENON FOLLOWS!
AND SHE'S BEEN TRANSFERRED INTO OUR FRESHMAN CLASS! THIS IS A BIG SCOOP!
BWAP
...
HMM
UH-HUH.
WHAT DO YOU MEAN "UH-HUH"?! IS THAT ALL YOU HAVE TO SAY?!
AIEEE!
take that!
thmp
klnk
DO YOU KNOW WHAT A POLTER-GEIST IS?
OF COURSE!
rub
IT'S GERMAN. IT MEANS "LOUD GHOST," OR SOMETHING.

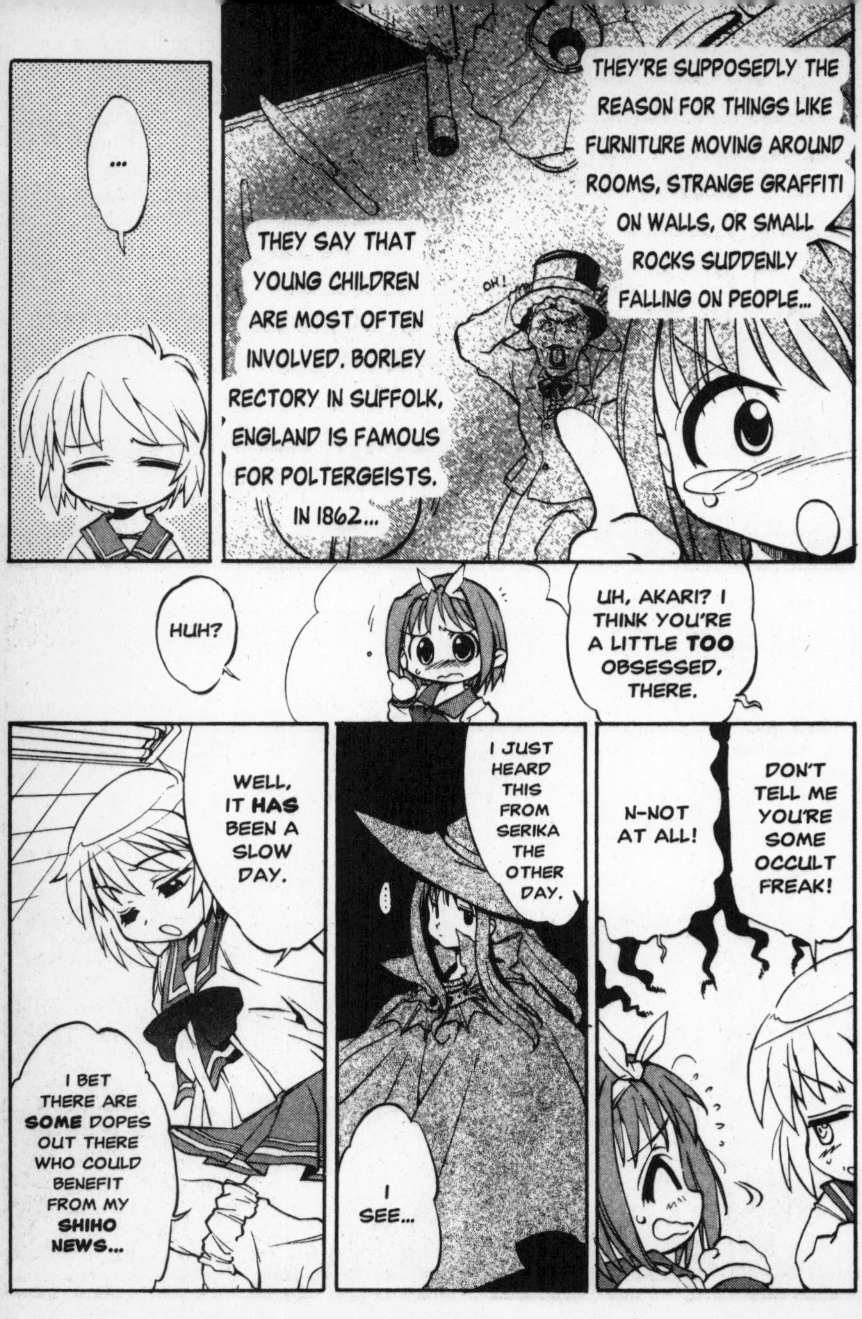
THEY'RE SUPPOSEDLY THE REASON FOR THINGS LIKE FURNITURE MOVING AROUND ROOMS, STRANGE GRAFFITI ON WALLS, OR SMALL ROCKS SUDDENLY FALLING ON PEOPLE...
OH!
THEY SAY THAT YOUNG CHILDREN ARE MOST OFTEN INVOLVED. BORLEY RECTORY IN SUFFOLK, ENGLAND IS FAMOUS FOR POLTERGEISTS. IN 1862...
...
UH, AKARI? I THINK YOU'RE A LITTLE **TOO** OBSESSED, THERE.
HUH?
DON'T TELL ME YOU'RE SOME OCCULT FREAK!
N-NOT AT ALL!
I JUST HEARD THIS FROM SERIKA THE OTHER DAY.
I SEE...
WELL, IT **HAS** BEEN A SLOW DAY.
I BET THERE ARE **SOME** DOPES OUT THERE WHO COULD BENEFIT FROM MY **SHIHO NEWS**...

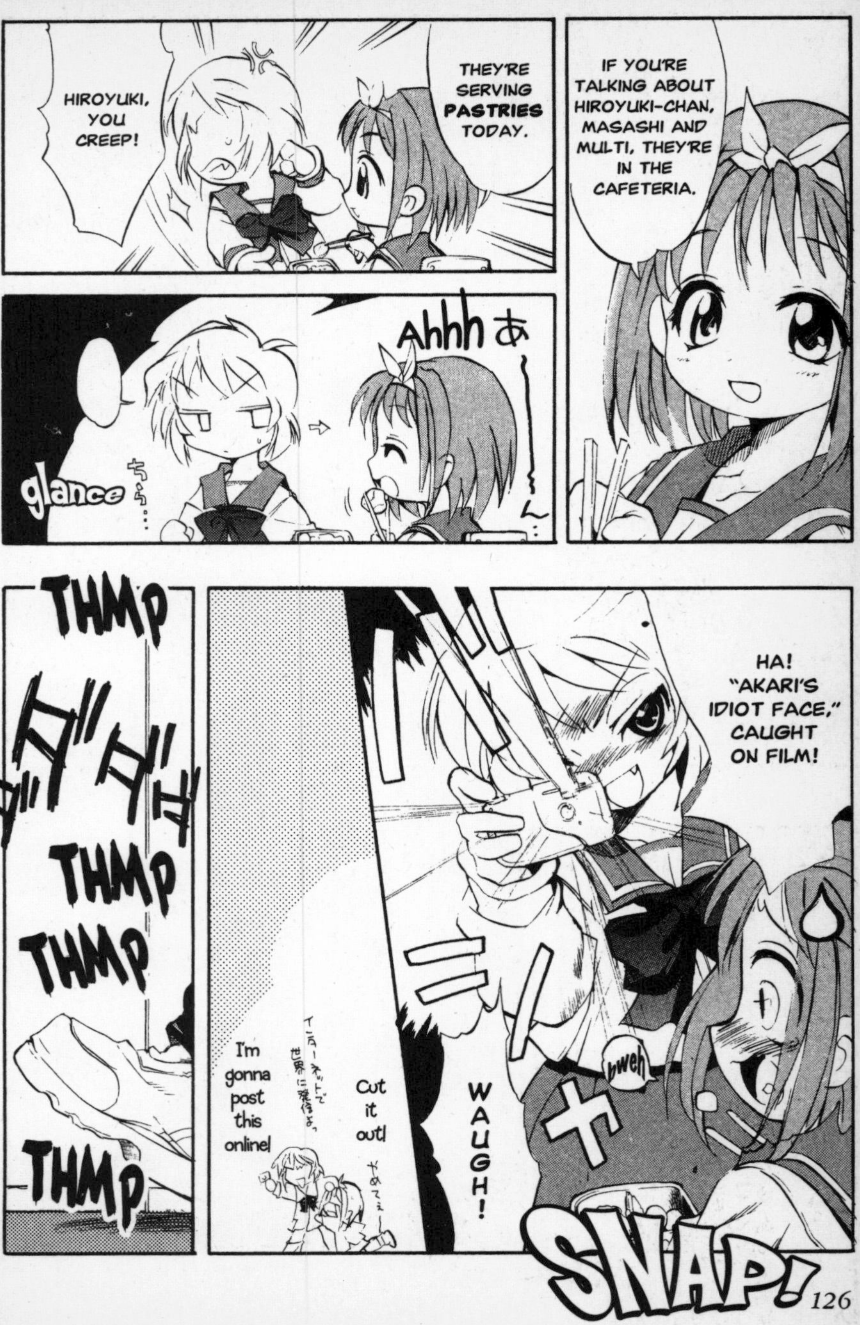
IF YOU'RE TALKING ABOUT HIROYUKI-CHAN, MASASHI AND MULTI, THEY'RE IN THE CAFETERIA.
THEY'RE SERVING PASTRIES TODAY.
HIROYUKI, YOU CREEP!
Ahhh あ～～ん…
glance ちら…
HA! "AKARI'S IDIOT FACE," CAUGHT ON FILM!
bweh
WAUGH!
SNAP!
Cut it out!
やめてぇ～
I'm gonna post this online!
インターネットで世界に発信よっ。
THMP
ダダダダ
THMP
THMP
THMP

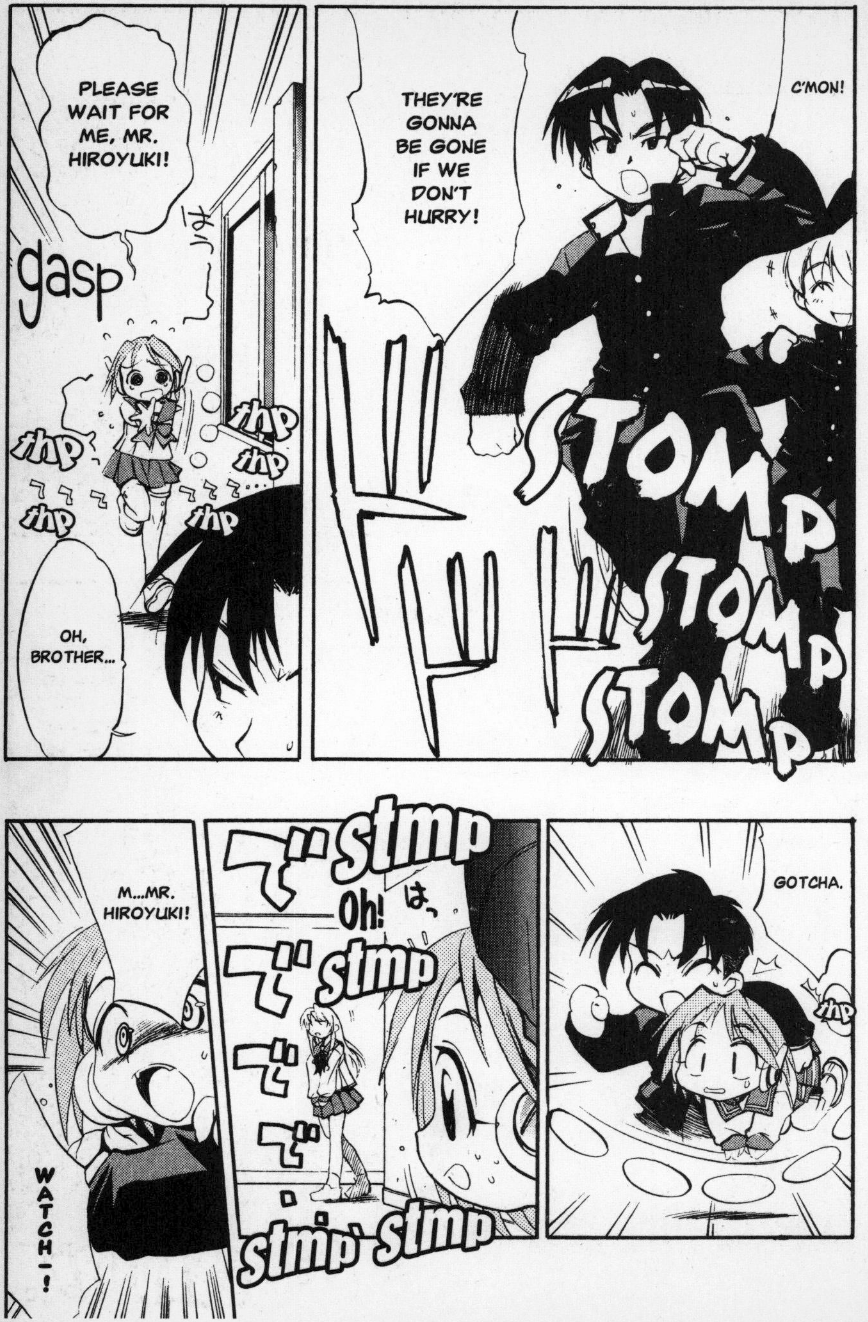

C'MON!
THEY'RE GONNA BE GONE IF WE DON'T HURRY!
STOMP STOMP STOMP STOMP
PLEASE WAIT FOR ME, MR. HIROYUKI!
gasp
thp thp thp thp thp
OH, BROTHER...
GOTCHA.
thp
stmp
Oh!
stmp
stmp stmp
M...MR. HIROYUKI!
WATCH—!

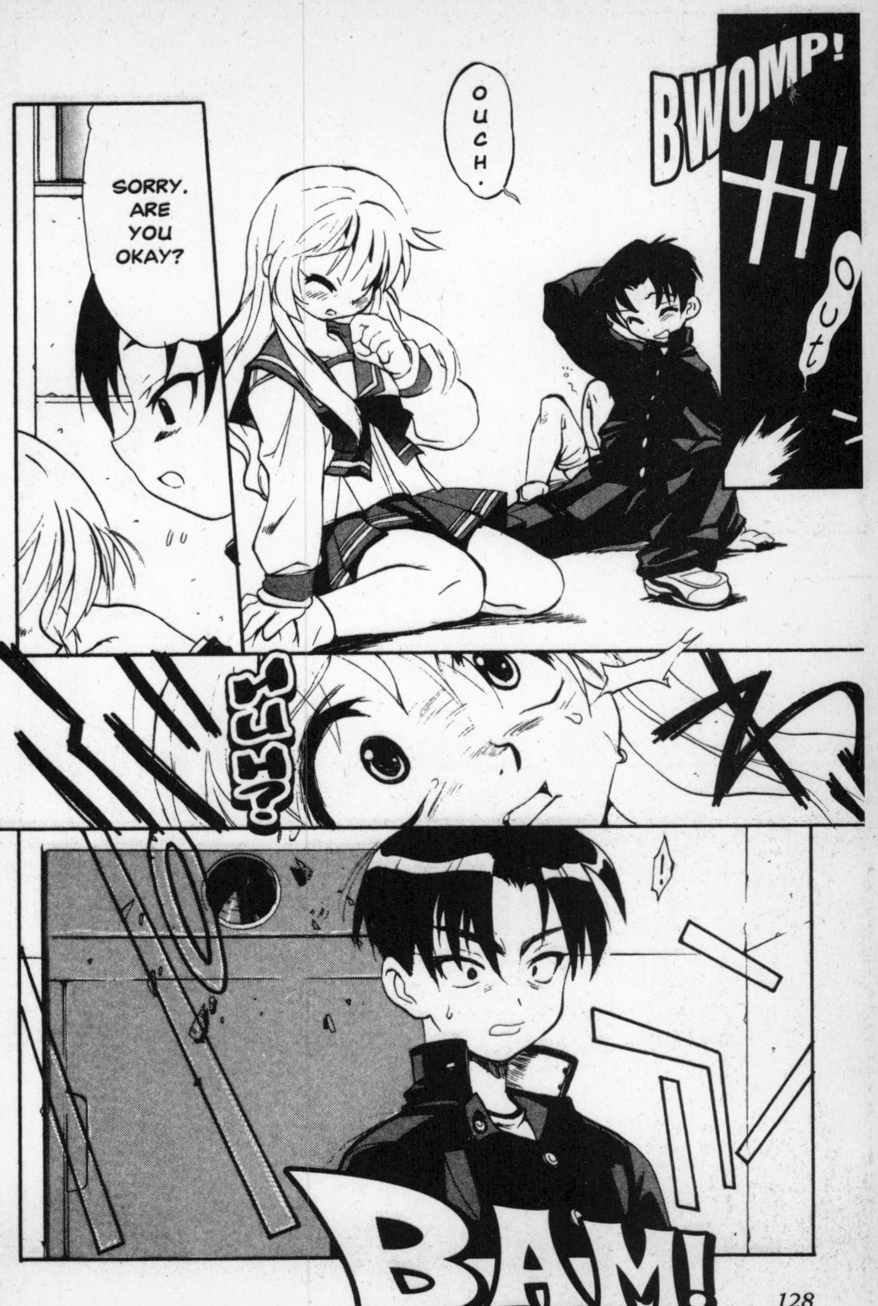
BWOMP!
OUCH.
SORRY. ARE YOU OKAY?
!
BAM!

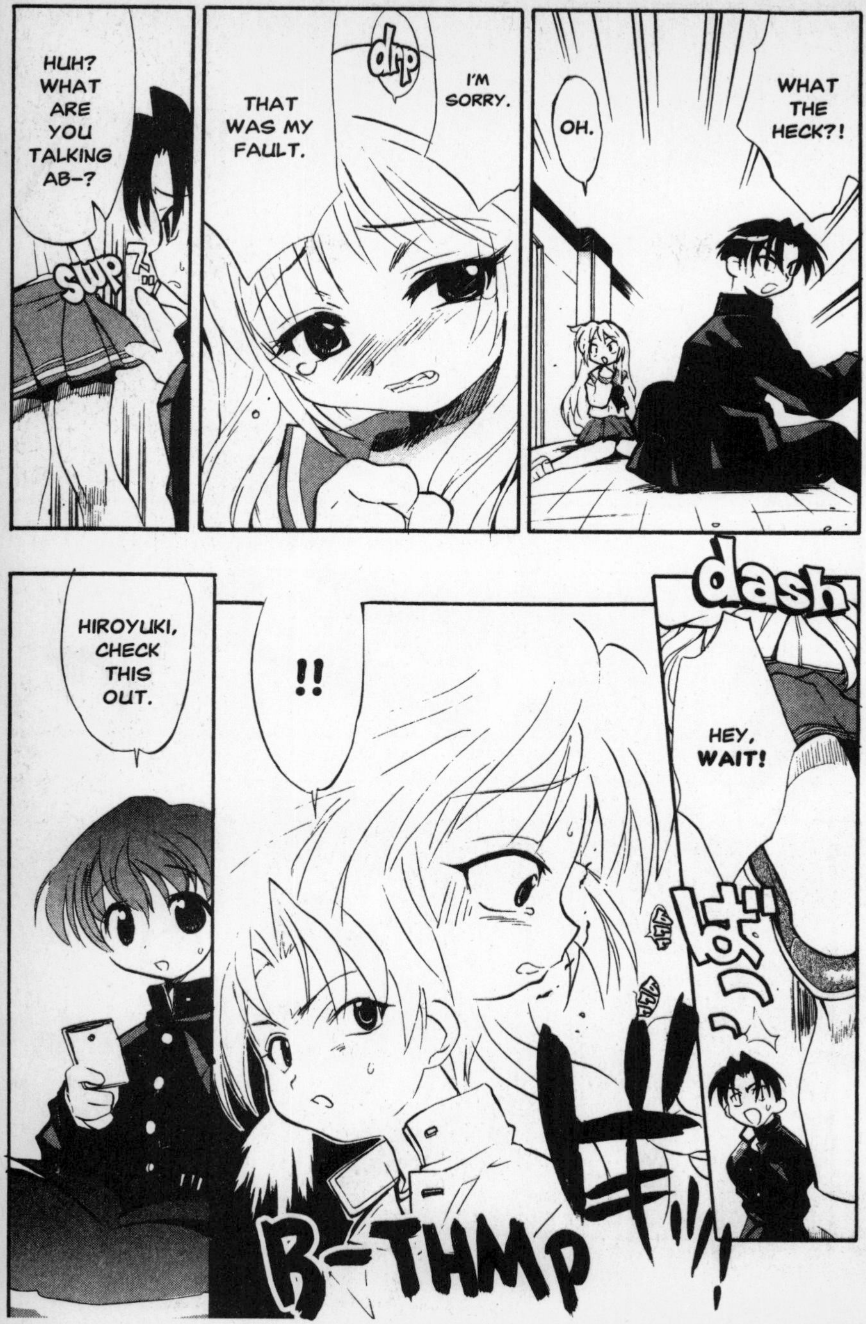
WHAT THE HECK?!
OH.
drp
I'M SORRY.
THAT WAS MY FAULT.
HUH? WHAT ARE YOU TALKING AB-?
swp
dash
HEY, WAIT!
B-THMP
!!
HIROYUKI, CHECK THIS OUT.

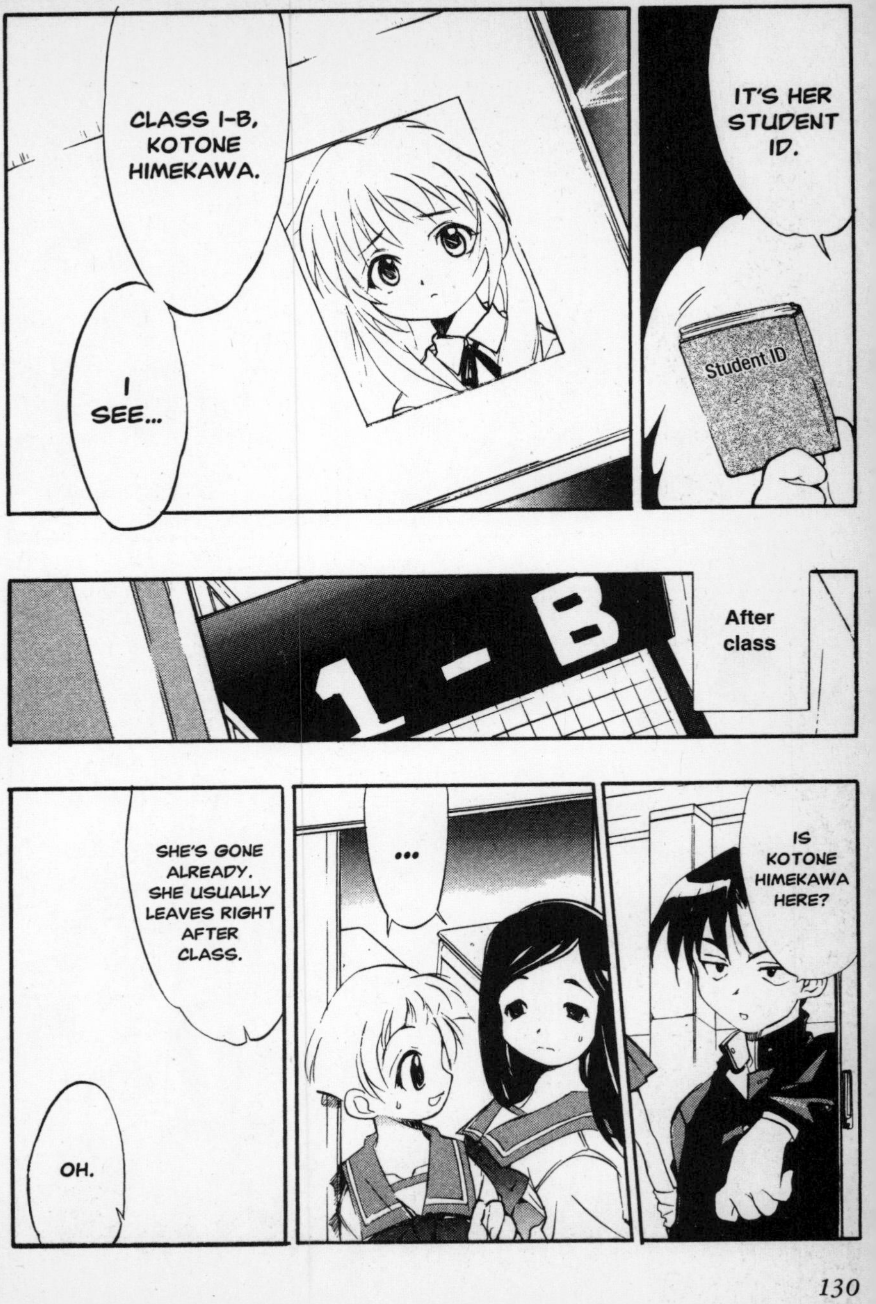

IT'S HER STUDENT ID.
Student ID
CLASS 1-B, KOTONE HIMEKAWA.
I SEE...
After class
1-B
IS KOTONE HIMEKAWA HERE?
...
SHE'S GONE ALREADY. SHE USUALLY LEAVES RIGHT AFTER CLASS.
OH.

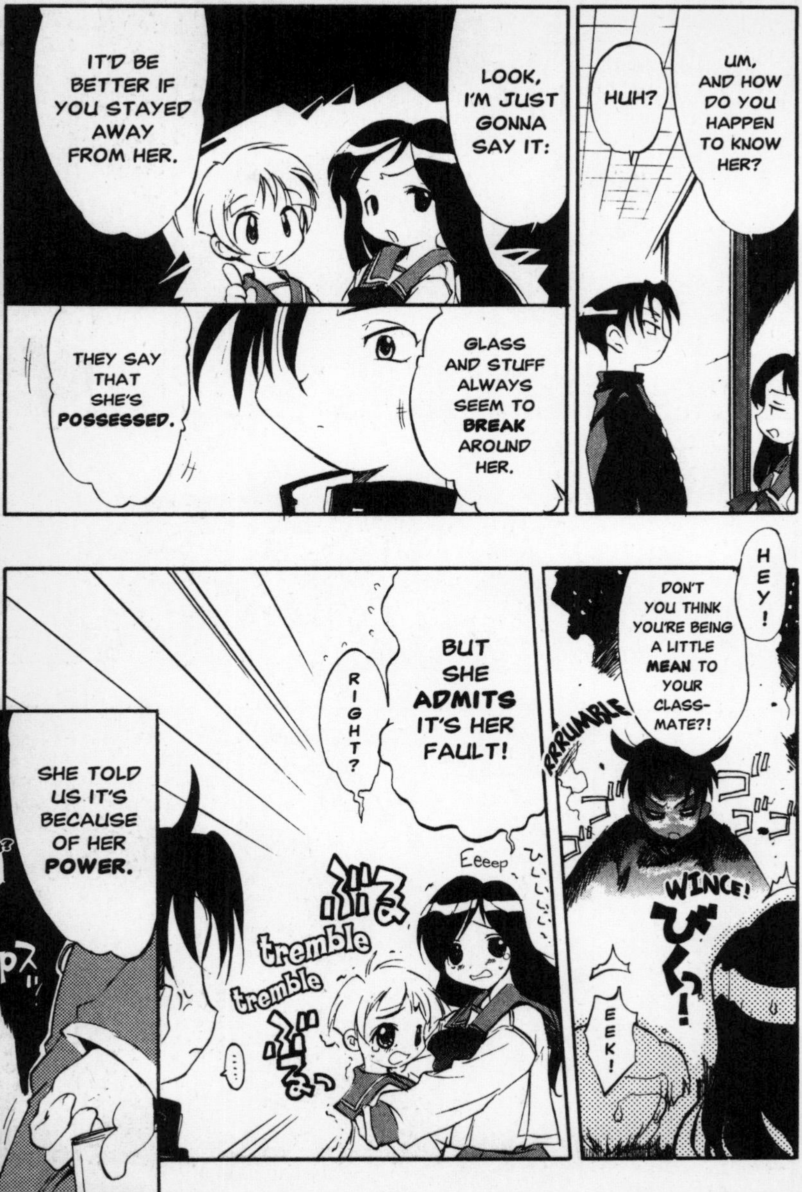

UM, AND HOW DO YOU HAPPEN TO KNOW HER?
HUH?
LOOK, I'M JUST GONNA SAY IT:
IT'D BE BETTER IF YOU STAYED AWAY FROM HER.
GLASS AND STUFF ALWAYS SEEM TO BREAK AROUND HER.
THEY SAY THAT SHE'S POSSESSED.
HEY!
DON'T YOU THINK YOU'RE BEING A LITTLE MEAN TO YOUR CLASSMATE?!
RRRUMBLE
WINCE!
EEK!
BUT SHE ADMITS IT'S HER FAULT!
RIGHT?
Eeeep
tremble
tremble
SHE TOLD US IT'S BECAUSE OF HER POWER.
Right?
swp

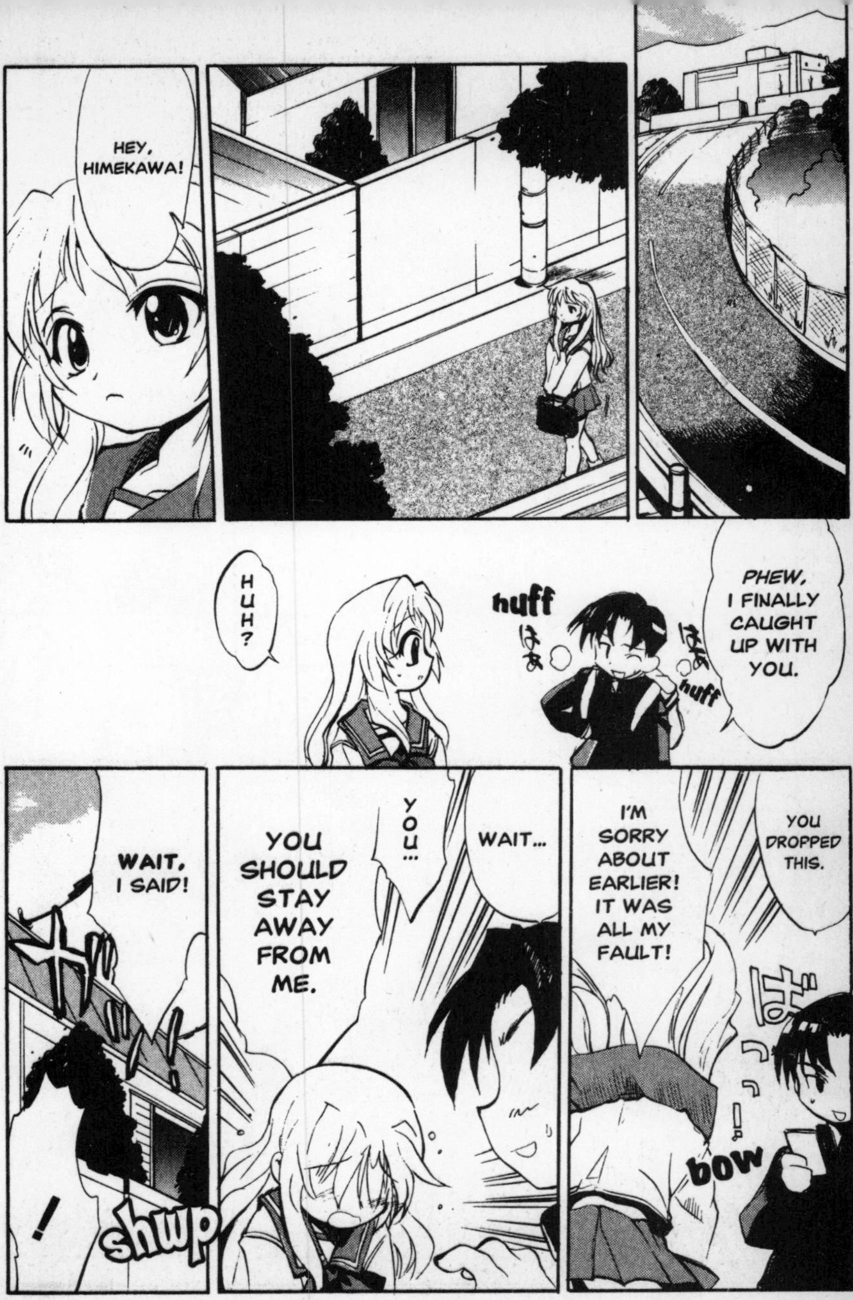
HEY, HIMEKAWA!
PHEW, I FINALLY CAUGHT UP WITH YOU.
huff
はぁ
はぁ
huff
HUH?
YOU DROPPED THIS.
I'M SORRY ABOUT EARLIER! IT WAS ALL MY FAULT!
bow
WAIT...
YOU...
YOU SHOULD STAY AWAY FROM ME.
WAIT, I SAID!
!
shwup

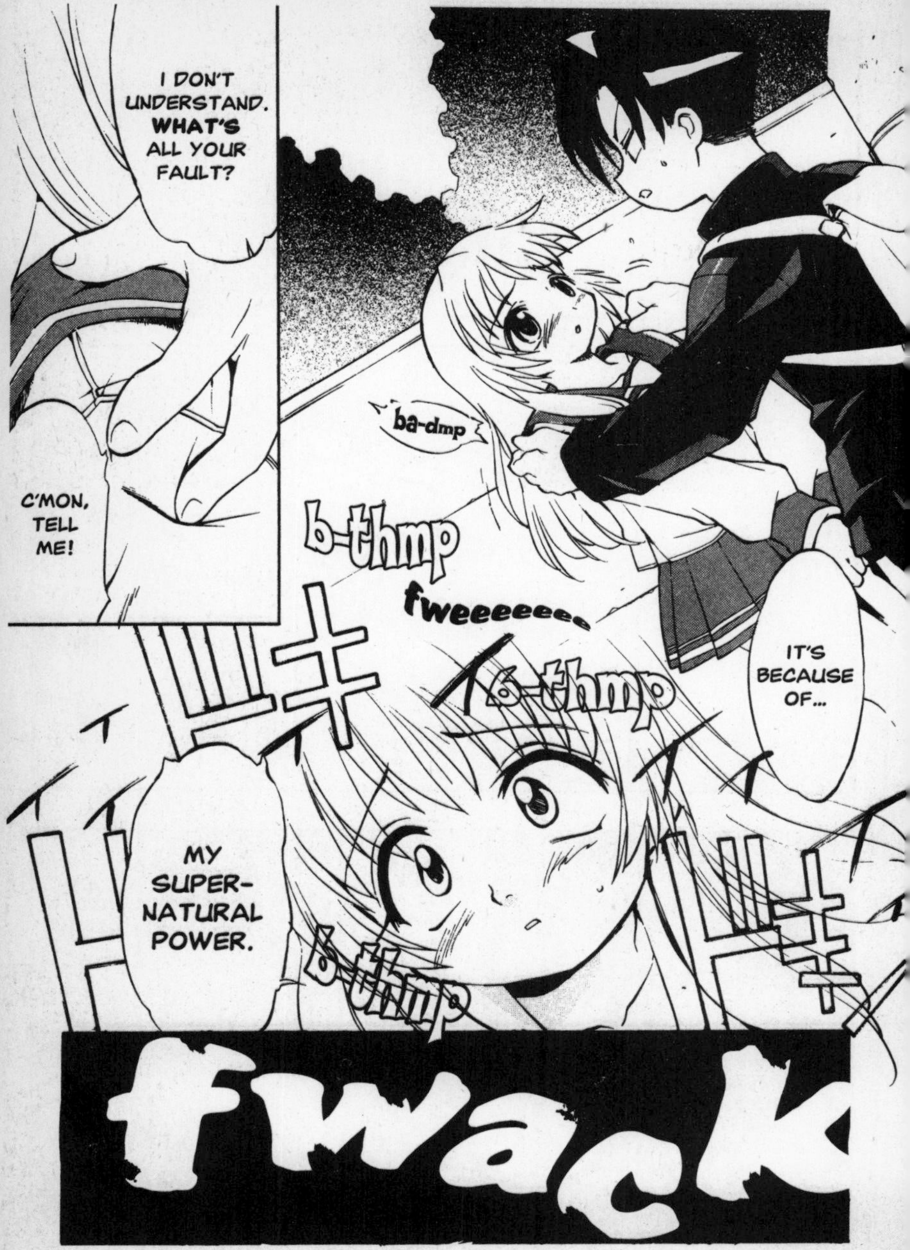
I DON'T UNDERSTAND. WHAT'S ALL YOUR FAULT?
C'MON, TELL ME!
ba-dmp
b-thmp
fweeeeeee
b-thmp
IT'S BECAUSE OF...
MY SUPER-NATURAL POWER.
b-thmp
fwack

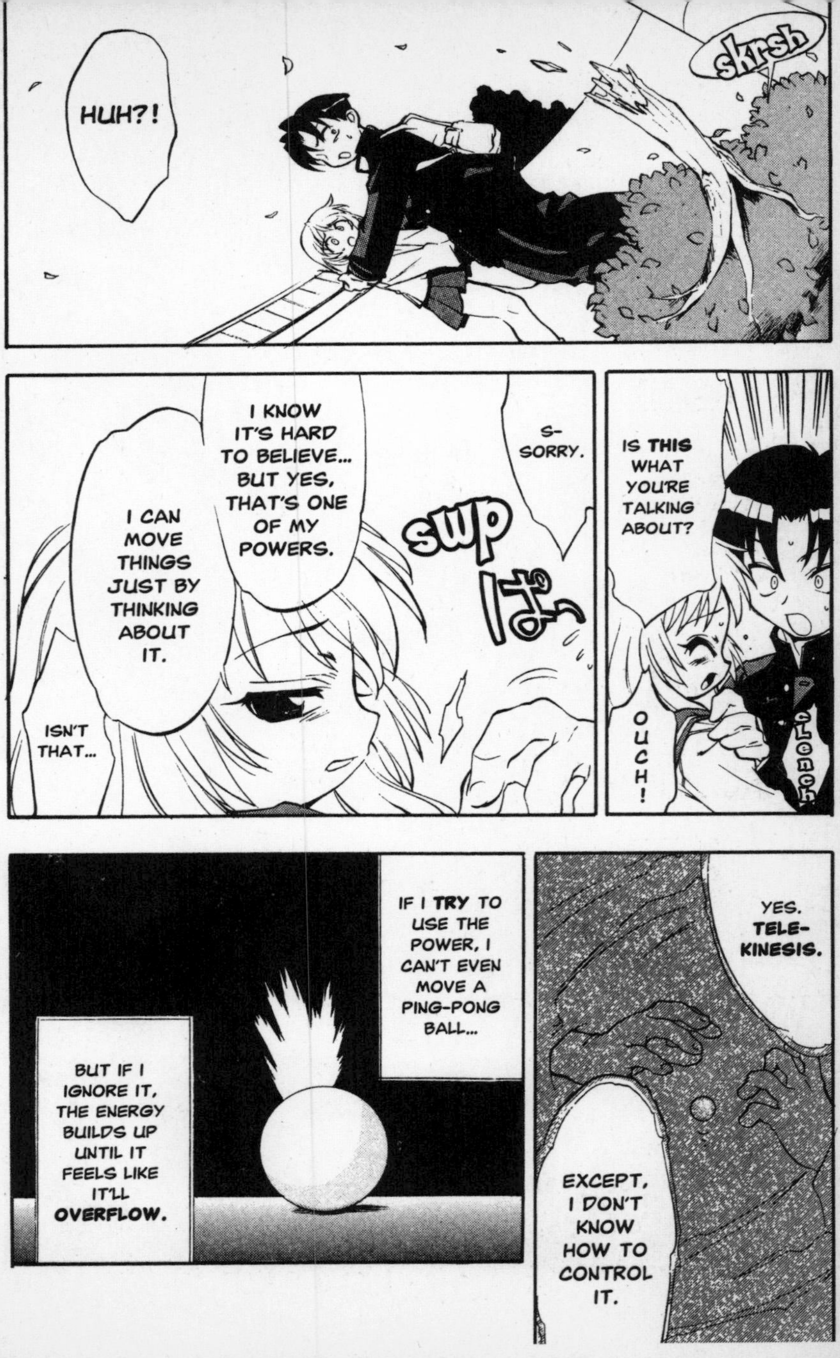
skrsh
HUH?!
IS **THIS** WHAT YOU'RE TALKING ABOUT?
clench
OUCH!
S-SORRY.
swp
ぱっ
I KNOW IT'S HARD TO BELIEVE... BUT YES, THAT'S ONE OF MY POWERS.
I CAN MOVE THINGS JUST BY THINKING ABOUT IT.
ISN'T THAT...
YES. **TELE-KINESIS.**
EXCEPT, I DON'T KNOW HOW TO CONTROL IT.
IF I **TRY** TO USE THE POWER, I CAN'T EVEN MOVE A PING-PONG BALL...
BUT IF I IGNORE IT, THE ENERGY BUILDS UP UNTIL IT FEELS LIKE IT'LL **OVERFLOW.**

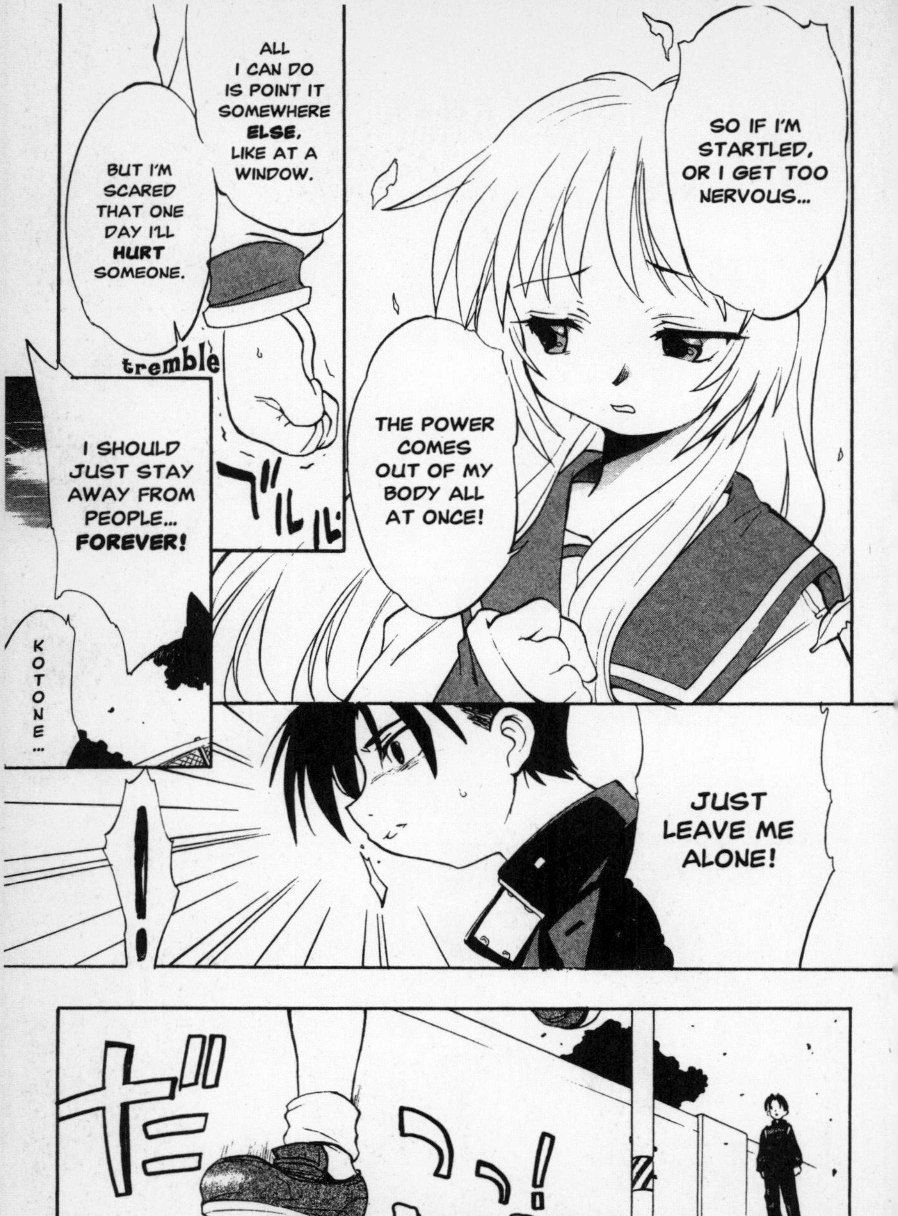

SO IF I'M STARTLED, OR I GET TOO NERVOUS...
THE POWER COMES OUT OF MY BODY ALL AT ONCE!
ALL I CAN DO IS POINT IT SOMEWHERE **ELSE**, LIKE AT A WINDOW.
BUT I'M SCARED THAT ONE DAY I'LL **HURT** SOMEONE.
tremble
ブルル
I SHOULD JUST STAY AWAY FROM PEOPLE... **FOREVER!**
KOTONE...
JUST LEAVE ME ALONE!
!
ダーっ!
dash!

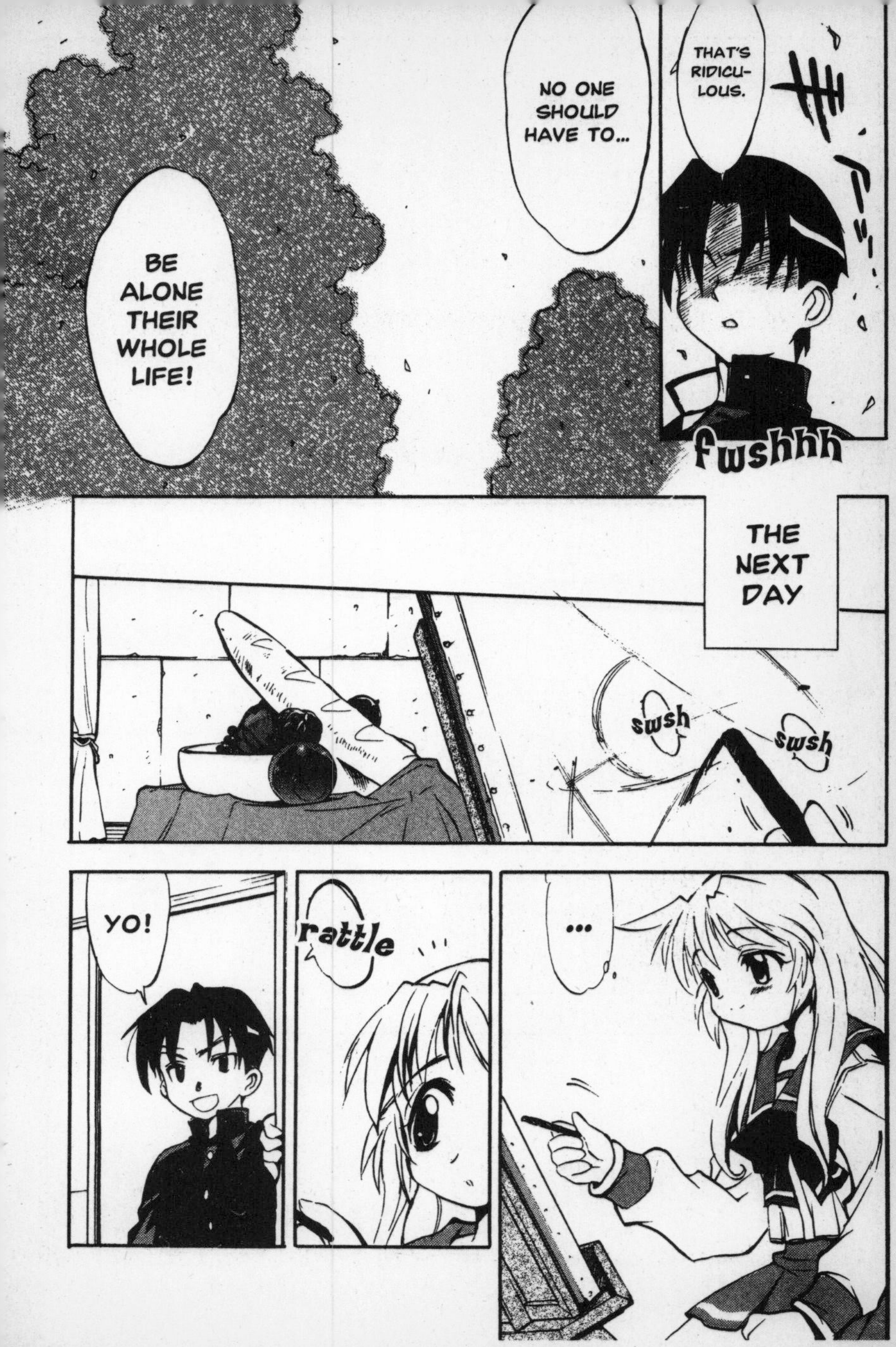
THAT'S RIDICU-LOUS.
NO ONE SHOULD HAVE TO...
BE ALONE THEIR WHOLE LIFE!
fwshhh
THE NEXT DAY
swsh
swsh
...
rattle
YO!

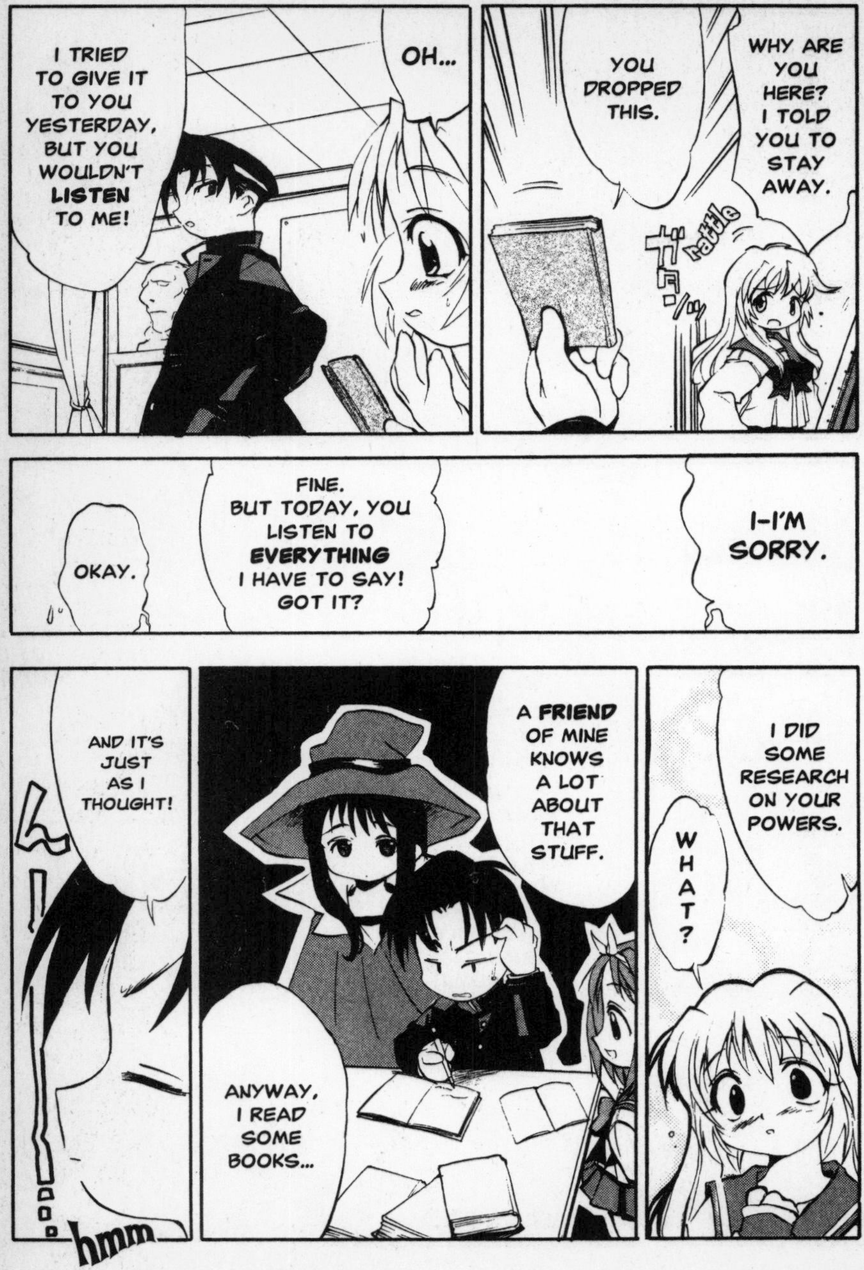
WHY ARE YOU HERE? I TOLD YOU TO STAY AWAY.
rattle
YOU DROPPED THIS.
OH...
I TRIED TO GIVE IT TO YOU YESTERDAY, BUT YOU WOULDN'T **LISTEN** TO ME!
I-I'M SORRY.
FINE. BUT TODAY, YOU LISTEN TO **EVERYTHING** I HAVE TO SAY! GOT IT?
OKAY.
I DID SOME RESEARCH ON YOUR POWERS.
WHAT?
A **FRIEND** OF MINE KNOWS A LOT ABOUT THAT STUFF.
ANYWAY, I READ SOME BOOKS...
AND IT'S JUST AS I THOUGHT!
hmm

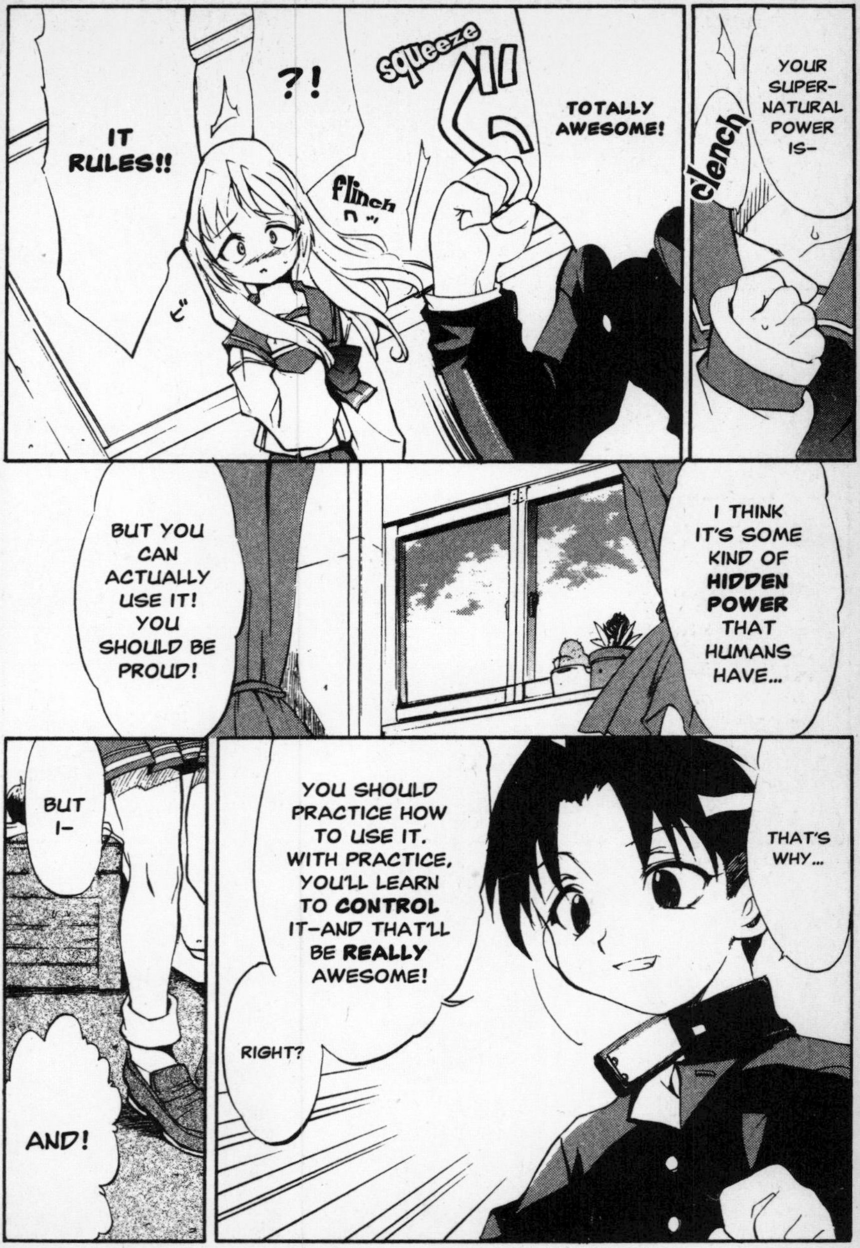
YOUR SUPER-NATURAL POWER IS–
clench
TOTALLY AWESOME!
squeeze
?!
flinch
IT RULES!!
I THINK IT'S SOME KIND OF HIDDEN POWER THAT HUMANS HAVE...
BUT YOU CAN ACTUALLY USE IT! YOU SHOULD BE PROUD!
THAT'S WHY...
YOU SHOULD PRACTICE HOW TO USE IT. WITH PRACTICE, YOU'LL LEARN TO CONTROL IT–AND THAT'LL BE REALLY AWESOME!
RIGHT?
BUT I–
AND!

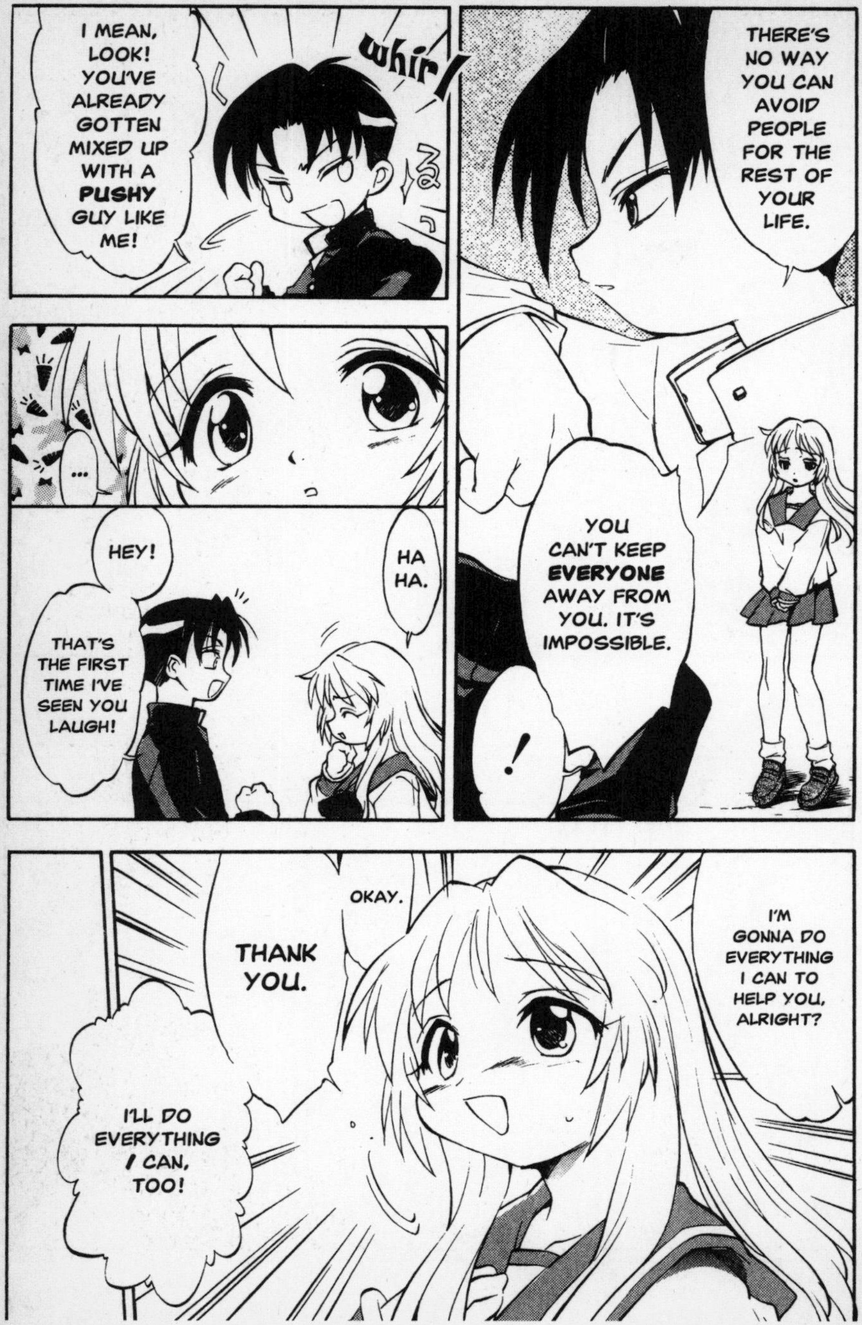
THERE'S NO WAY YOU CAN AVOID PEOPLE FOR THE REST OF YOUR LIFE.
YOU CAN'T KEEP **EVERYONE** AWAY FROM YOU. IT'S IMPOSSIBLE.
!
I MEAN, LOOK! YOU'VE ALREADY GOTTEN MIXED UP WITH A **PUSHY** GUY LIKE ME!
whirl
...
HA HA.
HEY!
THAT'S THE FIRST TIME I'VE SEEN YOU LAUGH!
I'M GONNA DO EVERYTHING I CAN TO HELP YOU, ALRIGHT?
OKAY.
THANK YOU.
I'LL DO EVERYTHING *I* CAN, TOO!

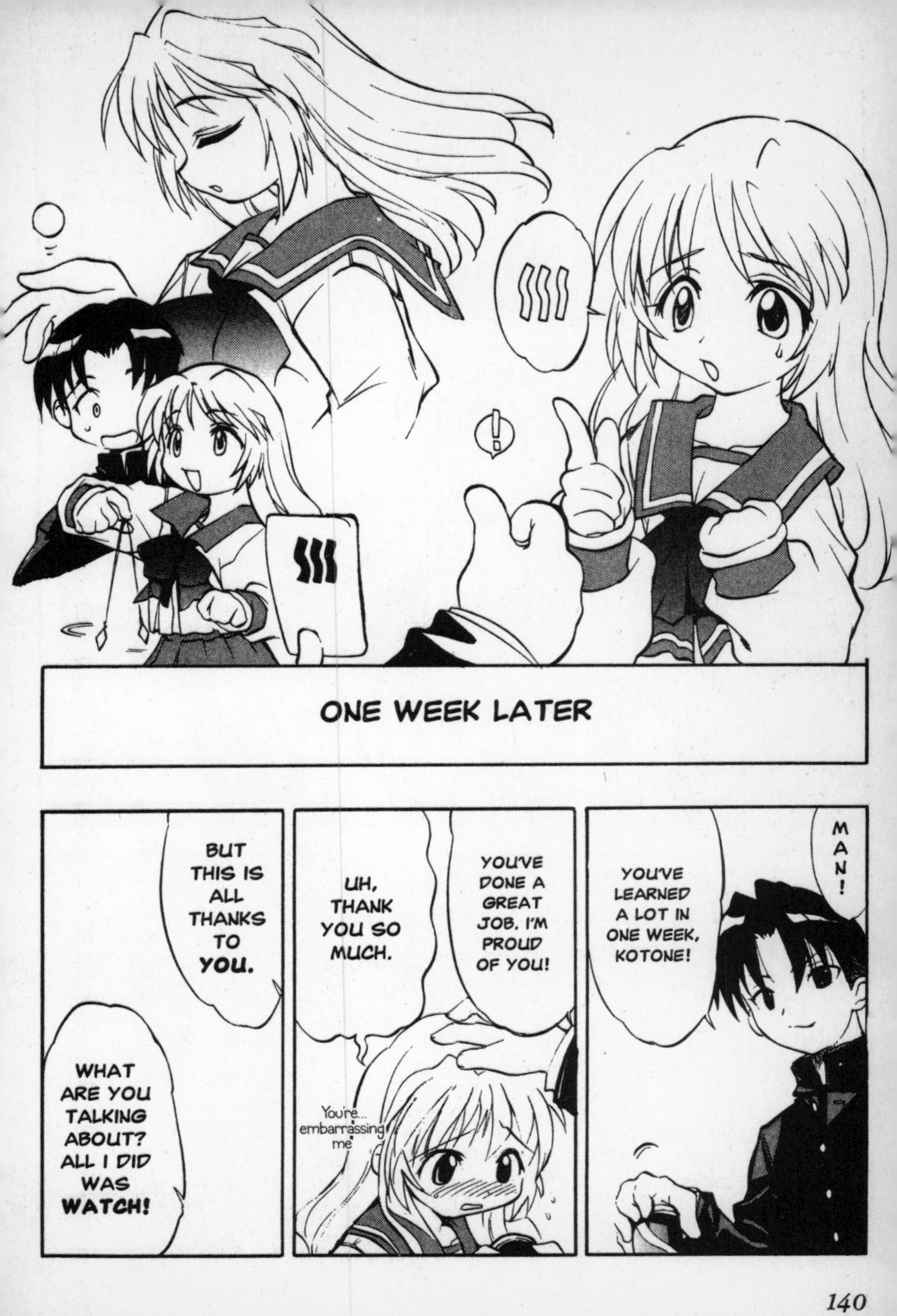
ONE WEEK LATER
MAN!
YOU'VE LEARNED A LOT IN ONE WEEK, KOTONE!
YOU'VE DONE A GREAT JOB. I'M PROUD OF YOU!
UH, THANK YOU SO MUCH.
You're... embarrassing me
BUT THIS IS ALL THANKS TO YOU.
WHAT ARE YOU TALKING ABOUT? ALL I DID WAS WATCH!

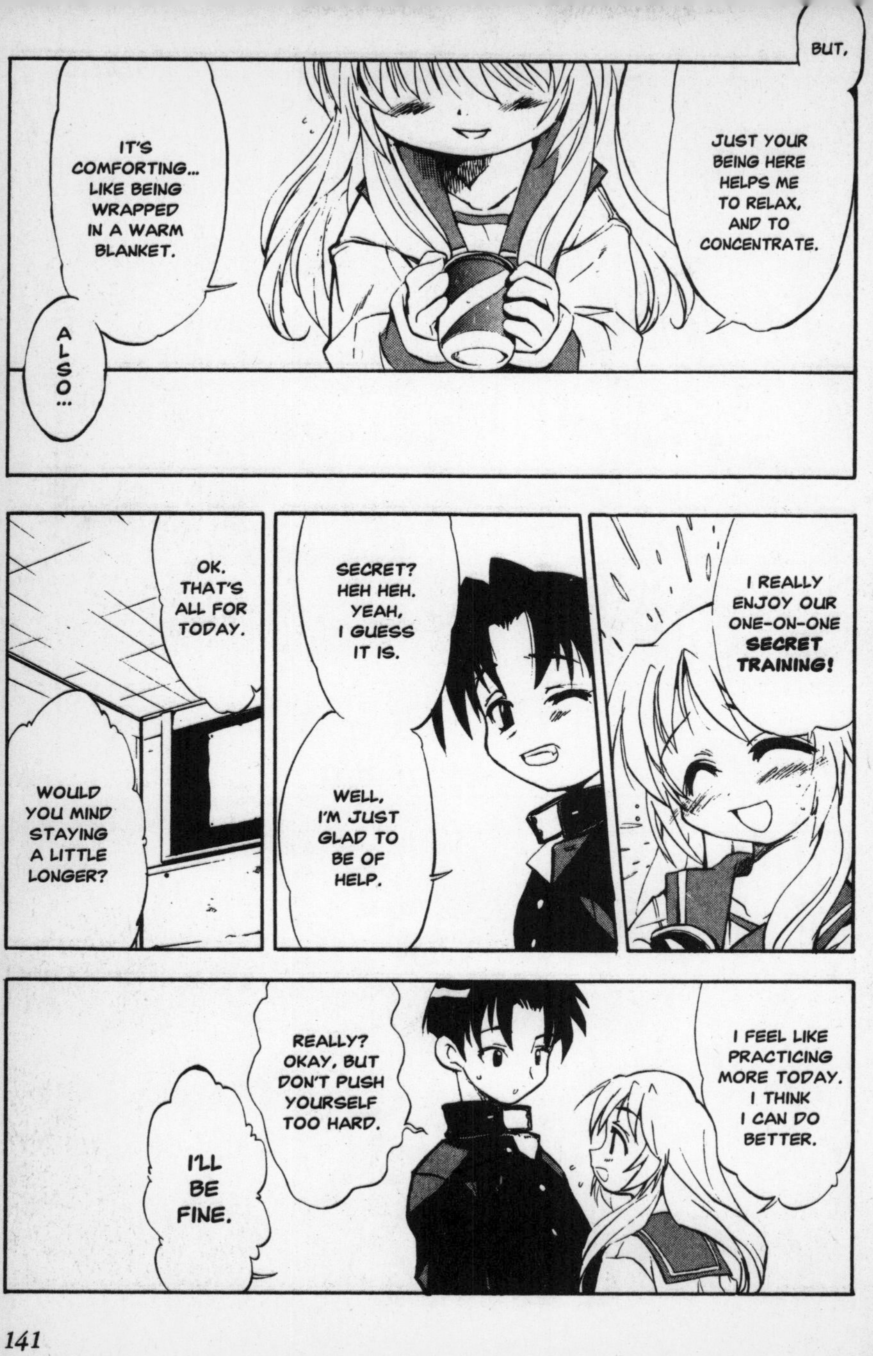
BUT,
JUST YOUR BEING HERE HELPS ME TO RELAX, AND TO CONCENTRATE.
IT'S COMFORTING... LIKE BEING WRAPPED IN A WARM BLANKET.
ALSO...
I REALLY ENJOY OUR ONE-ON-ONE **SECRET TRAINING!**
SECRET? HEH HEH. YEAH, I GUESS IT IS.
WELL, I'M JUST GLAD TO BE OF HELP.
OK. THAT'S ALL FOR TODAY.
WOULD YOU MIND STAYING A LITTLE LONGER?
I FEEL LIKE PRACTICING MORE TODAY. I THINK I CAN DO BETTER.
REALLY? OKAY, BUT DON'T PUSH YOURSELF TOO HARD.
I'LL BE FINE.

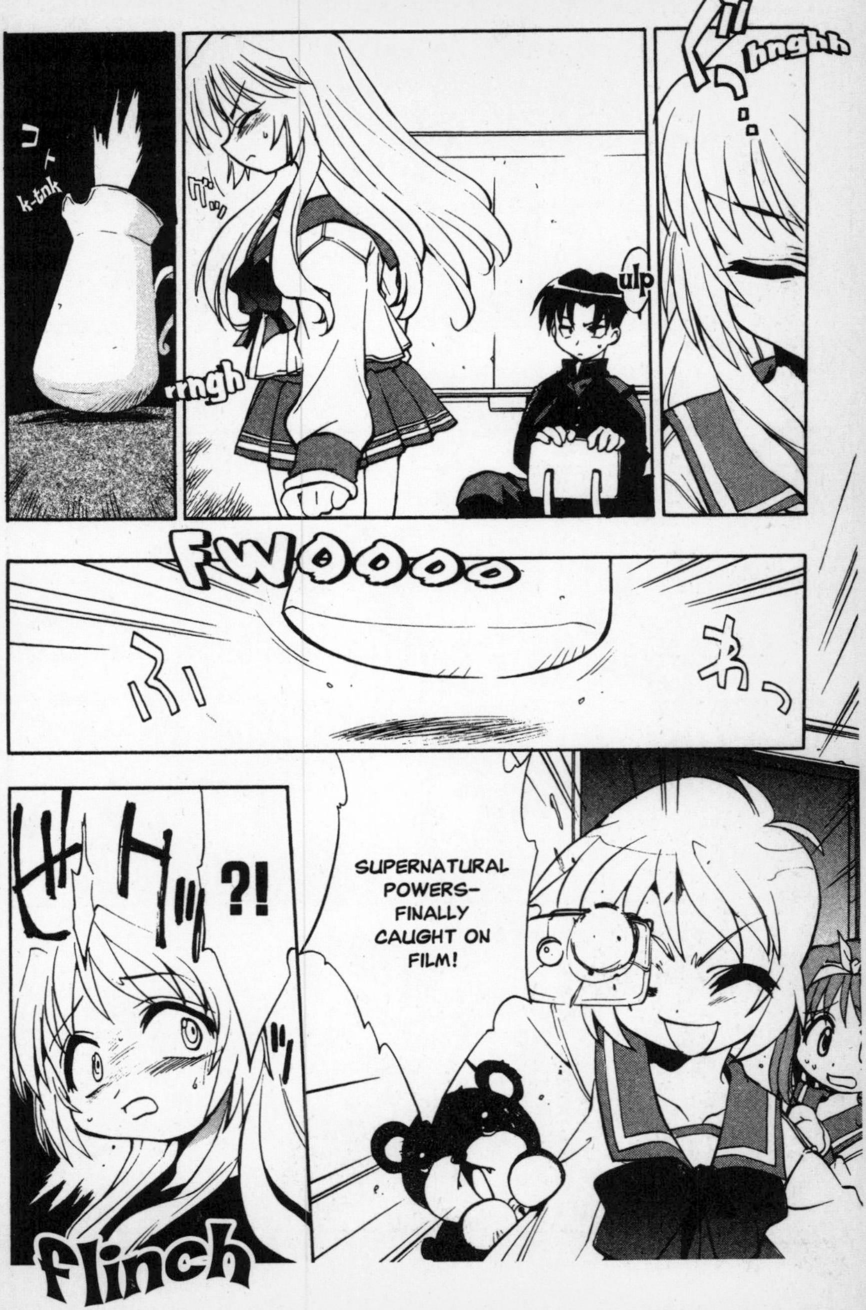

hnghh
ulp
rrngh
k-tnk
FWOOOO
SUPERNATURAL POWERS— FINALLY CAUGHT ON FILM!
?!
flinch

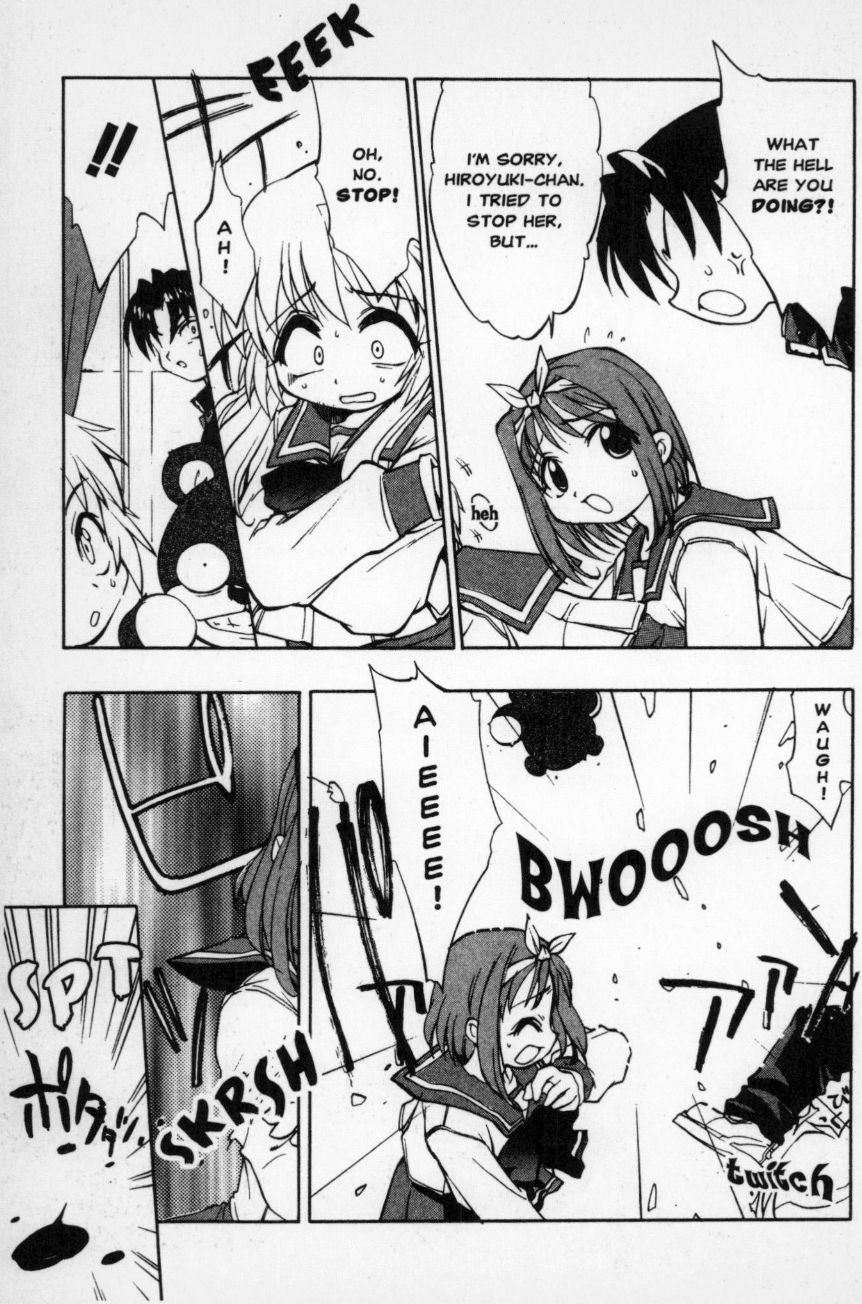
WHAT THE HELL ARE YOU DOING?!
I'M SORRY, HIROYUKI-CHAN. I TRIED TO STOP HER, BUT...
heh
EEEK
OH, NO. STOP!
AH!
!!
WAUGH!
AIEEEE!
BWOOOSH
twitch
SKRSH
SPT

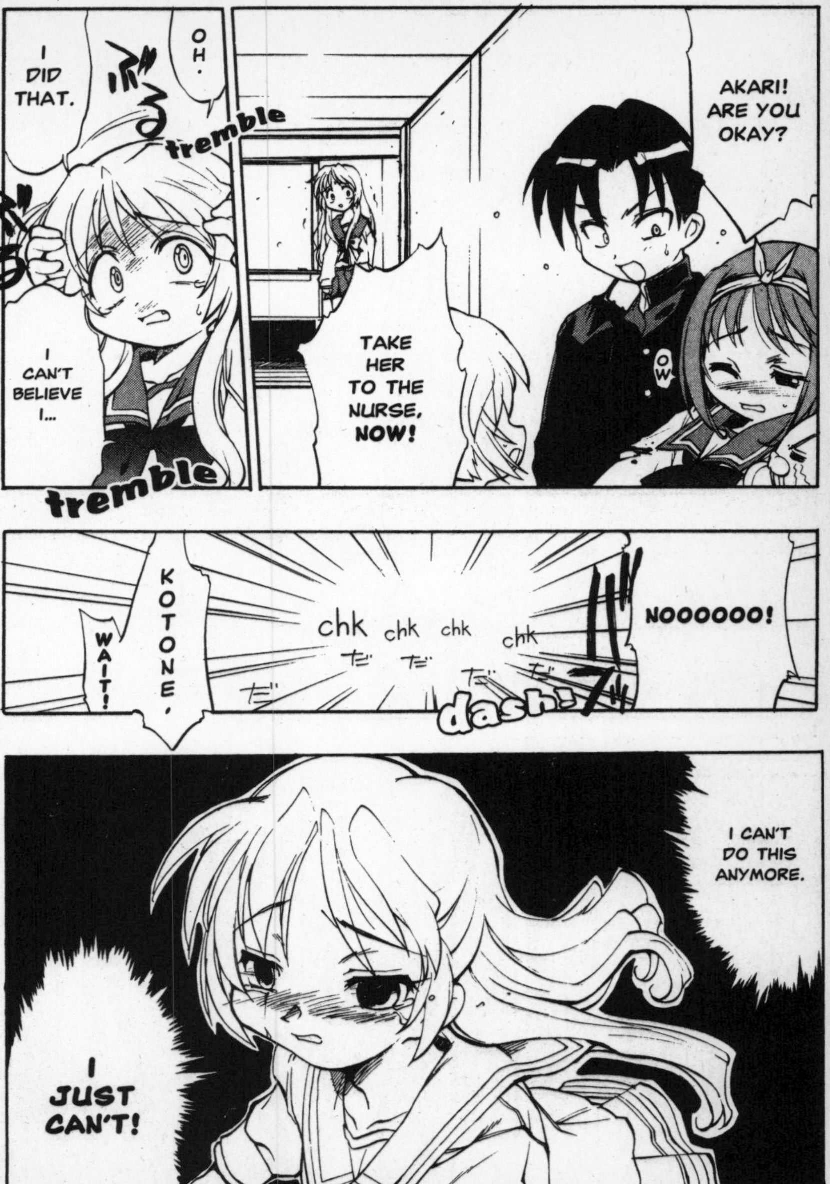
AKARI! ARE YOU OKAY?
OW
TAKE HER TO THE NURSE, NOW!
OH.
I DID THAT.
ぶる
tremble
ぶる
I CAN'T BELIEVE I...
tremble
NOOOOOO!
dash!
chk chk chk chk
だ だ だ だ だ
KOTONE, WAIT!
I CAN'T DO THIS ANYMORE.
I JUST CAN'T!

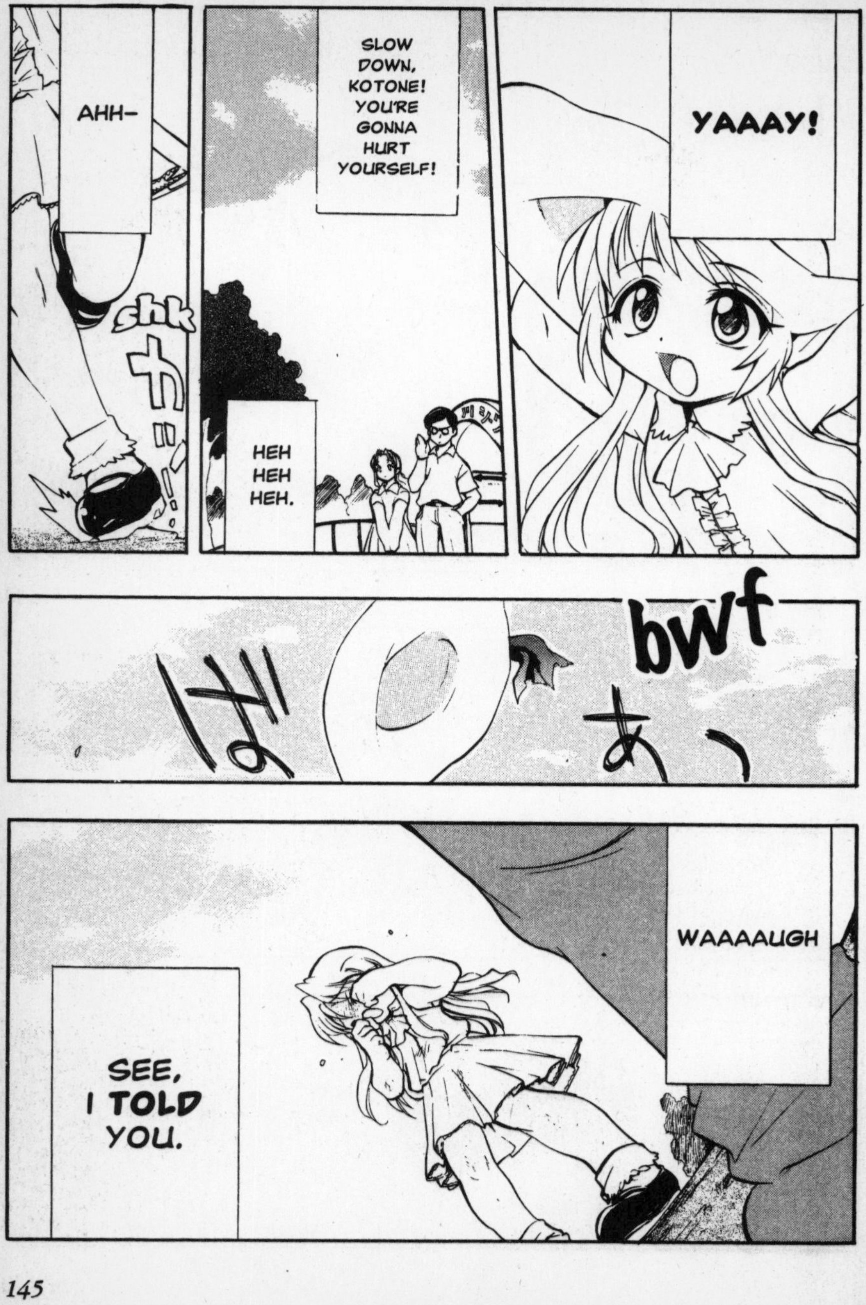

YAAAY!
SLOW DOWN, KOTONE! YOU'RE GONNA HURT YOURSELF!
HEH HEH HEH.
AHH-
shk
bwf
WAAAAUGH
SEE, I TOLD YOU.

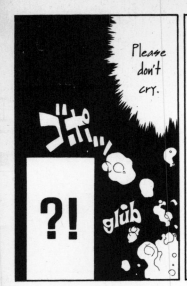

HEY, WHERE'S YOUR HAT?
hic
hic
Please don't cry.
ゴポ…
glub
?!
WHO ARE YOU? WHERE ARE YOU?
swp
WHAT? THAT'S RIGHT.
I CAN HEAR YOU.
THIS WAY, RIGHT?
HEY, WHERE ARE YOU GOING? KOTONE!

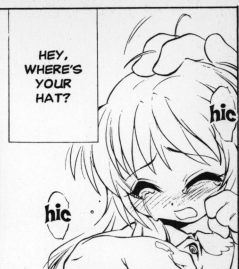

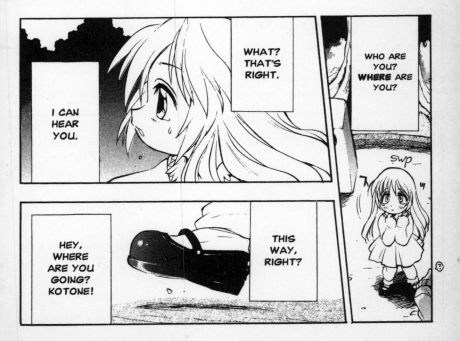

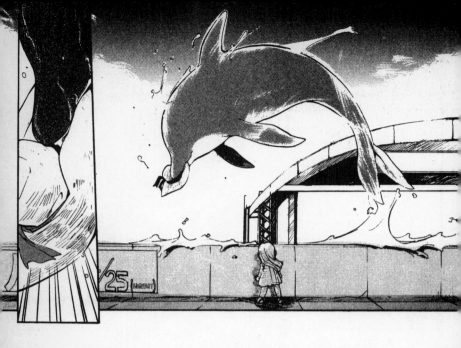

THAT WAS WHEN I FIRST REALIZED MY SPECIAL POWERS.

I COULD DO THINGS THAT OTHER PEOPLE—EVEN MY MOM AND DAD—COULDN'T DO! I DIDN'T KNOW HOW I COULD DO THESE THINGS, BUT I FELT A LITTLE **PROUD** OF MY POWERS.

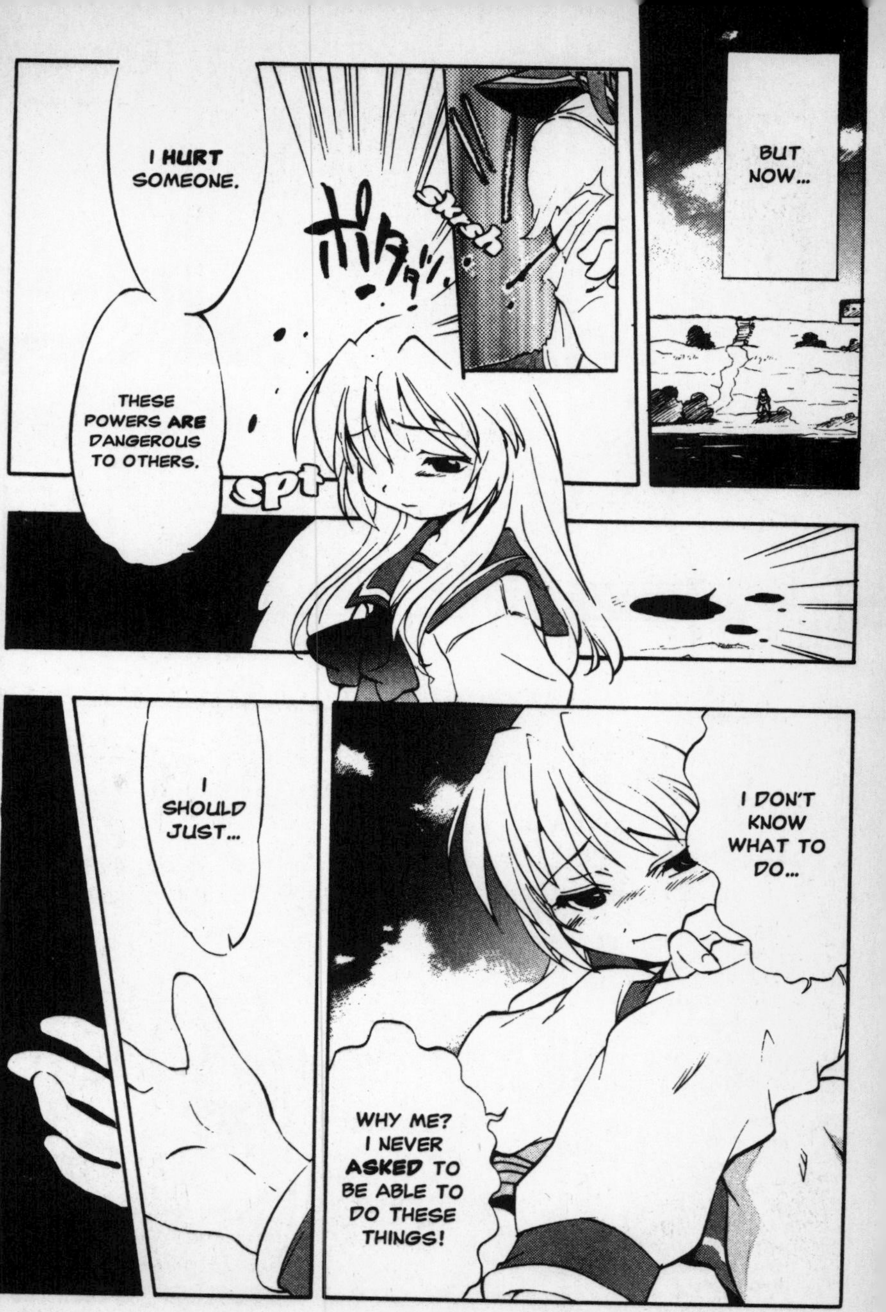

BUT NOW...
Skrish
I HURT SOMEONE.
THESE POWERS ARE DANGEROUS TO OTHERS.
spt
I DON'T KNOW WHAT TO DO...
WHY ME? I NEVER ASKED TO BE ABLE TO DO THESE THINGS!
I SHOULD JUST...

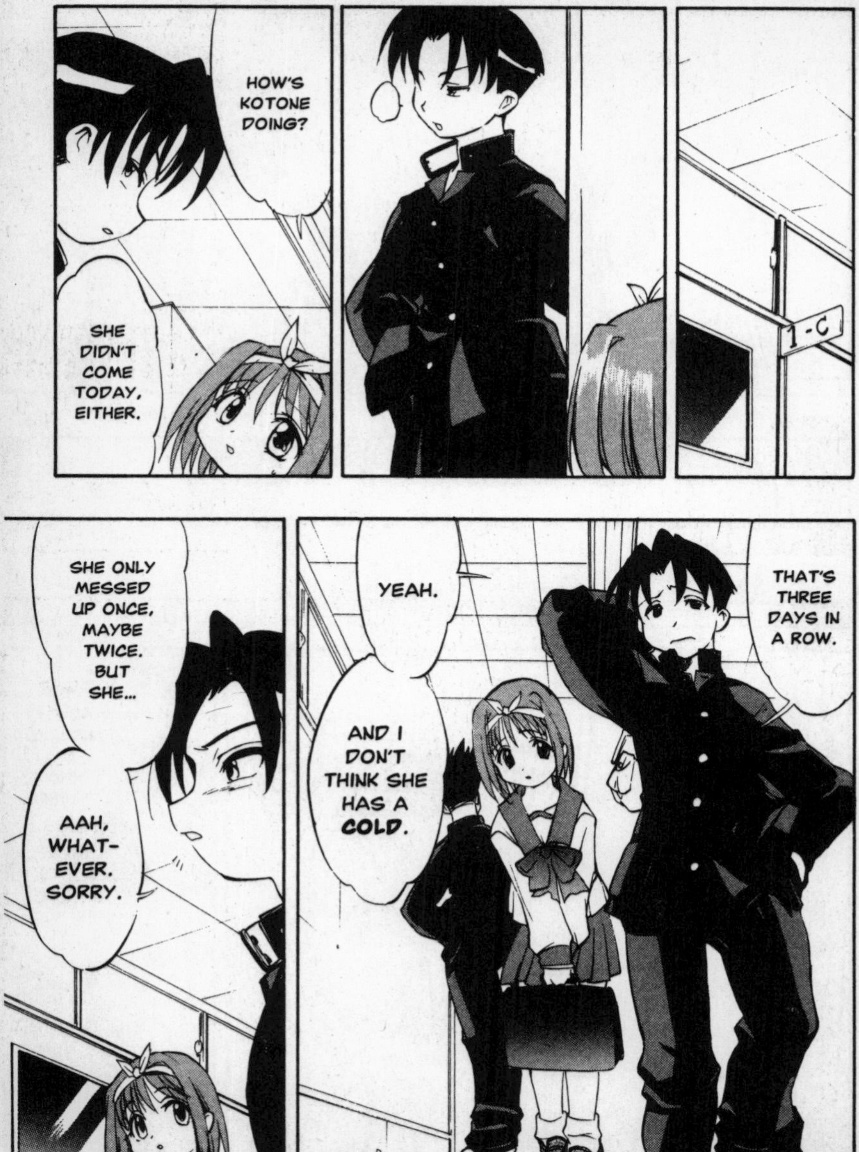
1-C
HOW'S KOTONE DOING?
SHE DIDN'T COME TODAY, EITHER.
THAT'S THREE DAYS IN A ROW.
YEAH.
AND I DON'T THINK SHE HAS A **COLD**.
SHE ONLY MESSED UP ONCE, MAYBE TWICE. BUT SHE...
AAH, WHAT-EVER. SORRY.

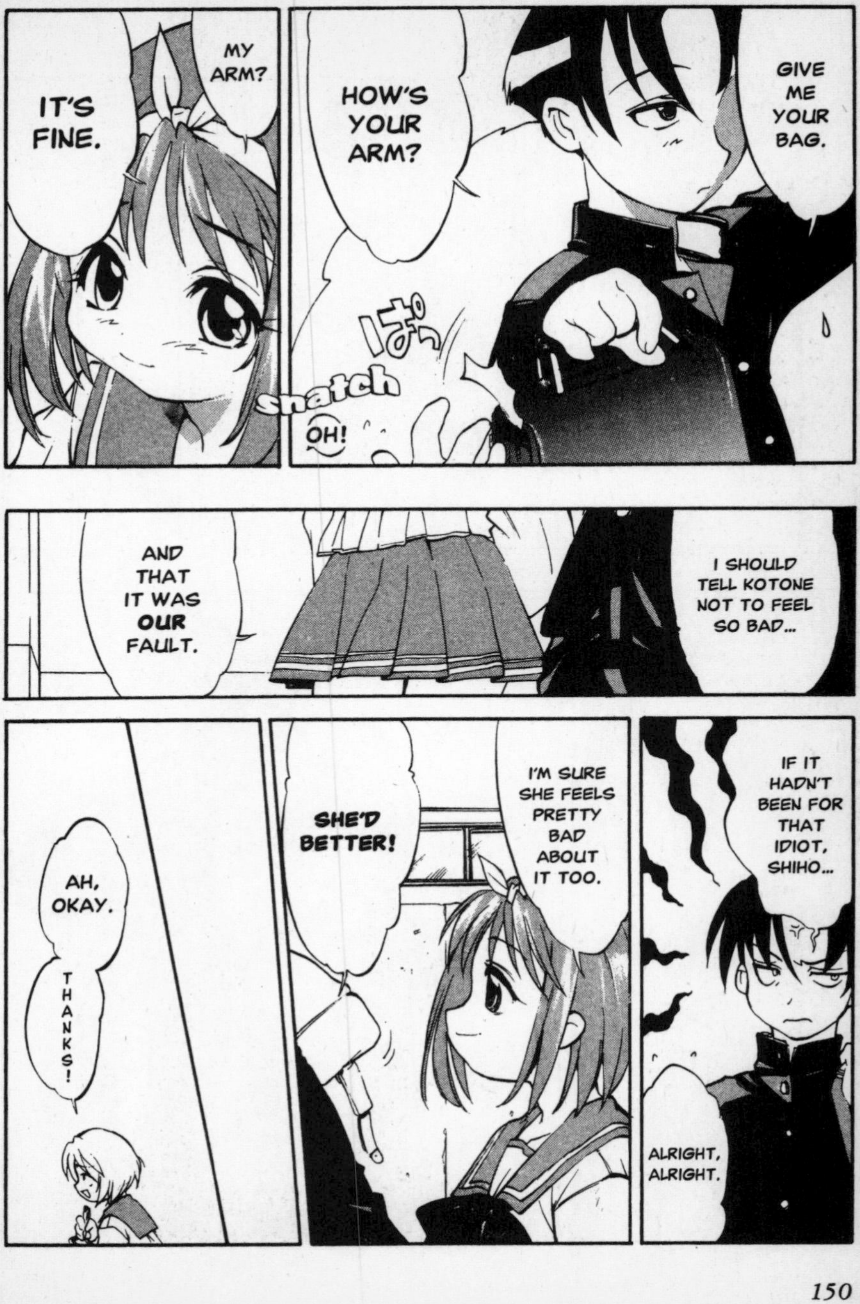
GIVE ME YOUR BAG.
HOW'S YOUR ARM?
ぱっ
snatch
OH!
MY ARM?
IT'S FINE.
I SHOULD TELL KOTONE NOT TO FEEL SO BAD...
AND THAT IT WAS OUR FAULT.
IF IT HADN'T BEEN FOR THAT IDIOT, SHIHO...
ALRIGHT, ALRIGHT.
I'M SURE SHE FEELS PRETTY BAD ABOUT IT TOO.
SHE'D BETTER!
AH, OKAY.
THANKS!

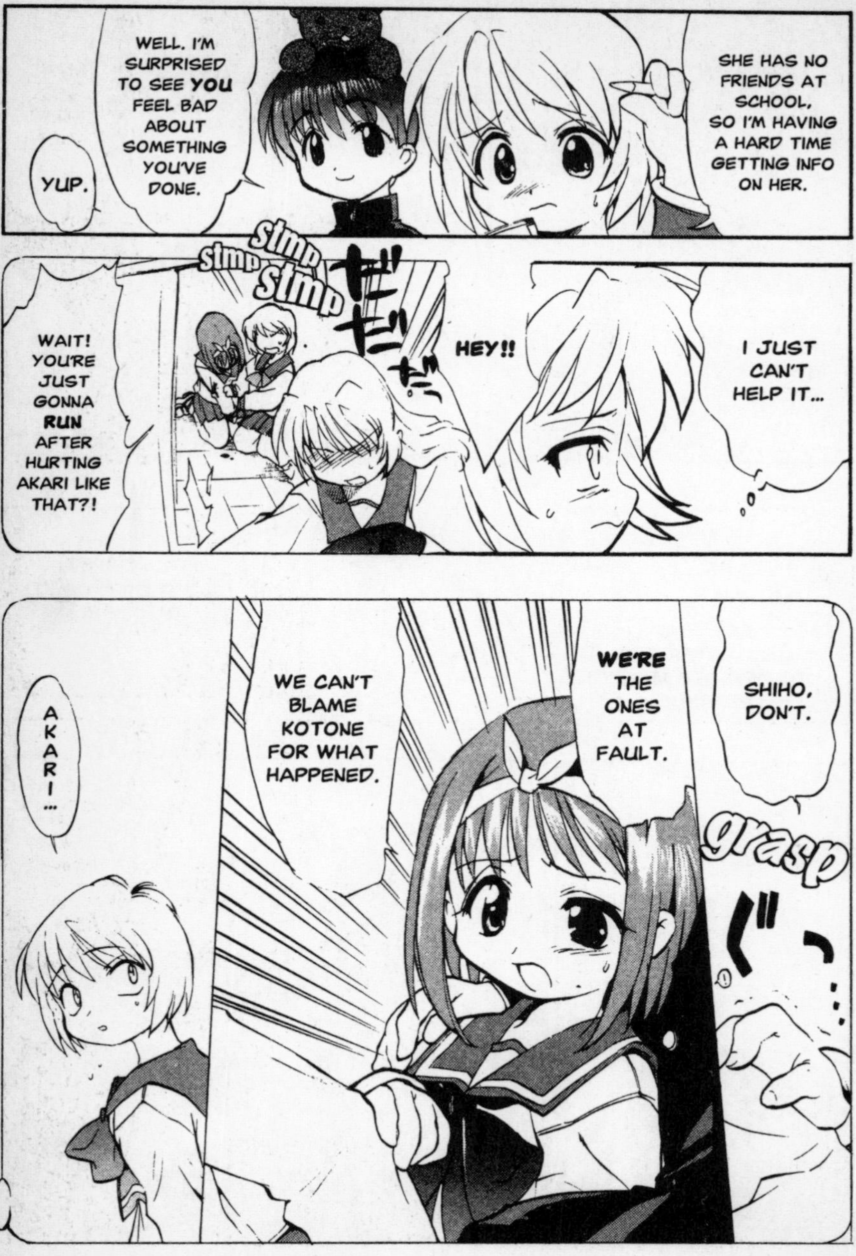
SHE HAS NO FRIENDS AT SCHOOL, SO I'M HAVING A HARD TIME GETTING INFO ON HER.
WELL. I'M SURPRISED TO SEE **YOU** FEEL BAD ABOUT SOMETHING YOU'VE DONE.
YUP.
I JUST CAN'T HELP IT...
HEY!!
stmp stmp stmp
WAIT! YOU'RE JUST GONNA **RUN** AFTER HURTING AKARI LIKE THAT?!
SHIHO, DON'T.
grasp
WE'RE THE ONES AT FAULT.
WE CAN'T BLAME KOTONE FOR WHAT HAPPENED.
AKARI...

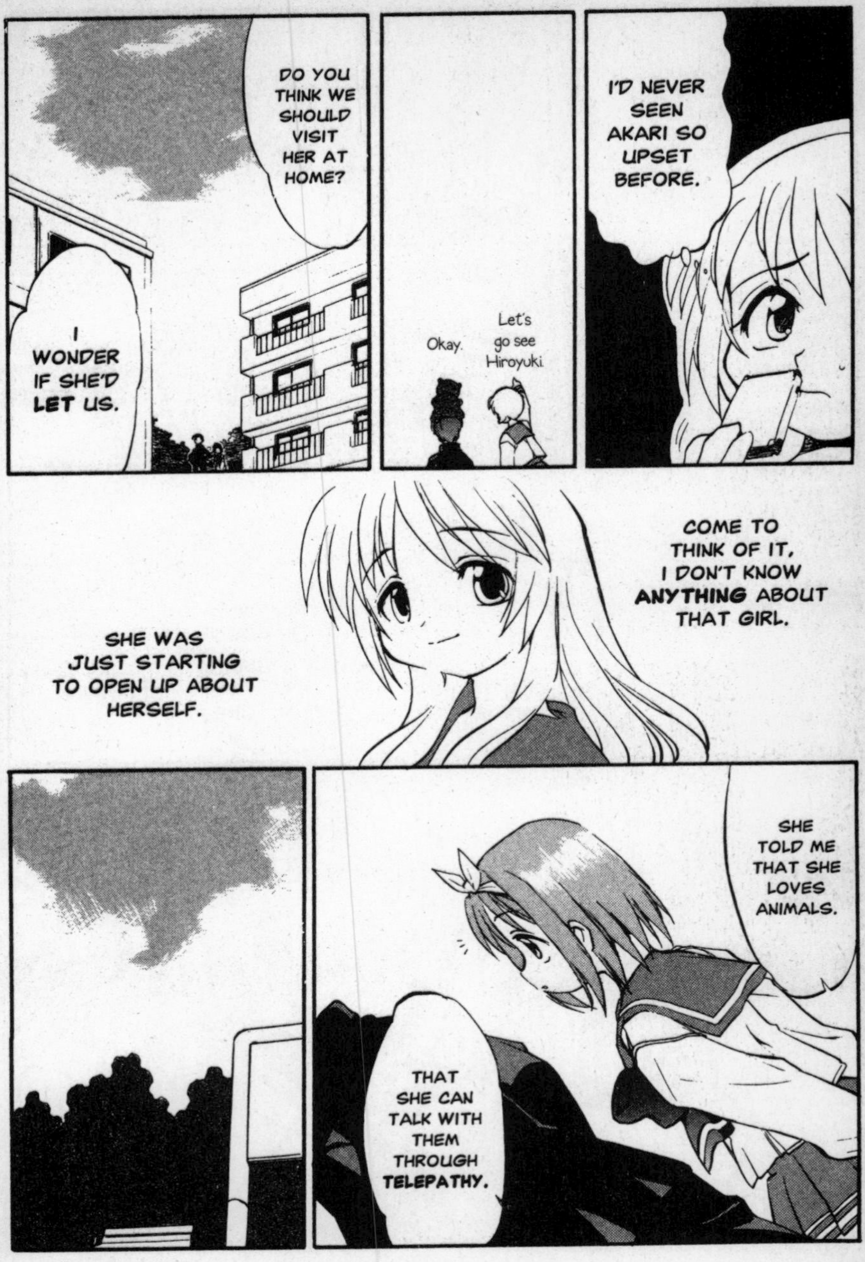
I'D NEVER SEEN AKARI SO UPSET BEFORE.
Let's go see Hiroyuki.
Okay.
DO YOU THINK WE SHOULD VISIT HER AT HOME?
I WONDER IF SHE'D **LET** US.
COME TO THINK OF IT, I DON'T KNOW **ANYTHING** ABOUT THAT GIRL.
SHE WAS JUST STARTING TO OPEN UP ABOUT HERSELF.
SHE TOLD ME THAT SHE LOVES ANIMALS.
THAT SHE CAN TALK WITH THEM THROUGH **TELEPATHY**.

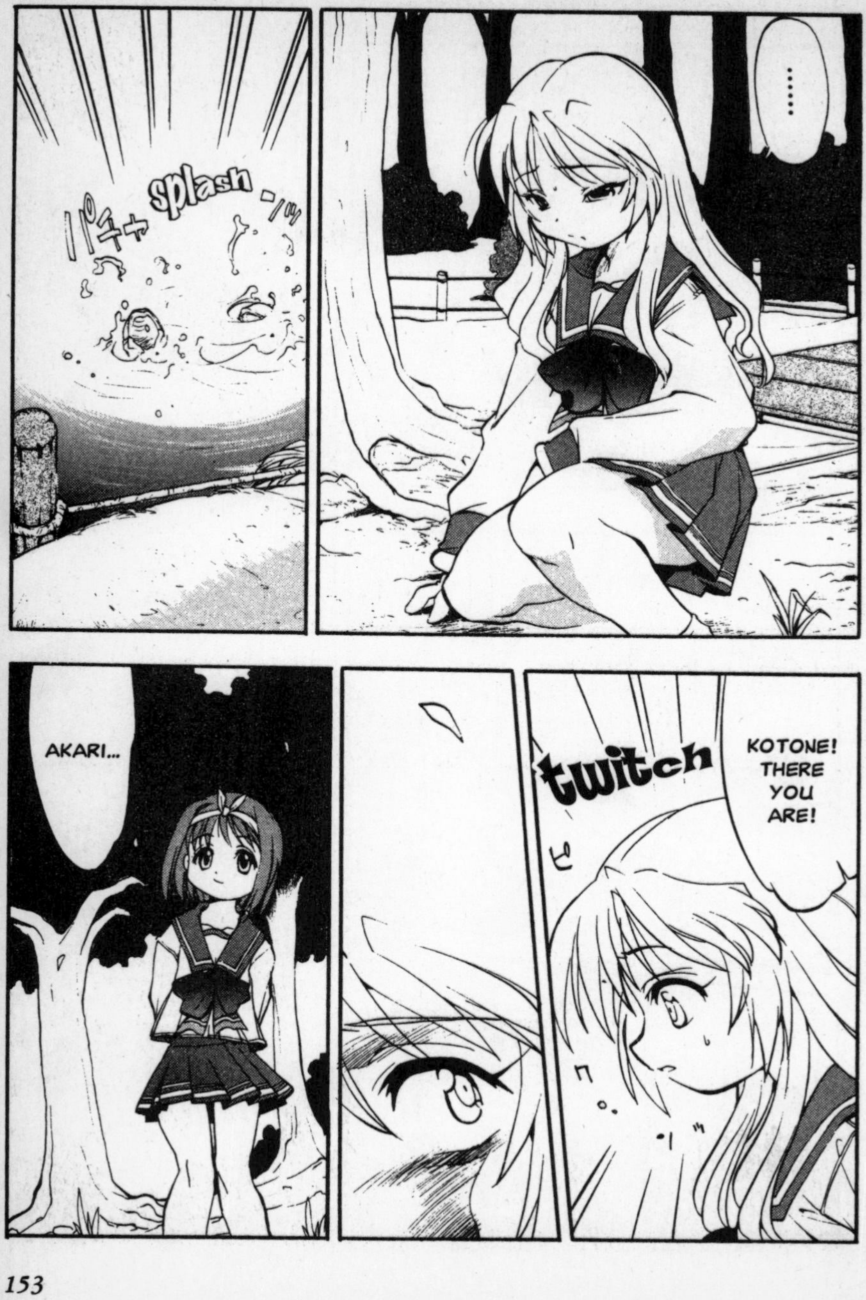
......
パチャ
splash
KOTONE! THERE YOU ARE!
twitch
ピ
AKARI...

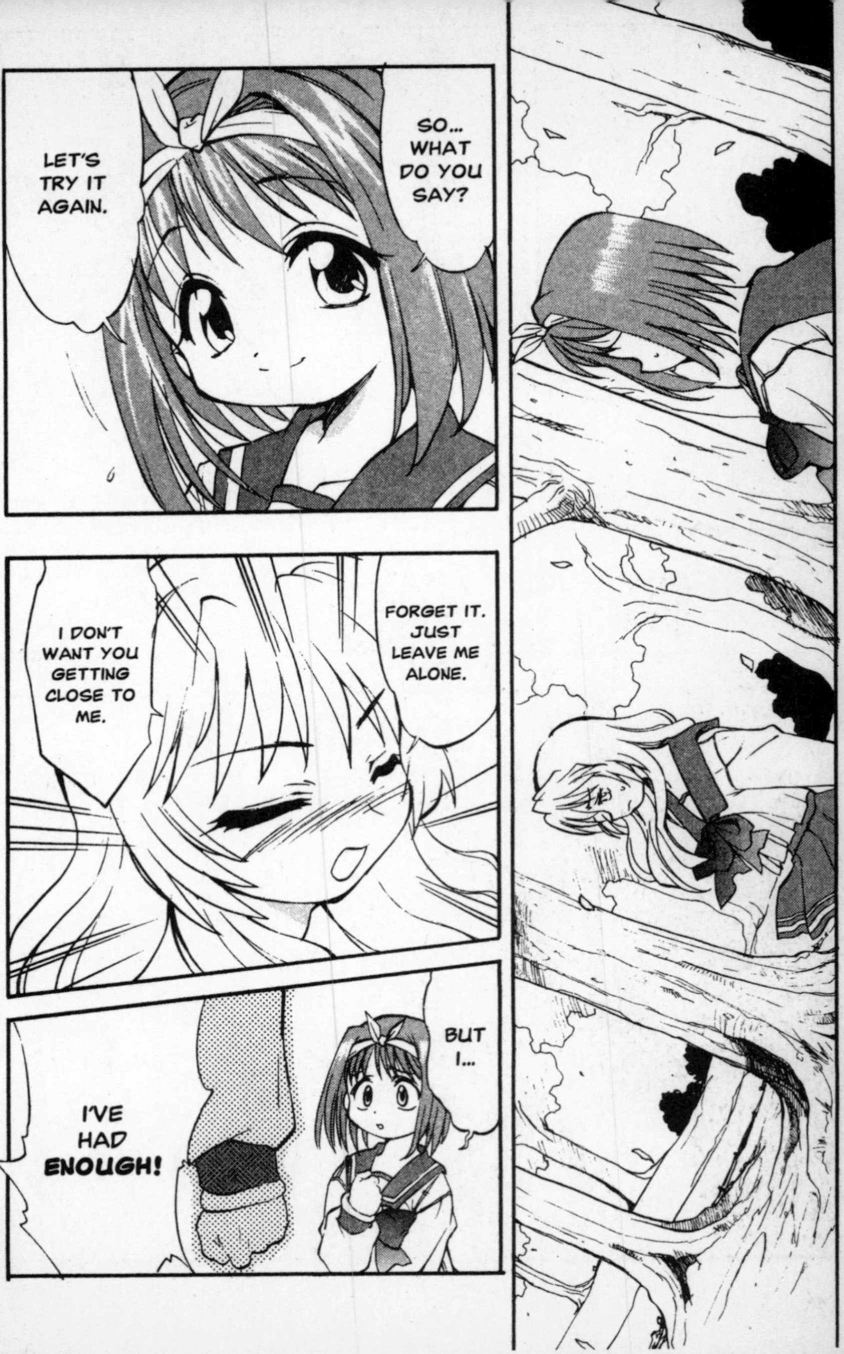
SO... WHAT DO YOU SAY?
LET'S TRY IT AGAIN.
FORGET IT. JUST LEAVE ME ALONE.
I DON'T WANT YOU GETTING CLOSE TO ME.
BUT I...
I'VE HAD **ENOUGH!**

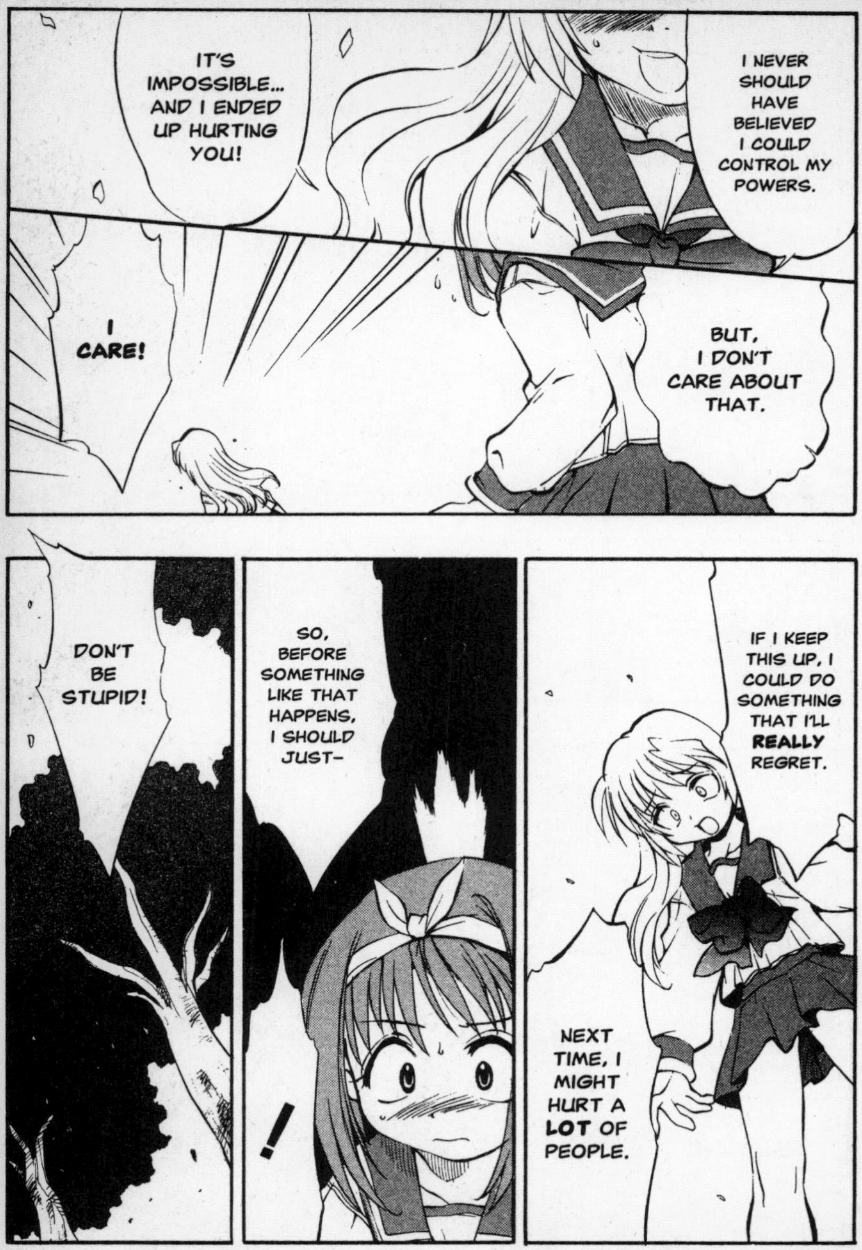
I NEVER SHOULD HAVE BELIEVED I COULD CONTROL MY POWERS.
IT'S IMPOSSIBLE... AND I ENDED UP HURTING YOU!
BUT, I DON'T CARE ABOUT THAT.
I CARE!
IF I KEEP THIS UP, I COULD DO SOMETHING THAT I'LL REALLY REGRET.
NEXT TIME, I MIGHT HURT A LOT OF PEOPLE.
SO, BEFORE SOMETHING LIKE THAT HAPPENS, I SHOULD JUST-
!
DON'T BE STUPID!

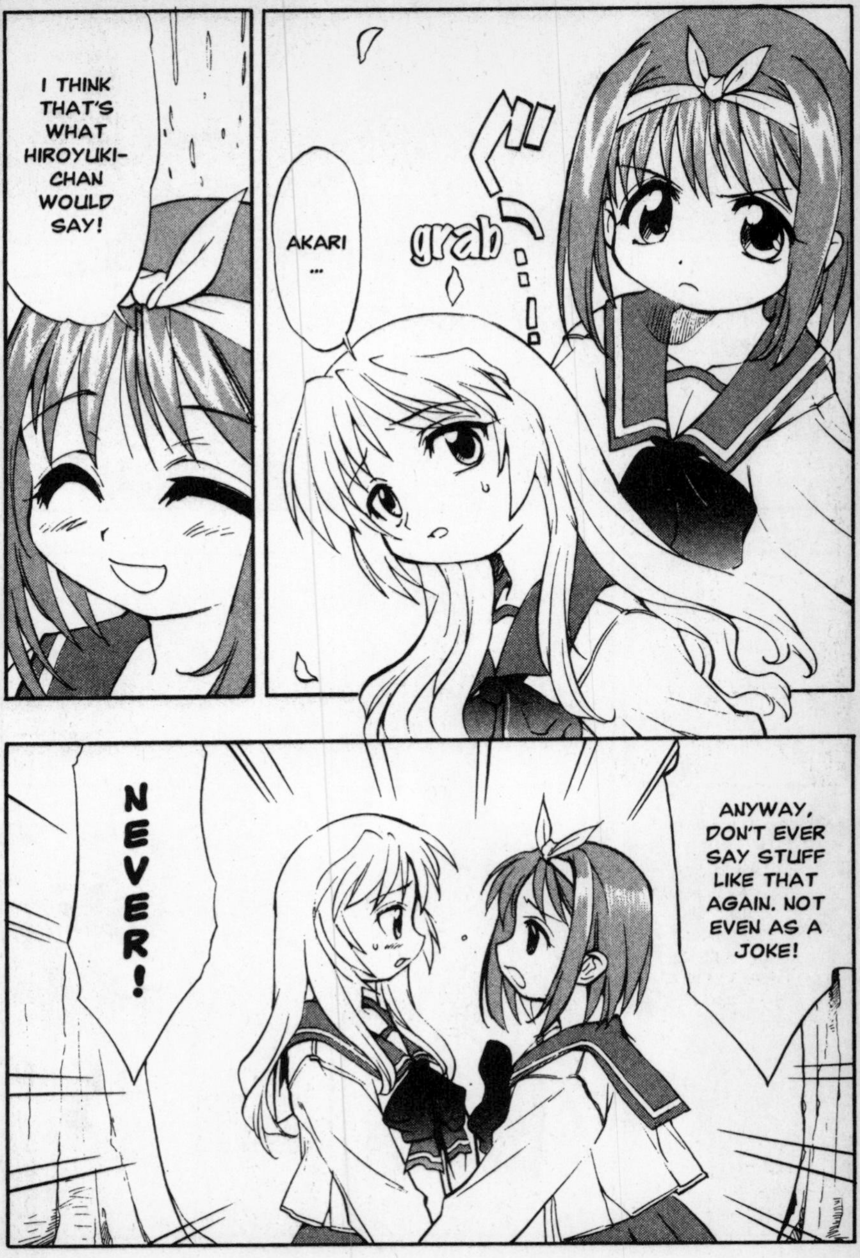
grab
AKARI ...
I THINK THAT'S WHAT HIROYUKI-CHAN WOULD SAY!
ANYWAY, DON'T EVER SAY STUFF LIKE THAT AGAIN. NOT EVEN AS A JOKE!
NEVER!

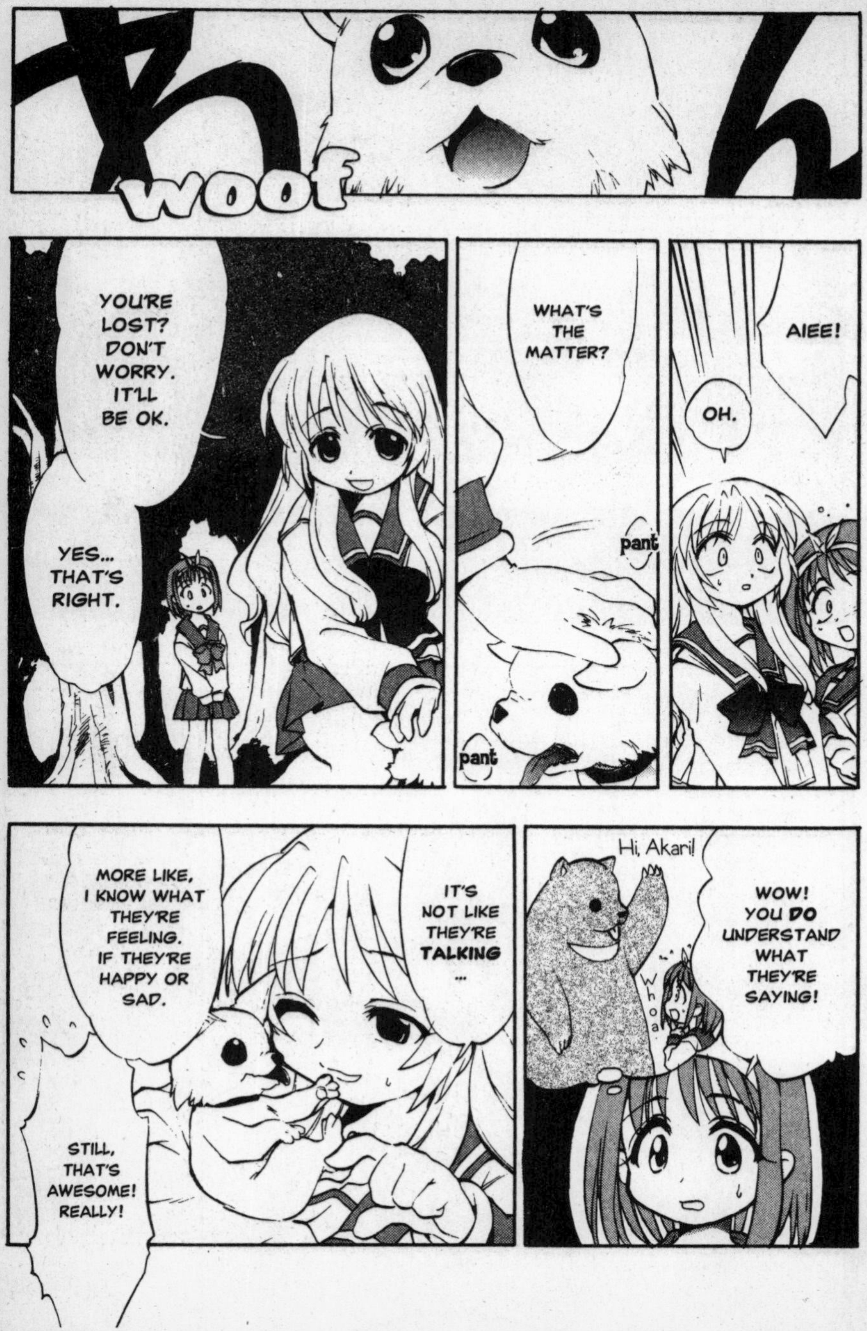
woof
AIEE!
OH.
WHAT'S THE MATTER?
pant
pant
YOU'RE LOST? DON'T WORRY. IT'LL BE OK.
YES... THAT'S RIGHT.
Hi, Akari!
Whoa
WOW! YOU **DO** UNDERSTAND WHAT THEY'RE SAYING!
IT'S NOT LIKE THEY'RE **TALKING** ...
MORE LIKE, I KNOW WHAT THEY'RE FEELING. IF THEY'RE HAPPY OR SAD.
STILL, THAT'S AWESOME! REALLY!

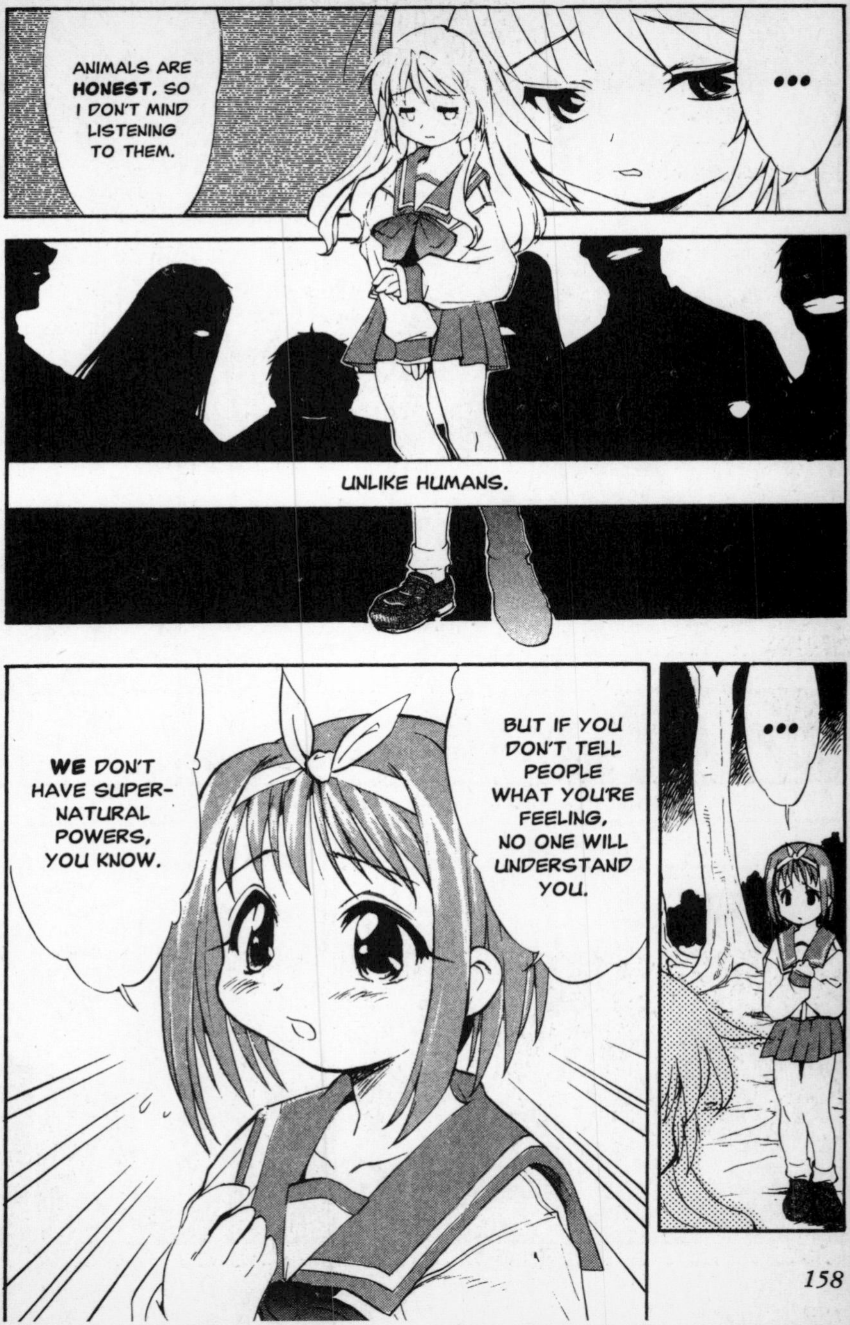
...
ANIMALS ARE HONEST, SO I DON'T MIND LISTENING TO THEM.
UNLIKE HUMANS.
...
BUT IF YOU DON'T TELL PEOPLE WHAT YOU'RE FEELING, NO ONE WILL UNDERSTAND YOU.
WE DON'T HAVE SUPER-NATURAL POWERS, YOU KNOW.

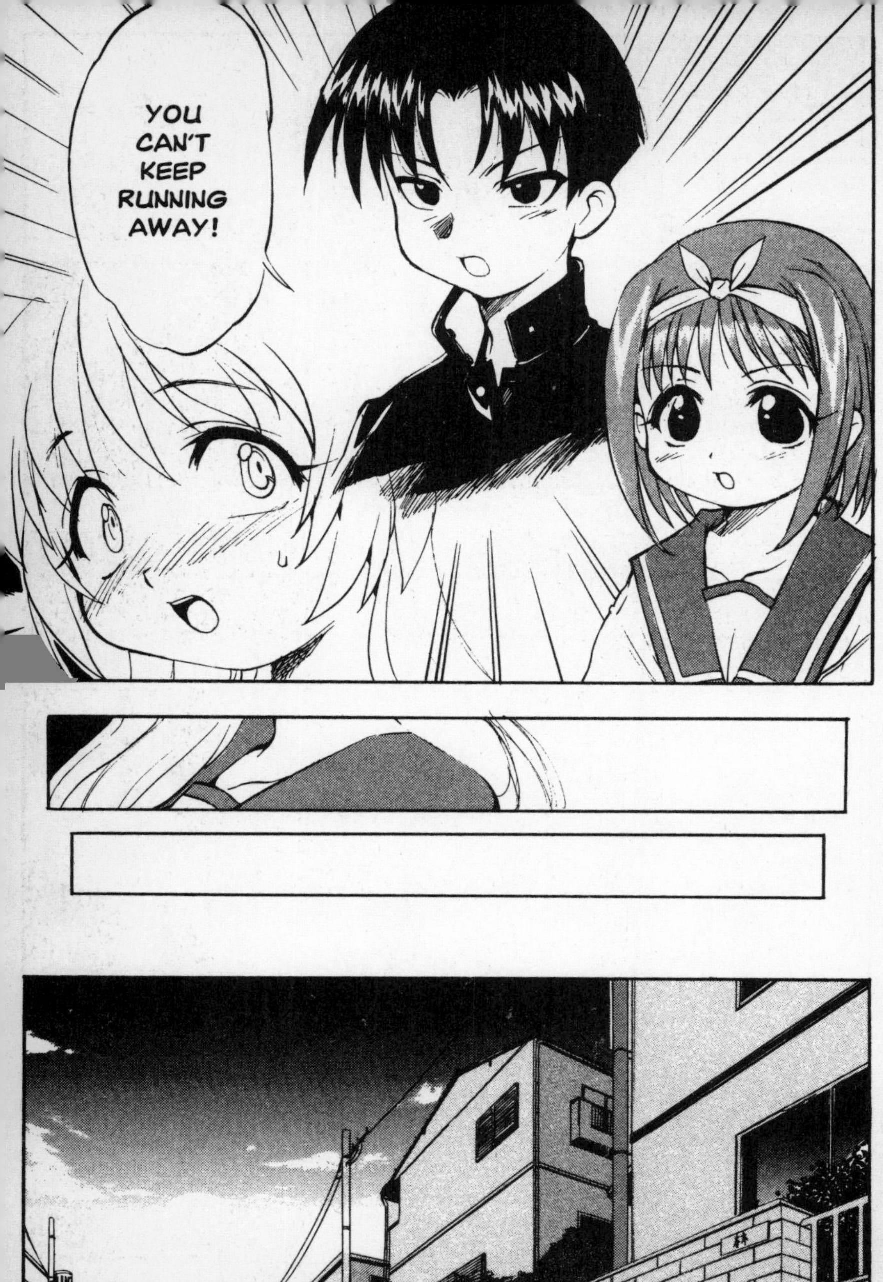
YOU CAN'T KEEP RUNNING AWAY!

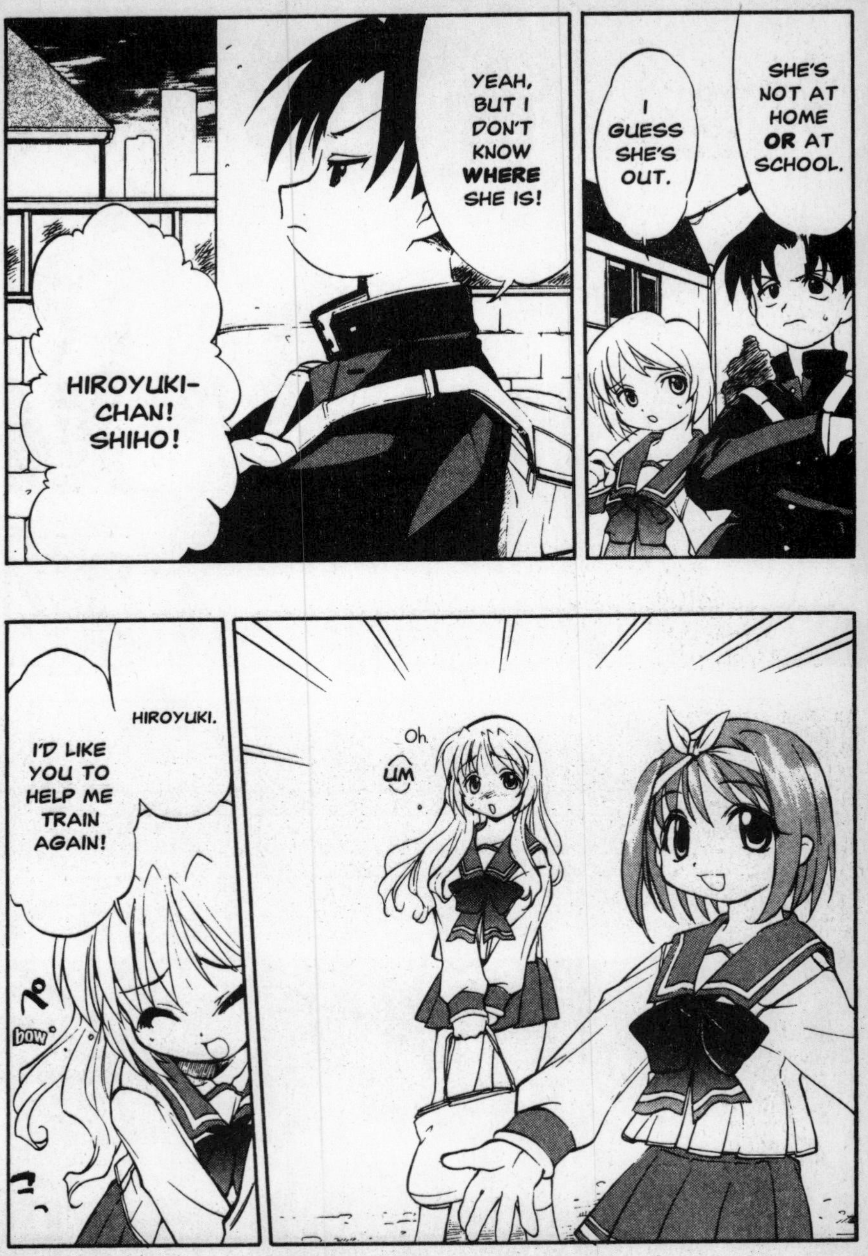
SHE'S NOT AT HOME OR AT SCHOOL.
I GUESS SHE'S OUT.
YEAH, BUT I DON'T KNOW WHERE SHE IS!
HIROYUKI-CHAN! SHIHO!
Oh.
UM
HIROYUKI.
I'D LIKE YOU TO HELP ME TRAIN AGAIN!
bow

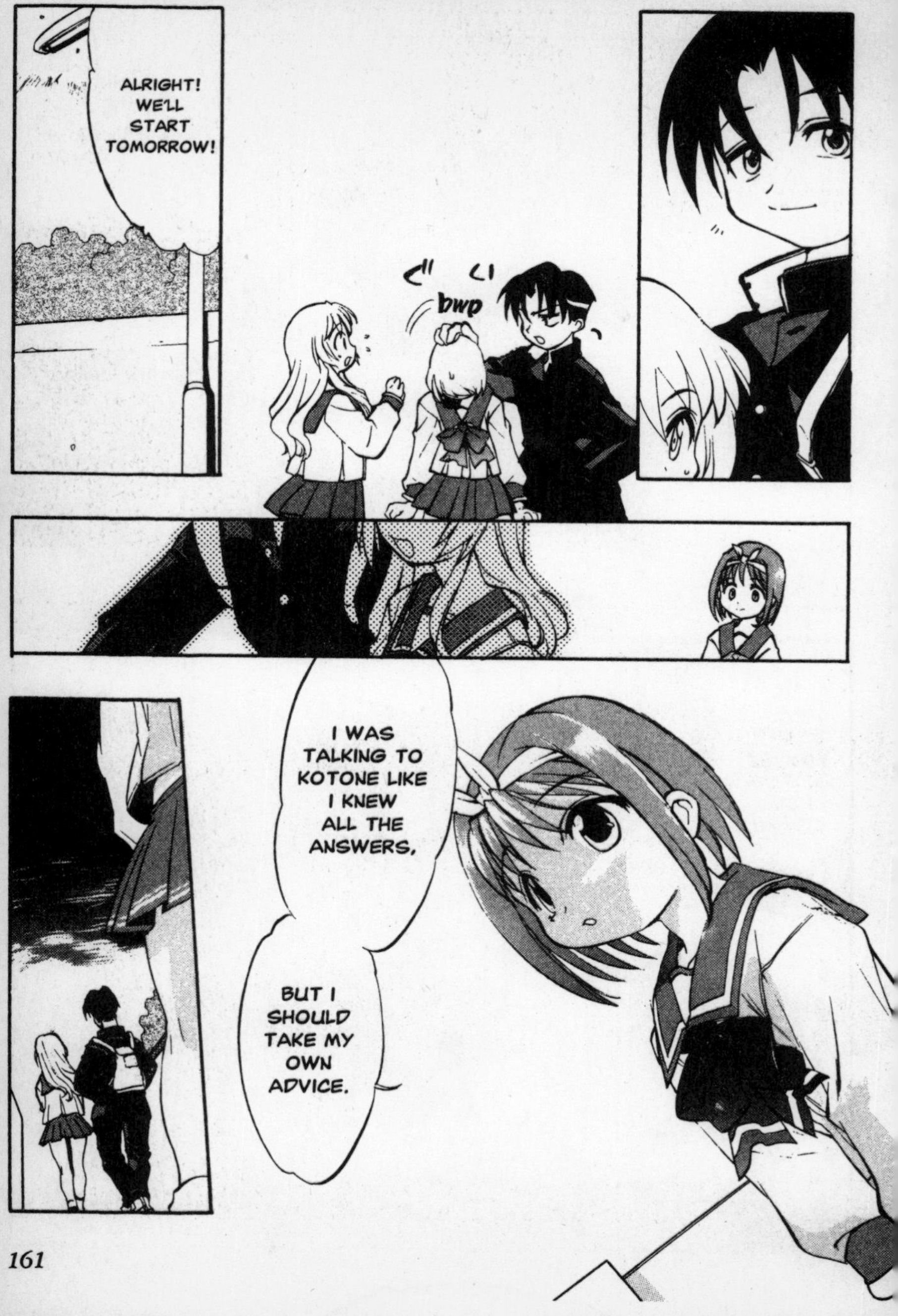
bwp
ALRIGHT! WE'LL START TOMORROW!
I WAS TALKING TO KOTONE LIKE I KNEW ALL THE ANSWERS,
BUT I SHOULD TAKE MY OWN ADVICE.

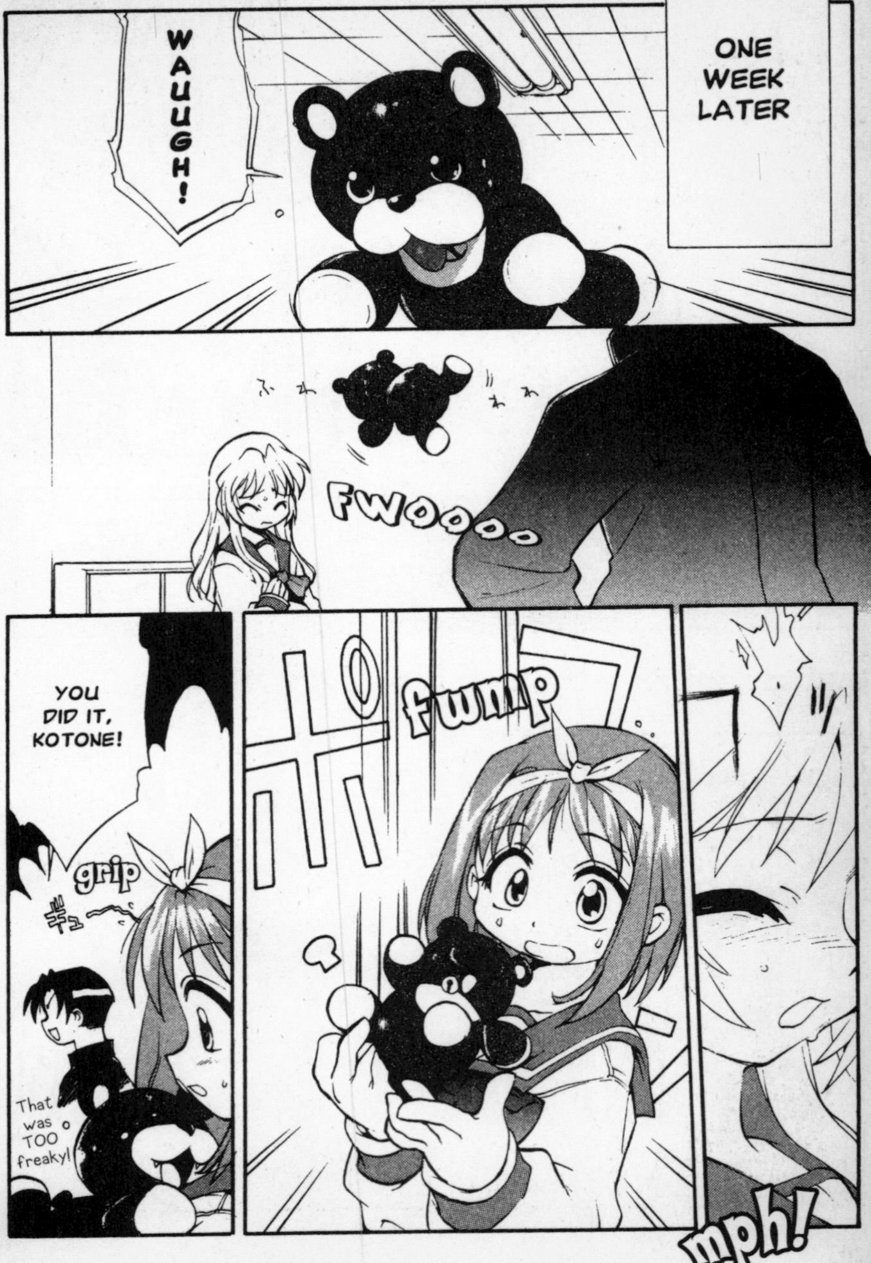
ONE WEEK LATER
WAUUGH!
ふわ
わ
FWOOOO
fwump
mph!
YOU DID IT, KOTONE!
grip
ギュ～
That was TOO freaky!

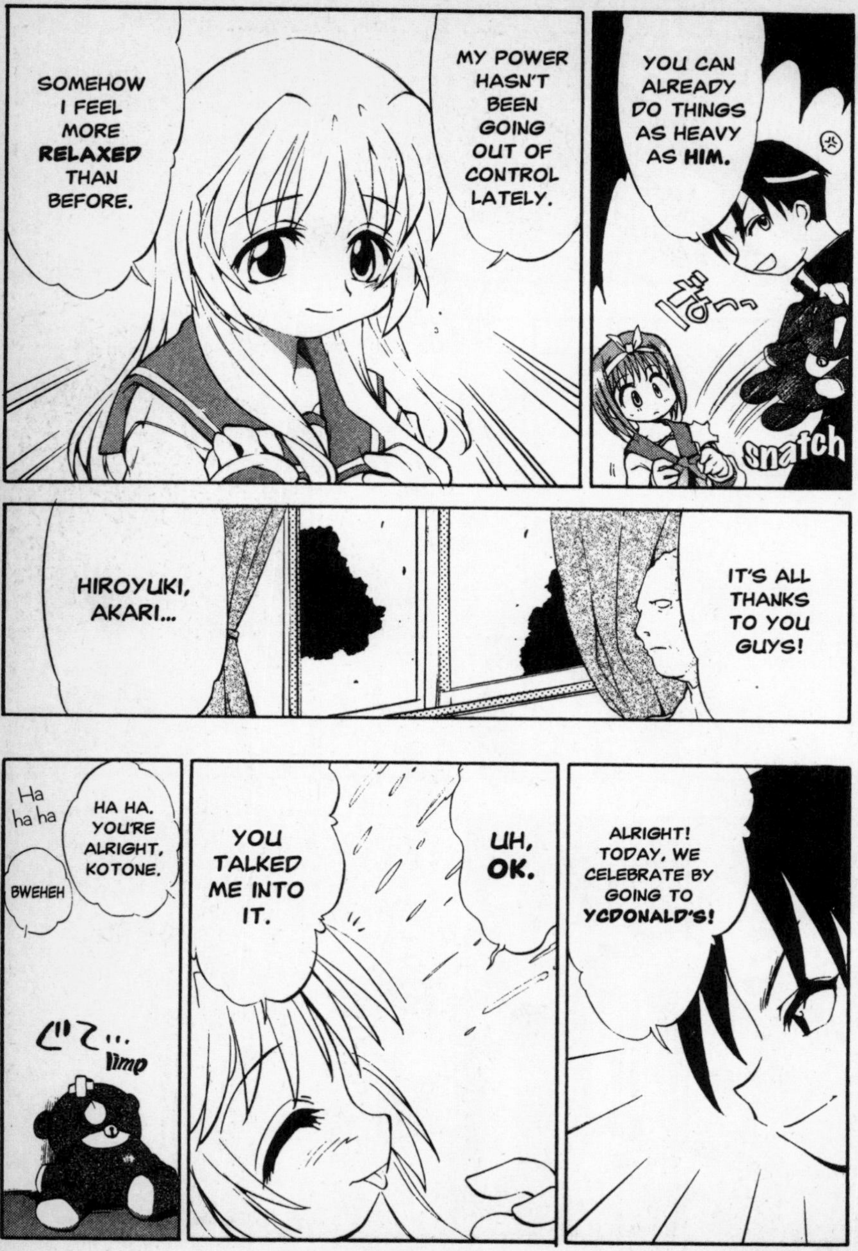

YOU CAN ALREADY DO THINGS AS HEAVY AS HIM.
ばっ
snatch
MY POWER HASN'T BEEN GOING OUT OF CONTROL LATELY.
SOMEHOW I FEEL MORE RELAXED THAN BEFORE.
IT'S ALL THANKS TO YOU GUYS!
HIROYUKI, AKARI...
ALRIGHT! TODAY, WE CELEBRATE BY GOING TO YCDONALD'S!
UH, OK.
YOU TALKED ME INTO IT.
HA HA. YOU'RE ALRIGHT, KOTONE.
Ha ha ha
BWEHEH
ぐて…
limp

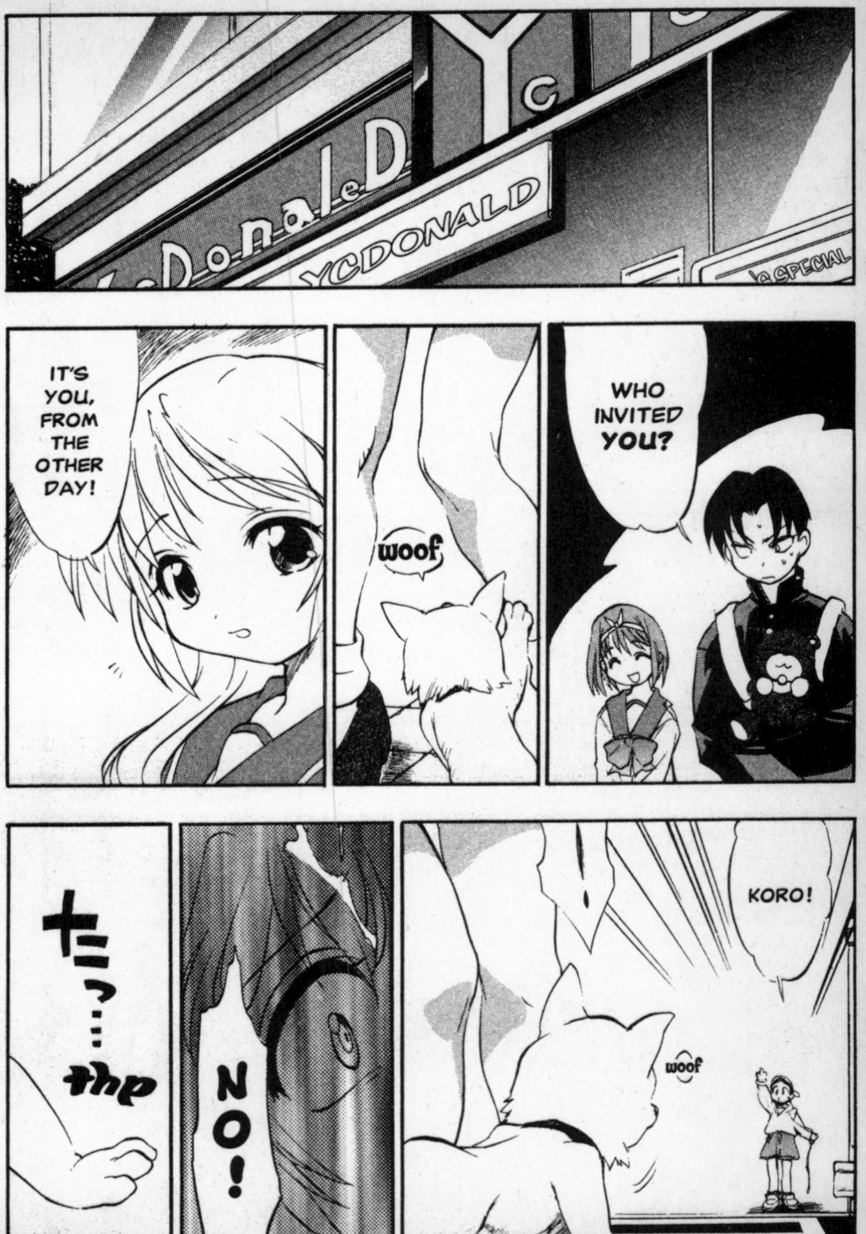
YCDONALD
'S SPECIAL
WHO INVITED YOU?
woof
IT'S YOU, FROM THE OTHER DAY!
KORO!
woof
NO!
たっ…
thp

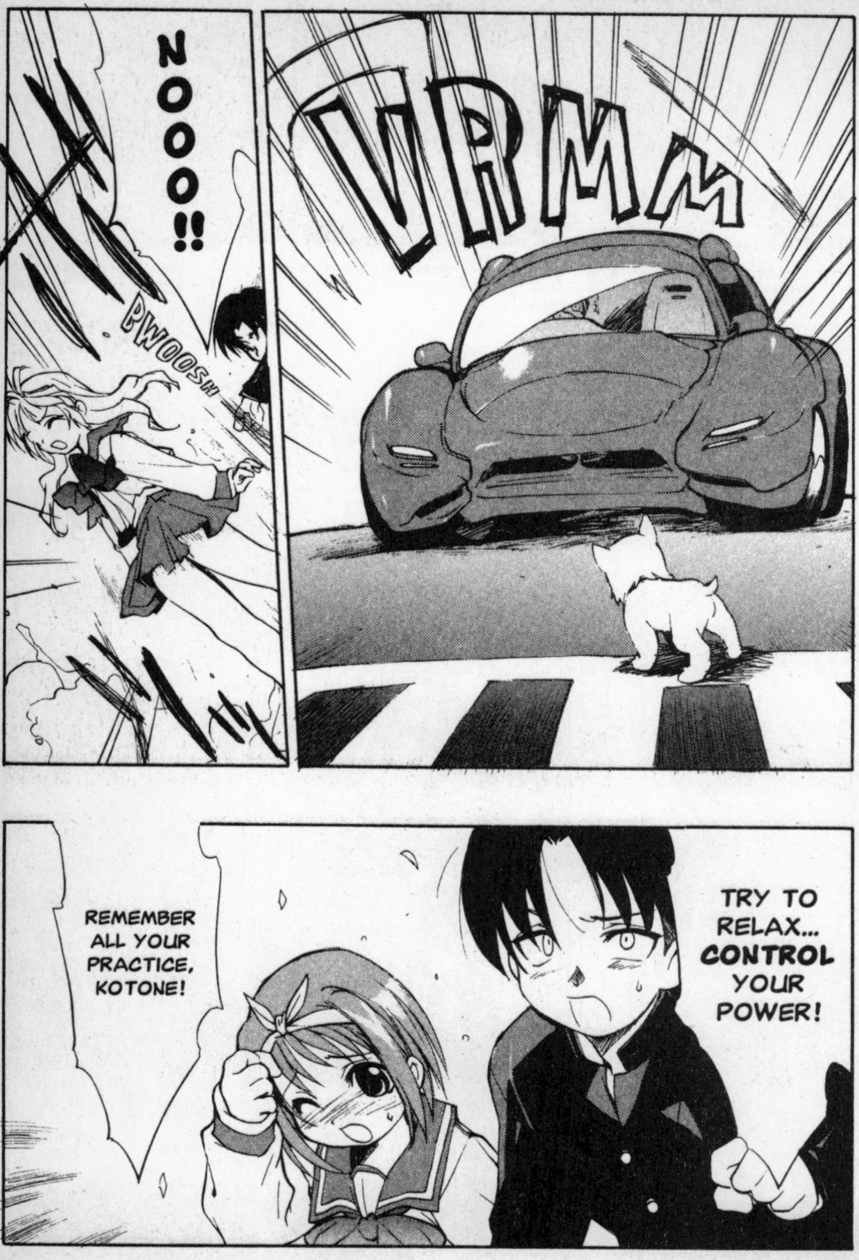
VRMM
NOOOO!!
BWOOSH
TRY TO RELAX... CONTROL YOUR POWER!
REMEMBER ALL YOUR PRACTICE, KOTONE!

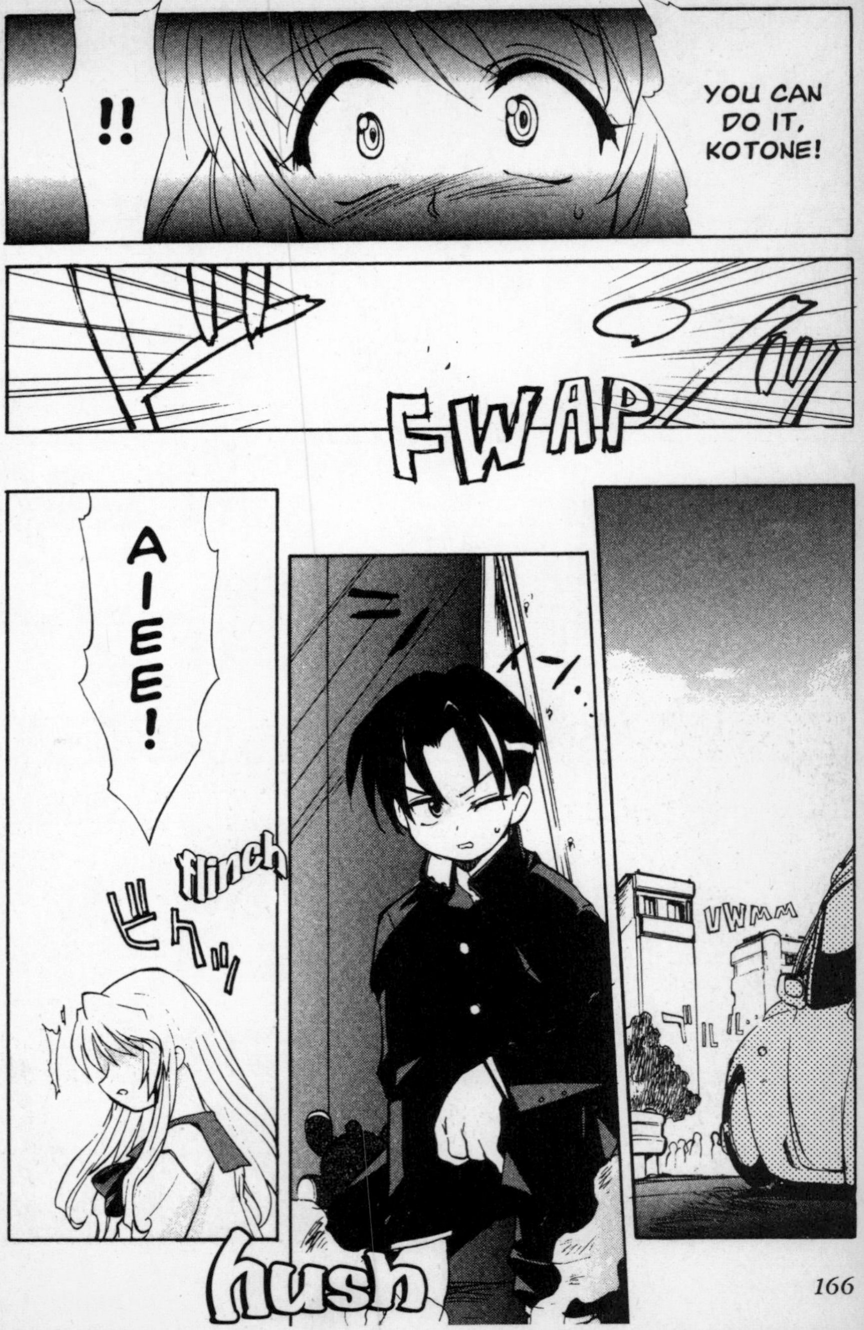
YOU CAN DO IT, KOTONE!
!!
FWAP
VWMM
hush
flinch
AIEEE!

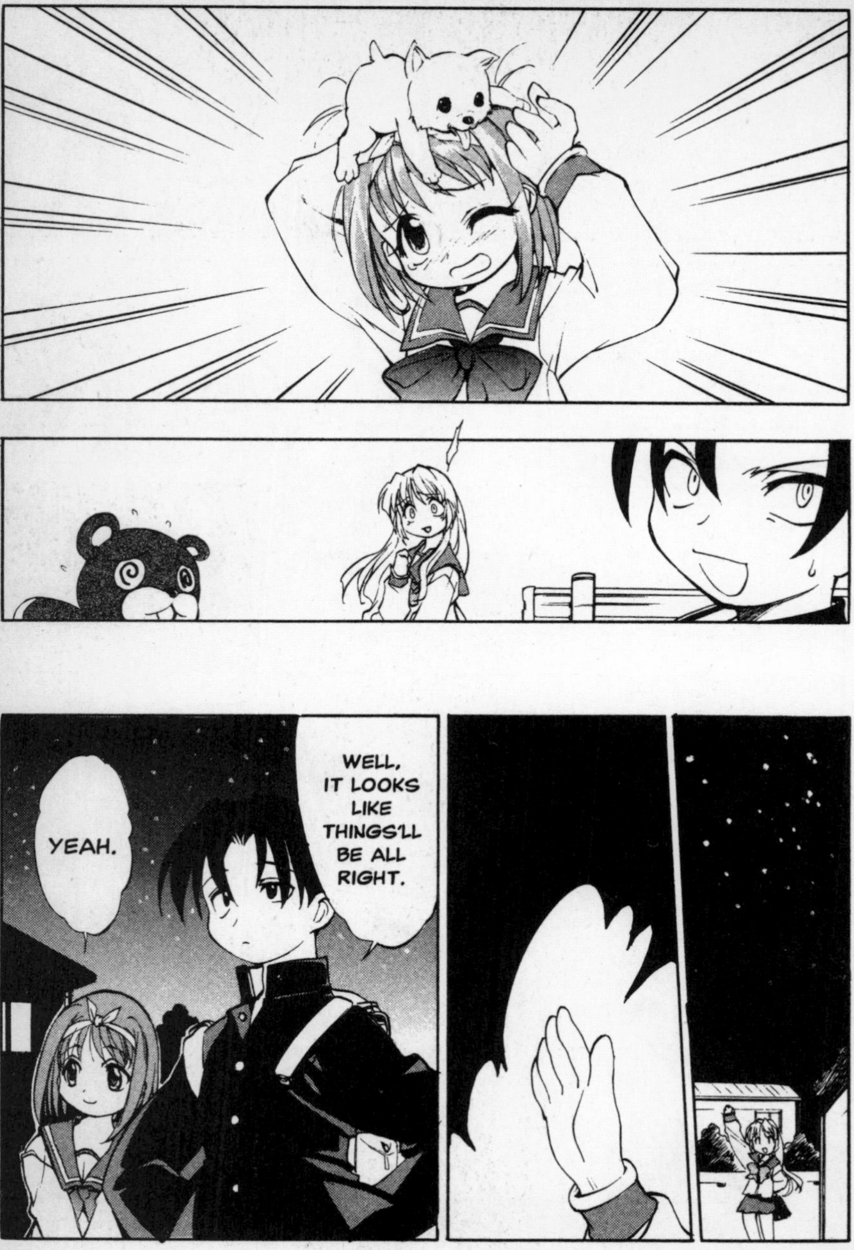
WELL, IT LOOKS LIKE THINGS'LL BE ALL RIGHT.
YEAH.

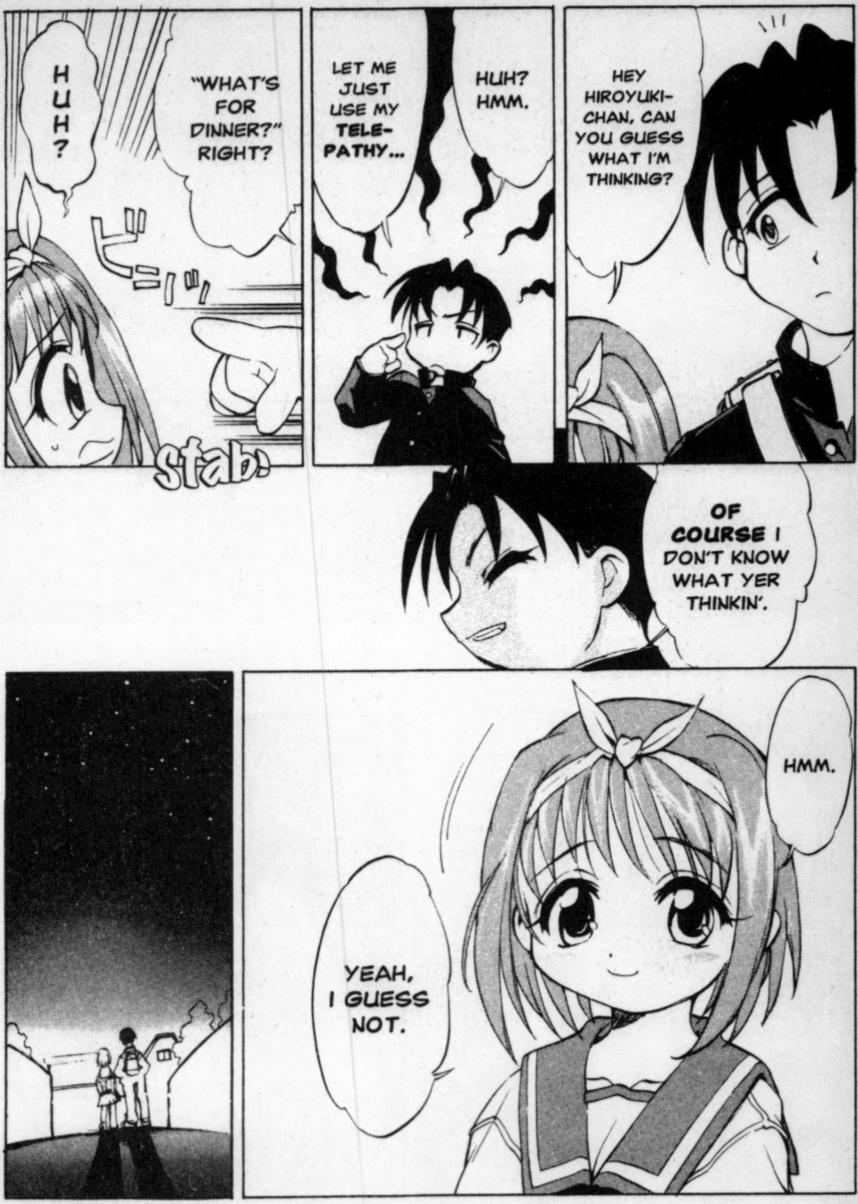

HEY HIROYUKI-CHAN, CAN YOU GUESS WHAT I'M THINKING?
HUH? HMM.
LET ME JUST USE MY TELEPATHY...
"WHAT'S FOR DINNER?" RIGHT?
HUH?
stab
OF COURSE I DON'T KNOW WHAT YER THINKIN'.
HMM.
YEAH, I GUESS NOT.

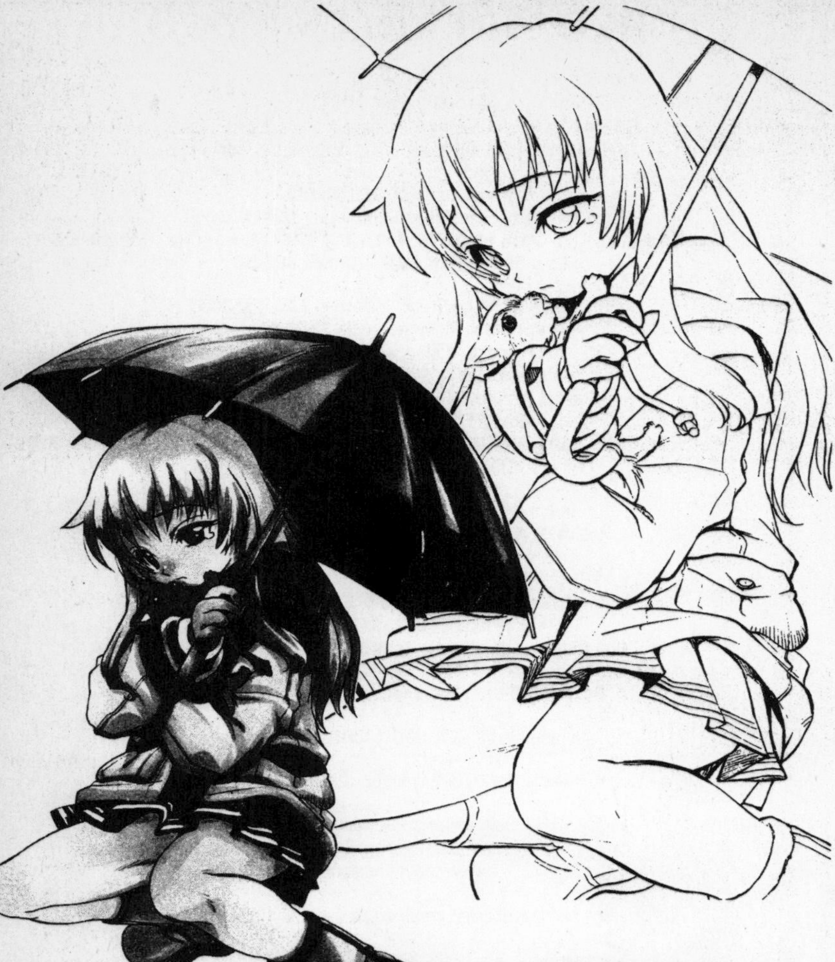

Kotone Himekawa

姫川琴音

HER MYSTERIOUS POWERS WILL HELP HER TO MAKE IT THROUGH THE SAD TIMES. SHE'LL SEE A SHINING RAY OF HOPE, EVEN IF IT'S THROUGH EYES CLOUDED WITH TEARS.

TO HEART VOLUME TWO

© AQUAPLUS
© UKYOU TAKAO 1999
First published in 1999 by Media Works Inc., Tokyo, Japan.
English translation rights arranged with Media Works Inc.

Translator **KAY BERTRAND**
Lead Translator/Translation Supervisor **JAVIER LOPEZ**
ADV Manga Translation Staff **AMY FORSYTH, BRENDAN FRAYNE, HARUKA KANEKO-SMITH,
EIKO McGREGOR AND MADOKA MOROE**

Print Production/ Art Studio Manager **LISA PUCKETT**
Pre-press Manager **KLYS REEDYK**
Art Production Manager **RYAN MASON**
Sr. Designer/Creative Manager **JORGE ALVARADO**
Graphic Designer/Group Leader **SCOTT SAVAGE**
Graphic Designer **LISA RAPER**
Graphic Artists **HEATHER GARY, SHANNA JENSCHKE, WINDI MARTIN AND GEORGE REYNOLDS**
Graphic Intern **MARK MEZA**

International Coordinator **TORU IWAKAMI**
International Coordinator **ATSUSHI KANBAYASHI**

Publishing Editor **SUSAN ITIN**
Assistant Editor **MARGARET SCHAROLD**
Editorial Assistant **VARSHA BHUCHAR**
Proofreaders **SHERIDAN JACOBS AND STEVEN REED**

Research/ Traffic Coordinator **MARSHA ARNOLD**

Executive VP, CFO, COO **KEVIN CORCORAN**

President, CEO & Publisher **JOHN LEDFORD**

Email: editor@adv-manga.com
www.adv-manga.com
www.advfilms.com

For sales and distribution inquiries please call 1.800.282.7202

ADV MANGA™ is a division of A.D. Vision, Inc.
10114 W. Sam Houston Parkway, Suite 200, Houston, Texas 77099

English text © 2004 published by A.D. Vision, Inc. under exclusive license.
ADV MANGA is a trademark of A.D. Vision, Inc.

All Rights Reserved. This is a fictional work. Any resemblance to actual events or locales,
or persons, living or dead, is entirely coincidental. Reproduction and, or transmission of
this work in whole or in part without written permission of the copyright holders is unlawful.

ISBN: 1-4139-0070-4
First printing, July 2004
10 9 8 7 6 5 4 3 2 1
Printed in Canada

To Heart Vol. 02

PG. 12 **On swimwear and uniforms**

Unlike Japanese secondary school students, children in Japanese elementary schools do not usually wear uniforms. One exception is P.E., where boys and girls wear generic, standard bathing suits. Though disliked for its blandness, the swimwear is not quite as infamous (or controversial) as the "bloomer" shorts which middle and high school girls must wear during P.E.

PG. 90 **Christmas**

Christmas in Japan is much different than in countries with a larger Christian influence. Rather than a family occasion, it's considered a romantic one, a time for couples and dating similar to what we associate with Valentine's Day (hence Akari and Hiroyuki's reactions). Christmas is still highly marketable in Japan, so familiar icons such as Santa Claus and Christmas carols (and George Michael's "Last Christmas," for some reason) are well-known to the Japanese.

PG. 100 **"Hot Hotel"**

If you've ever spent any time in Japan, you'll instantly recognize this as one of the many "love hotels" sprinkled throughout any of the major cities. Used primarily by couples who only need an hour or so to themselves, love hotels come decked out in a variety of themes and can include mirrored ceilings, disco balls and karaoke machines. Oddly enough, their rates for an entire night are often cheaper than "standard" hotels, as certain members of our translation staff (who shall remain nameless) can attest to.

PG. 126 **Borley Rectory**

Borley Rectory is widely regarded as the "most haunted house in England." Though the property itself has existed for hundreds of years with accounts of a Borley Manor existing even before the Norman invasion of 1066, it became world-famous in the early 1900s when paranormal researcher Harry Price visited and wrote about the place. There are many legends surrounding the property, and various accounts of poltergeists and paranormal activity.

PG. 130 **Student ID**

The Japanese *seito techo* is actually a combination ID and handbook.

LETTER FROM THE ADV MANGA TRANSLATION STAFF

Dear Reader,

On behalf of the ADV Manga translation team, thank you for purchasing an ADV book. We are enthusiastic and committed to our work, and strive to carry our enthusiasm over into the book you hold in your hands.

Our goal is to retain the spirit of the original Japanese book. While great care has been taken to render a true and accurate translation, some cultural or readability issues may require a line to be adapted for greater accessibility to our readers. At times, manga titles that include culturally-specific concepts will feature a "Translator's Notes" section, which explains noteworthy references to the original text.

We hope our commitment to a faithful translation is evident in every ADV book you purchase.

Sincerely,

Javier Lopez
Lead Translator

Madoka Moroe

Haruka Kaneko-Smith

Eiko McGregor

Kay Bertrand

Brendan Frayne

Amy Forsyth

ADV Manga™

A class trip leads to more romantic complications!

ToHeart
Vol.3

ISBN 1-4139-0087-9
Fall 2004
$9.99

And complete your collection with

To Heart vol. 1

ISBN 1-4139-0022-4

$9.99

© AQUAPLUS
© UKYOU TAKAO 2000

ADV MANGA

More Manga Monthly!

ADV MANGA™
www.adv-manga.com

One's just not enough.

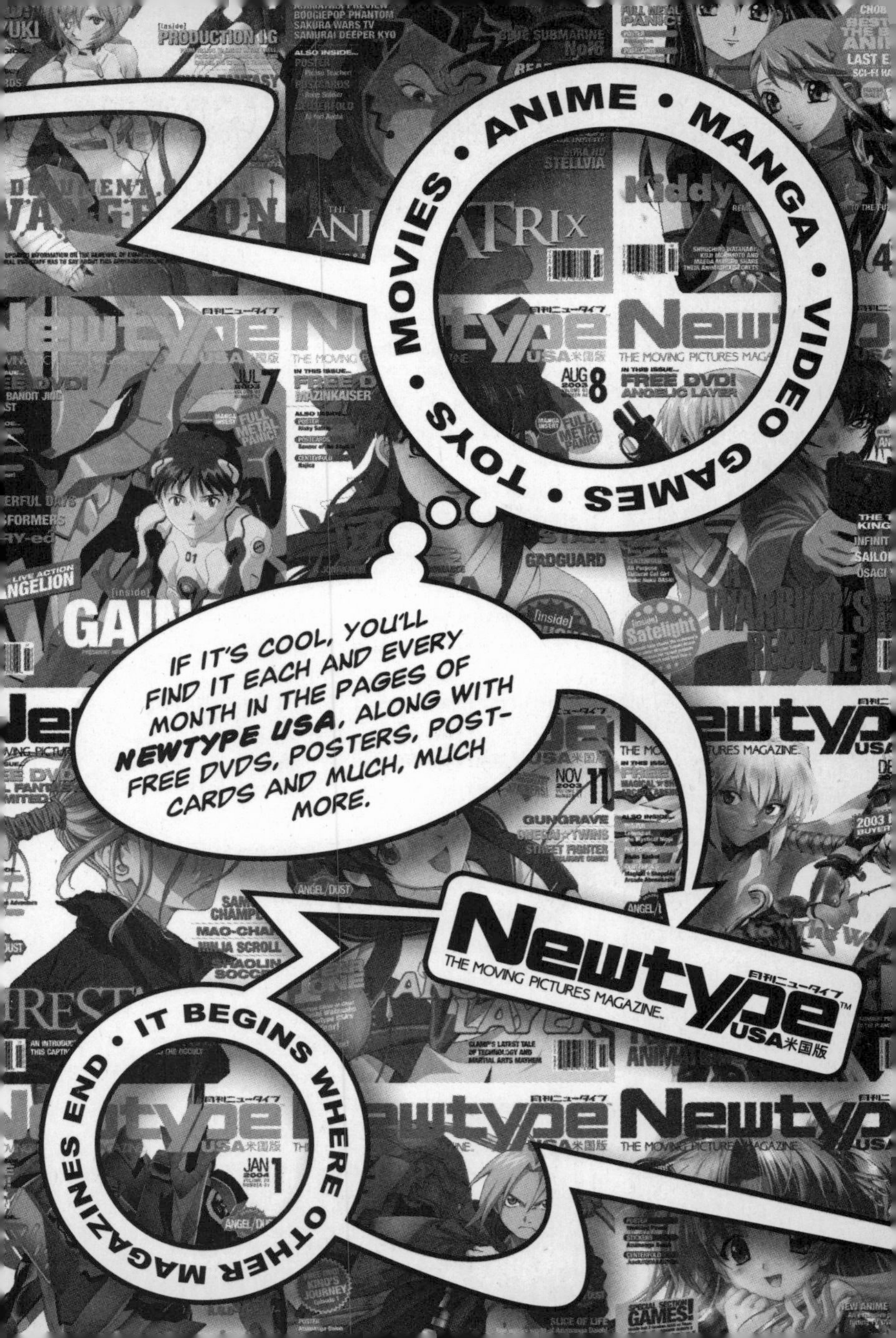
ANIME • MANGA • VIDEO GAMES • TOYS • MOVIES •
IF IT'S COOL, YOU'LL FIND IT EACH AND EVERY MONTH IN THE PAGES OF NEWTYPE USA, ALONG WITH FREE DVDS, POSTERS, POST-CARDS AND MUCH, MUCH MORE.
Newtype
THE MOVING PICTURES MAGAZINE.
USA 米国版
IT BEGINS WHERE OTHER MAGAZINES END •

MANGA SURVEY

PLEASE MAIL THE COMPLETED FORM TO: EDITOR – ADV MANGA
c/o A.D. Vision, Inc. 10114 W. Sam Houston Pkwy., Suite 200 Houston, TX 77099

Name:______________________________
Address:______________________________
City, State, Zip:______________________________
____
E-Mail:______________________________
Male ☐ Female ☐ Age:______________

☐ ***CHECK HERE IF YOU WOULD LIKE TO RECEIVE OTHER INFORMATION OR FUTURE OFFERS FROM ADV.***

All information provided will be used for internal purposes only. We promise not to sell or otherwise divulge your information.

1. Annual Household Income (*Check only one*)
- ☐ Under $25,000
- ☐ $25,000 to $50,000
- ☐ $50,000 to $75,000
- ☐ Over $75,000

2. How do you hear about new Manga releases? (*Check all that apply*)
- ☐ Browsing in Store
- ☐ Internet Reviews
- ☐ Anime News Websites
- ☐ Direct Email Campaigns
- ☐ Online forums (message boards and chat rooms)
- ☐ Carrier pigeon
- ☐ Other:______________
- ☐ Magazine Ad
- ☐ Online Advertising
- ☐ Conventions
- ☐ TV Advertising

3. Which magazines do you read? (*Check all that apply*)
- ☐ Wizard
- ☐ SPIN
- ☐ Animerica
- ☐ Rolling Stone
- ☐ Maxim
- ☐ DC Comics
- ☐ URB
- ☐ Polygon
- ☐ Original Play Station Magazine
- ☐ Entertainment Weekly
- ☐ YRB
- ☐ EGM
- ☐ Newtype USA
- ☐ SciFi
- ☐ Starlog
- ☐ Wired
- ☐ Vice
- ☐ BPM
- ☐ I hate reading
- ☐ Other:______________

4. Have you visited the ADV Manga website?
- ☐ Yes
- ☐ No

5. Have you made any manga purchases online from the ADV website?
- ☐ Yes
- ☐ No

6. If you have visited the ADV Manga website, how would you rate your online experience?
- ☐ Excellent
- ☐ Good
- ☐ Average
- ☐ Poor

7. What genre of manga do you prefer?
(*Check all that apply*)
- ☐ adventure
- ☐ romance
- ☐ detective
- ☐ action
- ☐ horror
- ☐ sci-fi/fantasy
- ☐ sports
- ☐ comedy

8. How many manga titles have you purchased in the last 6 months?
- ☐ none
- ☐ 1-4
- ☐ 5-10
- ☐ 11+

9. Where do you make your manga purchases? (*Check all that apply*)
- ☐ comic store
- ☐ bookstore
- ☐ newsstand
- ☐ online
- ☐ other:_____
- ☐ department store
- ☐ grocery store
- ☐ video store
- ☐ video game store

10. Which bookstores do you usually make your manga purchases at?
(*Check all that apply*)
- ☐ Barnes & Noble
- ☐ Walden Books
- ☐ Suncoast
- ☐ Best Buy
- ☐ Amazon.com
- ☐ Borders
- ☐ Books-A-Million
- ☐ Toys "Я" Us
- ☐ Other bookstore:
_____

11. What's your favorite anime/manga website? (*Check all that apply*)
- ☐ adv-manga.com
- ☐ advfilms.com
- ☐ rightstuf.com
- ☐ animenewsservice.com
- ☐ animenewsnetwork.com
- ☐ Other:_____
- ☐ animeondvd.com
- ☐ anipike.com
- ☐ animeonline.net
- ☐ planetanime.com
- ☐ animenation.com

All information provided will be used for internal purposes only. We promise not to sell or otherwise divulge your information.